Jochen Rindt

A touch of drift, no-one else in sight. What better image could capture the insouciant arrival of Jochen Rindt on the European scene? Crystal Palace, F2, 1964. (LAT)

Jochen Rindt
UNCROWNED KING
THE SUPERFAST LIFE OF F1's ONLY POSTHUMOUS WORLD CHAMPION

DAVID TREMAYNE
FOREWORD BY SIR JACKIE STEWART

CONTENTS

DEDICATION

To Uwe, Nina, Natasha and Bernie.

And to fans everywhere who applaud the gallantry of the fastest men of their eras.

© David Tremayne 2010

All rights reserved. No part of this publication may be reproduced or stored in a retrieval system or transmitted, in any form or by any means, electronic, mechanical, photocopying, recording or otherwise, without prior permission in writing from Haynes Publishing.

First published in September 2010

A catalogue record for this book is available from the British Library

ISBN 978 1 84425 472 9

Library of Congress control no. 2010924925

Published by Haynes Publishing, Sparkford, Yeovil, Somerset BA22 7JJ, UK
Tel: 01963 442030 Fax: 01963 440001
Int. tel: +44 1963 442030 Int. fax: +44 1963 440001
E-mail: sales@haynes.co.uk
Website: www.haynes.co.uk

Haynes North America Inc.
861 Lawrence Drive, Newbury Park,
California 91320, USA

Designed by James Robertson

Printed in the USA

Jacket photographs courtesy of LAT

LEFT *Jochen on his way to victory, British GP, Brands Hatch, 1970.* (Grand Prix Photo)

FOREWORD

Sir Jackie Stewart

First and foremost, Jochen Rindt was an extraordinarily fast racing driver; many people might have said he was the fastest of his time. His style of driving, until probably 1969, was what excited most people about Jochen. It wasn't just the spectators that were stimulated; it was the racing drivers who were following Jochen who were excited by the angles that his cars would take up, with handfuls of oversteer. If you were following him, your mindset was: "Which corner is the accident going to happen?", but of course it never did.

Equally, if you were leading Jochen in a race, your mirrors were full of a car going sideways behind you and the normal reaction might have been: "This won't last long; he's going to have a shunt," and again, it just never happened.

His exuberant driving was truly remarkable, his car control superb, but it wasn't always the fastest way. In a Formula Two car, somehow or other he made it happen. In a Formula One car, it took him a little while to realise that a heavier car carrying more fuel and with more power usually went off in performance as the race progressed and when tyre temperatures went beyond their best performance.

By 1969 Jochen had worked that out; Jim Clark had died the year before, which was a great loss for both Jochen and I. Jochen, in my mind, came of age; he moved on from that exuberance in driving, to be a much more calculated and more efficient racing driver.

Our British Grand Prix battle that year I think goes down as the most enjoyable race I ever had. We knew we could pass each other twice a lap at Silverstone; one slipstreaming down the Hangar Straight and passing before Stowe Corner and again, between Abbey Curve and Woodcote Corner in the slipstream. If we had been behaving stupidly, obstinately or selfishly, we could have blocked each other and used a bit of road that would not have allowed the pass to take place, but that would only have slowed us up and both of us understood that very well.

OPPOSITE *Jochen and Jackie, rivals but friends, Mexico City, 1969.* (LAT)

I would point to my inside, halfway down Hangar Straight, that Jochen should pass me before we entered the braking distance, so that we didn't slow each other up and likewise, Jochen would do the same before reaching Woodcote. It was a clear understanding of two people driving at the absolute limit, but knowing that if we were going to slow each other up it was only going to give the other people behind us a better chance of getting in the battle. It could only have happened with two people who truly trusted each other. Jochen and I were very good friends and I certainly trusted him.

Nina and Helen were the best of friends and have remained so for what seems to be forever. To this day, because Paul and Mark grew up with Natasha and, later, with Tamara when she arrived, and they stayed close, Nina, Helen and I have always retained lots of love and affection and a deep friendship.

Jochen's life was effervescent; he had a fantastic sense of humour and loved a good laugh. He skied like he drove racing cars in his early days; right on the edge at extraordinary angles at an on-the-limit speed.

He also had a wonderful relationship with Bernie Ecclestone and I am sure Jochen, had he not died at Monza in 1970, would almost certainly have retired after winning his World Championship. I am also certain he would have gone into business with Bernie in one form or another. He, like Bernie, loved wheeling and dealing and got as much excitement out of getting a deal done as he got out of winning a race.

The world became a duller place when Jochen lost his life at Monza; it was one of the most traumatic experiences that I went through during my racing career, and one that I don't think I will forget until my dying day.

However, the happy memories, the challenging races, the countless laughs, parties and going on holiday as a group, will also always remain as part of an extraordinary period of my life.

The life of Jochen Rindt has surely been celebrated many times over. David Tremayne is a wonderful writer who has done Jochen great justice in the words that he has chosen to depict a remarkable man and a remarkable career.

INTRODUCTION

It was a sunny day in Hendon Central, north London, a Saturday. September 5 1970. If the coach journey down from the Lake District was memorable, my mind has long erased the reasons. I'd just come back from a brief camping holiday with my elder sister and her husband, and quite why I hadn't driven up – I'd passed my driving test three months earlier – likewise escapes me now.

Perhaps that's because of the newspaper placard I saw, almost the moment I had stepped off the coach and picked up my luggage. I guess, given that it was afternoon, it must have been the *Evening Standard*.

"Rindt dead."

My heart sank, the way it always does at such moments. The way countless fans' hearts sink. And while I waited for my father to come and pick me up, I bought a copy of the paper to discover the Austrian's fate.

Jochen Rindt! The name demanded an exclamation mark, italics, too. For Jochen never did anything by halves. Like Ronnie Peterson and Gilles Villeneuve and Ayrton Senna, whose times were to come, he was the purest, most spectacular, kind of racer. Whether he was driving a Formula One Lotus or a Formula Two Brabham, or a road car or playing tennis with his buddy and neighbour Jackie Stewart or gin rummy with close friends Bernie Ecclestone or Piers Courage, or... Well, whatever he did, he had to compete. And he had to be doing it flat out, to win. There were no half measures.

Twenty years ago I wrote a chapter about him in a book called *Racers Apart*. It began: "Even now, 20 years after that day when tragedy snatched him from the world title that was to follow, it sets the mind tingling, instantly conjures up mental imagery of a car being driven to its absolute maximum. Of a long-faced man with a distinctively flat nose and tousled hair, who would inevitably seek the sustenance of a cigarette whenever he stepped from the cockpit".

OPPOSITE *Jochen watches as, clockwise, Eddie Dennis, Herbie Blash and Dick Scammell make last-minute adjustments to the DFV, Monza, 1970.* (LAT)

Another 20 years later, those words still ring true, still paint evocative images. But new generations of fans do not always remember those who went before. New heroes have basked in the spray of champagne, as the song has it. That was brought home to me very forcibly a few years back, I guess it would have been 2003, when I took a late flight out to Monaco one Wednesday evening. Across the aisle from me was an American dude, dressed top to tail in bright red Ferrari gear. He was a fan of the Scuderia, and was not afraid to share that with anyone who was prepared to listen. What he didn't know about Michael Schumacher could be written on the sharp end of a pin. After a while, listening to him made me feel like I was sitting on it.

It was, inevitably, the pretty stewardess who bore the brunt of all this expertise, and equally inevitably he asked her The Question. Was she going to the race? She handled his advance superbly, but the truth is that the guy really took himself out.

"I used to go," she said quietly. "But after what happened to Senna I didn't want to go any more..."

Our friend across the aisle ground to a sudden halt, the sort of bemused expression writ large across his face of a man who has just run head-on into a brick wall of ignorance. "Senna?" the suddenly desperate look in his eyes said, as this fount of all Formula One knowledge scanned his memory banks and his mental computer came up with the answer: "No matching files found".

That made a big impression on me. This guy was armed with all the latest mags, and obviously devoured information about Schumacher, but even though Ayrton had only been dead nine years, and had been The Man before Michael's era began – indeed had raced against and often beaten the German hero – this "uberfan" had not even heard of the Brazilian's name let alone knew anything of his towering achievements.

It shook me, frankly.

And it reminded me of a poignant line in that great song *Elegy to Campbell* written of speedking Donald Campbell by Andrew Wintersgill: "Speed is the king in the realm of ambition, great is the glory but short is the reign".

ABOVE *'Mano a mano', Jochen leads the Ferraris of Jacky Ickx and Clay Regazzoni, and Chris Amon's March, on his way to victory, Hockenheim, 1970.* (LAT)

The Lost Generation was my last book, published in 2006, in which I sought to preserve the memories of those three potentially great British racers Roger Williamson, Tony Brise and Tom Pryce, all of whom were taken so young. But even while I was writing it I was thinking ahead to what would follow. No matter which mountain you climb, you always need to have the next peak lined up, ready.

I knew then that I wanted next to write about Jochen, the sport's only posthumous Formula One World Champion. Not just to recapture his glories and perhaps to paint a sharper picture of his character and life, but also to put him into the true perspective in which he deserves to be remembered.

Trying to compare drivers across the eras is fun, controversial and, ultimately, frustrating. Pointless, even. Because it poses way more interesting questions than it ever provides answers.

Jackie Stewart will forever feature in my all-time Top 10, as he will in many others', for all sorts of reasons. But would Jochen? The truthful answer is probably no,

but if you really start to get into these things, the foolishness of the endeavour inevitably becomes apparent because of things like that. If anything, Jochen was slightly faster than Jackie, if not so polished overall; certainly, JYS always considered him his equal, the man he had to beat just as Jochen regarded Jackie as his potential nemesis. So how can one really separate the two? It would be like having Ayrton Senna in your Top 10, but not Alain Prost, the only man who posed a consistent same-level threat to the great Brazilian.

Judged by any standard, Jochen was a true great of the sport. In Formula Two he could beat Jim Clark and Jackie Stewart. That spoke volumes. In Formula One he showed the talent and the pace to see off anyone too, towards the end of a career that promised so much more. It seems ridiculous that the gods should grant him only six wins, just as it would Gilles Villeneuve. As Ernest Myers, writing of Achilles, put it: "What gifts hath Fate for all his chivalry? Even such as hearts heroic oftenest win; Honour, a friend, anguish, untimely death…"

The tragedy of his young life – he had just turned 28 – is that everything was finally coming together for him after all those wilderness years in poor or unreliable Formula One cars. On September 5 he knew that the summit of his great mountain was in sight, after he had

won half of the season's ten races. But as cruel as his ultimate fate was the fact that those fickle gods denied him the knowledge while he was alive that he had staked his own flag at the top. He had scaled the pinnacle, yet never knew it.

Jacky Ickx was always glad that he did not win the 1970 US Grand Prix, that his Ferrari let him down in the race he *had* to win in order to stay on target to overcome Jochen's World Championship points tally. The Belgian was something of a maverick in his heyday, a throwback to a bygone era who went his own way and raced with a fatalism that did not always sit well with peers who were set on trying to improve safety standards. Many people I spoke to for this book were adamant that Jochen really didn't like him, though Jacky says they never had any hard words. But Jacky would be the first to admit that back then, when he was himself a young god, he believed that all his dreams could come true and that he never fully appreciated the people all around him who contributed to the effort on his behalf. Not until much later in his life. "When you are young you think everything is somehow due to you..." Jochen's friends say he thought Jacky was arrogant, just as others thought Jochen was.

I saw Ickx race in the first event I ever went to, the 1968 Race of Champions. He was in a Ferrari 312, the

ABOVE Jochen always did have good taste in reading material. At the Race of Champions in 1969 he catches up on the March 13 issue of Motoring News. (LAT)

same car in which he would later win the French Grand Prix in pouring rain at Rouen. He's one of the drivers of that era that I didn't get to know; indeed, when we talked for this book in the paddock at Spa in September 2008, it was only the second time in my life that we had conversed. But I always had immense respect for him as a driver and as a sportsman. And he said something that I really appreciated.

"I think it is fantastic that you are doing a book on Jochen," he said, "and that there have been books on others too. Because all these guys deserve a piece of writing about what they did so they are not anonymous." I remembered that his father, Jacques, had been a leading motoring journalist, and thought that was a lovely thing for somebody of his calibre to say, though it's ironic because he steadfastly resists a book on his own remarkable career.

"The most important thing you have is time," Jochen once told writer Barrie Gill. "No one knows how long you have to live. So it is everyone's duty to put into his life all he can.

"You mustn't misunderstand me. I am not talking about life just for a racing driver. I'm not thinking of the danger. It's the same for a bank clerk. We must all use our life to the full."

This book has been a longer journey than intended. There were warm distractions in the winter of 2007, and part of the truth is that one of the reasons I welcomed them was because I had burned myself out emotionally on *The Lost Generation*. So my apologies to those who have admirably been keeping their impatience in check, most notably Mark Hughes and his great team at Haynes. Here it is at last. I hope it's been worth the wait. And that it does justice to a man I came very much to like as the story progressed, and of whom my friend Mike Doodson once wisely wrote: "Now he is gone, he must be given a place among the all-time greats as the amateur who became the reluctant, but dedicated, professional".

The man widely acknowledged to be the fastest driver of his era.

Jochen Rindt!

David Tremayne
Darlington,
June 2010

BIBLIOGRAPHY

BOOKS

Anatomy of a Grand Prix Driver, Richard Garrett (Arthur Barker)

Autocourse (Hazelton Publishing)

Brabham, The Grand Prix Cars, Alan Henry (Osprey)

Brabham Ralt Honda, The Ron Tauranac Story, Mike Lawrence (MRP)

Colin Chapman, The Man and his Cars, Jabby Crombac (Patrick Stephens)

Fast and Furious, The Story of the World Championship of Drivers, Richard Garrett (Stanley Paul)

Fifty Famous Races, Highlights from half a century of the world's most exciting sport, Alan Henry (Patrick Stephens)

The Forgotten Races, The Three Litre Formula One Non-Championship Races 1966 to 1983, Chris Ellard (W3 Publications)

Grand Prix Accident Survey 1966-72, Adrian Bell, Ray Crowther, Eric Dymock, Ray Hutton and Michael Kettlewell (The Jim Clark Foundation)

Grand Prix! Vol 1 & 2, 1950-1973, Race-by-race account of Formula 1 World Championship motor racing, Mike Lang (Haynes Publishing)

Grand Prix Greats, A personal appreciation of 25 famous Formula 1 drivers, Nigel Roebuck (Patrick Stephens)

Jackie Stewart, Winning is not enough, Jackie Stewart (Headline)

Jochen Rindt, Alan Henry (Hazelton Publishing)

Jochen Rindt, Bilder aus dem Leben des unvergessesnen Weltmeisters, Erik Thomas Neger (Styria Printshop)

Jochen Rindt, The Story of a World Champion, Heinz Pruller (William Kimber)

Lotus 72, Formula One Icon, Michael Oliver (Coterie Press)

Motor Racing, The Grand Prix Greats, Edited by Barrie Gill (Pelham Books)

Motor Racing Year (MRP)

Piers Courage, Last of the Gentleman Racers, Adam Cooper (Haynes Publishing)

Racers, The Inside Story of Williams Grand Prix Engineering, Doug Nye (Arthur Barker)

Racers Apart, Memories of motorsport heroes, David Tremayne (MRP)

Red-Hot Rivals, Ferrari vs Maserati. Epic clashes for supremacy, Karl Ludvigsen (Haynes Publishing)

Rob Walker, Michael Cooper-Evans (Hazelton Publishing)

Roy Salvadori, Racing Driver, Roy Salvadori and Anthony Pritchard (Patrick Stephens)

Team Lotus, The Indianapolis Years, Andrew Ferguson (Patrick Stephens)

The Formula 1 Record Book, John Thompson, Duncan Rabagliati, Dr K. Paul Sheldon (Leslie Frewin)

The Men, The World's Grand Prix Drivers Examined in Depth, Barrie Gill (Leslie Frewin)

PERIODICALS

Autocar

Auto Racing

Autosport

Motor

Motoring News

Motor Racing

Motor Sport

WEBSITES

www.jochen-rindt.at

ACKNOWLEDGEMENTS

So many people within the sport contributed to this book, and I am grateful to them all for their insights.

From the racers themselves, my thanks to Mario Andretti, Derek Bell and Herbie Blash for memories; Sir Jack Brabham for a great interview about a man he so evidently loved and respected; Lady Bridport, aka Nina Rindt, who was kindness itself during a lengthy telephone conversation in which she resolutely answered in details questions from even the darkest period of her life, and for suggesting that I speak with Erich Walitsch; Peter Collins for doing the interview with Sir Jack when I was otherwise occupied reporting a Grand Prix in Melbourne, and for his own memories of Warwick Farm; Bernie Ecclestone for a memorably candid, insightful and highly enjoyable if poignant hour together - without interruption - during the 2010 Chinese GP weekend in Shanghai; Nick Goozee, Howden Ganley and Dan Gurney for memories; Helmut Marko for the lowdown on far-off wild days in Graz and sharing some wonderful stories; Alan Rees, Dick and Frances Scammell and Tim Schenken for memories; Dick Sellens for his memories of rescuing Jochen at Levin; Sir Jackie Stewart for his candid memories of one of his closest racing friends whom he still misses 40 years on, and for writing the Foreword; John Surtees and Ron Tauranac for memories; Franz Tost for boyhood memories; Frank Williams and Roy Winkelmann for memories of a man who played such an important part in their lives.

From my colleagues in the writing fraternity: thanks to doyen Italian sportswriter Pino Allievi for his memories of Jochen; author Michael Argetsinger for his outstanding generosity in not only sharing superb memories of days spent in F1 with Jochen, but for writing them down electronically for me too; the late Jabby Crombac, our beloved and much-missed 'Legend'; Mike Doodson for memories and his wonderful writing in Motoring News; Hartmut Lehbrink for kind help; Hubert Lepka for contacts; Graham Heeps for contact details for John Miles; writer Gerhard Kuntschik for memories, help and kindness; Andrew Marriott, for so many great tales from his days as A.R.M. of Motoring News; Paddy McNally for memories; the late Pat Mennem who, until I understood both men, had always struck me as an unlikely ally for Jochen; Gregor Messer for boyhood memories; Doug Nye for memories from his excellent book on Williams, Racers; to Willy Pilz for his kind help in sourcing early images; Gerald Pototschnig for his photos and memories of Jochen's childhood and for a copy of Didi Hubmann's interview with Felizitas Zeller; Heinz Pruller, for friendship, memories and his own brilliant biography of Jochen that came out in 1971 when the pain was still so raw (and wishing him recovery from recent illness); Dieter Rencken for his habitual help and enthusiasm; Nigel Roebuck for memories; Erich Walitsch, Austria's indefatigable keeper of Jochen's flame via his www.jochen-rindt.at website, who reacted immediately when asked for help and never ceased to provide assistance of the highest quality thereafter; the incomparable Eoin Young, whose brilliant Straight From The Grid column in Autocar did so much to inform and inflame my early passion for F1 and to tell the world for the first time about the personalities behind the drivers' familiar faces; and the great Helmut Zwickl, writer, historian, gentleman and respected friend.

And to David Hayhoe for compiling his wonderful results table.

Words and pictures cannot be separated, and my thanks and respect go to Paul Cross, Andrew Frankl, Roger Lane, LAT Photographic, Nick Loudon and Peter Nygaard for their excellent photographs which bring this book to life. And to Paul Kelly for digging out the wonderful images from Indianapolis Motor Speedway.

And thanks also to Jonathan Gee for spotting an Internet plea I had posted and connecting me with Roy Winkelmann; and Mark Read on Rosco McGlashan's land speed team for likewise spotting the same plea and offering another Winkelmann connection.

And lastly to Jochen's half-brother, Dr Uwe Eisleben, for his unstinting help in providing memories and images of the Eisleben and Rindt families.

CHAPTER 1

Who the hell is Jochen Rindt?

Whitsun, 17/18 May 1964

"I think I've made it. BP has raised my contract money to such an extent I thought I was dreaming!"

Jochen Rindt

LEFT *Jochen reigns supreme, Crystal Palace, 1964.* (LAT)

So here's the myth about Jochen Rindt. Prior to 18 May 1964 nobody had heard of the flat-nosed Austrian, but that was the day that he came out of nowhere to beat Graham Hill – Mr Motor Racing! – in his own South London backyard at Crystal Palace to catapult himself on to the sports pages of national newspapers. He was, they said, the original overnight sensation. Everybody wanted to know: Who the hell is Jochen Rindt? So, in one bound he launched himself, fully fledged, on to the international motor racing stage.

The truth is even more intriguing, even if it didn't quite fit such a dramatic mould, because once anyone had seen him driving, they didn't forget it. Frank Williams, a legend today but back then a little-known wannabe racer cum race car dealer, had become a card-carrying Rindt fan after watching him racing his aged Cooper at Tulln-Langenlebarn, an airfield circuit in West Germany.

"I proudly claim the title of having become Jochen's first fan," he told writer Doug Nye in 1982. "There was a very fast fifth-gear curve, and I can still vividly picture Jochen flying through there in beautiful four-wheel slides. I thought it was splendid. I was sure he had a great future, and it's not putting it too strongly to say I worshipped him from then on…" A few years later, Williams told writer Alan Henry: "I went up to him and told him I thought he was brilliant. He liked that!"

Jochen was fast and he was fearless, and he got the job done with a flamboyance matched only by his choice of clothes. Racer Jonathan Williams remembers that he affected some startling apparel in their days on the Formula Junior trail, and while Jonathan had been impressed with the performances Jochen squeezed out of an elderly Cooper, he was less taken with his attire. He told Henry: "Rindt had a white Jaguar E-type, pink shirts. I remember thinking: 'Who the hell's that queer?'"

Frank remembers Jochen turning up to the 1964 Racing Car Show looking resplendent in a camel hair coat. His mission that day was to part with £4,000 of his inheritance (the equivalent of £60,750 today) to secure a brand-new Brabham BT10 single-seater from Jack Brabham, as part of his plan to graduate to Formula Two. Austria's FIA delegate, a Viennese clockmaker called Martin Pfunder, had been instrumental not just in helping him to move up the Brabham order list, but also to obtain one of the priceless 1-litre Cosworth SCA engines that, the BRM apart, would rule the roost in the new racing category. As we shall learn, however, Jochen also had his own ideas about how to get a decent engine from Cosworth…

If the truth really be told, which of course must be the object of this biographical exercise, Jochen was an over-weekend sensation, because even before he hit the little race track near Anerley in south-east London he had

electrified Mallory Park on the Whitsuntide weekend with a performance so accomplished that it established him immediately among the top rank of European racers.

Here is how he did it.

Jochen had never seen Mallory Park, but at the end of qualifying for Whit Sunday's Grovewood Trophy Formula Two race at the pretty little Leicestershire track there were few drivers or spectators who did not have his name on their lips. He was driving the Brabham-Cosworth with some sponsorship from Ford Austria, and against many highly respected names – none more than Jimmy Clark, who had hot-footed back from practice at Indianapolis to take the lead Lotus, his formidable team-mate Peter Arundell, Denny Hulme, Brian Hart, Richard Attwood, David Hobbs and Frank Gardner – he took pole position with seeming ease.

"It was my first race in England and I asked Denny Hulme if I could follow him round for a few laps," Jochen explained. "I was really surprised when I found I had done fastest time."

He wasn't the only one.

His best lap was 52.4s or 97.75mph, two-tenths faster than Grovewood Award winner Hart in the development Lotus 22-Cosworth, Hulme in a similar Brabham and Clark in a Ron Harris-entered Lotus 32. In the circumstances, it was an astonishing feat.

As a schoolboy, Nick Goozee had hung around Cooper's workshop in Surbiton until the mechanic there told him to make himself useful and put the kettle on. Subsequently he went to work with Jack Brabham, when the Australian set up his own manufacturing business.

"Of course, you really got to know everybody then," he recalled. "You *did* know all the drivers, you knew all the other teams. We used to travel in convoy on the continent. We used to share other people's problems, and them ours."

By force of circumstance, Goozee found himself working for Jochen that day at Mallory. "I'd started my apprenticeship at Brabham in December 1963, doing odd jobs. At the beginning of April 1964 the build programme for the smaller formulae – Formula Two and Formula Three – was getting really busy as the races were about to start. The drivers usually turned up with their mechanics to finish their cars off, or to pick them up. Drivers would either stand around waiting for them to be completed, or roll their sleeves up and get stuck in.

"Jochen turned up with a mechanic, but the guy seemed to go off somewhere and get lost, leaving Jochen looking slightly bemused. He stood around quite a bit, as I recall. I was only 18 and too inexperienced to work on cars just then, but because his needed some work I was asked to help the foreman Jerry Holmes to finish honing this very dark blue one for Jochen. Jerry was going to accompany Jochen to Mallory for that weekend's race, and they asked me if I'd like to go too. That was a big thrill! I had only done a couple of races, working with Denny Hulme on his car.

"We just went up there with the car on the trailer, a few spare wheels; no arrangements had been made. Jerry, the mechanic who had appeared again, and I all stayed in the same room in a local bed and breakfast. Jochen stayed somewhere else. We worked on the car into the early hours, finishing it off. It was very exciting, working with this very unknown person in a remote spot in the paddock."

Goozee remembers Jochen as a lonely, slightly aloof figure that weekend, something of a stranger in a strange land. "He was around us all the time. He was immensely quiet, just watched. He was just there on his own, he hadn't brought along any friends or companions; he was quite alone."

And, funnily enough, Goozee had no recollection of garish apparel. "His taste seemed normal, as I recall. At Mallory and Crystal Palace he had pretty much what he stood up in. It was in the pre-jeans days, but he was fairly sombrely dressed then, and he would be when we worked together in 1968. I don't remember anything outlandish."

What he did remember was the little bit of serendipity. "He put the car on pole, after Denny had shown him the way round, so the amusing thing was that the car I was working on that weekend was on pole, and the one I usually worked on was alongside it!"

BELOW *On his way to a sensational third place, after starting from pole but fluffing his start, Jochen leads Mike Beckwith and Alan Rees at Mallory Park.* (LAT)

Unfortunately Jochen fluffed the start, and condemned himself to a race of recovery as Clark sped away to win from Arundell in a Lotus 1-2. "At the start I was so tweaked up that I didn't get into gear properly, and I had to work really hard to finish third," he admitted.

As Tony Maggs narrowly avoided ramming the stricken Brabham with his MRP Lola, Hart sped into the lead chased by the Lotuses of Clark and Arundell, and Hobbs's Merlyn. Further back, Jochen was at the tail end of a dust-up for fifth with Bill Bradley's Lola, the Brabhams of Alan Rees and Hulme, and Attwood's Lola.

Clark took the lead from Hart on the third lap, round the outside of the very quick Gerards 180 degree sweeper at the start of the lap, where Bradley went off and crashed. Attwood also got involved, as did Kurt Ahrens in his Cooper. All three retired.

Arundell and Gardner both found ways past Hart, whose engine would eventually fail, and Jochen fought his way clear of his group and began to challenge upcoming Briton Tony Hegbourne's Cooper for fourth. He really got his head down and with three of the 30 laps left outfumbled both Hegbourne and Gardner at the Esses. Over the last two laps Rees closed up in his Roy Winkelmann Racing Brabham, but Jochen finished an unruffled third to set the seal on a dramatic debut.

Jackie Stewart was the coming man in Europe at that time, having just won the Formula Three race that supported the highly prestigious Monaco Grand Prix. He won the F3 encounter at Mallory, too, as well as the GT race in a Lotus Elan. He was sceptical about Jochen's pole, but subsequently concluded that he was worth monitoring. "He looks very young, like a schoolboy, lost and somewhat out of place," were his initial impressions of the man who would become one of his closest friends, as related to Jochen's biographer Heinz Pruller. "His helmet doesn't seem to fit him and I can't quite see how he made fastest time. An Austrian in England... must be a timing error."

Later, as he realised that Jochen's pole time had been no fluke, he took a closer look, and told Pruller: "He squats in front of his transporter and looks as if he couldn't care less whether anyone talks to him or not. He obviously wants to be independent and asks no one for any favours; a bit of a 'loner,' perhaps. A man who doesn't need any help and who doesn't want anyone to think he does."

Except that he had had no qualms about asking Denny if he could follow him round... Already, Jochen's somewhat hard-looking mien, which stemmed from that flattened, boxer's nose, could confuse people.

OPPOSITE *At Crystal Palace the following day, Rees had plenty of time to study Jochen's gearbox, but could never find a way past the newcomer in the blue Brabham.* (LAT)

If onlookers had been impressed at Mallory Park, they were to be stunned when Jochen headed down to Crystal Palace, where everyone who was anyone in the Formula Two world gathered the following day for the 11th running of the London Grand Prix at the tight little track that threaded its way around parkland in downtown south-east London.

"Jochen was very, very pleased to finish third at Mallory, there was a lot of joy," Goozee recalled. But that evening they had to throw everything on to the trailer and hot-foot it down to Crystal Palace, where qualifying would begin early the next day.

"We stopped by the side of a road outside the circuit, with the race car behind us on the trailer, and just went to sleep. It was all new to me, the first time I'd ever slept in a car! And uncomfortable!"

The race, the third round of the *Autocar* British Formula Two Championship, was to be run in the form of two 20-lap heats, one for the drivers who were expected to be the fastest and one for the upcomers, and a 40-lap final.

Jim Clark jumped into the lead of the first heat from the middle of the third row of the grid, as Brian Hart and Bill Bradley collided in the first corner and Mike Spence's clutch exploded as he tried to accelerate away. Graham Hill, driving a Cooper-BRM entered by John Coombs, soon caught Clark, and after passing the Ron Harris Lotus on the third lap he pulled away to an easy victory over Clark and Denny Hulme's Brabham. Hill and Hulme shared fastest lap, in 58.6s.

David Hobbs led the second heat in his Merlyn-Cosworth, but Jochen breezed by on the second lap, driving with huge assurance and all the panache he had demonstrated the previous day at Mallory. Poleman Alan Rees quickly moved on to his tail, however, in Roy Winkelmann's similar car, and observers who had not been at the Leicestershire circuit confidently expected that the experienced Welshman, a noted Palace expert, would soon put the Austrian upstart in his place. He couldn't, however, and eventually finished second to him, with Kurt Ahrens' Cooper third. Rees set fastest lap, in 58.4s.

Hill and Clark were expected to fight for the final, with Graham starting from pole. Jochen and Alan completed the front row with Jimmy and Denny on the second.

Graham asked somebody: "Who is the boy alongside me?"

"Jochen Rindt of Austria," came the reply.

"Never heard of him," Graham answered. "Is he a skier?"

As it happened, Jochen was a damn good skier. But in time Hill would come to know from the inside at Team Lotus just who Jochen Rindt was when it came to racing cars.

It was Reesie who burst into the lead at the start, intent on avoiding the need to follow Austrians in dark blue Brabhams, let alone World Champions. At the end of the opening lap he was still in front of Graham, with Jochen leading Jimmy, Peter Arundell and Denny. Hill moved ahead on the second lap, however, and to Rees's chagrin Jochen passed him on the third.

Now Jochen had a grandstand view of what happened to Hill's Cooper. "I was chasing him when his rear anti-roll bar broke," he reported (it was actually a mounting bracket that had sheared). "This made his car understeer violently, and I was able to pass him." That happened on the 15th lap at South Tower, and thereafter Jochen was away on his date with destiny. Behind him the track was littered with brutal battles all the way down the field. Rees moved in to challenge Hill, without ever finding a way by, and Clark headed Arundell in fourth place until a quick pit stop to have a spark plug lead re-attached dropped him to the back of the field. After 40 laps Jochen was 1.4s ahead of Hill, who had Rees less than half a second behind him. Arundell was another 4.8s adrift, with Hulme on his tail. And just to demonstrate his startling superiority that day, and that his form at Mallory Park had not been a flash in the pan, Jochen set fastest lap in 58.0s, a time nobody had got close to in qualifying.

A 16-year-old Alan Henry, still a long way from starting a distinguished career in motorsport journalism, was among the spectators that day, together with his father. "Watching from opposite the pits," he would write nearly a quarter of a century later, "I was captivated by the atmosphere, the sense of occasion, the tremulous excitement." Jochen's astonishing success was one of the things that would inspire him to get into the sport.

Rees, too, was impressed by what he had seen Jochen do. At Mallory Park he had been treated to a demonstration of the Austrian's stylish driving, and for much of his race in the second heat at Crystal Palace he'd been able to watch and analyse how Jochen found his speed. Lap after lap the Brabham would slither around, its tail well out, as Jochen sawed the wheel from lock to lock the way that the fastest saloon car drivers of the day did. But he was not losing time doing that, merely helping the car to turn into the track's tight corners without the need to shed speed on the entry.

"I hadn't even met him prior to that race," Rees would tell Henry years later. "He hadn't actually achieved much before, although I knew he had done pretty well at the Nürburgring, where he finished fourth.

"Nobody had taken him particularly seriously before that weekend. I was very close behind him during the preliminary heat at Crystal Palace, and on every corner he did what looked like a half spin. After pulling my foot off the throttle for about seven laps, I started to get the message that this bloke must have known partly

what he was doing, and I thought: 'Jeez, he's not going to lose it, even though he looks it every time,' so I kept my boot in, even when he was sideways in front of me. From then on I tried everything to get past, but I just couldn't do it, so he won the heat.

"Jochen was supremely confident, the complete extrovert. He was obviously pretty serious about his racing, but his whole outward demeanour suggested he was only doing it for fun – and having one hell of a good time."

That was one of the things that endeared Jochen to the British racegoing public that weekend, and which was to attract fans all round the world in the years ahead. He was blindingly quick, and spectacular enough to look it. Some drivers, such as Clark, Gurney and his own fellow upcomer Jackie Stewart, were so smooth that they looked slow. Jochen did not, yet his extrovert use of oversteer, like Ronnie Peterson's, Tom Pryce's and Gilles Villeneuve's in future years, never seemed to cost him time the way that physicists tell you it must.

"It was quite remarkable when Jochen won the race," said Goozee, "and this time a lot more people wanted to talk to him. He was overjoyed, though he didn't really express it."

Frank Williams, Jochen's "number one fan", had been handling the signalling duties for him in the pits, and was stoked for his hero. "It was fantastically exciting to see him win in such company," he told Nye. But Doug recounted that the new-found superstar image had been dented a little when Frank had picked Jochen up from Heathrow Airport in his regular road car, an elderly 1951-vintage Ford Consul whose driver-side doors would not open. "Here I was picking up one of the world's most promising racing drivers, and we had to climb in the passenger side door..."

On Tuesday morning after the race, one British national newspaper's sport headline read: "Unknown Austrian beats Hill at Crystal Palace". But he was no longer unknown by the time that hit the streets. In two days of racing he had catapulted himself on to the international stage. And though he did not seek to make a big deal about it, he was quietly pleased with what he had achieved. "I won fairly easily," he said, "as a result of which I was offered some sponsorship from British Petroleum. This didn't make a good deal of difference at the time, but at the end of the year BP persuaded John Cooper to give me a Formula One drive."

Denis Druitt, the competitions manager of BP, had been at Crystal Palace and had taken to Jochen

OPPOSITE *With a deft touch of opposite lock, Jochen powers his way round the south London track to a sensational victory that immediately put him on the international motor racing map.* (LAT)

ABOVE *Soon after the start of the upcomers' heat, Jochen is already in the lead and heading for victory, having wrested control from the following David Hobbs' Merlyn. Alan Rees lies third, chasing the Englishman.* (LAT)

immediately when he invited him to his London office in the week after the race. Jochen never forgot the lift that Frank gave him there in the Consul. "He hated being a passenger," Frank said. "And even though you couldn't get into much trouble in London traffic, he was on his feet most of the way, shouting: 'Slow down, slow down!'" The nerve-racking trip would prove worthwhile, however.

Before he headed off for his next race, which would be at Avus in Germany six days later, there was another little twist to an already remarkable story, as the race winner's Brabham was worked on... in a lock-up garage in New Haw.

"Jerry Holmes lived on a council estate there and for a few evenings we prepared the car in this quite tumbledown garage ready for Jochen's next outing," Goozee said. "Though we drained the fuel there were acetylene bottles in the back of the garage, so it was a total hazard! Jochen was extremely amiable, though he didn't say much. I did the little jobs on the car, but he was quite chatty with Jerry. He had a gentle laugh, like

he was being very polite." The future World Champion, the man who would establish himself as the fastest in Grand Prix racing, would hang around as they worked, then go and get the fish and chips...

"Back in those days I was earning £5 for a 60-hour week," Goozee continued. "And I remember when we were working in that council lock-up that Jochen gave me a £5 note to say thank you for helping on his car. It was unbelievable; that was a week's money, and I was getting paid for doing something I enjoyed! Looking back, I'm so glad I was around at that moment in time."

Before that historic Whitsuntide weekend, Jochen's BP contract was worth £25 per race (the equivalent today of £380); in that meeting on the Tuesday after Crystal Palace, Druitt had amended it to £1,200 (£18,250) for the season.

"I think I've made it," a stunned Jochen told Pruller. "BP has raised my contract money to such an extent I thought I was dreaming!"

The man nobody had heard of was on his way.

OPPOSITE *Unknown Austrian beats Graham Hill... Jochen's face reflects his pleasure in the immediate aftermath of the brilliant drive at Crystal Palace that showcased his ability to run with, and beat, the best.* (LAT)

CHAPTER 2

The Wild One

1942 to 1964

"That was typical of Jochen's character. Not where is the next horizon, but where is the biggest opposition? I want to beat them all. That was his attitude."

Helmut Marko

LEFT *Jochen in his Alfa in 1962, winning on Sudtirol.*
(E. Jelinek via Willy Pilz)

In the last week of July 1943 combined Allied forces of the RAF and the United States Army Air Force unleashed an unprecedented firestorm of bombing on Hamburg that materially changed the life of the infant Jochen Rindt.

Operation Gomorrah was a series of concentrated blockbuster bombing raids on Germany's highly significant port and industrial centre, which housed oil refineries and a dynamite factory and was a key location for shipyards and U-boat pens. It lasted eight days and seven nights and created an enormous '*feuersturm*' – a firestorm that virtually destroyed the city, killed an estimated 50,000 civilians and left over a million homeless. Approximately 3,000 aircraft were deployed, 9,000 tons of bombs were dropped, and more than 250,000 homes were annihilated.

Formulated by British Prime Minister Winston Churchill and Air Chief Marshal Arthur 'Bomber' Harris, it was revenge for the Luftwaffe's blitz on London and was at the time the heaviest assault in the history of aerial warfare. It was later called the Hiroshima of Germany by British officials, and Harris reportedly said of it: "For they have sown the wind, and they shall reap the whirlwind."

The strategy centred on relentless bombing of the city centre first, thus drawing in the local firefighters, then dropping delayed-action high-explosives in a ring around the centre, fatally trapping them. This was followed by the dropping of further napalm and white-phosphorus incendiaries in an outer ring, to ensure the destruction of the remainder of the city. The circular bombing pattern was combined with the unusually warm weather and

LEFT *This is the opulent house where Jochen grew up in Graz, 16 Ruckerlberggürtel – since commemorated with an appropriate plaque.* (Gerald Pototschnig)

JOCHEN RINDT
1942-1970

FORMEL 1-WELTMEISTER 1970

WOHNTE VON 1943 BIS 1962
IN DIESEM HAUS

was fundamental to creating the necessary vortex and updraft of super-heated air which generated a 1,500ft-high tornado of fire that reached speeds of 150mph and temperatures of 800 degrees centigrade.

On the night of July 27, shortly before midnight, 739 aircraft attacked the working class districts of Hammerbrook, Hamm, Borgfelde and Rothenburgsort in Hamburg. In the firestorm, asphalt on the road surfaces burst into flame and the waters of the canals and the harbour actually ignited because of the fuel and oil spilled from damaged ships and storage tanks.

Karl Rindt had been born on July 1 1903 in Mainz, and ran the family spice mill, Klein & Rindt, whose antecedents went back to 1840. He had not long been married to Dr Ilse Martinowitz, who came from Graz where she had been born on November 21 1913.

They were a very modern couple. A liberated woman at a time when such things were very far from fashionable – let alone acceptable – Ilse smoked in public, loved fashion, adored cars and reportedly asked for a sportscar when she first married. She skied and participated vigorously in other sports, and was keen to go rallying until she encountered paternal opposition.

Karl was also keen on the idea of racing, but was obliged to focus on the family business and confined himself instead to flying. Ilse was also interested in aeroplanes, and that was how they met. One day he flew his private plane to Graz and they fell so quickly for each other that even though she had a small child, Uwe, who was born in 1939, she quickly divorced her husband, Otto Eisleben. Ignoring the opprobrium in her social circles of the day, she followed her heart and married Karl, and their child, Karl Jochen Rindt, was born in Mainz on August 18, 1942. There seems little doubt that he inherited his mother's maverick genes.

Karl and Ilse shouldn't have been in Hamburg that fateful night in 1943. Klein & Rindt was based in Mainz, but the company had a branch office in Hamburg and they were there looking after some business. Nobody knows the exact details of their demise, for like many of those who perished their remains were never found. Many of those who succumbed died as the firestorm consumed all of the available oxygen from the cellars and bomb shelters into which they had fled, or its super-heated wind swept them off the streets and burned them like paper.

Jochen, his half-brother Uwe and their cousin Gert Mosettig, the son of Ilse Martinowitz's sister Elfe (Dr Elfe Hanus), had been evacuated to Bad Ischl in upper Austria, near Salzburg, a couple of weeks earlier, so the brothers were already in Austria when their parents died. Subsequently Otto Eisleben insisted on taking his son to Latvia, but logic dictated that Jochen and Gert stayed in Austria. They went to Graz, where Jochen was brought up by his maternal grandparents, Dr Hugo

and Gisa Martinowitz, and Gert by his mother. Ever after, Jochen fervently regarded himself as Austrian, not German.

"Jochen was not the sort of man to tell stories about his family," said the keeper of his flame in Austria, historian Erich Walitsch. "But one thing is true, he hated being referred to as a German, though for some reason he never applied for an Austrian passport. He and his whole family were victims of World War Two, and that perhaps was the reason why Jochen just did not like Germans in general."

Later, when he was racing abroad, Jochen was referred to by one mistaken commentator as Jochen Rindt, the Australian driver, rather than Austrian…

Jochen and Uwe grew up separately after their respective first and fourth birthdays. Otto and Uwe lived in Riga for just under a year before moving to Hamburg. "In Riga my father was the chief of a firm producing coatings," Uwe explained. "We stayed there about ten months and then we had to flee when the Russians came. In Hamburg he was a self-employed technical businessman.

"The first time I again saw Jochen was in summer 1951 when my grandfather, Dr Hugo Martinowitz, invited me to Graz. As far as I remember, Jochen and I understood one another from the beginning. We often played table tennis and made trips on our bicycles. The entertainment at that time was not so developed as today, but we had a lot of fun together. For a week we made vacations with our grandparents at the Turacher Höhe in Kärnten.

"There in the evening after dinner we played at cards – Tarock, a special game. The first who had got free from his cards was the winner and had to proclaim loudly: 'Virgin!' My grandparents and I were concentrating very hard, when Jochen suddenly jumped up and cried loudly: 'Virgin!' He really had won. The whole room, with the other guests, was suddenly quite still and then all the people cordially began to laugh and Jochen sat down, blushing a little bit."

Over the next ten years the two brothers met on several occasions. "Beginning in 1951, we met up during our school holidays in summer and two times in the winter at Christmas for skiing in Austria, always together with our grandparents. In 1952 and '53 we had nice holidays in Rottach Egern at the Tegernsee in Bavaria. At that time our grandfather visited with Jochen for some days the spice mill in Mainz to clear up his inheritance there. In 1956 we had fantastic holidays at Maria Wörth at the Wörthersee, in Kärnten.

"During the summer holidays I had also often been to Graz, where Jochen and I had a nice time together. On all these vacations we had a lot of fun, swimming in the lake, hiking with Grandpapa, rowing small boats, playing table tennis. There were no extraordinary happenings, but we were happy."

ABOVE *Dr Ilse Martinowitz, pictured aged 25 in 1939 when she had four years left to live, was a very modern woman with a penchant for smoking, skiing, fashion, driving fast cars and flying.* (Uwe Eisleben)

Dr Martinowitz was a solicitor – "very respectable!" Jochen laughed, in an interview with *Autosport's* David Phipps in 1968 – and Jochen lived a comfortable, self-sufficient life with his grandparents in their sizable house – 16 Bruckerlberggürtel – not far from a small hill known as the Ruckerlberg in one of the opulent areas of Graz. His primary school, Nibelungen Volksschule, was nearby.

It was perhaps unsurprising given his genes and the indulgence of kindly grandparents that he grew up an independent, headstrong character. One of his very first teachers, Felizitas Zeller, was interviewed by writer Didi Hubmann and photographer Gerald Pototschnig in 2000.

"See how my hands are starting to shake," she said as she held an old class photo in her hands, and skimmed her eyes over the faces of the little boys and said their names and told their stories. Until she found Jochen. Then she stopped the flow of reminiscence momentarily, before a greater flood began.

"Hardly a day goes by when I don't think about that little boy," she said. "For many he became a great racing celebrity but to me he remained my little Jockerl. He was

full of life and vitality. All children were drawn to him. He was a natural leader who possessed special qualities. One always knew that he was going to lead a blessed life and career."

She told stories of post-war hardships in Austria, of children who came to the school barefoot. And she remembered that Jochen owned a little wooden scooter, the latest piece of gadgetry of the time, the equivalent of today's high-tech must-have aluminium scooters. "I must say, although he rode like a mad thing as he took to the curves, he never crashed into anyone!" She shook her head, as she cast her mind back. "Yes, Jockerl was a very obliging child, reading out loud to his grandmother when her eyesight started to fail; he was always very affectionate. Later, yes, he drifted into a difficult period and attended a string of different schools, before finally settling at the boarding school at Bad Aussee."

Later, school studies would interest him little, but he excelled at sports such as tennis and football, and skiing, where balance and hand/eye coordination were important.

"I was always in trouble at school," Jochen confessed cheerfully, "partly because I didn't work very hard, and partly because I was always fighting. I was quite good at mathematics, but I didn't find the other subjects very interesting so I didn't bother much with them."

By the time he had reached his mid-teenage years his streak of rebellion had its expression in his hedonistic lifestyle, where the search for kicks far outweighed schoolwork. And as his competitive spirit really developed his latent need for speed, first demonstrated on that wooden scooter, became a major attraction, first on skis, then on a succession of mopeds, motorbikes and cars. He remembered once coming perilously close to running over a teacher – his chemistry professor – who was intemperate enough to step in front of his moped. That was the final straw that hastened his departure from the Pestalozzi School, and he lasted an even shorter time at his next educational establishment after apparently sabotaging an excursion intended to acquaint students better with Vienna.

Dr Martinowitz despaired of ever taming his unruly 15-year-old grandson, and finally decided to send him as an exchange student to England. He ended up in Chichester, on the south coast, to learn the language and, hopefully, calm down a bit and acquire some discipline. The Goodwood circuit was only a stone's throw away, so it was almost inevitable that Jochen would be tempted to go and see the motor racing that was held there. Initially, however, his favourite pastime was sailing.

"I spent most of my time doing that," he explained. "But I was staying not far from Goodwood, and one Saturday, because I had nothing else to do, I went to a club race meeting. There were no famous drivers there but there were some D-Type Jaguars, and I thought they looked marvellous."

It wasn't as if a sudden light was turned on in his head, no neon arrow was illuminated to point to a career in motor racing, but a seed had definitely been sown.

Upon his return to Austria Jochen fell in with several of his moped partners in crime, most notably Andy Zahlbruckner, the son of a local doctor, Stefan Pachanek, who would become a six-day trials rider, and Helmut Reininghaus, whose family owned the well-known brewery. But his closest soul brother was a schoolmate called Helmut Marko, the son of an electrical dealer, who would also go on to pursue a career in motor racing, and for a brief time, become a Grand Prix and sportscar star in his own right. Together they would all do the stuff that renegade teens are feared for, especially scaring the hell out of civilians who were going about their lawful business on the twisty B-roads outside Graz...

"We had been together in school at Graz, aged 16 or 17," Marko explained, "and that was when we got our first wombats – motorcycles – and there it started. Whatever we did on these motorcycles, it was on a competitive level."

Jochen borrowed his from a policeman who lodged with his grandparents, after convincing him that he was old enough. He rode it in many moto-cross events, and since the machines could reach more than 60mph there were inevitable injuries to go with the foot he had once broken while competing in a downhill provincial

ABOVE Half brothers Uwe Eisleben and Jochen Rindt, photographed together as infants in Graz late in 1942, were brought up separately but saw one another regularly throughout the Fifties. (Uwe Eisleben)

championship ski race, and the leg broken in a similar incident when he was 14. Like French-Canadian racing legend Gilles Villeneuve in later years, he did not seem overly bothered by broken bones.

The other thing that he and Marko had in common was that they were both expelled from the Pestalozzi School in Graz. "Let's put it this way," Marko explained: "If we left, they would give us a positive report. If not, we wouldn't make it. So it was a very attractive offer. We messed about, we skipped lessons. We were a wild age and we really didn't fit in this system of nice boys.

"So then we went to a boarding school called Bad Aussee, in the mountains, and that was a really wild time because whatever you had to do, you had to organise yourself. Climbing out of the windows during the night... We had to walk to school, because from our boarding house to where the school was, was about a half hour walk. And in the mountains Jochen was a very good skier, but at that time there was no safety, bindings and all that stuff. One day we went skiing and he broke his thigh. It was the second time he had broken that leg, so it was more complicated and the healing took longer."

Years later, in the Tasman series in 1969, Jochen told writer Eoin Young that the reason he limped was that one leg was significantly shorter than the other after these boyhood accidents.

And he later explained to Jack Brabham why he had such a distinctive nose. "Yeah, I found out how it came to be so flattened," Jack chuckled. "He'd broken it once before, I think, but one day he was skiing and hit a tree, and the skis went either side. Bang!" Early photographs, however, suggest that Jochen's nose always had that shape, and that he might have been pulling Jack's leg.

Jochen had inherited Klein & Rindt, but would not be eligible for any money from it until he had turned 21. The broken thigh had a silver lining, however, as Hugo Martinowitz organised for him to have a chauffeur from Klein & Rindt, to ferry him to and from school.

"I learned to drive while I was in England," Jochen explained, "but I was too young to get a licence. Then, when I went back home, I broke my leg skiing, and had to have a car to get to school – I had been readmitted by then – so my grandfather arranged one. At first a

BELOW *Ilse's parents Hugo and Gisa Martinowitz, pictured with their surviving daughter Elfe and a 14- year-old Jochen on holiday at Ehrenbachhohe, Kitzbuhel, in 1956.* (Uwe Eisleben)

colleague drove me, but then I decided I was perfectly capable of driving myself – even though I had no licence and one leg was in plaster. I actually drove without a licence for 18 months, and then got caught the day before I was eligible to collect it!"

He had annoyed the authorities so much that Dr Martinowitz had to step in on his behalf to pour legal balm on his troubled licence waters.

"The car was an old VW Beetle that smelled of pepper," Marko recalled with a snort of laughter. "No synchronisation on the gears, and the throttle was a little button. The brakes were operated by cables, so you had more or less in winter an independent braking system, depending on the temperature, and it was never braking like nowadays' cars!

"And Jochen very quickly got a good solution, telling the grandfather that we had someone who had a licence in our class so we are saving him money and he can send off the chauffeur. You know of course how this story ends!

"We had a car, no licence, and we managed to go nearly every weekend to Graz where we had our parties, and there was a good system. Most of the time we managed someone in the car who had a licence and the system was like this: everybody gets a drive, but only as long as he doesn't make a mistake. A mistake means he was not on the limit, so he was judged by all the others. And let's say some wild driving started!"

Marko chuckled again as the question arose who was quicker, he or Jochen. "I can't say because it was a normal road, but it was competitive."

He admits that the things they did were the things that you lie in bed at saner times in the middle of the night thinking about in a cold sweat.

"To survive this era was already some achievement. It was unbelievable! There are so many stories, we would sit here for hours... We had this German licence plate on the VW and normally we wouldn't stop for policemen, there weren't so many, but once we had to stop at the level crossing at the railway and we were very much in the countryside, and the police came, a big queue of people behind us all getting agitated by what they had seen us doing. So, 'Driver licence...' Jochen showed his passport and the police guy said, 'No, driver licence.' Jochen said that in Germany if you want to go abroad you get your passport and if you go abroad you need a car, so the same thing counts for both..."

The passion that had already raged on two wheels flared even more when Jochen persuaded his grandparents to help him acquire a Simca Aronde Montlhéry, as he turned 18. Perhaps as a quid pro quo part of the deal, he enrolled at Vienna's Polytechnic for World Trade.

"As soon as I had a driver's licence I started to tune the Simca and enter it into rallies," Jochen revealed.

The Simca featured in Uwe Eisleben's last sighting of his younger brother, and he later came to understand the strain Jochen's juvenile behaviour had put their grandparents under, after reading Hugo's letters to Elfe.

"Before the Simca Jochen had a small motorbike and with some other friends he was driving very fast through the streets in Graz and my grandfather often had to clear problems with the police. He was a very patient and kindly gentleman, and with Jochen during this stormy period it was not easy."

Uwe and Jochen met up for the last time during a week in Schruns, in the Montafon area of Austria, in 1960. "At that time as a high school graduate I worked as an apprentice at the airplane building plant Hamburger Flugzeugbau, as my intention was to become an engineer of airplane technics. My grandfather invited me. He and Jochen drove there from Graz. Jochen was just 18 years old, and had just got his driving licence. That was very important to him."

Uwe never forgot the driving demonstration his younger sibling gave him.

"Even at that early time he had fun driving mountain races. For that purpose, he had taken out everything that was not really necessary in order to save weight for the races. It was not very comfortable! When I had to go back by train to Hamburg, Jochen took me to the station, but as we had some time to spare he suggested we had a short drive on a mountain road. Now Jochen

was in his element! This was my first and only private race with him, and I sat in that car like I was sitting on eggs. As there were only the front seats and no seat belts I clamped to the seat beside him and prayed that this race would not last too long. It's hard to describe, but it really was a race. Fortunately my time of departure put a limit on it.

"Jochen was young and just at the beginning of his career, and at that time for me it was not easy to get comfortable and familiar with that. But now, looking back so many years, I realise that he had driven 'my' race with him very well.

"I never went to any proper races with him, as I had no time during my years spent at the university. But whenever there was an opportunity I watched his races on television."

Jochen first cut his teeth with the car – registered G.22.849 – in speed trials. As he remembered it he finished third in the first one, at Innsbruck airport. In his biography, Heinz Pruller related event organiser Udo Poschmann's first impressions of the Simca's driver.

"A former champion sold his Rallye-Simca to some

BELOW *Jochen and Uwe enjoyed many activities on their frequent summer and winter holidays together as young boys in the Fifties. Here they are skiing at HoheSalveWeihn in 1954.* (Uwe Eisleben)

toff in Graz. When the toff arrived to sign on he had a wild hairdo and was wearing odd lengths of string instead of shoelaces."

The results suggest, however, that Jochen was unplaced in his first event, the Steirische Bergwertung at Strassrennen, and that he finished sixth next time out at Innsbruck, where he was right in among the dominant Alfa Romeos...

"It's a funny thing," he said in an interview with *Auto Racing* magazine in March 1970, "but most of today's top Grand Prix drivers seem to have taken up motor racing almost by accident. I certainly did; I started with a secondhand Simca, which was in the same class as the Alfa Romeos and thus didn't have a chance."

Marko recalled of that time: "We had our final examination. I studied law and Jochen was 19 and I was 18, and he said now he wants to go racing. He made a deal with his grandfather, because he had money but he couldn't use it, and for relatively cheap money he started. It was a combination of rallying and running in these airfield races, because we didn't have a permanent circuit in Austria at this time."

Jochen and Helmut attended their first Formula One race together, when they took the Simca across to the Nürburgring for the German Grand Prix in 1961.

Marko recalled that Jochen forgot his wallet, and by the time they reached Mainz they were out of fuel and out of cash. So without batting an eyelid Jochen knocked up the night porter at Klein & Rindt, but the man was unimpressed by the self-confident teenager's tale of owning the factory and it wasn't until Jochen had insisted that he should rouse a secretary that they were able to go on their way with adequate funds.

"That was a trip of 14 hours or so, and at that time the roads became already like a race track, and we enjoyed all that," Marko remembered. "So when we arrived I remember Schwalbenschwanz, where we went on the grass with a blanket and we fall to sleep. Not even the noise of the Ferraris really woke us up. So that was our first contact with Formula One!"

They had gone to see Count Wolfgang Alexander Albert Eduard Maxmilian Reichsgraf Berghe von Trips, the debonair young German aristocrat known more conveniently in racing circles as 'Taffy' von Trips, who was fighting with the American driver Phil Hill for that season's World Championship. Their two powerful Ferrari racers were soundly beaten that weekend, for the second time in an otherwise dominant year, by the great Englishman Stirling Moss in Rob Walker's private Lotus-Climax, but that did not affect their enjoyment in the slightest. That weekend marked the first time that Marko ever remembered his friend outlining his motorsport ambitions.

"We were hanging on the fences and Jochen said: 'I want to do that.' So I said, 'Okay,' like somebody was talking in a bar in the evening. But there it was the first time from him, very clear, 'I want to do that.'"

It was a neat touch that it should be Trips who inspired Jochen. The German was a snappy dresser who often drove faster than others considered it wise for him to, and to young men of a similar mind he made a fine role model. Poignantly, Fate would engineer another connection. Trips was touching the helm of the World Championship later that year when he started the Italian Grand Prix at Monza on September 10. Starting from pole position, he was killed in an accident with Jim Clark's Lotus on the approach to the Parabolica curve on the second lap, the overall circumstances chillingly similar to what lay in store for Jochen, only nine years hence.

Jochen and Marko were on their way back to Graz from a hillclimb, the day Trips died. "At that time in Graz we had a light writing on a building which gave you all the news," Marko remembered, "and it was evening otherwise we wouldn't have seen it. And there on that sign there was the news about Trips' death at Monza. That was where we learned about it."

Despite their support for Trips the tragedy touched the pair lightly, for they were young and blithe. "At this time my intention was just to have a bit of fun," Jochen said of his own racing, "and then get down to studying economics. But I couldn't have much fun with the Simca because I was in the same class as the Alfas and they were too fast for me."

The Simca eventually met a nasty end. To begin with Marko raced against it on the roads with a little Steyr Puch, but before long he took to 'borrowing' his father's more powerful Chevrolet for the nocturnal activities, as they did their best to close the roads between Graz and Bruck off to 'civilians' by telling them that an "Official Test" was taking place. The deal was that Helmut could only attempt to pass Jochen in corners, as the Chevrolet had such a clear power advantage on the straights, but one night things came to a sticky end when, in trying to do this, he encountered a truck coming in the other direction and had to take sudden avoiding action. The Chevrolet ended up teetering on the edge of a precipice, down which it slithered as Marko tried single-handedly to rescue the situation as his watching friends dissolved into helpless laughter.

"We belonged to the same gang, but were not considerate to one another," he explained. "Being over-sensitive was regarded as a weakness, so if you got into trouble, you were on your own... Nobody would have dreamt of asking for help."

Jochen was always the ringleader in these madcap escapades at school. The best tennis player. The best skier. "The James Dean films were simply fairy tales compared with what we did," he boasted. That was apposite, since to many Austrians he was their own incarnation of the ill-starred actor.

ABOVE *Jochen remembered taking third place at Innsbruck in 1961 on his competitive debut in the much put upon Simca Aronde Montlhéry, but in reality was unplaced on the Steirische Bergwertung.* (Archive Erich Walitsch)

That episode created plenty of trouble for Marko, but it didn't stop the gang from moving on to the next game. First it was being towed up to 45mph on a sledge. Then being towed behind a car on skis. Eventually the Simca met its end when Jochen slid into what he thought was a snowbank, only to discover that it hid a snowplough.

When his grandfather died, Jochen persuaded his grandmother to buy him a new car. Not surprisingly, it was an Alfa Romeo Giulietta TI. Even then, he possessed a financial acuity that would stand him in great stead in the business side of his life. It wasn't enough just to acquire an Alfa, he had to have it tweaked by the best tuner in the business, "having first persuaded my local dealer to sell it at cost as I was going to race and get a bit of publicity for him! The dealer also made arrangements for me to get it tuned by Conrero, and I tipped everybody in sight to make sure they did a good job."

On top of that he got his indulgent grandmother to pick up the tab for the tuning... Gisa Martinowitz, it transpired, was a friend of the Alfa dealer, Ossi Vogl.

Jochen competed in a mixture of races, rallies and hillclimbs in the Alfa. He won his first event, the Flugplatzrennen at Aspern, despite the presence of potent 3.8-litre Jaguar Mk2s. Third time out he won the Timmelsjoch hillclimb at Sudtirol. He and mechanic Kurt

Broder won their class and finished fourth overall on the Grosser Semperit Rallye at Waidhofen, he was second in the Italienische Bergrennen hillclimb, and then won the similar Trieste-Opicina event. The results suggest that he was embroidering things a little when he claimed that, "I won almost everything I went in for." But it was true when he added: "I even went to Italy and blew off the local champion in a hillclimb."

Years later, Vogl remembered that his partnership with Jochen didn't always run smoothly because his protégé wasn't always focused wholly on the job in hand.

"At a drivers' training run in Kottingbrunn I found him involved with a girl instead of being on the track," he said, "and I asked him, 'What are you here for exactly – the driving or the girls?'"

"My first really exciting moment was when I had my first race in the Alfa," Jochen remembered in the *Auto Racing* interview, when it was safe to assume that he was referring to moments on the race track rather than to other episodes from his wanton youth. "It was at Aspern, near Vienna. There were several other Alfas in the race, and a very quick Jaguar, but I managed to beat the lot of them – and as a result the local dealer agreed to look after the car for me free of charge. I naturally felt very pleased about this, not only because I had won the race but because I had organised everything so well. Motor racing looked pretty easy to me at this time."

The distinguished Italian racing journalist Pino Allievi met Jochen long before his own writing career took off, and immediately became animated and wreathed in smiles at the very mention of the Austrian's name when we conversed at Vodafone's headquarters during the launch of McLaren's MP4-25 contender, late in January 2010: "I knew him! We spoke many times! He did not know my name, but he was very, very kind, very easy to approach, just like Jo Siffert. Normally drivers don't speak with very young people, but Jochen did. He was totally open. He was one of the best guys I have ever known. He was trying to use proper words in Italian, to show us that he understood, that he cared."

BELOW *First time out in the Alfa Romeo Giulietta TI that he persuaded his grandmother to fund and dealer Ossi Vogl to sponsor, Jochen delivered by beating this 3.8-litre Jaguar at Aspern in 1962.* (Archive Erich Walitsch)

"I know the Italians loved him! Even when he was very young he had a great reputation in Italy, because he raced the Alfa Romeos, and then he won there in Formula Junior at Cesenatico. He was very well known by groups of tifosi, particularly expert tifosi, for his incredible style of driving. He braked later and harder than the others…

"He was a fantastic guy! So nice. So sweet. Not a hard guy. When I first met him I was still just a fan. I saw him race the Alfa, perhaps round the lake of Garda? I went to many races then."

Marko was impressed by his friend's progress and the spirit with which he went racing. "He kept going, and immediately he was fast and he got some support from the local dealer and the Grandmother Institution in the second year when he got the Alfa Romeo, and with that he won nearly everything. What was untypical for a German-speaking area was that he was always looking for the competition, and when he saw that there was nothing which was anywhere near him in Austria he went with the Alfa Romeo in Italy, and some other European races."

Jochen was due to come into his full inheritance in August 1963, when he turned 21, but he was able to borrow against that expectation and celebrated by buying a secondhand Formula Junior Cooper T59 from promising Austrian Kurt Bardi-Barry, who had been victorious with it on one occasion in 1962. Bardi-Barry himself moved up to a newer T67, and they agreed to join forces for the new season to race under the aegis of Ecurie Vienne.

"Jochen inherited approximately $80,000 ($563,000 in today's money) from his parents," Roy Winkelmann said. "He used this money to further his motor racing career but made one investment that did not pay off; that was in a friend's laundromat in Austria. He often joked about this and said that everyone should have a similar laundromat experience in their life."

Jochen first drove the Cooper for a couple of laps at Aspern airfield south of Vienna, before deciding whether to buy it. "Kurt was a very good friend of mine," the distinguished Austrian writer Helmut Zwickl recalled, "and I was there that cold day in March 1963 when Jochen made his first run in a monoposto. He pulled into the pits after two laps and declared: 'This is shit! I can't see anything!' He was really pissed off!

"Kurt didn't know him well then, so he said to him, 'Look, Herr Rindt, this is a racing car, not a touring car. Try again.' So Jochen did, went quicker, and bought the car."

"My next big moment was when I first drove a single-seater racing car," Jochen himself recalled in that *Auto Racing* story. "Even a bad single-seater is a lot more responsive than a production car, and it's a terrific feeling when you drive one for the first time."

That year Ecurie Vienne ran in selected races across Europe, starting with the opening round of the Italian Formula Junior Championship, the GP Caltex at Vallelunga, where Jochen made his open-wheel debut on April 7. He was second fastest to Bardi-Barry in the first heat and had qualified on pole position for the Final, but his starter jammed on the grid and Bardi-Barry went on to score a fine victory in his new car. A week later they went to Cesenatico, a tricky little track close to the town of the same name on the Adriatic coast in the province of Forli-Cesena in the Emilia-Romagna region, for the Circuito Riviera di Cesenatico. There, Jochen finished second in Heat One and won the Final quite easily to the surprise of many, not the least Bardi-Barry.

"Admittedly there was not much opposition," he said, "but it was nice to win."

Jochen was putting himself down rather than disparaging the depth of his opposition. There were actually some pretty good pedallers out there. The Italian Giacomo Russo, who raced under the soubriquet 'Geki', was second in the works Madunina de Sanctis, with another favoured Italian, Corrado Manfredini, third in a Wainer. Geki went on to win races that year and to clinch the championship title, while upcoming Frenchmen Jo Schlesser and Jacques Maglia were also

victorious, and both would later show strongly in Formula Two.

"Kurt told me that the move that won Jochen the race came where there had been an accident," Zwickl said. "Jochen drove straight through the gap between the ambulance and the straw bales, where there was hardly room for his car! Later Kurt said to me, 'Helmut, if Jochen Rindt survives he will be World Champion in two years!'"

The Cooper's clutch broke at the Nürburgring, the meeting that also marked Frank Williams' first-ever single-seater outing, when he drove an old Lotus 20 that belonged to a Parisian taxi driver/cum racer called Gabriel Aumont, who towed it around Europe behind his Peugeot 404 cab. Frank loved the experience and felt he was doing reasonably well running at the pace of the also-rans at the back of the field in practice, until the car broke down.

"I amused myself by watching Jochen's progress thereafter," he told Doug Nye, "slithering by on opposite

BELOW *After practice for Monaco's Formula Junior race in 1963 Jochen had to buy another engine, but finished fourth in his heat in his old Cooper and was fifth in the Final until a driveshaft broke.* (Schlegelmilch)

lock, smoke puffing from the hard-pressed little Cooper's tyres and his foot hard down the whole way. Of course, he fell off into the ditch eventually, and I walked up after the finish and helped him hoick it out and back on the road."

And he remembered, in 2010, "He climbed back in to drive back to the pits and told me to hop on the back. I sat there astride the engine, hanging on to the rollover bar. But once he set off he seemed to forget the wheels were all buckled and pointing in different directions, and that I was on the back! He just drove off like I wasn't there! Faster and faster, steam pouring out of the broken radiator. I was frantically tapping his helmet to remind him I was there. Fortunately it was only about half a mile to the pits, but it was a ride I've never forgotten. Absolutely typical bloody Jochen…"

At Monza he was third behind winner Geki and Bardi-Barry in the Trofeo Bruno e Fofi Vigorelli in May; second in the Race for Friendship of Nations at Brno in August; second in the GP Portoroz in September; and fourth in the Internationales Flugplatzrennen in Achum a week later.

Interestingly, Zwickl recalled that in Monza Jochen was particularly taken by the looks of a very pretty girl who sat in the pits. She was the 20-year-old daughter of Finnish racer Curt Lincoln, a regular winner with a Brabham Ford in Formula Junior in Finland, Sweden and Europe. "'That's a nice girl,' he kept telling me."

The season got tougher as the T59's performance faded, though it might be unfair to suggest that more attention was focused on Bardi-Barry's newer car after Jochen's surprise victory. It was all a bit of fun as he toured Europe in his grey E-Type Jaguar, with a little financial assistance from the Austrian equivalent of the Automobile Association, the ÖASC. But while he was clearly very fast, it was Bardi-Barry who had the experience to score several podium finishes.

One of the highlights came upon his first experience of Monaco, where such glory lay ahead for him. He was a strong fourth in his heat and was lying fifth in the final when a driveshaft broke.

Zwickl remembered that race fondly. "There was Kurt with his Ferrari 2+2, Jochen with his E-Type which I would drive from the paddock, which was almost in a desert, to and from the shops in Monaco to get provisions; sausages, bread, mineral water.

"All the German spectators were talking about this fool driving like a devil in this blue racing car… Jochen really drove like a mad man. In practice he destroyed the engine and the gearbox as he drives like hell, but we heard of a Formula Junior car in a garage in Nice; the driver was a British man, Dennis Taylor, who had been killed in Monaco in the previous year's Formula Junior race. Jochen said to me, 'Are you coming with me to Nice, to buy this engine?' The engine was bigger than the

E-Type's boot and we drove home with it sticking out! I asked him was he scared to use a dead man's engine, and he said no.

"After he broke the driveshaft in the Final, the mechanic that Kurt employed to work on both cars said to him, 'Jochen, you are an asshole. I work day and night to maintain the car, and you break it with your crazy driving.' Jochen just said, 'Sorry, excuse me'."

He left his mark that weekend. Less than halfway through his first single-seater season he was, for those wise enough in the ways of motorsport, a man to watch.

"I was really wild then," he laughed. "I wore a red shirt and pink trousers, and I kept going off the road. But I enjoyed it tremendously."

1963 also gave him the experience of his first big accident in a race car, as opposed to on skis. Running again at the Nürburgring, on the South Loop during practice for the ADAC-Eifelpolak-Rennen late in September, he crashed quite heavily: "A backmarker got in my way, and I went off the road and through a hedge trying to avoid him. I wasn't badly hurt, but it was a nasty shock nevertheless."

"The car was pretty badly bent where it had overturned," Zwickl recalled. "I took Jochen to the hospital in Adenau in Kurt's Opel Kapitaine, with him lying forlornly on the back seat. At one stage I remember he said to me, 'Helmut, my nerves are not cut out for this life. This was a serious warning that I am not born for racing. I'm going to quit.' He had a medical check and though he was bruised everything was okay, but it hurt him mentally.

"The next day his spot on row two, behind the Ron Harris Lotus team of Peter Arundell and Mike Spence, was empty. I have a photo of Jochen spectating, with a very glum face… He said 'Helmut, I'm pissed off. I could win this race…' Twenty-four hours later, and he had forgotten all about quitting!"

The fact that in his first season of single-seaters Jochen could lap the Nürburgring at comparable speed to Arundell spoke volumes about his potential. The Englishman had been racing Formula Junior since 1961 in a works Lotus and was a multiple champion whose victories in the category ran into double figures.

Zwickl recalled a day when he was at home in the suburbs of Vienna one evening when Jochen pulled up outside in the E-Type and rang the doorbell. "We went out for a drive through the city, and he was drifting the car round the ring road at 120kph. It was incredible. You couldn't drive that fast there now. We stopped for a coffee, and all the people in the place knew that this was Jochen Rindt, the mad racing driver."

Marko found his own inspiration in his friend's increasingly impressive performances and profile, believing that if they had possessed similar speed in their various 'Graz to Bruck' competitions, he too might be able to make a go of racing.

"When he got the Formula Two car he quickly found out that there was no opposition for him, that he had to go to England. Being an Austrian, our English was just from schooling, a very low level, and he did this decision and went, as you say, to the place of the lions. And that was very, very brave, and I think not many non-English-speaking people at that time would have done that. The Germans stayed in Germany and did sportscar races, the French stayed in France.

"That was typical of Jochen's character. Not where is the next horizon, but where is the biggest opposition? I want to beat them all. That was his attitude."

But Marko, who knew him better than most, did not perceive that as arrogance, though that tag would stick to Jochen for much of his career with those who did not know him well. "No, he was just confident. I never would say he was arrogant. Through the language problem maybe it sounded a little bit like that, but he never was. And he was very faithful and you could rely on him, handshake quality and all that."

They stayed close as Jochen's career burgeoned so quickly. "In the meanwhile I had to do my studies because my parents said first finish University then you can make whatever you want, but before, not a penny.

So I personally would never have done what I did, had the confidence to go into international racing, without him. But I saw what he did so I said, 'Oh, good.'"

Ironically, when both had established themselves, each found he could no longer match the old times between Graz and Bruck, even though they were in infinitely better machinery, and were themselves better drivers.

In September 1963, the irrepressible Jochen's onward progress continued as he raced in Formula One for the first time. The Austrians had organised a non-championship 80-lap Austrian Grand Prix to be run on the bumpy concrete airfield at Zeltweg, and he was determined to participate. He borrowed Kurt Bardi-Barry's T67 Cooper and installed a 1.5-litre Ford pushrod engine, as his fellow Ecurie Vienne racer had switched to drive Carel de Beaufort's spare Porsche 718 under the Dutchman's Ecurie Maarsbergen banner. Jochen's car would be hopelessly underpowered against opposition that included a works Lotus 25-Climax V8 for Jim Clark, Lotus 24s for Innes Ireland, Jim Hall and

BELOW *At Monza in 1963 he finished third behind winner Giacomo Russo and team-mate Kurt Bardi-Barry. It was also the first race at which he registered the presence of 20-year-old Nina Lincoln.* (Massimo Lelii via Archive Erich Walitsch)

Jo Siffert, Chris Amon's Lola, Jo Bonnier's Cooper T60 and Jack Brabham's BT3.

Clark took pole with 1m 10.2s with Brabham next up on 1m 11.4s, and Hall on 1m 12.1s and Ireland on 1m 12.7s completing the front row. Bonnier, Siffert and Amon filled row two, while Jochen was on the inside of row four, 12th fastest, on 1m 17.7s. It wasn't a bad effort, given that he was quicker than more experienced drivers in better cars such as Ian Burgess (Scirocco-BRM V8), Gunther Seifert (Lotus 24-BRM V8), André Pilette (Lotus 18/21-Climax 4), Bardi-Barry (Porsche 718 4) and Tim Parnell (Lotus 24-BRM V8).

Brabham won as he pleased once Clark and Ireland had retired with a broken oil pipe and a broken cam follower respectively. Jochen gave a good account of himself, pushing hard throughout to keep ahead of more powerful machinery until his overworked Ford engine broke a connecting rod on the 21st lap.

Though *Motor Sport* referred to him in the text of Denis Jenkinson's report as Jochem Rindt [sic], the famed writer praised his efforts and said: 'young Rindt was going extremely well and leading all the others with his Cooper-Ford, being sixth overall.' Subsequently, however, Jenkinson's comments would become barbed and markedly less benign.

"It was in 1963 that I recognised that motor racing suited me better than anything else," Jochen told Pruller. "This discovery pleased me, because otherwise I would have wasted two years."

Heinz once asked him how often in those days he drove beyond his limits, and Jochen had smiled at him and replied, "Did I ever drive within them?"

The year 1963 was also crucial for him for a very different reason. It was when he made the acquaintance of the beautiful fashion model he had spotted at Monza, Nina Lincoln. Her father and Jochen were both racing in Budapest in June, when Jochen nearly had a major accident after trying too hard and aquaplaning on a puddle on the tight street circuit. Nina thought he looked "amusing", but once again Jochen appeared not to have noticed her.

Later she was in Zurs that winter when a skier slewed to a dramatic halt in front of her: Jochen, of course. Yet when later she met up with him in the 'Kuhbar', with her father and brother Lasse, a talented tennis player, she was disappointed when he paid more attention to his friends, only danced with her when others prompted him to, and thereafter only seemed to accompany her on the ski slopes.

"I *saw* him in Budapest, when my father was racing in Formula Junior," Nina remembered. "But we didn't actually *meet* there. We were actually introduced by my father in Zurs. And, yes, it's true, Jochen did ignore me and hung out with his friends in the bar, though we talked on the slopes. I certainly don't think that was

because he was shy! He just said I was the youngest girl he'd ever been out with! That was a bit weird, maybe, but we were both very young."

The relationship blossomed, however, and she saw more of Jochen in 1964 after she moved to Belgium.

"I was attending school in Brussels, learning French and studying haute couture. Jochen lived in Vienna. We used to go out for dinner when he was passing through, and skied in Zurs, while he was courting me. Very quickly, he asked me to get engaged.

"He was always driving from Vienna to England, where he was chatting up the secretary at Cosworth in the hope of getting the best engine out of her. That was annoying!

"I thought of joining PanAm as a stewardess, as I was modelling at the time in New York and Paris, but Jochen didn't like that. Eventually I dropped the idea."

She immediately dismissed suggestions that she was a modelling star in her own right, however. "I was a star in Finland, which meant nothing! People might say I was a star elsewhere, but that wasn't true. I'm flattered if people suggest I was like a Claudia Schiffer, but I wasn't. Now, Twiggy *was* somebody back then.

"I was working as a model, but I didn't take it seriously. Even then, if you wanted a career in modelling you had to focus on it seven days a week, and I was travelling around with Jochen to races in 1964…"

In the end, however, she admitted that she got fed up with him just coming and going with no apparent sign of commitment, and they didn't see anything of each other for a couple of years. She even gave him his engagement ring back, but he returned it with the words, 'Keep it, Jochen'.

"He was travelling so much, and I didn't think he really cared," Nina explained. "Those two years were difficult, and I'm sure he saw a whole lot of women. At 22 he was quite impossible. He was so full of life and energy, very avant garde, but he was always showing off his cars, the E-Type, his pink trousers… He wanted to impress me with his money and his racing, but I made it clear I wasn't interested in either."

She went back to photographic modelling, posing for magazines such as *Elle*, *Vogue* and *Life*. It was lucrative work, despite her modest assessment of her career.

Though they might have separated, however, Nina Lincoln was to become the love of Jochen's short life.

As we have seen, one of the emergent racer's biggest fans was Frank Williams, himself an erratic man behind a steering wheel. "I first saw him in Formula Junior in 1963," Frank reiterated in 2010. "I was his number one fan, and proud to be so. He was very happy when I told him that! He was in this dark blue Cooper. He was magic! His driving stood out like the rock of Gibraltar. He was hurtling round this flat-out corner in a classic four-wheel drift on every lap."

It wasn't just Jochen's driving that attracted Frank's attention, or anyone else's, for that matter. "As far as dress sense was concerned, he was the prototype cool dude," Frank smiled. "Very attractive to women. He had wealth, and because of that he had this air about him."

Zwickl said: "He was always very cool, just like James Dean. He was the type of boy every grandmother wanted. Niki [Lauda] was never as cool and spoke only of his March understeering or oversteering when he was starting out; he had no charisma then, though it is a very different story now! But Jochen had charisma right from the start. He was larger than life. Everybody loved him."

Early in 1964 Frank offered to drive Jochen's new Formula Two Brabham out to Vienna for him, in time for his first race with it. Sadly, this would be the Kurt Bardi-Barry memorial race, on April 12. Tragedy had touched Ecurie Vienne early in the new season as Bardi-Barry was killed in February when his car collided with a tram while he was on his way home from an evening at the opera.

In April Frank loaded the sparkling new BT10 on to its trailer and hitched it to Jochen's new twin-rear-wheeled Ford Transit van. He and Jochen's mechanic got to Vienna from London in 23 hours.

"That trip has caused a lot of trouble at my team ever since," Frank told Doug Nye, "because if a truckie moans that he's only got two days in which to drive to Vienna I trot out this story, and that really stirs them up. Jochen was a hard man, though. I wasn't used to driving a longish vehicle with twin rear wheels, and by the time I pulled up in triumph at his place both outside wheels had blown tyres where I had crashed them over kerbs. It was very deflating. He was furious. It cost 20 quid for new tyres. Jochen counted every penny…"

Speaking in 2010, Frank smiled at that memory.

"He was really mad about the wheels and very ungrateful, and we did have a furious row about it, but that probably lasted all of two minutes! Later that night he took me out on the Danube in his boat, and we nearly crashed at high speed into a barge that he only saw at the last minute!"

Frank has often suggested that Jochen Rindt was the fastest human God ever put on earth to drive a racing car, a view he doesn't see any reason to correct today. "It wasn't the sort of thing you saw on a stopwatch, but he was just brilliant to watch. He was a good friend, though we weren't particularly close. But he always had time for me. Was always very chatty, talkative. He stayed at our Harrow Road flat a lot. When I stood back from the adoration – because I was a young man back then, remember – the guy was just magic."

Jochen just made that Bardi-Barry Memorial race at Aspern, for his Formula Two debut. The series attracted him for a number of reasons. He had seen talented racers such as Chris Amon, Mike Hailwood, Peter Revson and

ABOVE *Jochen, 1963 vintage, a young guy in a big hurry whom spectators at Monaco deemed a mad man. But team-mate Kurt Bardi-Barry predicted that if he survived he would be World Champion.* (Schlegelmilch)

Jim Hall trudging round in uncompetitive Grand Prix cars, and didn't figure that was the right way to go. "I didn't think that trailing along at the back of the field could help me very much," he said. "The new Formula Two racing was going to make its debut. I guessed that for the first season at least most cars would be pretty equal. I might even have a chance to meet the big names on fairly level terms." It would be a very prescient line of thinking, though that first race was a disappointment because of carburettor trouble. "Then I finished fourth at the Nürburgring behind Clark, Attwood and Spence, and I might have done better if I hadn't over-revved the engine." By any standard, that was a more than worthy performance from a rookie in such company.

Now, as he prepared to travel to England, and the wholly unfamiliar Mallory Park and Crystal Palace tracks, Jochen was Austria's sole hope for international honours. It was a mantle he was to assume with spectacular effect as the year progressed. And he would prove the late Kurt Bardi-Barry both wrong and right, even if the latter's estimation of the time it would take him to rise to the top would prove a little premature.

CHAPTER 3

Fast rise, slow burn

1964 to mid-1965

*"It's not yourself that
makes a career, just a lot
of circumstances."*

Jochen Rindt

LEFT *Jochen hustles Rob Walker's Brabham BRM,
Austria 1964.* (LAT)

It was inevitable that Jochen would make his World Championship Formula One debut sooner rather than later after his spectacular drives at Mallory Park and Crystal Palace, and the opportunity arose in his home race in August 1964. But before then, he tried his hand again in other Formula Two events. The pickings, however, were slim, with five retirements in the remaining seven races, and there was to be no repeat of the Crystal Palace giant-killing act.

Avus, in his homeland, was a crazy track that was effectively two long straights joined by a hairpin at one end and a steep banking at the other. It was famed for races in the Thirties and Fifties, but had been sullied in 1959 by the fatal accident to the French Grand Prix driver Jean Behra in the Formula Two race, and a massive accident from which Germany's Hans Hermann was incredibly lucky to escape completely uninjured in the second heat of the Grand Prix itself after his BRM suffered brake failure.

The weekend after his stunning success in London, Jochen found himself beaten to pole position by upcoming British driver Tony Hegbourne, and then suffered a retirement with broken suspension in the first heat of the Pries von Berlin, with no chance of taking part in the final.

That was followed soon after by an abortive first visit to the 24 Hour classic at Le Mans (see Chapter Four), and then the Formula Two Grand Prix de Rheims. This was held early in July on the fast, public road course in France's champagne fields, where the drivers had to slipstream one another to get really quick lap times. Jochen and Alan Rees teamed up to do just that in practice, as their friendship blossomed. Rees went on to win the race from Jack Brabham, but as Jochen was chasing Peter Arundell and Richie Ginther the upcoming Englishman, twice a winner of the Monaco support race, spun and the American could not avoid him. Jochen was caught up in the accident, which put Arundell out for the rest of the season and most of 1965, and effectively blighted a hugely promising career. The Lotus's engine cover struck the Brabham and Jochen subsequently pulled into the pits once he had stopped at the scene to render assistance. He was scolded by his mechanic for stopping, and later told Heinz Pruller: "I didn't know at the time that that one must stay in the race as long as one's car is halfway driveable. You just don't stop on the track. This is the sort of mistake only a beginner makes."

That was the race at which Jochen and Jackie Stewart met properly. Jackie and Helen were travelling round Europe in a Mini, as he competed in Formula Three races with Ken Tyrrell's Cooper-BMC. Jochen was driving in the Formula Two race and Jackie won the Formula Three, but there was another reason why the Scot found it such a memorable weekend… Nina was there and she had with her another Finnish girl, Bebo,

who was just as attractive. The two of them, they attracted the full attention of the entire Rheims paddock that weekend.

"I remember we all went to the public swimming pool! It must have been a quiet day. Nina and Bebo were wearing teeny-weeny bikinis and everybody well remembered that!" Stewart chuckled. "And Jochen was very much just a sidebar to that. A shadow. But already everybody was talking about him being a hotshot. I think we were all at the pool together and everyone congregated round the same area, which was probably Jochen's territory! And he and I got talking there. But I don't remember much else about Jochen that year other than him doing Zeltweg in Formula One, and being a hotshot."

Nina had cause to remember that meeting for different reasons. "I went so that I could see Jochen, but he was more concerned with that secretary girl from Cosworth. I can't remember her name. He was always chatting *her* up!"

Stewart also admitted to Alan Henry: "Jochen was more fundamentally polished and worldly than I was at the time. In relative terms we were the hicks, the new boys. Jim Clark, Graham Hill, John Surtees, Lorenzo Bandini…they were the big stars. We looked up to Jo Bonnier as the super international sophisticate. We were just a couple of youngsters sharing hotel rooms and meals. We really were not very sophisticated at all!" In the ensuing years they would mature quickly together, as their camaraderie grew ever stronger.

Some of the Crystal Palace sparkle came back on July 19 in the Trophée d'Auvergne. Round Clermont-Ferrand, France's answer to the Nürburgring, Jochen chased Denny Hulme and Stewart home to finish on the podium with third place. Thereafter things went downhill again, mainly because he lost the services of his mechanic and had to handle most of the preparation of the Brabham himself. In the British Eagle Trophy clash at Brands Hatch on August 3 his famed luck on British soil dimmed as he brought the Brabham home only sixth.

To help make ends meet for Rob Walker's eponymous racing team, his Swedish number one driver Bonnier came up with the idea of hiring out the second car to a local driver at each race. Rob remembered in his autobiography that Bonnier's plan was to "make them pay through the nose". It was Jochen's flattened nose that attracted Bonnier when the Austrian Grand Prix was held for the first time on the bumpy Zeltweg airfield circuit on August 23. Jochen, desperate to graduate at any speed, jumped at the offer.

Rob, who listed his occupation in his passport as 'gentleman', was the scion of the Walker scotch whisky family, and was very taken with him. "He had been driving brilliantly in Formula Two but this was his first Formula One race and he was absolutely thrilled about it," he told his biographer Michael Cooper-Evans. "I remember that he had taken the trouble to find out when I was arriving and meet me at the airport. He was such a charming young man, so full of youthful enthusiasm, and so grateful for the drive. He never forgot that I gave him his first Formula One drive and when the Osterreichring was inaugurated some years later he said to me, 'I want you to be the first person I ever drive round this circuit' – and he took me round in a Mercedes 500SEL. It was very touching."

Jochen qualified Rob's BRM-engined Brabham BT11 in 13th place out of the 20 entries, only three places behind the infinitely more experienced Bonnier in Rob's Climax-engined BT7. The Swede lapped in 1m 11.59s, Jochen in 1m 12.00s, and among those behind him on the grid were future stars such as Chris Amon and Mike Hailwood, and 1961 World Champion Phil Hill in the second works Cooper. Unfortunately, Jochen was afflicted first by a brake problem and then by a steering problem when the pinion in the rack jumped a tooth, and he was forced to retire after completing 58 laps. Bonnier was sixth in a race of attrition in which only winner Lorenzo Bandini and runner-up Richie Ginther made it through without trouble.

Jochen was desperately keen to carry on racing with Walker in 1965, and privately fretted for years when

BELOW *Young and very fresh-faced, Jochen holds the obligatory cigarette as he discusses the performance of the Rob Walker Brabham with his mechanics on his Grand Prix debut.* (LAT)

Rob turned him down. "He was all bounce and joy," Rob told Alan Henry, "a charming boy. He was really most attentive. After the race he kept ringing me up and asking whether he could drive for me in 1965."

Finally, years later Jochen asked Rob why he had not wanted him. Part of the problem was that Rob's cars ran on Esso fuel, whereas Jochen had been associated with BP ever since he burst on to the European scene. Indeed, BP's Denis Druitt was already starting to negotiate a deal on his behalf with Cooper, and Winkelmann Racing with whom he was close to forging Formula Two ties was also affiliated to the British company.

"And, quite simply," Rob explained, "I thought he would be better off in a works team such as Coopers, which would have guaranteed entries".

Walker's impressions of Jochen are a crucial adjunct to the story, because they so firmly refute the suggestions that he was arrogant. And given how positive they were even at that early stage, it is interesting that he penned a story in *Road & Track* in 1970 in which he expressed the view: "The greater Jochen's successes, the nicer a person he becomes."

There wasn't much success in September, however. He was as fast as ever, but the preparation of the Brabham began to let him down as three final Formula Two races each brought retirement. At Albi on the 13th the battery failed; at Oulton Park's Gold Cup meeting on the 19th it was the clutch; at Montlhery on the 27th the suspension.

Frank Williams remembered a disturbing moment in the journey back from Oulton. "Jochen was a terrible passenger, but it was a different matter when he was driving," he told Nye. "Coming back in a Peugeot he suddenly just let go of the wheel and climbed into the back, saying 'I'm tired, now you drive,' and you had to grab the wheel, clamber over and take control; there was no question of stopping."

By late September, however, John Cooper had made his mind up whom he wanted to partner Bruce McLaren in place of former champion Phil Hill in 1965. There were several upcoming young British drivers he could have chosen, but he had long been convinced by Jochen's talent and character. He was 20 years old and had just some 30 races under his belt, whereas the alternatives were more experienced, but Cooper was minded to go for youth and vigour. Since 1962 the 29 Formula One Grands Prix had been dominated by four drivers: Jim Clark, Graham Hill, Dan Gurney and John Surtees, with occasional interlopers such as Bruce McLaren and Lorenzo Bandini. Clark was the top dog with 13 victories, followed by Hill with eight, Gurney and Surtees with three apiece, and McLaren and Bandini with one each.

Clark, Gurney and Surtees had each made their mark early in their career, and Cooper bore that in mind when he offered Jochen a ride in the opening race of the 1965 season, the South African Grand Prix. The stunning

Formula Two drives at Mallory Park and Crystal Palace notwithstanding, that was still a gamble. But Cooper reasoned that Jochen had the potential to run with the established hot dogs, as he so often did in Formula Two, and that it made sense to go with a driver who clearly had the speed and could soon gain the experience to complement it. Besides which, he could get him cheaply, and he liked Jochen's fundamentally cheerful character and his innate intelligence and honesty.

So did Alan Rees. One version of the story has it that he suggested to team owner Roy Winkelmann that he should run a two-car team in 1965, pairing him with Jochen. Rees told Henry that it never occurred to him for a minute that he was inviting the wolf in through the door. "In my mind I was going to be World Champion, so it didn't make any difference to me having Jochen Rindt in the team with me," he said. "But, except on odd occasions, Jochen was quicker than me. We never needed team orders because he was always going to beat me anyway, as things turned out!"

Winkelmann was a reserved expatriate Briton who was born in Hendon in north London and, after two years conscription in the Royal Navy, emigrated to America with his parents in 1950. Initially against the move, he came to love the States. "I first got involved in intelligence work in the Korean War," he revealed, "which is where I made my money."

He subsequently set up successful businesses there before returning for a while to the UK where he established the country's first high-security armoured car service, which he later sold to Securicor. From 1964 he was busy developing a motor racing accessory business, and the Roy Winkelmann Racing team operated out of premises in Slough beneath a bowling alley that he also owned.

Everything about the operation was first class, because that was the only way Winkelmann wanted to do anything. The cars were immaculately prepared, and he involved himself in every decision regarding chassis, tyres – and drivers. Sometimes he would even visit races without people being aware of it. "I'd just sit in the stands, and watch how things were done. People say that Alan chose Jochen, but that's wrong. I did," he said in 2010. "I had first met him at Crystal Palace, where he'd just got his car and then went out and showed everyone how to do it. He went round the outside of them in the first corner – it was just incredible! I knew I had to have him and we talked and he was very polite. Alan was a little bent out of shape by that, but it was my team and in 1965 I told him that Jochen was the number one. Jochen was just outstanding, words fail me. He once told me, 'If I'm not scraping the paint off the car in the corners, then I'm not driving fast enough!'"

Everything thus seemed rosy as Jochen looked forward to the next step in his burgeoning career, but while

Formula Two would smile upon him again it would gradually become clear to him just what sort of situation he had so willingly stepped into in Formula One.

Unfortunately, Cooper's fortunes were in decline, and in October 1964 came another blow when John's father, Charles, died. He had run the team with his son, and while he did not exactly have an iron fist he certainly knew the value of a dollar. John, more of a racer than a businessman, was devastated, and it would take him a long time to get over his bereavement.

Behind the scenes, he discussed the situation with a close friend, the racing driver Roy Salvadori who was preparing to retire and who suggested that the Chipstead Group might have an interest in acquiring the Cooper Car Company in Surbiton. A deal was thrashed out with directors Jonathan Sieff and Mario Tozzi-Condivi whereby Cooper kept the freehold premises and Chipstead paid £200,000 (the equivalent of £2.8m today) for the Cooper Car business. Chipstead appointed Salvadori as racing manager.

In the company's heyday in the late Fifties, the Coopers *père et fils* had helped to revolutionise Grand Prix design by developing their cars along the lines of the rear-engined 500cc specials with which they had initially entered the sport at the beginning of the decade. They won their first Grand Prix courtesy of Stirling Moss in Argentina in 1958, and Jack Brabham took his first two World Championships, and the Coopers theirs, in 1959 and '60. But already Colin Chapman at Lotus was building a better mousetrap, and from 1961 Cooper never got a look-in apart from Bruce McLaren's

fortuitous victory at Monaco in 1962 after Jim Clark and Graham Hill, in Lotus and BRM respectively, had run into trouble.

What Salvadori – and Jochen – inherited was a team on its way down, with cars for the new season that were really only warmed-over versions of the 1964 machines which McLaren and Phil Hill had been unable to persuade to perform. Where Lotus had introduced the monocoque chassis in 1962, and been followed by BRM, Ferrari and Brabham successfully stuck with the tubular spaceframe; Cooper's challenger, the T77, a modified version of the 1964 spaceframe T73 with riveted aluminium panels for added torsional strength, was no match for any of them. That was not something that Cooper found easy to accept. Salvadori felt that John believed the cars were competitive, and that he would come to convince himself as the season went on that the drivers were simply not trying hard enough. In racing terms, it was an old story.

Not even Bruce's excellent technical understanding or Jochen's flamboyant brilliance could turn the cars they were given to race in 1965 into silk purses, and Salvadori tried to look ahead to the arrival of a new 3-litre Formula One that would replace the existing 1.5-litre category for 1966.

The ramifications of all this lay in the future as Jochen journeyed to the East London circuit in South Africa at the end of December 1964, for the opening race of the new season. He knew it would be a try-out. That if he did well there, he might just have a future in the Big League.

He was under no illusions about his dramatic rise to the top. In a profile written by journalist Bill Gavin for *Autosport* in February 1965 he said, with disarming lack of pretension: "It's not yourself that makes a career, just a lot of circumstances." But you also make your own luck, and he had done that with his bold decision

to move into Formula Two for 1964. Now it was paying dividends.

The South African GP was notable for several reasons. Clark celebrated Hogmanay with a stunning victory that would set the tone for what his rivals could expect that season, starting from pole, leading every lap and beating Surtees by 29sec, with Hill a further 2.8sec adrift.

Goodyear made its grand prix debut, and also that other upcoming young driver, Jackie Stewart. The 25-year-old Scot, the reigning British Formula Three champion, scored a point for sixth on his debut for

BRM, chasing home fourth-placed Mike Spence in the second Lotus and Bruce McLaren in the lead Cooper.

Jochen was unclassified after electrical failure stopped his T73 after 39 laps. But he had impressed in qualifying. Clark had won his pole with a lap of 1m 27.2s. McLaren had wheeled his newer T77 round in 1m 29.4s for eighth place, ahead of Gurney's Brabham on 1m 29.5s. Jochen was 10th, completing the fourth row with 1m 30.4s, which beat Stewart by a tenth. Jochen experimented with gear ratios and a wider front track, while Jackie's practice was interrupted by a misfire generated by a faulty water filler cap, and a clutch problem.

"Jochen and I both stayed in the King's Hotel in East London," Jackie remembered. "We went to the drive-in movies on Hogmanay. The two of us in a car together. Today, people would talk! Perhaps they did then! Two guys never went to drive-in movies. But there was so much noise in our hotel, which was the hotel to stay at – Bruce, Graham, Jo Bonnier, they were all there. Jochen and I decided to have an early meal and then went to this drive-in movie. I can't remember what we saw, but I remember I was nervous because it was my first Grand Prix, and I had done well with the Lotus at Kyalami and wanted to do well here with the BRM. I remember Bruce beat me in qualifying and Ken had had a bet with John Cooper that I would be faster than Bruce. So Ken, back home, was well upset! Jochen and I got to know each other well then. That's where the friendship really began."

It's almost impossible to imagine such a scenario in the modern F1 era, such is the way in which the sport has changed. Kimi Raikkonen and Fernando Alonso looking for a drive-in theatre near Albert Park in 2001? It's unlikely, isn't it?

It was unusual even back then, that the two upcoming men should befriend one another rather than treat each other circumspectly, which would more likely be the case today. It said much for both of their characters, and their inner confidence.

"By then I had got very friendly with Jimmy, not really with Graham, and also with Bruce and Pat McLaren because I'd gone down to stay with them on my way to Monaco in 1964," Stewart continued. "Bruce had been driving the Cooper Formula Three car at Goodwood, when I first tested it for Ken, so that's where that friendship started. So really the friendship with Jochen was a very natural thing, and even back then we hung out occasionally."

Before long they were firm friends, and Jackie spoke warmly of Jochen's character. "He was very exuberant as an individual, when he got excited or happy he couldn't contain it, it was so obvious. He was never cool, if you know what I mean. Other people would see him as cool, but when he was amongst friends, whether it was good or bad, it was very vocal. If he was angry it was a high anger.

"There was one photographer – I'd better not name him – and he was the most hated of Jochen's hated people. Even more than Denis Jenkinson. Jenks was an original, this other guy was oily, and smarmy. He was always too much, and Jochen hated that. He just thought he was trying to get something out of him all the time.

LEFT *In Roy Winkelmann's immaculate F2 Brabham, Jochen fought his way to third place at a slippery Pau behind winner Jimmy Clark and Richard Attwood.* (LAT)

Jochen wouldn't talk to him…he was rude about it. But once he had decided something wasn't on it was closed doors, there was no way back. I saw him a lot with this photographer; the guy would often come out to our house. He was a guy who would really service that entrée, and Jochen did not like any of that."

Nina and Helen Stewart got on well, and had their own long-term relationship. "We still see a lot of Nina, and Helen is a godmother to her daughter Tamara," Stewart continued. "And Natasha is godmother to my son Mark's first child, Leona, because she and Mark were great friends when they were children."

Stewart remembered that, back in 1965, Jochen's wit was quite dry. "I don't think he had a very happy childhood. That was my interpretation. I think he was a problem at school, and he was quite arrogant when he wanted to be. If he had a waitress and he thought she was quite good, then there was no bad in that person. I mean, it was like lock, stock and barrel good.

"He got together with an architect in Switzerland and he was going into property development with him. And I got this same architect to do my coalhouse, and afterwards I said to Jochen, 'Are you absolutely sure about this guy?' because I knew, having done what he did for me, that there was something left in the bucket that wasn't being used. And Jochen said, 'Oh no, he's fine.' And then of course the guy goes bankrupt, and Jochen lost money. I'm not saying that decision was wrong, but he was with the guy lock, stock and barrel. That was how Jochen was if he liked people."

So what was it that made the two of them click? "I don't know. He was much more active than I was. He was a very good skier. Motorcycles, he loved motorcycles. He got me a KTM. I moved to my place in 1968, and before I got the pool built or the tennis court, there was a big flat area and a drop with steps down it to another flat area and then another drop down to a vineyard. And he used to get on this motorbike and then fly down the steps and then take off like you only see them do nowadays. I mean, back then nobody did that shit! The bike was in the air…It wasn't a drop like from the ceiling to the floor, it was two or three times that. It was beyond me. I wasn't a motorbike guy, but to me it was like a good skier, and he was just very good on a bike and very good on skis. And even when Francois [Cevert] decided to come around, in 1970, I suppose just before Jochen died, the two of them and the other one would have been Piers, they did the same sort of tricks. But nothing as extreme as Jochen.

"Jo Bonnier was close by but he was older and much less active. We were the puppies, sort of thing. And Piers came over and stayed both at Jochen's and mine. Nina, Helen and Sally were very close, and at that time we were all one big happy family. That was a totally different era of friendships and communications."

Jochen got away 12th at the start of that South African Grand Prix, momentarily lost a place to Gurney until the American's Brabham faltered with electrical problems, then had electrical trouble of his own as two pits stops were required to investigate broken wires in the ignition's transistor box. On the 39th lap the Climax engine cut out altogether, and his first Formula One 'works' drive was over. He had, however, done enough.

There was one final key factor in South Africa, for that was where Jochen hooked up with the man who would become his closest confidant in racing: Bernie Ecclestone. "I think the first contact we had was when he was going to drive for Cooper," Ecclestone remembered. "I can't think where we went, but we were in South Africa and did some testing. The top of some mountain there. It was because of my contact with Roy and Cooper."

Like Stewart, Ecclestone never figured out quite why they hit it off so well, but like most really close friends they never bothered to analyse the root of their friendship. "We just got on well together. I have no idea why. We just clicked."

Jochen was even then very outspoken, and their 12-year age gap was generally deemed a large one back in those days. Ecclestone laughed at that one. "We never thought of things like that, it never came into discussion. I just liked the way he'd call a spade a spade. And I think the good thing was that I could trust him with anything, you know. He was thoroughly trustworthy. To me it's important, that sort of thing. We just got on well together."

That was where they began their fascination for playing gin rummy that would last throughout a relationship that would have very far-reaching and beneficial consequences for both of them.

When Jochen returned to London in January, Heinz Pruller accompanied him to the Racing Car Show where John Cooper had a contract waiting for him to sign. The choice of venue was what sowed the first seed for his first Jochen Rindt Show in Vienna later that year.

The Cooper contract was for three years, and he would be paid a retainer of £2,000 (the equivalent of £29,000 today) and £200 (£2,900) per race in that first season. Again, Jochen modestly put that all down to good luck, as if he had just been in the right place at the right time. But he mused, "Three years is maybe too long, but I don't have much other choice."

Jackie had the magic carpet ride early in his career, because his winning in Formula Three was done with

OPPOSITE *Jochen was never too serious for long and was always up for a laugh, as he demonstrates with a small motorbike in the paddock at Pau.* (LAT)

Ken Tyrrell and was all part of the established UK racing scene, whereas Jochen raced "on the continent", as it was referred to at that time, and was thus less well-known to the people who mattered in Formula One teams. Where Jackie made his Grand Prix debut with BRM after racing briefly in F1 for Lotus in South Africa, Jochen had to settle for a lesser team just to get his foot in the door. His three years with Cooper would significantly influence the speed at which he could graduate to better things.

At Brands Hatch in March for the non-championship *Daily Mail* Race of Champions, he outqualified McLaren for the first time, now driving a similar T77. As Clark took pole in 1m 34.9s, Jochen placed ninth on 1m 37.7s; Bruce was tenth on 1m 38.00s.

He began Heat One in eighth place but steadily lost

BELOW *The 1965 season saw Jochen drive anything and everything to further his experience. At the Nürburgring he raced this Porsche Carrera 8 to third place in the 1,000kms, with Jo Bonnier.* (Porsche)

places to Gurney, Richard Attwood and Frank Gardner, before surrendering 12th place to Bruce when his engine went off song. Mechanics worked on it in the interval, and the two Coopers went to the start of Heat Two in team order in 12th and 13th places. As Mike Spence won for Lotus after Gurney pressured Clark into a rare mistake, Jochen spun twice – at Hawthorn and then Bottom Bend – on oil dropped by Bob Anderson after the privateer's Brabham had split its final drive. McLaren placed fifth, Jochen seventh. Spence won overall from Stewart and Bonnier. Bruce was sixth, Jochen seventh. In *Motoring News* Mike Twite praised him for "a very good drive following his two spins".

Next up were two Formula Two meetings, at Oulton Park on April 3 and Snetterton a week later. The former was the *Daily Express* Trophy meeting, where Jochen made his debut with the Winkelmann Brabham BT16-Cosworth. He was upstaged in qualifying when Richard Attwood put his Lola on pole and was only sixth equal with Rees, two seconds off as they sorted their new cars. Rees led initially before being overtaken by Jackie Stewart's Cooper-BRM, and he then fell back into a

tough scrap with eventual winner Denny Hulme's Brabham-Cosworth, Jochen and Graham Hill's Brabham-BRM. Jochen's gear linkage then fell apart, forcing him into retirement with only two gears, and Denny passed Jackie's misfiring Cooper to win, with Reesie recovering to third.

Jochen was on pole for the first heat of the *Autocar* Trophy at Snetterton, lapping at the same speed as Hill but doing the time sooner. However, on the way to the grid the Cosworth engine in the Winkelmann Brabham overheated so much that it took two bucketfuls of water – and then refused to restart. Hill was adjudged to have won the heat even though he and Clark finished side-by-side with the same race time, with Jack Brabham's new Honda-powered contender third. Jochen started the second heat from the back, but was out after eight laps with more engine trouble, leaving Hill to beat Attwood's Lola and the Cosworth-engined Brabham of Mike Beckwith. On aggregate, Hill won from Beckwith and Clark, but as a sign of what lay in store Brabham set fastest lap in his Honda-powered car.

Stewart's star remained on the ascendant as he took

pole position for the non-championship *Sunday Mirror* International Trophy Formula One race at Goodwood in April with a lap of 1m 19.8s, ahead of Hill and Clark. Reality had set in for Jochen, who jockeyed his Cooper round to 13th place in 1m 24.2s, compared to McLaren's seventh fastest time of 1m 21.4s. Clark beat Hill in the 42-lap race, in which Bruce was placed fourth. Jochen ran eighth initially in a tough scrap with Anderson and Jo Siffert, then Anderson found his way by only to get it wrong and smash a hole through the wall at the chicane. He was subsequently disqualified, as was Jochen who emulated the error soon afterwards and went through the hole the Englishman had created.

Back in Formula Two, for the Grand Prix de Pau a week later, nobody could hold a candle to Clark as he ran away and hid on a wet track. Stewart took pole,

BELOW *Monaco 1965 was the nadir of his career, after a throttle problem remained undetected for too long and he failed to qualify for the first and only time.* (LAT)

ABOVE *There was to be no fairy tale at Crystal Palace this year. As Jim Clark dominated, Jochen had to settle for fourth behind the Scot, Graham Hill and Richard Attwood.* (Nick Loudon)

from Hill and Clark, while Jochen and Rees were tenth and 11th. As Jimmy sped away, Jochen worked up to fifth by the sixth lap at Beckwith's expense, as Attwood, Stewart and Hill battled over second. Jochen had the Brabham at some lurid angles on the slippery surface, interestingly keeping it on the island as both Hill and Stewart uncharacteristically did not. It was another sign that he was now undoubtedly a world class talent. But then his turn to push too hard came on the 65th lap when he slid off the road momentarily at the Buisson hairpin as he was making inroads into Attwood's advantage. That did not deter him, but as a majestic Clark reminded everyone what he could do despite the Lotus 32's shortcomings as he lapped the field, Jochen was still 40 seconds shy of Attwood by the finish.

While Jochen's F1 stock remained static, Jackie's had risen further as he shared a new lap record with Jimmy at Goodwood. Now it went higher still at the *Daily Express* International Trophy race at Silverstone in May, when he scored his first F1 victory as he beat reigning World Champion Surtees in a straight fight after Brabham and team-mate Hill had hit trouble. Bruce and Jochen qualified ninth and 11th respectively (1m 33.8s and 1m 34.1s compared to Hill's pole time of 1m 31.4s), but Jochen gave a sign of what was to come with a super-aggressive performance in the opening laps. Hill

led Surtees, Brabham, Stewart and Bandini (in a flat-12 Ferrari) across the line at the end of the opening lap, with Jochen right on the red car's tail having overtaken fifth fastest qualifier Spence. In a preview to the battle he would enjoy with Jackie four years later, Jochen continually passed and was repassed by Bandini as they, and later Gardner and McLaren, scrapped furiously for sixth place. Inevitably the treatment Jochen was meting out just to stay anywhere near Bandini took its toll on his tired Climax V8, which expired with a broken con-rod at Copse just after the start of the 24th lap.

Things picked up a little in Formula Two with third place overall in the Gran Premio di Roma at Vallelunga in the middle of May, where Richard Attwood won in the MRP Lola-Cosworth ahead of team-mate Tony Maggs, a former Cooper F1 incumbent, in a Lola-BRM. The MRP drivers each won a heat, with Jochen third each time.

A week later he expanded his experience when he shared a works Porsche Carrera 8 in the Nürburgring 1,000km with Jo Bonnier. John Surtees and Lodovico Scarfiotti won easily in their Ferrari 330P2 by 45 seconds after 44 laps from works team-mates Mike Parkes and Jean Guichet in a 275P2, but as Ford's challenge crumbled Jochen and Jo pressed on as hard as they could and were still on the lead lap, albeit seven minutes in arrears, after nearly seven hours of racing. They set the fastest lap in their class while coping with a carburation problem that caused the engine to bog down when they stood on the gas accelerating out of corners, so it was a highly creditable performance. For Jochen, it was a harbinger of what was to come at Le Mans.

Hill, Bandini and Stewart were the stars when Grand Prix racing resumed in Monaco, the Englishman scoring the third straight victory of his five in the Principality, but the meeting was a disaster for Jochen. For the only time in his career he failed to qualify even though Team Lotus elected to miss the race as Colin Chapman's focus was on the Indianapolis 500 which Clark would win. Monaco would highlight the growing tensions within the Cooper camp.

In practice Jochen just couldn't get full revs from his Climax engine and was unable to better 1m 37.5s, which left him half a second shy of penultimate qualifier Ronnie Bucknum in a Honda. Richie Ginther was actually 2.2s slower than Jochen, but got his place on the grid by virtue of the lead Honda's guaranteed start status.

Team manager Salvadori explained the situation to writer Anthony Pritchard, in his book *Roy Salvadori – Racing Driver*. "In practice he [Jochen] seemed to be trying really hard, but despite stopping at the pit for minor changes to be made to the car by the mechanics, he was unable to achieve a good time. Jochen was very despondent, I was unhappy too and the atmosphere in the team was even frostier than usual." At one stage Jochen turned to Salvadori and asked: "Would you like to drive instead?"

"After practice began to draw to a close Jochen complained to John [Cooper] that his Climax engine was no good," Salvadori continued. "John, like everybody else frustrated by our poor showing, exploded. It was only too clear that John, used to working with Jack Brabham who was so full of constructive ideas and happy to work on the cars himself, lacked the patience to deal with Jochen who could not put his finger on the precise problem. After the final practice session it was discovered that one of the mechanics had carried out a private modification to the car, hacking off a lug supporting the throttle cable to make tank installation easier. He replaced the lug with tape which allowed the cable outer and inner core to move together and thus prevented full throttle being used.

"Jochen was understandably furious and so I suggested that I tell the press his failure to qualify was the team's fault and the team would recompense him with the starting money. Jochen was not the easiest driver to get on with, but this was the start of an improved relationship in which we could understand each other and work better together."

Typically, Bruce McLaren took a little time in his *Autosport* column the following week to offer his embattled team-mate a little succour. "Jochen was bitterly disappointed at being the only non-qualifier," he wrote. "His Formula Two drives indicate that he has the ability, all he needs in F1 is the right break." Cooper, it was increasingly clear, was unlikely to be the team to provide that. And when tensions one day spilled over,

Jochen told Salvadori: "I can change my team much easier than you can."

His Formula Two outing at Crystal Palace in 1964, of course, had been his springboard to the big time, but this year there was to be no fairy story. Once again Clark was dominant, setting fastest lap as he won the first heat from Hill and Attwood and repeating the feat in the second, when Attwood shared fastest lap with him. Jochen, however, having finished fourth in the first heat, was a dogged contender for second in the second but had to be satisfied with fourth place again in Hill and Attwood's wheeltracks. Thus the order overall read: Clark, Hill, Attwood, Rindt and Rees.

The relationships gelled well at Winkelmann. Rees' mechanic John Muller knew a guy back home in New Zealand who was every bit as good as he was, and thus Jochen was introduced to Pete Kerr, with whom he would forge a lasting friendship. "Jochen was a great driver to work for," Muller told *Motor Sport* writer Paul Fearnley. "He could drive consistently near the limit without making mistakes, and he was sensitive to the most minute changes. At one race he came into the pits because of a vibration. We couldn't locate it and felt it unwise to continue. We eventually found the fault: a minute piece had broken from the magnesium spacer in the multi-plate clutch. It weighed so little that an average driver would not have felt it. Jochen was one of those few drivers who stand above the rest."

Muller's comments make interesting reading when compared to Jack Brabham's. "I got to know him in Formula Two when he was driving for Winkelmann, he used to come into the factory, that sort of thing, we saw quite a bit of him," the Australian said. "He had little mechanical sympathy. He completely relied on the team about the mechanics of it. He didn't know anything about the engineering, he just got in the car and drove. But he would know if something was wrong with the car, and he'd come in."

While things improved off-track in Formula One after the venting in Monaco, the Belgian GP brought Jochen little better fortune on his first visit to the super-fast Spa-Francorchamps track in the Hautes Fagnes region. While Hill, Clark and Stewart occupied the front row, he could only qualify 14th, five places and two seconds adrift of Bruce. To compound that he stalled at the start when caught unawares as the starter dropped the flag the moment the grid formed. His recovery drive drew praise, but later he had to stop in the pits when, of all things, the rev counter fell into his lap. He finished a disgruntled 11th, three laps down on the unbeatable Clark, as Jackie polished his reputation yet again with a superb run to second.

A week later, however, Jochen would be lapping Stewart with monotonous regularity, on his way to the greatest victory thus far in his career.

CHAPTER 4

Flat out to the finish

Le Mans, 19/20 June 1965

"Jochen had got the wreckers and they were moving cars in the car park, and one of the crew guys said, 'Jochen, don't leave, man, you're up again soon'."

Leo Mehl

LEFT *Jochen and the NART 250LM, flat out at Le Mans.* (LAT)

Irony embraced every turn of Jochen Rindt's journey to Le Mans in 1965. He didn't really like the place. He had gone in 1964, but never got the chance to race. And his co-driver would be Masten Gregory, a fast but erratic racer better known for jumping from out of control cars just before they hit something hard.

They made an odd couple. Jochen was coming up to 23 and still yet to shed the impetuous flamboyance that had characterised his teenage years in Graz. Masten was ten years older and they knew one another already from Formula One. Their remarkable weekend drive in France would forge their friendship, and Gregory would forever after smile at mention of Jochen's name and refer to him fondly as "that mad sonofabitch!".

Gregory, however, was hardly mainstream himself. Born in Kansas in 1932, he was one of three children whose father owned an insurance company but died when Masten was only three. Married by 18, Masten was able to inherit money his mother had set aside for him, and went racing. He did not look the part; he was five feet eight inches tall, weighed only 140 pounds, chain smoked and wore thick-framed glasses. He had a sharp, witty sense of humour not dissimilar to Jochen's, and told his jokes in a deep Mid-western drawl. Veteran writer Al Bochroch, in his book *Americans at Le Mans*, related a tale told to him by fellow writer Ken Purdy of travelling with Gregory on an occasion when he had to deal with some rough characters who cut them up. "Masten kept right on talking as he stalked the offender, pulled alongside, leaned his car against theirs and, with a twitch of the steering wheel, sent the culprit over the curb."

He first performed his trademark bailout during a sportscar race at Silverstone in 1958. Faced with an impending shunt, he stood up in the seat and leapt overboard just before the moment of impact. When his astounded brother Riddelle asked him why on earth he had done that, as he recovered in hospital, Masten simply replied: "You should have seen what I was going to hit! A huge earth embankment!".

In 1959 he did the same thing in a Tojeiro Jaguar at Goodwood, when the steering failed. That was the race in which an emergent Jim Clark, to whom Gregory was a hero, finally realised his own true level of talent when he lapped the car they shared faster than the American could. Gregory, 'The Kansas City Flash', also believed that he had been fired by Cooper, as third string driver to Jack Brabham and Bruce McLaren in 1959, because he was quicker than either of them. When he had first come to Europe, Stirling Moss counselled him that he would kill himself if he didn't calm down a little.

These, then, were the two drivers that Luigi Chinetti had lined up for his Ferrari 250LM prototype. For a 24-hour race…

And they were far from the stars of a show whose box office draw was the fabulous battle between the works Ferraris and the works Fords, as the might of Detroit was set on crushing the favourites and multiple winners from Maranello. Indeed, Jochen was such a late inclusion on the 1965 entry that when *Motoring News* published it in its preview the week before the race, he wasn't even listed.

Everyone's attention was focused elsewhere. Ferrari's challenge centred on 330 4-litre P2 prototypes for John Surtees/Lodovico Scarfiotti and Mike Parkes/Jean Guichet; a 275 3.3-litre version for Lorenzo Bandini/Giampiero Biscaldi; 4.4-litre cars from NART for Pedro Rodriguez/Nino Vaccarella and privateer David Piper for himself/Jo Bonnier. Then there were numerous back-ups: 275LMs from Maranello Concessionaires for Lucien Bianchi/Mike Salmon and from Ecurie Filipinetti for Dieter Spoerry/Armand Boller; 250LMs from Ecurie Francorchamps for Pierre Dumay/Gustave 'Taf' Gosselin and Langlois/'Elde' and a 275GTB from Ecurie Francorchamps for Willy Mairesse/'Beurlys'. And, of course, the late NART entry for Jochen/Masten.

Ford, launching another multi-million dollar onslaught, intended to wipe out the embarrassing stigma of expensive public failure the previous year, had two 7-litre Mk2s for Chris Amon/Phil Hill and Bruce McLaren/Ken Miles, and sundry 5.3-litre and 4.7-litre versions for the likes of Scuderia Filipinetti for Innes Ireland/Herbie Muller and Rob Walker for Bob Bondurant/Umberto Maglioli, Ford France for Maurice Trintignant/Guy Ligier and John Willment for Frank Gardner/Alan Rees. There was also a host of Cobras to battle in the GT category, driven by pilots of the calibre of Dan Gurney/Ronnie Bucknum and Jerry Grant/Jack Sears. Just to add to the pressure on the Americans, Henry Ford II was there in person on race day, expecting to see the massive investment paying off.

Jochen's ride with Luigi Chinetti's second-string North American Racing Team entry came via the famed Swiss journalist Jabby Crombac, a very good friend of Jimmy Clark's who also became close with Graham Hill, and then Jochen. "I had been helping Jochen quite a bit early in his career," Crombac said, "and I was helping these guys not because they were racing drivers but because they were friends. For me, the fact that a man is a racing driver doesn't make him a special hero. In those days we were the same age, we were chasing girls together." His true heroes were men such as Colin Chapman as he was more attracted by the technical side, and he would name his son Colin James after Chapman and Clark.

OPPOSITE *When a distributor problem brought the NART Ferrari into the pits early on Saturday afternoon it all seemed to be over, until Jochen and Masten Gregory staged their remarkable comeback.* (LAT)

"I was the one who brought Jochen to Le Mans," he explained. "He came in 1964 with Chinetti, who was very, very close with my partner Jean Lucas in the French magazine that I started, *Sport Auto*. Jean started his career as Chinetti's right-hand man and was his co-driver in some races. They won together the race at Spa following Le Mans in 1949, which Chinetti had won with Lord Selsdon. So when we started *Sport Auto*, Chinetti helped us. He was putting advertising for his racing team on the back cover, which was bringing us a lot of money and for him, absolutely nothing.

"He was always totally disorganised and he would turn up at Le Mans with a fleet of cars; he would have entered four, five, six cars. In each of them was a paying American customer, and for the rest he would come and ask me who we should put with them. I would help him pick the best available drivers.

"In 1964 he wanted a driver and I was quite friendly with Rolf Markel, an Austrian Formula Junior driver, who was very friendly with Jochen. And Markel was in my office and we were discussing Jochen and I said, 'This fellow Rindt, I don't know him but he really is impressive.' And he said, 'Yes, and he'd like to drive at Le Mans.' I said, 'Tell him, if he wants to drive in Le Mans I can get him a ride with Chinetti, no problem.' So we phoned him and Jochen took the next plane and did practice, but he didn't drive in the race that year because David Piper had the oil filter burst in their NART 250LM at the start because the team hadn't warmed up the oil enough. But Jochen had been so impressive in practice that Chinetti told him straight away that he wanted him next year…"

Jochen recalled: "In 1964 I had my first experience of real speed when I drove that Ferrari at Le Mans. It was rather scary to go down the straight at 180mph, and I didn't enjoy it because I didn't know what to do if anything went wrong. I still don't know, of course, but I have now had a bit more experience at high speeds."

This time around Jochen got a late call. He was at his flat in Vienna, and had decided to go water-skiing. "I had my suitcase in my hand and I was outside the door. I wasn't quite sure whether to answer the phone. When I did, it was the offer to drive in a Ferrari. I said I'd accept it if I could get there. My luck stayed with me. There was one seat left on the plane and I made practice in time to qualify." When he got to Le Mans, there was another nice surprise: his car was number 21. That was highly significant to him, as we shall see.

Leo Mehl, the former guru of Goodyear's racing programmes, told *Autosport* a story which endorsed Crombac's take on Chinetti's level of disorganisation. Chinetti hadn't even checked with Goodyear whether it had allocated any tyres to NART.

"The first day I was there this short Italian man came up to me. He said his name was Luigi Chinetti, that he was running a production Ferrari 275LM [sic] and that Mr Hartz (Vice President of Goodyear's development team) had promised him that I would bring along some tyres for him. I told him that I didn't know anything about it. I said: 'Well, we've got plenty of tyres for these big Fords, but we don't have anything that even fits on a 275LM…'"

When Chinetti insisted, Mehl was forced to improvise. Rain was always a likelihood at Le Mans so he had brought along a batch of narrow wet weather tyres and gave him a set of those to be getting on with. "Amazingly," Mehl said, "the drivers loved them…"

Phil Hill, a three-time winner, slaughtered the opposition in qualifying with a 142.25mph lap of 3m 33s, which was 5.1s faster than the closest Ferrari. Jochen only arrived in time for the final practice session, but lapped 11th fastest.

The Dearborn iron dominated the early stages of the race, too, with McLaren and Amon leading the way. Bruce set a new lap record on his second tour – 3m 45.2s – and soon trimmed that to 3m 41.2s or 136.13mph. Amon then cut that to 3m 37.7s or 138.32mph. They were leaving the Ferraris at five seconds a lap in a crushing demonstration of outright speed. Eventually Hill would leave the lap record at 3m 37.5s.

The Ford challenge did not last long, however. The McLaren/Miles car quit with gearbox failure after four hours, and clutch problems delayed the Hill/Amon car and it was through by midnight.

Now the works Ferraris surged to the front as Surtees/Scarfiotti led into the new day in a tense nip and tuck battle with Parkes/Guichet. Behind them the Fords had all wilted, generally with transmission maladies or blown cylinder head gaskets. But the red cars were also beset with problems, centring on cracked brake discs. Surtees/Scarfiotti dropped back, and eventually retired when their overworked gearbox cried enough; Parkes/Guichet lost 50 minutes in the pits with similar problems, while Bandini/Biscaldi dropped a valve and Rodriguez/Vaccarella were also hampered by gremlins in the brakes and transmission.

Jochen and Masten had been as high as eighth at the end of the first hour as Jochen battled with Bandini. He carried on for another 15 minutes, but when he handed over to Masten they lost three laps while an errant starter motor had to be changed. Less than 90 minutes after Masten had begun his stint the American was back in the pits with what sounded to Jochen like a dropped valve. The engine was actually running on only half of its 12 cylinders. "The distributor must have packed up," Masten suggested, but Chinetti and team manager Johnny Baus both believed the "Kansas City Flash" had over-revved it and damaged a valve. They sent Jochen out to do a looksee lap, and he came back in to confirm Masten's diagnosis: their V12 was a straight six. Chinetti

ABOVE *Exiting Mulsanne Corner, Gregory keeps number 21 ahead of the David Piper/Jo Bonnier Ferrari 365P2 and the works 275P2 of Lorenzo Bandini/Giampiero Biscaldi.* (LAT)

was all for withdrawing the car, but after the mechanics had finally changed the distributor they discovered a faulty condenser. While they were dealing with it all, Jochen was getting ready to leave.

Masten went looking for his co-driver, and found him in his civvies in the car park, preparing to drive home. Fortunately, his hire car had been boxed in. "Masten had gotten in the race car and then somebody said, 'Where's Jochen?'" Mehl remembered. "Well, Jochen had got the wreckers and they were moving cars in the car park, and one of the crew guys said, 'Jochen, don't leave, man, you're up again soon.'"

When Masten broached him and asked what he was doing, Jochen said: "We've had our race; we can't possibly win." "Are you mad?" Masten responded in his deep drawl. "It is impossible for us to lose as long as we don't have any more problems. Le Mans is a peculiar event. Losing ten laps means nothing."

Masten, of course, was bullshitting. By any standard, they were screwed. Jochen knew that. But there and then they made a pact. They would drive the thing flat out to the very last lap, and if it got to the finish it got to the finish. If it broke, well, it broke.

Jochen's good friend Michael Argetsinger, the son of US

GP promoter Cameron Argetsinger, remembered talking to him about that when they first met at Watkins Glen later in the year. "I recall congratulating him on the win at Le Mans. He told me the story about that race in some detail – and I was later to be present to hear him repeat the story at various times over the next several years. The importance of this is that I believe – based upon hearing Jochen tell it – that the generally held view of what transpired has, in my opinion, become greatly distorted.

"The way the story is often told today is that after the Ferrari had its early troubles Jochen and Masten tried to blow it up so they could leave early – and that the surprise was that it kept going and they won the race. There is a subtle but important difference in what is the truth. They did not have the intent to deliberately blow it up, nor did they hope that would be the outcome. What they did agree to was that since they were so far behind they may as well drive it flat out and see what they could make of it. If it blew up, well that was the risk but it might last and it was the only possibility of a good outcome.

"I remember Jochen's words on the subject: 'It was a great joke, it kept going and we won the race.' At no time did I ever hear Jochen say they intended to blow it up, rather they accepted the possibility of that happening and just reached a mutual pact that they would go all out and see what happened. I think this an important distinction to make."

Masten resumed the race in 18th place, but by midnight they were 14th and as the works Ferraris ran into trouble they moved steadily up the leader board. By dawn they found themselves in second place, behind the Ecurie Nationale Belge 250LM. By six o'clock the yellow car was averaging 121.56mph and had covered 203 laps. Of the works cars, only Parkes/Guichet were in with a chance, but they were still cracking brake discs and then when their overworked gearbox jammed in fifth it became a clear-cut two-horse race. By ten o'clock the Belgians were still half a lap ahead, but Jochen and Masten were turning traditional Le Mans practice on its head, driving as if this was a Grand Prix not a day-long endurance race.

Dumay and Gosselin were amateur racers, the former a nightclub owner, the latter a wealthy industrialist; breathing down their necks were two of the hardest chargers in the business, one an experienced international racer, the other a man who would in the coming years establish himself as the fastest man in Grand Prix racing. It was no contest. Jochen was taking five seconds a lap off them, Masten four. Their stunning pace, however, came at a price. They would use six sets of Leo Mehl's skinny wet weather Goodyears and six sets of brake pads, which added up to time lost in the pits as the car was serviced.

Things were shaping up for a dramatic denouement, much to the concern of Ferrari's team manager Eugenio Dragoni. A man whose Machiavellian demeanour would ultimately prove to be his undoing at Le Mans the following year, he unwisely attempted to prevail upon Chinetti to slow his drivers down in order not to jeopardise the marque's chances of victory. Chinetti had heard all that guff before, four years earlier, when Pedro Rodriguez and his late younger brother Ricardo had scared the hell out of the works team with their blistering speed in NART's entry. He took no more notice now than he did then. While Chinetti laughed at the suggestion, Jochen simply treated it with the disdain it deserved and ignored it.

During their extraordinary drive, they lapped the tardy gas turbine-engined Rover-BRM many times, as Graham Hill and Jackie Stewart soldiered dutifully on. "Jochen lapped me… I'm inclined to say every five laps," Stewart recalled. "Graham had stuck our car in the sandbank at the end of Mulsanne on the very first lap, and it had digested loads of sand which had blunted all the blades in the turbine. So we had to drive at reduced revs. Instead of 71,000 it was something like 55,000! I was also getting passed by Triumph Spitfires on the straight!" He broke off to laugh.

"That was a big deal, Jochen was pissing himself. Every time this red 250LM came by me it seemed to be at some impossible angle and he was flicking vee signs out of the window. And he would pass *close*, if you know what I mean! I would nearly get blown off the road…"

The turning point came soon after dawn, at 4.50am, when Jochen took Ferrari number 21 into the lead briefly before having to make a scheduled pit stop. By ten o'clock the two 250LMs were still within a lap of each other. At 12.13pm Dumay made a routine pit stop, enabling Jochen to get back on the same lap, albeit three minutes behind. When Gosselin then made a very short stop to hand back to Dumay, he closed to within 53 seconds, then hacked off another 11 in one lap. Within another lap he'd stolen another 13, and the two cars were only 29 seconds apart when the Belgian Ferrari threw the right rear tyre tread on the Mulsanne straight after Dumay ran over debris. The rear bodywork was badly damaged and the rear wheel collapsed as he nursed the car back to the pits. That was when the lead changed hands for good. Dumay lost further time as repairs were made until officials were satisfied that the car was no longer in a dangerous condition.

"The big excitement came when we passed the Belgian Ferrari," Jochen said. "We had been catching it slowly for a long while and then it blew a tyre on the straight; when I saw it crawling around to the pits on the rim I knew we had the race in our pockets." This was manna from heaven for Mehl, as the Dumay/Gosselin car was running on Dunlops.

Jochen pitted soon after taking the lead to hand over to Masten and have the final set of tyres and brake pads fitted. By the time Dumay crept into the pits the American had a two minute lead, and by the time Dumay got going again after two further stops to satisfy the officials that the jagged rear bodywork was safe, they were five laps behind and their sole hope remained that the Rindt/Gregory car would break. They had no way of knowing it, but that was a distinct possibility. The fearsome pace had taken its toll on the brakes and steering, both of which were juddering violently. And the engine had been down on power by 300rpm ever since the change of distributor. No longer charging, Jochen and Masten were now having to nurse their machine. And it got worse. Masten had been trying to win Le Mans for ten years, and now there was every possibility that the great prize was about to be snatched away at the last moment.

Jochen understood his partner's hunger for the

victory, and sportingly let him handle the final 90 minutes. Almost certainly that was what got them through. Belying his reputation as a car breaker, the American dealt with an increasingly worrying graunching noise from the limited-slip differential by dipping the clutch and coasting through the corners, before gently feeding it back in when the car was pointing straight again. Jochen was later honest enough to admit that he would never have been able to discipline himself to do that. In the pits, he told Heinz Pruller: "If he manages to pull through, I'll be deliriously happy!"

Masten's nursemaiding worked. As Dumay stopped the yellow Ferrari by the finish line just before four o'clock, rather than risk having to run a further lap, Masten came round and was greeted by delighted whoops from the Chinetti squad as he brought the red 250LM over the line having covered 348 laps or 2,906.23 miles at

an average speed for the 24 hours of 121.09mph. Dumay and Gosselin were almost 47 miles behind.

It was the first time that one of Chinetti's own cars had won the race, though the man himself had been victorious for Alfa Romeo in 1932 (with the incomparable Raymond Sommer) and '34 (with Philippe Etancelin), and again in 1949 (with Peter Mitchell-Thomson, Lord Selsdon) in the first post-war race. On that occasion he had secured the first win for Ferrari at La Sarthe. Now, as Jochen and Masten celebrated their first, nobody could know that NART had won Ferrari's

BELOW *Towards the end of a gruelling race the NART Ferrari suffered from brake vibrations and a grumbling differential, as Jochen and Masten Gregory nursed it towards a fabulous and unexpected victory.* (Grand Prix Photo)

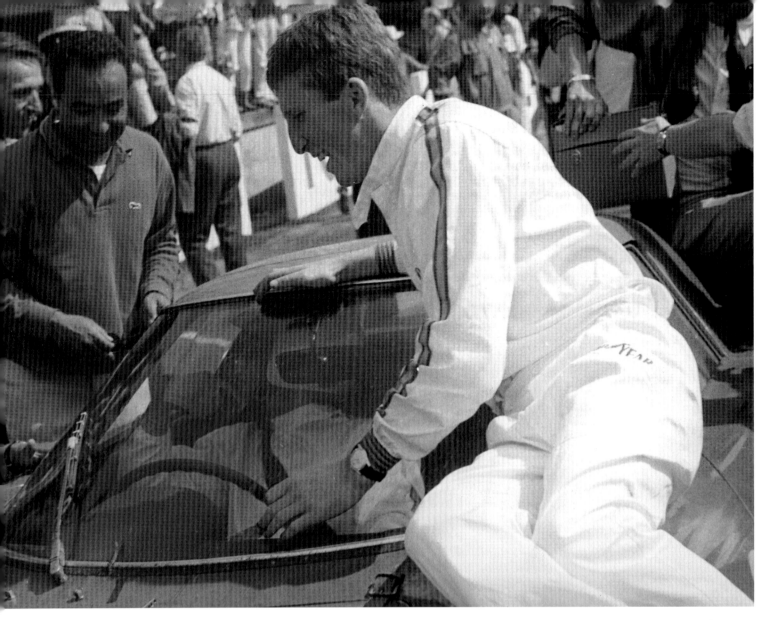

ABOVE *Jochen sportingly let Gregory finish the race, and leapt aboard the car as they celebrated their triumph. Moments later, the hard-worked differential failed en route to the paddock.* (Grand Prix Photo)

ninth and final victory there. It was also the first victory for a privateer since Ecurie Ecosse won in 1957.

In the moment of triumph, an ecstatic Jochen celebrated the biggest moment of his burgeoning career as he joined the mechanics atop the dirt-streaked car. Somehow it was totally apposite that he should win the race in such a dramatic fashion.

There were four intriguing postscripts to the fairy story. The first came almost immediately. Masten had been right to nurse the car for those closing hours. As one of the mechanics drove the Ferrari back to the paddock, the differential seized. Victory had been that close-run...

Meanwhile, Mehl was on the phone to Akron, desperately relieved that he'd had a decent supply of those wet tyres on hand and that nobody else had needed them during what turned out to be a dry race,

and excited to have the news to impart that Goodyear had just won the big race for the first time. "I'll never forget it!" he said. "I called Mr Hartz and said: 'Mr Hartz, you remember Mr Chinetti?' He said, 'Yeah, yeah...' I said: 'You remember telling him that I would take care of the tyres?' 'Yeah, I do remember that...' I said: 'I've got news for you; we won the race!'"

The third postscript arose via the late American driver Edgar Hugus who had raced at Le Mans nine times since 1956 with best finishes of seventh in a Ferrari 250 TR and a 250 GT in 1958 and 1960 respectively.

"This year I was to drive a Ferrari of Luigi Chinetti in the race," Hugus said of that 1965 epic, as he went on to make a remarkable claim. "However, the factory did not finish the car in time, so Luigi put me on as reserve driver on the 250 LM. During the night, about four o'clock in the morning, Masten had gone out in the LM. A famous Le Mans pea soup fog moved in and Masten with his bad eyesight and very thick glasses came in; he couldn't see well. Rindt had disappeared, no one knew where, so Luigi told me to get my helmet on and go. So I finished the last hour or so of Masten's part. Luigi told

me many times later that he had informed the pit official about this. However, as Luigi said, maybe they were too busy with a wine bottle behind the pits. He was disappointed and so was I. C'est la vie!"

The irony was that after his debut at La Sarthe when he and racing writer John Bentley took an 1100cc Cooper to eighth overall, ACO Clerk of the Course Jacques Loste had told Hugus: "Look Ed, you've done very well here with the Cooper. You have an entry for the race any time you want," yet there he was, ignored by officialdom in what seemed to be his greatest hour. His driving was never officially registered, and his claim would forever go unsubstantiated, but those who knew him well confirmed that he was not a man given to flights of fantasy nor to beating his own drum. By the time he made his way through the gathered throng to the victors' ceremony, it was all over, and it appears that a self-effacing racer was never credited with his part in his more illustrious co-drivers' triumph.

Writer Barrie Gill had filed his story of the race, minus winners' quotes because Jochen appeared to have decamped, but later happened upon him. "I was leaving

ABOVE *The joy of victory is evident in Masten and Jochen's gestures, and cemented their friendship. Co-driver Ed Hugus was unable to get to the rostrum, and his role was overlooked by officialdom.* (LAT)

for my hotel when I heard a shout from a car parked by the press box staircase," Gill wrote. "It was Jochen. He had escaped from the crowds with Heinz Pruller. Jochen was quite overwhelmed at the victory. He had to talk to someone though, and what a story he had to tell.

"'It's fantastic!' he kept saying. 'I won in car number 21.' Then the whole story flooded out. He had driven car number 21 on his first victory at Cesanatico. The car in which he won at Crystal Palace was also number 21. 'And now this – I still can't believe it,' said Jochen. We talked for a long time. He seemed to be trying to convince himself that he had really won and how much it would all mean.

"'It really is the big one to win,' he said. 'Everyone knows who the winners of Le Mans are – I'll be all right now.'"

CHAPTER 5

Making points

June to December 1965

"He was a serious man and highly focused but he balanced it with a great sense of humour and fun. He was outspoken and, as the saying goes, 'did not suffer fools gladly'. But he was seldom unkind."

Michael Argetsinger

LEFT *Flying high at the Nürburgring.* (LAT)

If the gods of one French circuit had smiled on Jochen at Le Mans, those at Clermont-Ferrand did not. The week after his sensational victory he found himself back in the normal situation with Cooper on a demanding circuit that cruelly highlighted the T77's shortcomings. Jimmy put his Lotus on pole position with a lap of 3m 18.0s, but Jochen could not wind the Cooper round faster than 3m 23.6s, which left him three places and four-tenths shy of Bruce who qualified ninth. His style, however, drew praise yet again as he attacked the dips and climbs of a circuit deemed a 'mini-Nürburgring', clipping apexes and earth banks as he slid his way around with abandon. Eventually his enthusiasm got the better of him and he lost it and spun at the pits hairpin, graunching the front suspension on a bank. The car was rebuilt, with a fresh engine, and as Clark and Stewart reprised their runaway one-two from Spa, Jochen recovered from another spin at the pits hairpin on the warm-up lap only to run into the back of Chris Amon's Parnell Lotus-BRM on the third. As he retired, Bruce brought his car home fifth, bringing his points tally to eight. Jochen had yet to open his account, and in later years would describe the shunt into Amon's Lola as his one major mistake up to that point in his F1 career. Thus far Bruce had shown him the way, and after Clermont-Ferrand there was a school of thought that perhaps Jochen was too fiery for his own good as he tried to make up for his car's evident inadequacies.

He had no such problems at Rheims for the Formula Two race which supported the 12 Hours endurance event the following weekend, where his split-second victory provided one of the most exciting results ever witnessed at the circuit amid the champagne fields. Jochen, Reesie and Jack Brabham wrapped up the front row of the grid, with respective times of 2m 29.5s, 2m 30.7s and 2m 31.2s, with Clark and Hill on row two in Lotus-Cosworth and Brabham-BRM respectively. Stewart was sandwiched on row three in his Cooper-BRM by the similarly powered MRP Lolas of Gardner and Attwood.

As expected, the race instantly developed into a slipstreaming epic, and Jochen made life harder for himself with a quick visit to the escape road at the Thillois hairpin on the fourth lap. He resumed in 13th place, fortunate not to have lost the tow as the field was still closely bunched. Rees, Clark and Gardner made the pace as Jochen launched a frantic recovery which took him back into contention for the lead by the 15th lap. From that point on he led across the line 11 times, as he and Rees beat up Clark. Several times Jimmy seemed to have made the crucial break to throw them out of his draft, but each time the two Winkelmann drivers worked perfectly together to exploit their greater straightline speed and tow themselves back up to the Lotus. Gardner, meanwhile, was never more than three feet adrift of them over the line, just biding his time.

After 36 nail-biting laps the leaders headed into the final one, while further back Stewart, Attwood and Brabham were locked in similar combat. On the exit to Thillois the four leaders were still absolutely locked together, weaving and jockeying for position. Jochen just managed to keep the lead over the line to score his first Formula Two success since Crystal Palace the previous year, and he got there a mere two-tenths of a second ahead of Gardner who had slipstreamed from fourth to second ahead of Clark, another tenth down, and Rees, three more tenths in arrears. Just over half a second thus covered all four.

The British GP at Silverstone on July 10 brought Jochen back down to earth. Clark was again unstoppable, as Bruce and Jochen qualified 11th and 12th, two seconds off his pace on this quick track but separated from one another by just one-tenth. Bruce fought over seventh place initially with Jackie, whose BRM was on wet tyres, as Jochen gave distant chase from ninth place until he spun at Becketts. He recovered to eighth until engine failure intervened on the 63rd lap. Bruce finished tenth after a pit stop to sort out the gear selection.

On the Thursday, photographer Nick Loudon had bumped into Jochen. "After practice *Autosport* reporter Mike Kettlewell and I went to see our good friend David Hobbs at Stoke Mandeville Hospital," Loudon recalled. "He was recuperating from a broken jaw, as a result of a road accident, and when we arrived at the ward who should we find there also visiting David but Richard Attwood and Jochen. Having said our 'hellos' and congratulated Jochen on his Le Mans win, I had a copy of a photo of him that I had taken earlier that year at Crystal Palace, and had not had an opportunity to give it to him. I duly produced it, and recall that Jochen was most impressed."

There was no respite in Holland eight days later. In practice Jochen experimented with the spare car, equipped with a Hewland transmission, without drawing any firm conclusions. As Bruce qualified ninth on 1m 32.6s, Jochen lined up 14th on 1m 33.7s. He overtook Bruce for ninth place on the ninth lap of a cloudy and windy race, and the two team-mates had a strong battle until McLaren lost a tooth on his crown-wheel and pinion and retired on the 37th lap. There was no joy for

OPPOSITE TOP *Cooper's T77 was an unsuccessful car that was troubled, among several things, by horrible understeer. Here at Silverstone's International Trophy, Jochen suffered engine failure.* (Nick Loudon)

OPPOSITE BOTTOM *The faces of Jochen and team manager Roy Salvadori (by rear wheel) tell the story at the British GP, where the engine failed again. Designer Derrick White takes notes.* (Grand Prix Photo)

Jochen, however, as his oil pressure began to fade and an exhaust pipe split; he joined McLaren in retirement on the 48th lap.

Jimmy could not be beaten the following day, either, after the leading runners had made a mad dash to Rouen for another Formula Two race. On a circuit that did not give the Brabham the straightline speed advantage it had enjoyed at Rheims, Jimmy was able to fight tooth and nail with Jochen after Jack had upstaged them both to take pole position. This was the fight so many wanted to see between the two men acknowledged to be the fastest in the formula, and they swapped the lead many times.

BELOW *Relations between Salvadori (left) and Jochen were often tense during their three years together at Cooper. In the background, influential Austrian writer Helmut Zwickl looks on.* (LAT)

Jochen led away only for Jimmy to take the lead at the Nouveau Monde hairpin. Jochen was in front when they went past the pits, but Jimmy had the lead back there on the third lap. Rees lost contact and retired with driveshaft failure after 14 laps, while Hill and Brabham indulged in their own battle further back for third. From the eighth lap Jochen began to feel his engine losing power and dropped back into Hill and Brabham's clutches before retiring on lap 31. Later, as it began to rain, Clark rubbed in his dominance by pulling further ahead of Hill and Brabham, leaving Jochen once again to wonder what might have been.

There was finally some light on the Formula One horizon, however, and fittingly it came on the circuit where a year earlier he had first shown what he could do in a Formula Two car: the Nürburgring. The place where his own racing ambition had been fired just four years earlier.

Clark took his inevitable pole with a lap in 8m 22.7s, with his Scottish shadow Stewart alongside for BRM with 8m 26.1s, Hill on 8m 26.8s and John Surtees in the Ferrari on 8m 27.8s. Jochen was a promising eighth on 8m 37s, with Bruce tenth on 8m 39s and swaddled in plasters on his neck after his McLaren Elva sportscar had caught fire the previous week at Silverstone. Such was the pace of development that the first nine drivers lapped beneath Surtees' lap record, and McLaren equalled it.

Jochen got away seventh as Surtees fluffed his start, behind Clark, Hill, Stewart, Dan Gurney, Lorenzo Bandini and Mike Spence. McLaren soon passed him, and Jochen settled into a fight with Spence, Bandini, Jo Bonnier and Jo Siffert in Rob Walker's Brabham-BRM. Bruce retired on lap seven with a detached gear selector rod and Spence with a broken driveshaft a lap later, while Bonnier pitted to investigate a vibration and Siffert over-revved his engine when his car jumped out of gear. Bandini, who had been holding Jochen up in the early laps, dropped back after spinning at the Karussel, dislodging his Ferrari's alternator drivebelt and closing up one of its exhaust pipes.

By the flag, as Clark led Hill and Gurney home, Jochen finished an excellent fourth to earn the first three World Championship points of his career, on the most daunting circuit in the world. The crowd was jubilant, for despite his Austrian licence they firmly regarded him as "theirs".

Jochen was back in Victory Lane in the Formula Two race at Enna-Pergusa the following week. He was so quick in Friday's practice that he didn't need to run on Saturday. The two heats were decided on practice times, odd numbers going into heat one, evens into heat two. Jochen won the first easily, as did Reesie the second. When it came to the Final Jochen showed his sporting nature by deciding that it was time his Winkelmann team-mate did some winning. They sped into the lead with Peter Revson, Mike Beckwith and Chris Amon in pursuit. Soon Jochen deliberately hung back to play with this trio, letting Rees break the tow. In the closing laps Alan's engine began to lose its edge but though Jochen closed up he refused to overtake and they crossed the finish line two-tenths of a second apart. Beckwith won the scrap for third, unable to challenge the beautifully prepared Winkelmann cars as his engine had now done four races without a rebuild.

With the prize money Jochen decided to take a brief holiday in Taormina where, according to Pruller, he spent most of his time trying to tip Rees out of their boat once the Welshman had been incautious enough to divulge that he couldn't actually swim.

A week later the Winkelmann BT16s were in action again in Italy, this time in the Formula One Gran Premio del Mediterraneo at Enna-Pergusa. They were up against

the likes of Jimmy Clark and Mike Spence in the works Lotuses, Jack Brabham and Denny Hulme in the works Brabham BT7s, Jo Siffert's private Brabham BT11, Chris Amon's Parnell Lotus 25 and Frank Gardner's Willment Brabham BT11, with their Climax and BRM V8s. For Jochen it must have been the 1963 Austrian Grand Prix all over again, as the Formula Two cars proved woefully underpowered even though they had been fitted with 1.5-litre twin-cam Ford engines. Both cars had to be ballasted to Formula One weight, and that seriously offset the power gain. Reesie qualified ninth, three seconds off Clark's pole time, while Jochen was 11th, six-tenths further down after his engine had puked its oil out of a blocked breather. As Siffert pipped Clark by a hair for the second year in succession, after a race-long duel which saw fellow dicer Spence land upside down in the lake after a huge accident caused by a stone being thrown up by one of his rivals, Jochen lasted ten laps before a driveshaft doughnut broke, and Reesie dropped out four laps later with piston failure. Stark contrast to their Formula Two success seven days earlier.

There was another little boost when Jochen went home briefly to race the Ferrari 250LM belonging to his friend, Viennese jeweller Gotfrid Koechert, in the 200-mile Austrian Grand Prix, which had reverted to sportscar status. He had quite stern opposition, with Lotus sending a 40 for Mike Spence, Frank Gardner in John Willment's 30, Mike Parkes in Colonel Ronnie Hoare's Maranello Concessionaires Ferrari 365P2 and erstwhile privateer David Piper in his own 250LM. Chris Amon was also entered, albeit in an Iso Grifo A3C.

Unshaken by his Enna experience Spence was fastest in practice with 1m 8.46s which was well below Gurney's lap record of 1m 10.56s set during the previous year's car-breaking Grand Prix. Then came Gardner on 1m 9.76s, Parkes on 1m 10.29s and Piper on 1m 12.85s; they filled the front row of the four by three grid, with Jochen taking the inside of the second row with 1m 13.41s while nursing a stomach still upset after he suffered food poisoning at the Enna Formula Two race.

There was a brief shower at the start, but Spence's early lead was stymied when his Ford engine overheated. That left Parkes out front, chased by Gardner and Jochen. Jochen's race nearly came to a premature end as he lapped privateer Kurt Rost's Ecurie Biennoise-entered Lotus 30 in the Hangar Bend. Jochen was going for the outside line and they rubbed bodywork as the Swiss failed to see him. Both made investigatory pit stops, the 250LM requiring some quick panel-bashing where the bodywork was fouling the tyres.

That little incident enabled Parkes and Gardner to increase their lead, though both knew they would have to make refuelling stops. Each came in at the halfway mark, and as Parkes switched to a fresh set of Dunlop's R7 tyres Jochen swept into the lead. The question now was

whether Jochen had sufficient fuel to make it through without the stop that would undoubtedly lose Koechert the race. Not to mention whether his Goodyears would last or an oil leak would create problems of its own. In the pits his old friend Kurt Bardi-Barry's ace mechanic Joschi Borka began to get nervous.

Lap by lap Parkes took a second off Jochen, and with seven left to run the 365P2 was only 11 seconds adrift. However, a washer on a bolt securing the fuel pump filter was leaking, starving the V12 of fuel. The problem came just as Borka and Koechert were imploring Jochen to ease back to be sure of maintaining his dwindling supply of fuel. By the finish he was 40 seconds ahead, his Goodyears still showing plenty of tread. "It was right that you won here," Hoare told him sportingly, before privately confirming his intention of switching to the American rubber forthwith.

Neither the Nürburgring nor Zeltweg results signalled an upturn in Jochen's fortunes in the remaining Grands Prix, but both did a great deal for his self-confidence. At Monza, on a circuit where the Cooper's chassis shortcomings were less of a disadvantage, he lapped within 1.8s of poleman Clark to take seventh on the grid, half a second ahead of tenth-placed McLaren. Unfortunately, the engine in his T77 then cracked a cylinder liner, obliging him to race the spare T73 with the Hewland gearbox. He got away badly in a traditionally ragged Monza start, and settled into a slipstreaming battle for ninth place with Richie Ginther and Ronnie Bucknum in their Hondas, Richard Attwood and Innes Ireland's Parnell Lotus-BRMs, McLaren and Denny Hulme. It was the typical drafting situation: the moment you lost the tow you were history, but Jochen kept the Cooper firmly in play until his engine went off song and he was dropped by the group. As Jackie Stewart scored his first Grand Prix victory ahead of BRM team-mate Graham Hill, followed by Gurney, Bandini, McLaren, Attwood and Bonnier, Jochen droned home a frustrated eighth.

"In Formula Two you usually beat Jackie," Pruller observed to his friend, who grinned and replied: "That's because Jackie is driving a Cooper in Formula Two!" And to Salvadori, he asked ironically: "Roy, why do our cars never look like real racing cars?"

There were two more Formula Two races on the calendar. For the Gold Cup at Oulton Park he qualified second, behind Hulme and ahead of Hill, Clark, Spence and Rees. Jochen led away and then engaged in a fraught battle in which he swapped the lead with Hulme, Rees

OPPOSITE Enna was always famous for its flying stones so Jochen took suitable precautions prior to the start of the F2 race, where he won his heat but let team-mate Alan Rees take the Final. (LAT)

and Clark. It was Rheims all over again, albeit without the slipstreaming on long straights, as the quartet ran only inches apart. Jochen was in his element, while Jimmy made one of his very rare mistakes and spun out of the lead on the eighth lap. Soon Hill and John Surtees in the Lola-Cosworth also came into the picture, but on lap 32 Jochen went out with another broken driveshaft doughnut.

The following weekend the Grand Prix d'Albi was another cracker. Jochen led away, as usual, from Clark, Hulme, Rees and Brabham, who was back out in the Honda-powered BT16. However, Clark, Hulme and Brabham shoved him down to fourth after four laps. Brabham had a spell in the lead before Clark reasserted himself, and as the Scot and the Australian duked it out Jochen kept a close watch with Hulme breathing down his neck. Denny overtook with 35 laps left, and as Clark and Brabham continued their duel the New Zealander moved into a safe third. In the end Jimmy won by six-tenths of a second from Jack with Denny another 22 seconds adrift. Jochen stayed fourth, half a minute behind the second works Brabham, with Rees a lapped fifth on a rare day when the Winkelmann team was completely overshadowed.

Nobody was going to stop Graham Hill in the US Grand Prix at Watkins Glen, where he won the most lucrative race of the season for BRM after starting from pole. Dan Gurney and Jack Brabham made it a good day for Brabham, as the two Scots were each out of luck. Jochen qualified only 13th, four places and half a second slower than Bruce, but fortune smiled upon him as he worked up to join a battle for seventh place with Jo Siffert in Rob Walker's Brabham-BRM and American Bob Bondurant in the third Ferrari. After 40 of the 110 laps he had moved ahead of Jo Bonnier's Brabham-Climax for sixth place, and the highlight for his race in cold and wet conditions came when he caught and passed Bandini's Ferrari flat-12 for fourth.

Just as it seemed that he might reprise his Nürburgring result the road began to dry out and the Italian repassed as he was able to make full use of his power advantage. At the same time Jochen was beginning to struggle to find second gear, and as the problem worsened he was challenged by Pedro Rodriguez's Ferrari V8 for fifth. With eight laps to run Pedro got right in the Cooper's slipstream, and that was it. Jochen was eventually lapped for the second time, finishing one lap down on the Mexican. But he had scored another point and, as organiser Cameron Argetsinger's son Michael confirmed, he was quite happy with that. Argetsinger Jnr met Jochen for the first time at the upstate New York circuit, and their friendship gelled quickly.

"It was in the pits after the race," he recalled. "My father was the race director and organiser and I worked in the press room as assistant to the press director. I

RIGHT *Jochen applies his customary touch of opposite lock at Oulton Park, as he battles with the similar F2 Brabhams of Denny Hulme and Winkelmann team-mate Alan Rees before a driveshaft broke.* (LAT)

introduced myself to Jochen and invited him to come to the Paddock Club. He did and we walked up the hill to the Club.

"As for that first conversation, I can't recall it in detail. I know he liked Watkins Glen and the feel of the place – I know we talked about that. And he was pretty happy, as he had scored a World Championship point there. We talked a fair amount about my own ambitions as a driver. And I have a clear recollection of him telling me in some detail about the Le Mans win with Masten Gregory, on which I had congratulated him. We got to know one another better the following year."

There was one Grand Prix left, in Mexico that October. It was to be the swansong of the 1.5-litre formula, and for Jochen the end could not come soon enough. He was sick and tired of the sight of his woefully uncompetitive Cooper T77. Almost inevitably, it let him down yet again.

In the rarefied air at the high-speed track that was located six thousand feet above sea level in Mexico City, he and Bruce struggled. McLaren qualified 15th in 1m 59.15s, Jochen 16th in 1m 59.3s. To put that into perspective, Jimmy Clark had taken pole position for Lotus with 1m 56.17s.

As Richie Ginther headed for his day of days, and an historic maiden F1 victory for himself, Honda and Goodyear, Jochen overtook Bruce early on and was running in ninth place when his Lucas electronic ignition went on the blink. And so ended his first season in Formula One. Within Cooper he had established a reputation as a hard trier who didn't take kindly to slights on his talent at the wheel, and had an edgy relationship with Roy Salvadori. He was once moved to tell the former racer: "The best thing about you is your wife!"

"When you say they didn't get on…" Ecclestone mused. "You know when it's somebody who's competitive and people aren't getting the equipment, they get upset. That's more or less what happened. When we met, at the top of that mountain in South Africa, they'd had problems with the engine, something like that… Jochen used to get upset about those things."

Those less involved in the maelstrom that was the Cooper team that season, liked him. Certainly Michael Argetsinger found him good company straight away. "I was impressed with him from the outset on several counts. He was a serious man and highly focused but he balanced it with a great sense of humour and fun. He was outspoken and, as the saying goes, 'did not suffer fools gladly'. But he was seldom unkind. If provoked he

ABOVE *Watkins Glen brought Jochen another World Championship point with sixth place. He's about to be lapped here by winner Graham Hill, but in the years to come he would put a stop to that.* (LAT)

could be so. He had a biting wit and was not afraid to be unpopular.

"He epitomised cool, at least as I saw it at that time. This translated, too, to behaviour in and around the car. He was very intense but evidenced none of the nervous habits or manifestations one associates with some drivers before going out for a race or practice. He was calm, collected, and very confident in his talent. He knew how good he was."

Jochen also knew how good his machinery was, and as 1965 drew to its close he found himself in a situation familiar to many young drivers. He had craved a way into the Big League and been very grateful when John Cooper made his offer. But it hadn't taken him long to figure out that a three-year contract with his fading team had been a serious mistake. In the chassis department the cars were no longer a match for Brabham and Ferrari, let alone Lotus, as once they had been, and as a corollary of the general decline the team no longer received the best engines from Coventry Climax. There was a pecking order based on a unit's ultimate specification, and predictably the latest-spec engines went to Lotus and Brabham.

"For a long while I didn't do very much," he admitted of his initial performances in Formula One, when perhaps his ebullient style overwhelmed his underpowered machinery. "Quite honestly, the cars weren't really competitive, and our Coventry Climax engines weren't anything like as good as the ones Lotus had. But I managed that fourth in the German Grand Prix and sixth at Watkins Glen, and I learned a lot about the proper way to go motor racing."

His driving attracted attention, however, and many appreciated that McLaren, as the senior driver, probably got the best of the equipment that Cooper could muster. Bruce finished the year ninth in the World Championship with ten points; Jochen was 13th with four; in the constructors' stakes, Cooper was fifth. At the end of the year Gregor Grant, the founder and editor of *Autosport*, unsurprisingly placed Clark head and shoulders above his rivals with five stars, then grouped Graham Hill, John Surtees, Jackie Stewart, Dan Gurney and Jack Brabham on four. After that came McLaren, Jo Siffert, Jochen, Lorenzo Bandini and Denny Hulme, together with three apiece.

"Let's look closely at the Cooper Climax pair, Bruce McLaren and Jochen Rindt," Grant wrote. "Both appeared to be at a disadvantage as regards equipment, for the 1965 Cooper has not progressed to the extent as have BRM, Lotus and Brabham. McLaren cannot be overlooked, and for that matter neither can the meteoric Rindt who on occasion has shown the ability to drive very fast indeed. However, his exuberance, if anything, is even more than that of Stewart." High praise indeed.

Jochen and Bruce got along okay, but nothing more. "We didn't become great friends, we didn't come close to each other," Jochen said, "but I don't think that we wanted to". That was interesting because New Zealanders tend to be as blunt as Austrians, without meaning any offence. They just speak their minds. "It happens in every team," Jochen continued. "The number one and the number two are not such big friends."

Alan Rees would in later years speak very highly of his friend's performance and character. "Yes, Jochen was arrogant," the Welshman said, "but not in the way people talk about him. You could say anything to him. In relation to joking with him and saying what the hell you liked to him, he wasn't arrogant. To people who didn't know him though, I'm sure he came across that way. Once you were accepted by him it was all right. If he accepted you and got on with you and liked you, he wasn't at all arrogant. He was a funny person, really.

"We worked together from 1965 to '68. He had his own car in 1964 and I also had my own car that year and we got quite close during the season because we were the only private owners who were anywhere near competitive. It was after that that we got together in the same team.

"I only really knew him from a Formula Two point of view, and there's no doubt that we had the best cars, which suited me fine! Those Brabhams were definitely the best cars. They were better than the Lotuses and the Matras.

"In those days we just got in and drove, and all the set-up was really in the design of the car. We didn't even change dampers and rollbars! You didn't have this fantastic downforce that they do now, and if the thing understeered, really you just changed the way you drove into a corner. Jochen would just drive round everything, absolutely everything, no matter what. He could do anything."

There were, however, some people who were disappointed that Jochen had not produced fireworks in Formula One the way he had at Crystal Palace, that he had not blown Bruce McLaren away. Jack Brabham did not agree. "He just didn't have the car, really. Look at it from the point of view that Brucie drove that bloody car forcibly but he had a much better engineering feel for getting more out of it, and that's what counted."

As 1965 drew to its close Jochen looked forward to exploiting all his hard-won experience in the new 3-litre formula, which was being touted as the "Return to Power". Cooper was one of the first manufacturers to source a new engine, and it came via the Chipstead Motor Group's links with the Italian Maserati company, once Ferrari's deadly rival. Chipstead's Mario Tozzi-Condivi had a close relationship with Maserati chief Adolfo Orsi and held the British concession for the marque, and he, Salvadori and Jonathan Sieff made frequent visits during the course of the year to thrash out the rudiments of a deal with enthusiastic chief engineer Giulio Alfieri once they had all convinced influential chief mechanic Guerrino Bertocchi and his son that it was a desirable undertaking.

At that time it was confidently believed by many that multi-cylinder engines would be required to generate the 400bhp that was being predicted as the benchmark. Maserati happened to have a 60-degree V12 in its armoury. It had initially appeared in 2.5-litre guise for Formula One as long ago as 1957. Jean Behra had raced it in the Italian GP, but while it was potent, producing a claimed 320 bhp, none of the drivers who tried it were taken with its narrow torque band. Subsequently 3-litre and 3.5-litre variants appeared for sportscar racing in the early Sixties, after the company had withdrawn from Formula One, and Alfieri opted for the bore and stroke of 70.4 x 60mm of the 1961 Le Mans engine as the basis for his 2,989cc 1966 Tipo 9 version.

Various modifications were effected to suit the mid-engined installation in a new monocoque chassis, the T81, penned by amiable crew-cut South African Derrick White. Cooper underwrote the development of the engine in return for a favourable loan deal on a dozen of them and the UK franchise rights.

Rumours that had been circulating since October continued to associate Hulme with the drive alongside Jochen in a Cooper-Maserati in 1966 as Bruce McLaren headed off to form his own Formula One operation, but Denny denied them. However, early in November he was reported to have helped out when he and Salvadori tested a hybrid Cooper. This was the spaceframe T80 chassis that had been built to take the stillborn flat-16 Coventry Climax engine that did not, after all, race in the 1965 season. Now it was powered by the first version of the Maserati V12. Hulme lapped Goodwood in 1m 19.5s in this prototype, which was a competitive time for the period. On Monday December 5 Jochen got behind the wheel at the Sussex circuit and also lapped easily beneath 1m 20s. Subsequently, at the end of the month, both he and Denny were lapping the developing car consistently in the 1m 18s bracket.

Hulme was always going to stay with Brabham, so Cooper opted initially to hire Richie Ginther. The crew-cut Californian had done sterling work as number two at Ferrari and BRM and had won the final race of the 1.5-litre formula – the Mexican GP – for Honda. But the Japanese manufacturer's 3-litre contender would not be ready until partway through the new season, and until such time as it was raceworthy he was available to Salvadori. Richie wasn't in Jochen's league, his victory in Mexico City notwithstanding, and the Austrian thus faced 1966 with high hopes that he would finally have the equipment with which to run at the front in Formula One the way he always did in Formula Two. And, as de facto team leader, to win Grands Prix.

Instead, another two years of disappointment and frustration lay in store.

CHAPTER 6

Treading water

Formula One, 1966

"*I had several exciting moments. First I had this tremendous spin about 180mph…*"

Jochen Rindt

RIGHT *Jochen, in a class of his own at Spa.* (LAT)

The *Daily Express* International Trophy at Silverstone kicked off Jochen's first F1 season as Cooper's team leader. Jack Brabham and John Surtees tussled for the pole, which went to the Australian with a lap of 1m 29.8s in his light and driveable Brabham-Repco, with the Englishman stopping the clocks in 1m 30.0s. Jochen went well, taking the third slot on the four by three by four grid with 1m 30.8s, ahead of Mike Spence in Tim Parnell's 2-litre Lotus-BRM.

In a sign of what lay ahead, Brabham led Surtees all the way from start to finish, in a result that was a serious embarrassment for the Scuderia, which had already seen Big John dominate the non-championship Syracuse Grand Prix in Sicily a fortnight earlier. Surtees and Ferrari were the pre-season favourites after Ferrari had been one of the first to reveal its new car, so the Australian's success came as a major surprise, especially as Black Jack finished seven and a half seconds ahead.

It wasn't a great race for Jochen. He followed Brabham and Spence off the line, but neither could prevent Surtees from slipping ahead under braking for Club corner as he set out on his fruitless pursuit of the green and gold Brabham. By the end of the lap Jochen had also disposed of Spence, but immediately he was repassed as he ran into gear selection problems. At the same time the handling of the Cooper also began to deteriorate, something which at the time both driver and team put down to problems with the locking mechanism of the ZF differential but whose real cause would not become apparent until much later in the season. These problems saw him upstaged by the privately owned Cooper-Maserati of his old former Rob Walker team-mate Jo Bonnier, and Denny Hulme's 2.7-litre Brabham-Climax. They passed him on the tenth and 13th laps respectively. When Spence stopped with a seized engine Jochen was promoted a place and hung on to finish fifth, already aware that the Cooper-Maserati needed a lot more development if it was ever to get on even terms with Brabham and Ferrari.

Brabham's domination caused much head-scratching in the weeks leading up to the Championship opener at Monaco. After all, the Ferrari was thought to have close to 350 bhp, the Repco V8 around 320. As it transpired, the Ferrari probably didn't have much more than 280, while the early Repco was good for 285 and had better torque. The spaceframe car was significantly lighter and its Goodyear tyres had an advantage over Surtees's Dunlops.

The race around the streets of Prince Rainier's Principality was eagerly awaited, for it truly heralded the much-vaunted 'Return to Power', though reality revealed that only seven of the 16 cars that qualified actually had pukka 3-litre powerplants. The rest used either 2-litre bored-out versions of the Coventry Climax and BRM 1.5-litre V8s, or 2.5 or 2.7-litre variants of the four-cylinder Climax motor, or, in Lorenzo Bandini's case, the 2.4-litre V6 Ferrari.

Clark put his 2-litre Lotus-Climax on pole with a lap in 1m 29.9s, just ahead of Surtees. The Englishman was not happy that he had expressly been denied access to the 2.4-litre V6 car, which team manager Eugenio Dragoni insisted Bandini alone should drive. Surtees knew that the V12 had been two and a half seconds slower around Modena when he tested both, and was adamant that the smaller, 150lb lighter car would be a much better bet on the tight circuit. That, of course, was entirely what Dragoni believed, though he was certainly not going to tell Big John that. There was method in his plan to keep his innocent young protégé in a car in which he could not be compared directly to Surtees, in order to maintain the promising Italian's currency. These increasingly evident ploys to further Bandini's cause would eventually have significant repercussions for both Surtees and the team.

The 2.1-litre BRMs of Stewart and Hill occupied the second row, and with Bandini and Hulme in the 2.5-litre Brabham-Climax taking the third, Jochen had to be satisfied with seventh place in his Cooper-Maserati after lapping it in 1m 32.2s.

Surtees led the BRMs off the line as Clark lagged on pole, unable to select first gear. And at the end of the opening lap the order read Surtees, Stewart, Hill, Brabham, Bob Anderson, Jochen, Bruce McLaren (in his first outing as a constructor), Richie Ginther and Bandini. Jochen, however, soon moved up to fourth behind the BRMs, as Clark began to scythe through from the tail of the field. Jochen was flying, and despite the unsuitability of the Cooper to the course, slipped ahead of Hill on the eighth lap and set his sights on Stewart. The two leaders, however, were fighting over the lap record, and soon Jochen was having to pay more attention to a closing Hulme in fourth place.

Things suddenly looked rosier for him on the 14th lap, when both Hulme and Surtees met trouble; Denny's car developed a driveshaft problem, and Big John pitted to investigate a clicking noise in his transmission. That promoted Jochen to second, albeit more than half a minute adrift of Jackie, but that position was soon snatched away as Bandini hit his stride. Driving with great elan Jochen dragged the lumpy Cooper round in the nimble Ferrari's wheeltracks, never giving the Italian a moment's peace. Graham, however, had got his second wind and was pushing back at Jochen's third place. It was tiring hefting the Cooper round, and by the halfway point, lap 50, both Graham and Jimmy had demoted the big

OPPOSITE *Jochen threw the hefty Cooper Maserati around Monaco with aplomb and ran as high as third before the handling went off, allowing Graham Hill to catch and pass him before the T81's engine broke.* (LAT)

green car as its handling yet again seemed to go off. Seven laps later the Maserati engine failed. Thus Jackie scored his second Grand Prix victory in style, with Lorenzo the hero after an aggressive drive which undoubtedly left Surtees pondering what might have been.

The former motorcycle champion got his revenge when he dominated qualifying at Spa-Francorchamps for the Belgian Grand Prix three weeks later, as the drivers really got a chance to extend their 3-litre machinery. Nobody came close to his lap of 3m 38.0s, but Jochen drove his heart out again to take second slot with 3m 41.2s ahead of Stewart who wound his little BRM up superbly for a lap of 3m 41.5s. Jack Brabham was fourth in the 3-litre Brabham-Repco on 1m 41.8s, and Bandini fifth in the V6 Ferrari in 3m 43.8s.

"When I went to Spa for the first time I soon realised that the speeds there were beyond anything I was used to, and I took things fairly easy for a while," Jochen admitted. "Now I am more accustomed to high speed, but I appreciate that you can't treat a three-litre car like the one and a half-litre car I first drove there. I think I can drive as fast as most people, and I have a strong instinct of self-preservation which prevents me from doing anything really stupid."

There would be more than one of his peers who seriously questioned that final sentence, after the sensational performance he put up in the race. If Crystal Palace marked the day on which he arrived in Formula Two, Spa would be the point at which he truly arrived in Formula One. The race was very nearly a complete disaster. The 15-car field set off on a dry road and on dry weather tyres, only to encounter torrential rain at Burnenville, a frighteningly fast right-hander beyond the hill that led from Eau Rouge up to Les Combes. The brooding atmosphere of a dark race was brilliantly captured by the camera car, driven by Phil Hill, that was filming for John Frankenheimer's movie *Grand Prix*.

Surtees led Jochen and Brabham into Eau Rouge, but soon the Australian used his lighter car's momentum to move ahead. The previous day he had been informed that he was being awarded the OBE in the Queen's Birthday Honours List, and he was feeling pretty good about life.

"In those days we all had to start on dries or all start on wets, remember?" Brabham said, referring to rules governing the use of tyres. "The organisers said all right, it's dry all round the circuit so all start on dries. And I was on the front row and first up the hill and first over the top of the hill and down to Burnenville. I arrived there in the lead and suddenly realised, 'Shit, this bloody road's wet and I've got dries on!'" The road there was more than wet; it was awash thanks to torrential rain.

"I gradually sort of turned the motor car because I couldn't do anything else 'cause it was too late," Brabham continued. "And I was heading for a bloody

house, and that's where I thought I was gonna go because there was no way of stopping, no way of doing anything about it. Luckily, at Spa they had a concrete strip round the outside, holding the road together, about that much higher than the road." He indicated perhaps half an inch, with his thumb and forefinger. "And as I was sliding out there was nothing was gonna stop me going straight into this bloody house, and suddenly I just touched this strip of concrete and it was just enough to straighten me up. I was that bloody close to going off."

Jack was incredibly lucky. Behind him there was mayhem as two separate accidents developed. Jo Bonnier spun his private Cooper-Maserati and tagged Spence's Lotus-BRM. Both of them went off the road, and by sheer good fortune the Swede escaped a very nasty accident as his car stopped with its front half overhanging a 20ft drop into a farmyard. Only the bulk of its Maserati V12 kept it from teetering over the precipice as JoBo beat a hasty retreat.

Then Denny Hulme and Jo Siffert tangled, in Brabham-Climax and Cooper-Maserati respectively, neither going any further. Behind them Jim Clark, who had started from the back row after a litany of problems in qualifying and a suspension failure in the morning warm-up, ran fewer than two kilometres before his Lotus's Climax engine broke.

Already five cars were out, and three more were lost before that fateful lap was over. At the Masta Kink Stewart's BRM, lying third, behind Surtees and Rindt, aquaplaned into a 170mph spin that sent it crashing through a woodcutter's hut, which it demolished, then sideways into a telegraph pole. It then sheared off the road, down an eight-foot bank and into the lower patio of a farmhouse. The chassis was bent around him like a banana after sustaining a hefty side impact, and the Scot was trapped for more than 20 minutes in a fuel bath in the damaged cockpit, with a fractured shoulder and bruised kidneys. Simultaneously, team-mate Graham Hill spun and abandoned his P261, while American Bob Bondurant rolled his similar Chamaco Collect BRM on to the grass. Both men ran across to Stewart's wreck, intent on freeing the Scot.

In those days steering wheels were not detachable, and they had to borrow spanners from the tool kit in a spectator's car before they could remove Stewart's and release him. The petrol bath had already started to burn Jackie's nether regions, to his considerable discomfort. Hill and Bondurant took him to a barn and, heeding his semi-conscious pleas, stripped him out of his fuel-soaked overalls and underpants. He was lying there naked when three nuns arrived on the scene.

In happier times Stewart would joke that the first thing the nuns did was gawp in surprise at the sight of a naked man; the second was to be impressed by what they saw because they had only ever seen naked

ABOVE *Jochen crosses the finish line second at Spa after a mighty drive that saw him survive multiple spins on the Masta Straight and lead comfortably until his Dunlop tyres went off and John Surtees slipped by.* (LAT)

(nationality inserted here to suit that of his audience) men; and the third was to try to get him back into his overalls. But at the time it was no laughing matter and it would be hours before he was finally taken to hospital in Liège. That was the day that his unstoppable safety crusade truly began. Jackie was determined that he was not going to become a statistic on motor racing's roll of honour, and he didn't want any of his colleagues on the list, either. Jochen, who that day was driving out of his skin, would himself come to appreciate that only the fickle moving finger of fate decided which of them would survive and who would not.

While this tragicomedy was being acted out, there was consternation in the pits when the field was long overdue. Eventually Surtees screamed past in the red Ferrari, a ridiculous nine seconds already ahead of Jack, Lorenzo Bandini and Jochen. Behind them came Dan Gurney, debuting his Eagle-Climax, and the Cooper-

Maseratis of Richie Ginther and Guy Ligier. Seven cars… All that remained of the 15 that started.

Jack, who thought he had been about to meet his maker, was by his own admission seriously chastened, and taking things very easy. Jochen was not chastened, despite a drama of his own. And he was not taking things easy at all. On that opening lap he had spun the big Cooper on the Masta Straight, and even he didn't know how many times it rotated, though some of his fellow drivers believed it might have been as many as nine. "I had several exciting moments," he said with commendable understatement. "First I had this tremendous spin about 180mph…"

Gurney said: "I can remember seeing Jochen spinning through 360 degrees in a ball of spray on the Masta Straight at well over 150mph, yet somehow he managed to gather it all up and carry on again!"

Amazingly, Jochen got the Cooper pointed in the right direction and lost little ground, and Brabham remembered being really mad that the Austrian overtook him on the second lap. "I didn't like him passing me! But I'd got such a bloody scare long before I got that far. And when I came round the next lap there were about ten cars in the paddy! Unbelievable! I think Jochen passed me on the Masta Straight, but I really don't remember. I lost interest in the rain, a bit! I really thought I was gone there."

Bandini momentarily poked the V6 Ferrari's nose ahead of Surtees's V12 on the second lap, but as the rain hit the whole circuit and the skies darkened, Jochen was simply flying. He hurled the Cooper on to Surtees's tail, and on lap four dived ahead before Malmedy. By the time they reached the pits, he'd opened a lead of two and a half seconds.

Ron Dennis was working as a junior mechanic for Cooper that weekend, though he freely admits today that he doesn't remember his exact capacity. "That was the famous race that was portrayed in *Grand Prix*," he said. "At that time I was assembling Formula Two cars at Coopers, and every now and then there was an opportunity to go to a Grand Prix. The cars all went away, and we were stood in sunshine, and we were all waiting for them to come back… Where are they? And then after a few laps Jochen came round, miles in the lead, and it seemed like there was no other noise. And then after a while Surtees came round. Jochen was just amazing that day."

Lotus's Dick Scammell was also impressed. "I went up by the Armco coming into the hairpin, and stood there every lap. And every lap I thought: 'This car is never, ever going to stop this time.' And it always did. It was incredible! This big old Cooper came down there and it was all over the place, but it always stopped, and went round the corner. I couldn't believe it. It was incredible car control."

"I found I was leading the race," Jochen chuckled when recalling his wonderful performance a few years later, and for a while it seemed that, like his friend Jackie Stewart, he was about to bag his first really big win early in his F1 career. By half distance, 14 laps, he was averaging 110mph and leading Surtees by a few seconds. Bandini was two minutes behind. But the weather gods had other ideas.

On lap 18 Surtees set the fastest lap at 121mph, 4m 18.7s, and from the 21st lap the road was beginning to dry. Now, as the Cooper began its usual handling problems, he began to pare down the advantage that Jochen had been maintaining without too much effort.

Again, Jochen surmised that the locking mechanism in the ZF differential was playing up because the behaviour that he began to encounter on the drying track was consistent with what he'd experienced in previous races whenever the track got greasy or oily rather than being wholly dry or wholly wet. It was only later that season that the team finally came to realise that the real reason why he started to struggle was a combination of a drying track and his Dunlops going off.

"As the track began to dry out," Jochen told Salvadori, "the car became almost uncontrollable." In his book, Salvadori explained: "We knew that we had a major problem, but we had not yet analysed it. As we realised later, Jochen's trouble was attributable to the Dunlop tyres which were causing handling problems on oily surfaces. There were no problems in practice, when there was little or no oil on the track, and there were no problems on a really wet track, but on a drying, oily track the cars' handling deteriorated substantially.

"Ferrari was the only other team running on Dunlop tyres and I believe that Surtees, with his vast racing experience, had instinctively grasped the situation. As Spa dried out, Surtees was avoiding the oiliest parts and slowing down where absolutely necessary only, while Jochen was slowing all round the course. Jochen suspected that the self-locking mechanism of the ZF final drive was at fault and we gave the ZF factory a terrible time, as they tried to trace a fault that did not exist."

"It was a good, controlled race, very fast," Surtees said. "Jochen was going really well, and when the track was at its wettest he cleaned a drier line for me to follow. I really needed to win as slowly as possible because of the conditions. He drove a very good race, but I saw my opportunity and was able to win it. Afterwards, Dragoni was upset with me – I had let a Maserati lead a Ferrari! But I was there to win the race, and I did."

Surtees put his Ferrari ahead of the Maserati at Malmedy on the 24th lap and immediately left it behind. Jochen was philosophical, after finishing 42.1s adrift when the flag finally came out. "In the end, after several more frightening moments," he said, "I finished second. But really I was quite happy just to be alive".

The race would feature strongly in Frankenheimer's movie, which highlighted Jochen's sense of humour. It contained a little vignette filmed in the Grand Prix Drivers' Association meeting at Spa, in which fictional racers Jean-Pierre Sarti (Yves Montand), Pete Aron (James Garner) and Nino Barlini (Antonio Sabato) are mixing in with Graham Hill (playing Bob Turner) and

OPPOSITE *Jochen had many reasons to look solemn at the wheel of the Cooper Maserati. It handled well, but was a heavy car that lacked the nimbleness of the Brabham Repcos, and often the reliability.* (LAT)

Phil Hill (playing Tim Randolph). Jochen, Dan Gurney, Jo Schlesser, Jo Siffert, Jo Bonnier, Guy Ligier, Bob Bondurant and Mike Spence are all in shot. At one stage Graham moves towards the back of the room, past the sitting Jochen who is reading a paper. Jochen playfully grabs Graham's foot at the last moment, nearly tripping him, and dissolves into laughter. It was a clear adlib that Frankenheimer chose to keep in.

Writer Michael Argetsinger remembered the Belgian Grand Prix fondly. "That was sensational! One of my jobs at Cooper was to keep the official lap chart. At the end of the first lap the seven surviving cars came by really strung out, with large gaps between each. It's a long lap at Spa. It was dry at the start/finish line – at least on lap one. Eventually it was raining everywhere on the circuit.

"Jochen led most of race and should have won. John and Jochen ran closely together throughout – except for the first lap! – and the race was hotly contested. I think Jochen drove one of his greatest and bravest races that day. It's hard to say precisely how our friendship developed, but it was during that 1966 season when I would see him at every race weekend. He was only two years, or less, older than me. I think he empathized with my passion to move forward in racing.

"I remember him picking me up at the hotel I was staying in at Stavelot to drive to the victory party, though I have no recollection of where that party was. I do remember that Jochen was still genuinely thrilled from the race and he was particularly animated. Stavelot was where Cooper had a garage and we worked on the cars. Because Stavelot was on the circuit, the most senior mechanics got to drive the race cars from there to the pits and paddock. I'm pretty certain Trevor Orchard drove Jochen's car. It was something they looked forward to each year. They did this at some other circuits as well, but Spa was a particular treat because there were several miles involved. They didn't just trundle along either.

"I also remember that Guy Ligier's light blue Cooper-Maserati was housed with the works team for this race and the Ligier team treated me to lunch on Thursday. I had been helping them do a petrol check. I remember, too, that Roy Salvadori picked me up on Monday morning and drove me to Spa where Keith Greene was staying; Keith was the Armstrong rep at that time and would help to set up the cars. I rode back to England with Keith and George Phillips, who was the *Autosport* photographer. We flew across from Ostend on the air ferry. Keith had a Cortina GT. I saw Peter Garnier at the airport and he asked me if I would deliver Gregor Grant's *Autosport* race story to the office in London, which I did." That was how it was often done back then, in those pre-telex, pre-fax, pre-email days.

"Jochen was really brilliant at Spa," Jack Brabham said recently, looking back fondly on a man he greatly admired. "That was fantastic. He got past me without any trouble and just disappeared. Incredible! He was a fantastic driver. And the wet was right up his street. I used to like driving in the wet, I never had any problem with that. I thought I was pretty good then, and I used to win quite a lot of wet races. But Jochen was fantastic that day. But to be honest, it didn't matter whether it was wet or dry, he was able to sort it out, no problem. He was really good. It was just everything about him, reflexes, balance, just a bloody good driver, he really was."

That didn't stop Cooper bringing in a new number one driver for the French Grand Prix at Rheims at the beginning of July, however. Though it was only the third round of the World Championship, it would prove a highly significant race. While it marked the real start of Brabham's title run and the historical milestone of the first time a driver had won a Grande Epreuve in a car bearing his own name, it also marked a turning point for Jochen as John Surtees joined Cooper after an explosive exit from Ferrari at Le Mans in June.

To this day the Englishman has never disclosed the full circumstances behind it, but it would have far-reaching effects for Jochen. Surtees had no beef with Enzo Ferrari, and they would retain their mutual respect, but was at the end of his tether with the Machiavellian machinations of Eugenio Dragoni. Monaco had just lit the fuse, and what fanned the flame was when Dragoni also cast aspersions on John's fitness even after the pace at which he had recovered from the pelvis-breaking accident he'd suffered at Mosport in a Lola T70 late the previous year had amazed his doctors. Dragoni even suggested that Surtees had dishonoured Ferrari by running behind Jochen at Spa, even though he had gone on to his excellent victory…

The final eruption came at Le Mans when Dragoni let it be known in the most public manner that he doubted Surtees' ability to maintain fitness throughout the race by nominating Lodovico Scarfiotti as a reserve driver for the car Surtees was to share with Mike Parkes. Big John had little time for his fellow Englishman because he believed him to be agitating the political situation behind the scenes to suit his own F1 driving aspirations, and nobody in the sport seriously considered either Parkes or Scarfiotti, nice, quick guys though they were, to be remotely in his league.

"The politics had got too much," Surtees admitted. "During my break due to my accident there had been a lot of, shall we say, undermining going on by certain persons. Two people in particular. One who wanted a Formula One career that was totally unsuitable for him, and who thought that the best chance was to make certain that I was out. The only trouble was that he could never match my times, so that lost him a bit, but he found an ally in Dragoni. The whole thing also got very political because of the increasingly strong likely involvement of Fiat to whom promises had been made, I think, about making an Italian champion." The upshot was that Surtees quit Ferrari there and then.

The jungle drums beat quickly, and by three o'clock the next morning Mario Tozzi-Condivi had received a call from a mole in Modena to inform him that the 1964 World Champion was footloose and fancy free. Salvadori had talented upcomer Chris Amon under contract to replace Ginther when the time came, but the New Zealander had yet to get the opportunity to demonstrate in F1 the fearsome ability that would, over the next six years, make him the greatest driver never to win a Grand Prix. A deal with Surtees was a no-brainer for Cooper, and after the directors agreed that day to ready a car for him for Rheims, Salvadori set about contacting John and, once his level of interest was apparent, getting a release (temporary at first, but subsequently season-long) from his Shell contract so that he could drive a BP-sponsored car.

Surtees' arrival was not without other complications, not the least of which was that Jochen had his nose put well out of joint because he was no longer the number one driver. Salvadori went to great lengths to keep his Austrian driver happy. "We were anxious to avoid any clash between Jochen and John," he wrote in his autobiography, "so we set up what were virtually two teams. Each driver had his own chassis, engines and mechanics. John had two ex-Aston Martin mechanics, Jim Potten and Jerry Holmes, whom he knew when he was racing for the Bowmaker team and whom he liked and trusted."

The new set-up was also good news for that youngest mechanic Ron Dennis, who would later mastermind McLaren's fabulous success from the Eighties onwards. Jochen chose Ron as his chief mechanic, despite his youth and inexperience. Generally, the arrangement would work quite well, with neither driver able to feel that the other was being favoured.

BELOW *Jochen reckoned that he sweated off ten pounds of body weight hauling the Cooper round Rheims, but it was the key race where he argued for, and got, rookie Ron Dennis as his personal crew chief.* (LAT)

Argetsinger was perfectly placed to observe some of the dynamics that weekend. "That year I was with Cooper for the season, and that's when I came to know Jochen much better. I didn't have a full-time job with Cooper, nor was I on the payroll. I had a job in Bristol with Harris & Co. But the Harris family wanted me have every chance to pursue my racing opportunities and gave me free rein to travel with Cooper and to stay on the continent as much as necessary and as often as I wanted. It was a dream job and they remain great friends.

"What happened for me at Cooper was thanks to

Roy. John Cooper was also a friend but he didn't have a really active role with the race team that year. Roy and Cooper took care of all my hotel arrangements and most restaurant bills. Roy also helped me get to and from the races, sometimes riding with him and Susan, and often with others. Sometimes I rode in the transporter with the mechanics.

"To understand my role it's important to understand the make-up of the team. The three cars – two race cars plus a spare – were looked after by seven mechanics. There were others back at the works, but that was the total that travelled to the races. Guys like Trevor Orchard, Jim Potten, Dennis Davis, Jerry Holmes and Ron Dennis. Therefore, one extra hand to be a 'go-fer' – I didn't know the term at the time – was most welcome. I made myself useful in just about any way you can imagine – I would help load and unload the transporter,

BELOW *At Rheims Jochen (left) passes Chris Amon, who is driving the prototype Cooper Maserati as Roy Salvadori's apology for signing John Surtees to the ride the New Zealander had been promised.* (LAT)

I polished and cleaned, helped move things from the paddock to the pits and back again, I would shuttle the churns to the BP truck to have them filled with petrol (we had a little cart we put them on). I would arrive at the given circuit either with the mechanics or later the same day. Usually we were setting up on the Wednesday before the race weekend.

"In addition to the seven mechanics there was engineer/designer Derrick White. By the weekend, Jonathan Sieff, who owned the team, would turn up. And of course there was Roy, running the whole thing. That was everyone. Hard, I'm sure, for some to believe given the size of Formula One teams today. And Cooper was by no means the smallest team. I am certain that Brabham and, I think, AAR Eagle too, had fewer people.

"Throughout the year I enjoyed easy access back and forth between the mechanics and to Roy and the drivers.

The team was very hierarchical, but being an American I guess I was somewhat immune to that and appeared to be welcome with both groups."

Argetsinger, as a friend of Jochen's and Salvadori's, got to see both sides of the Surtees coin. "Yes, there was occasionally tension there, between Jochen and Roy," he confirmed. "However, I think the supposed conflict between the two is somewhat overblown in latter day accounts. For the most part they got along fine. It is worth mentioning that Roy was the complete gentleman. He was then, and remains, my ideal of everything a Grand Prix driver of his era was thought to be. He was sophisticated, had a wide range of interests, was passionate about his racing, enormously entertaining and a great deal of fun, and was extremely loyal. He was also a great driver whose Formula One results would look very different if he had not possessed the

characteristic of loyalty. He had an opportunity to be number one driver at Cooper just at the time they were coming into their own in 1958. He turned it down out of loyalty to David Brown at Aston Martin. Roy knew at the time he did it that it was the wrong decision in terms of his career. The Aston Martin Formula One car was the wrong choice, but Roy made it out of loyalty to the team that had meant so much to him in his early days.

"The big confrontation between Roy and Jochen came over John Surtees joining the team. Jochen made some specific demands of Roy that were difficult for Roy to agree to because of the existing culture of the team. That he managed to accommodate Jochen speaks volumes for Roy's ability to make things happen. Ron Dennis was part of the compromise. The bottom line here is that Roy and Jochen were two very strong and outspoken individuals, each used to getting his way, but with very different backgrounds and world views.

"Ron was the junior mechanic, and it was hierarchical, based on seniority. When Surtees came into the picture, Jochen was upset that he would no longer be number one driver. Roy and Jochen went round and round on this and it was a tough negotiation. I heard this from both parties. The compromise they reached was that Jochen's car would run as an equal number one beside Surtees's, and that Ron Dennis would be the chief mechanic on the car. That was Jochen's demand and it only happened because he put his foot down. It was the hardest thing for Roy to make happen because Ron was the most junior member of the team. This was a big deal and Roy made it happen to appease Jochen. But it was Jochen who made it happen for Ron and it elevated him to a new prominence. He was very talented, no doubt, and likely would have found his way. But those who were part of the team believe this was the big break that propelled him on his way."

Surtees promptly upstaged Jochen in qualifying in France. Bandini put his V12 Ferrari on pole position in 1m 7.8s, but to Jochen's chagrin Surtees spoilt the symmetry for Ferrari by inserting his Cooper-Maserati between the Italian and Mike Parkes, who lapped in 1m 9.1s. Surtees's time of 1m 8.4s was 2.5s faster than Jochen could manage, but Big John had grabbed a tow when it mattered. Jochen lined up fifth alongside Brabham. Jo Siffert in Rob Walker's Cooper and Chris Amon were next up. The New Zealander's one-off drive, which had significantly increased the workload, was Salvadori's way of saying sorry to Chris Amon that he wouldn't, after all, get the regular ride in Richie Ginther's place that he had been lined up for, now that Surtees had joined the team.

Bandini led at the start, determined to prove his worth as team leader, and took the slipstreaming Brabham with him. Black Jack would discover that drafting the Ferrari increased his Brabham-Repco's

maximum speed from 176 to 182mph. Lorenzo had Jack covered, however, but after opening a lead of more than 30 seconds thanks to a record-smashing run that left the lap record at 141.43mph, his throttle cable broke at Thillois. Jack swept home to a great victory, his first in a Grand Prix since 1960, and, at 136.9mph, the second fastest in history at that time. Parkes finished second, nine seconds back, with Hulme two laps down leading fourth-placed Jochen home. Jochen's engine had frequently threatened to cut out, while Surtees' fuel pump had quit after five laps; both problems had their root in a fuel vaporisation problem in the tremendous ambient temperature that Cooper had not been able to rectify. He admitted he thought "at least ten times about retiring," and lost ten pounds in the sauna-like race conditions.

For the rest of the season, Surtees would generally have the upper hand at Cooper. The nimble Brabhams were dominant in qualifying for the British Grand Prix, where Brands Hatch did not prove a circuit to which the Cooper-Masers were ill suited. They were separated from the Australian's car by Dan Gurney's 2.7-litre Eagle-Climax, Graham Hill's 2-litre BRM and Jimmy Clark's 2-litre Lotus-Climax. On the third row, Jochen had Surtees to his right, Stewart's BRM to his left. Strikes in Italy kept the Ferraris at home.

Nick Loudon had been out at Stirlings taking photographs on Friday afternoon. "I was on the outside of the track, but after the inside of the corner, another favourite place of mine," he recalled. "Only Jack Brabham, Jim Clark and Jochen were circulating, in that order and not far apart. Now, at the same place in practice for the Race of Champions the previous year, I had seen Jochen spin off. His driving now seemed a touch hairy and I felt a little exposed, and therefore decided to move. After Jack went by I took refuge in the bushes, but left my camera bag. Both Jimmy and Jochen were quite mystified, peering here and there for me. I moved the camera bag on the next lap, and they continued searching for me for two or three laps till the end of practice.

"I saw Jimmy in the paddock after practice and he said to me wryly: 'Was I that bad?' I said, 'No, I had moved because Jochen, who was behind you, was a touch hairy'. Jimmy found this entertaining. I later saw Jochen in the restaurant at the top of the paddock, and wished him a good afternoon. His reply, 'You are a chicken!' I said, 'Yes, I suppose I am'. He then seemed to become quite upset, in complete contrast to Jimmy, and in his lovely fractured accent said: 'A bloody shicken!' and stalked off. Sadly, we did not speak again for some three years. However, I am glad to say that we 'kissed and made up' during practice for the Race of Champions in 1969."

In the race the usual handling problems dropped the

Coopers back, as both Jochen and JS had spells in
second place. Surtees' car retired with rear suspension
and differential problems after 67 laps, but Jochen eased
his home fifth as Brabham won again from Hulme, Hill
and Clark.

Jack and Denny were well into their stride again at
Zandvoort, as Clark joined them on the front row from
Gurney and Parkes. Jochen wrestled the big Cooper
round for sixth fastest time ahead of Hill and Stewart,
while Bandini was ninth and Surtees tenth. Both Coopers
had a troubled time, Jochen's dropping a valve and
Surtees's suffering a broken crankshaft.

Jochen's joy at outqualifying Surtees was short-lived.
On the second lap a problem with the gearlever gate
interlock mechanism let the downshift to second go into
first instead and he spun off into the chicken wire
fencing. Not long afterwards Parkes arrived at the same
corner with a boxful of neutrals and parked the Ferrari
where the Cooper was already parked, doing neither car
any good. Surtees, struggling in the poor-handling spare
car after his practice engine drama, retired with an
ignition problem.

Brabham, who made an amusing riposte to those
who regarded him as old at 40 by walking to the grid
wearing a false beard and leaning on a walking stick,
won again from Hulme, but only after a brilliant drive
by Jimmy Clark in the Lotus-Climax had been damned
by overheating.

ABOVE *The Cooper was quite well suited to Brands Hatch
thanks to its supple suspension, but after a spell in second
place Jochen dropped back to an eventual fifth after the
inevitable decline in handling.* (LAT)

The German Grand Prix was much more fruitful for
Cooper, though Surtees again overshadowed Jochen in
practice and the race. Clark took his almost inevitable
pole position even though he was still in the 2-litre
Lotus-Climax. The Scot lapped in 8m 16.5s, and Big
John took second place with 8m 18.0s to pip Stewart on
8m 18.8s. Scarfiotti, Brabham, Bandini, Parkes and
Gurney were all faster than Jochen, whose 8m 27.7s left
him only ninth on the four by three by four grid, nearly
eight seconds off his team leader's time.

It rained at the start and Surtees immediately pushed
ahead of Brabham. Jack overtook at the end of the lap
but John repassed as they began to draw away from
Jochen, whose T81 developed early braking problems.
Surtees spun but recovered and never let Brabham have a
moment's peace until the Cooper lost its clutch with two
laps to go, and ran its last one stuck in fourth gear.
Brabham won with Surtees second, 44 seconds behind,
and Jochen brought his troubled machine home third,
almost two minutes further back.

The Italian Grand Prix at Monza marked the point at
which the majority of teams had their pukka 3-litre cars.

OPPOSITE At a wet Nürburgring Jochen couldn't hang on to team-mate John Surtees, who challenged winner Jack Brabham, but joined them on the podium after a strong performance. (LAT)

Hill and Stewart finally had BRM's ambitious H16 cylinder cars, and Clark had a new Lotus equipped with the same multi-cylinder engine. Gurney had the 3-litre Weslake V12-engined Eagle, and Ginther was there with Honda's 3-litre V12. But the tifosi really wanted to see how their beloved V12 Ferraris and Cooper-Maseratis fared.

Parkes became their hero when he took pole position in 1m 31.3s from Scarfiotti on 1m 31.6s, while Clark was menacing with 1m 31.8s in the Lotus-BRM. Bandini and Surtees made up the second row in 1m 31.9s and 1m 32.0s respectively, followed by Brabham in 1m 32.2s, Ginther in 1m 32.4s and Jochen in 1m 32.7. Stewart and Hulme shared row four.

Monza marked two major turning points for the Cooper team. The first was Salvadori's decision to switch from Dunlop to Firestone tyres after they finally figured out what was causing the persistent handling problems. The second concerned the Cooper family's involvement in the team it founded. John Cooper was still in charge of preparation and refused to fuel Surtees' car overnight in order to let the load settle so that more might be persuaded into the tanks for a race that was traditionally hard on consumption because of its very high speed. When the car was finally fuelled at noon on raceday, a leak was discovered that could not now be corrected. Surtees had initially run in third place behind the dreaded Ferraris of Scarfiotti and Parkes, but subsequently had to withdraw because of the fuel bath he was forced to sit in. Tozzi-Condivi went ballistic with Cooper afterwards, with the result that his race preparation role was handed over to Salvadori.

Scarfiotti became the last Italian to win the Italian Grand Prix as he led Parkes home by a hair under six seconds. Hulme was the last runner on the lead lap, hounding Parkes and finishing only three-tenths adrift. Jochen, using a newly revised and more compact Maserati V12 with the inlet ports inclined inwards was

BELOW As young crew chief Ron Dennis checks out the front end of his T81 in practice for the Italian GP at Monza, Jochen ponders the benefits of a timely switch from Dunlop to Firestone rubber. (LAT)

fourth, a lap down. The consolation was that the Firestones maintained their performance all through the race; the handling problems were resolved by the switch, and ZF could finally relax.

There was another good haul of points at Watkins Glen in the US Grand Prix, where for a while Jochen even entertained thoughts of scoring his first F1 victory. But that would have to wait another three years on an historic day when Clark nursed the normally hideously unreliable BRM H16 engine to the sole victory of its inglorious career, ironically not in a works BRM P83 but in Lotus's slimmer 43.

Brabham had taken pole position in 1m 8.42s with Clark next on 1m 8.53s, Bandini on 1m 8.57s, Surtees on 1m 8.73s, then Hill and Stewart in their H16 BRMs on 1m 8.87s and 1m 9.17s respectively. Then came Hulme and Ginther on 1m 9.28s and 1m 9.37s. Jochen was only ninth, on 1m 9.63s, after needing an engine change when his oil-guzzling V12 was suspected of having devoured a piston.

Bandini and Brabham immediately began scrapping over the lead, but while Surtees was chasing along in third he tripped over backmarker Peter Arundell in the works Lotus-Climax. Both spun and pitted for inspections. Salvadori believed that a furious Big John spent so long going down the pit road to rant at Arundell that by the time his car was ready he had lost three laps and any chance of victory. Typically, Surtees drove like fury when he finally got back into the race, unlapping himself once on the leaders.

Bandini's hopes evaporated when his new 36-valve V12 Ferrari engine broke after 34 laps when a spark plug electrode fell into a cylinder and resulted in catastrophic failure, and Brabham, having now done enough to clinch the World Championship, also retired from the lead when a cam follower in his Repco V8 broke after 55 laps.

That left Clark in the lead in the Lotus-BRM, with Jochen second and Surtees a long way back but setting lap records in his frantic recovery. Such was the unreliable pedigree of Tony Rudd's BRM H16 that everyone believed it was a matter of time before Clark coasted to a halt somewhere around the picturesque track and began a long walk home. But it was Jochen who struck trouble, running out of fuel on the last lap. He maintained second place, while Surtees was an heroic third.

"If you take into account the time wasted by Surtees in the pits and the distance he was behind Clark at the finish, then if he had gone straight off when the car had been checked, he would easily have won the race," Salvadori said glumly.

The Mexican Grand Prix brought the season to a conclusion, and saw Surtees redress that by storming to a superb victory for Cooper-Maserati after starting from pole position. Brabham led Hulme home in second place, to sign off his third World Championship, and Ginther gave Honda points with fourth. Jochen was on target to score points as he shadowed Surtees and Brabham initially, after qualifying fifth, a second off Surtees's time. But his T81 broke its left front suspension when a balljoint failed on the Peraltada banking after 32 laps.

Looking back on his time at Cooper recently, Surtees smiled. "I was able to make Dragoni eat his words when I joined Cooper! We could also have won at the Nürburgring, where I had gear selection problems; at Monza, where I had the fuel leak; and at Watkins Glen…" He laughed when reminded of Salvadori's judgement about spending so much time in the pits haranguing Arundell. "Yes! Absolutely! That was my mistake. But I was really angry with him…

"Jochen was a good team-mate. He very much had his own group, but we talked about how to improve the car. Some things he liked and some he didn't. Despite the Cooper being heavy, it was actually quite a good car, and in general it was a good little team."

Louis Stanley, the husband of Jean Owen whose brother Sir Alfred owned BRM, was frequently derided for a streak of pomposity that occasionally saw him declining to correct waiters who mistakenly addressed him as if he too was a knight of the realm. But his candour and perspicacity made his poorly photographed *Grand Prix* annuals an interesting read. At the end of 1966, lining him up sixth behind champion Jack Brabham, John Surtees, Jackie Stewart, Jimmy Clark and Graham Hill, and ahead of Denny Hulme, Dan Gurney, Lorenzo Bandini and Mike Parkes, he wrote of Jochen: "This young Austrian must be judged, as anyone should be, on the merits of his best drives, and there were several in 1966. Cooper-Maserati were fortunate to have such a forthright No. 2 driver to Surtees. At times he takes unnecessary risks as some of his colleagues would testify, but he is greatly improved. He is submerged in his job. Whether the sum adds up to greatness remains to be seen. He appears to have the assets for championship honours".

When Surtees's points from Spa were added to his total, he finished runner-up to Brabham in the World Championship for drivers, with Jochen third, and Cooper was third in the Constructors, 12 points behind Brabham-Repco but only a point behind Modenese arch-rival Ferrari. All things taken into account, Jochen had had a good season, even if victory had eluded him. "I think I always managed the maximum with the car," he said.

If only he'd been on Firestones from the start…

OPPOSITE *Jochen spent much of the US GP at Watkins Glen expecting to inherit victory when Jim Clark's BRM H16-engined Lotus broke, but had to settle for second when the Scot nursed it to the finish. (LAT)*

CHAPTER 7

Tensions mount at Cooper

Formula One, 1967

"He was very competitive, intensely so. Whatever you were doing he had to beat you, even if it was noughts and crosses, skiing, anything he had to do he had to win."

Pat Mennem

LEFT *Gurney, Brabham, McLaren, Ginther, Hulme, Jochen and Hill hang out prior to the start of the 1967 Race of Champions.* (LAT)

Jochen's new Formula One season could not have got off to a worse start. For the second time in months, when Cooper-Maserati won a Grand Prix it was with a new team-mate at the wheel. He had got on fine with John Surtees when the 1964 World Champion was drafted into the team at Rheims the previous year, but he took against Mexican Pedro Rodriguez almost immediately and the dislike became deep-rooted after Pedro lucked into victory first time out in the South African Grand Prix at Kyalami on January 2.

The heat always caused teams problems at the track, and Jochen's Maserati V12 persistently misfired at high revs. While he was struggling with this in practice, Rodriguez had a dream debut to qualify fourth, starting behind Jack Brabham and Denny Hulme in their Brabham-Repcos and Jim Clark in the Watkins Glen-winning Lotus-BRM H16. He and Jimmy had gone out in Saturday's final session and towed one another round in fine style. Jochen was only seventh, a second slower than his new team-mate.

Pedro immediately endeared himself to the team, not just because he was fast but because he never complained about the car but just got on with driving it. "For some reason Jochen took an instant dislike to Pedro and was terribly rude to him all the time," Roy Salvadori remembered. "The situation was not helped by the fact that we were having problems with Jochen's car which we did our damnedest to cure. But all Jochen wanted to do was to get into Rodriguez's car. I said, 'Jochen, you have just finished a season with John Surtees and at no stage did he ask for your car and at no time would I have given your car to Surtees. Why are things so different now that we have got Rodriguez in the team?' Jochen's retort was that Rodriguez was not an established Formula One driver."

Compounding this, Pedro had a smoother driving style that got similar speed without taking so much from the Firestone tyres as Jochen did. Salvadori pleaded with Jochen to ease back on the flamboyance, and got annoyed when other drivers, including Denny Hulme, took up Jochen's cause to have Pedro give up his seat. "This rather upset me," Salvadori admitted, "as it was purely an internal team matter and a decision for me to make."

Hulme and Brabham squeezed Clark at the start, and led third-placed Surtees in his Honda over the line at the end of the opening lap. Pedro was fourth from a disgruntled Clark and Jochen, Jimmy believing the Coopers had ganged up on him too.

Jochen spun early on after moving up to third, but was back in that position after 30 laps, with Pedro fighting over fourth with Surtees and Brabham. But as expected Jochen was eating up his tyres, and then the gearbox failed after 38 laps. He was notably hard on that part of the car.

Hulme had the race in his grasp until he had to stop on lap 59 to inform his crew that he needed brake fluid, and make another call next time round to have them top it up. Then he had to stop three laps later to have the system bled. He would finish fourth. That left Rhodesian John Love in the lead in his elderly 2.7-litre Climax-engined Cooper, but then the fuel pump failed that he had rigged up in the reserve fuel tank fitted for this long race, and he came into the pits with eight laps remaining to take on more fuel. That elevated Pedro to the lead. After successfully getting the better of Surtees in the Honda he had deliberately driven smoothly and gently to preserve his car and stake his claim to a full-time ride with the team. He was, after all, leading the World Championship. Prior to the Mexican Grand Prix the previous year Cooper had not won a race since Monaco 1962; now it had won two in a row.

On other fronts, things began looking up. Jochen had to travel to Daytona to race for Porsche in the 24 Hours at the beginning of February, and he arranged to meet up with Nina Lincoln in New York while he was in the United States.

"It turned out that he still wanted to see me," she remembered. "That was pretty good! And he'd grown up fast. He was not a boy any more, but a real adult. Actually, it was like he was 40, which is probably why he liked Bernie so much because he really *was* 40! Jochen was quite romantic, though he didn't really show it. I would get flowers and nice letters… I hope he only wrote to me! One New Year's Eve there were red roses on our dining room table at home – my mother was totally impressed. He scored points there!

"I don't know what the attraction was. He was just very special. You can't always pinpoint why you like or love somebody, can you? But it was everything about him. He was never, *ever* arrogant. He'd have a beer with anyone, he didn't have any hang-ups about that sort of thing. But he was terrible with people he didn't like!"

Often he kept his own counsel, mainly because there was so little free time for other things or there were always so many people around them, but Nina remembered that he would share his thoughts when they were on long drives to and from races.

She went with him to Daytona, and when co-driver Gerhard Mitter burst in on them in their caravan to inform them that he'd shunted the car, Jochen could barely have cared less. "We got married two months later!" Nina said.

Jochen's next free weekend was March 5, and on that day they were married in Helsinki's oldest church.

OPPOSITE *Driving just the way he drove at Crystal Palace three years earlier, Jochen hustles the Cooper in the South African GP at Kyalami. He was incensed when team-mate Pedro Rodriguez won.* (LAT)

Legend has it that she spent her honeymoon sat huddled on a pile of tyres in the Cooper pit at Brands Hatch during the Race of Champions the following week, but she says they'd fitted in a couple of days' skiing in Zurs beforehand. "That was our honeymoon!"

They would settle initially in Paris to enable Nina more easily to find modelling work, moving into 137, Rue de la Tour in the opulent 16th Arrondissement. Subsequently they would rent boxer Ingemar Johansson's house near the Stewarts in Begnins, in Canton Vaud not far from Geneva, after Jochen fell out of love with the Parisian way of life "because the traffic is horrible, the telephoning complicated and there is never any parking place at the airport".

Cooper had entered both cars in the *Daily Mail*-sponsored non-championship race in England. Dan Gurney was in blistering form in practice to take pole position in the Eagle-Weslake, with team-mate Richie Ginther sandwiching Surtees's Honda on the front row. Jochen was sixth, two seconds down on the Eagle, with Pedro tenth, four-tenths of a second slower.

The race was run in two ten-lap heats and a 40-lap final, and the first heat proved a disaster for Jochen as his clutch let go as he left the line. He struggled round for three laps before pitting for repairs. Gurney won easily from Surtees, Ginther and Bruce McLaren in his BRM-engined M2B. Pedro was eighth after several feisty battles. Dan won the second heat from Ginther and Surtees, with Pedro fighting to fifth behind Lodovico Scarfiotti's Ferrari. Jochen's clutch failed again.

Gurney just fended off an on-form Lorenzo Bandini by four-tenths of a second to win the final, as Jo Siffert in Rob Walker's Cooper-Maserati fought tooth and nail to hold off Pedro and Scarfiotti to the flag. There was less than a second between the two Coopers after the 40 laps, and they were within three seconds of the leaders after impressive performances on an oily track. Pedro impressed Cooper with his coolness under pressure from Scarfiotti. Jochen lasted 14 laps this time, before pitting to retire with gearbox, clutch and handling maladies.

In Monaco Jochen and Pedro had handling and engine problems respectively and shared the back row of the 16-car grid, upstaged again by Siffert in Rob Walker's car who qualified ninth. Salvadori remembered: "Jochen had been bouncing the car over the kerbs, finishing practice with a broken wheel and damaged suspension. Poor Ron Dennis had to work overnight to rebuild the car virtually in time for the race, and was so exhausted that he spent the race sleeping under the pit

counter. At least Jochen had confidence in Ron and it was only through his untiring devotion to the car that we were able to keep Jochen happy".

Jochen drove his usual feisty race and at one stage had climbed to fourth when the track was at its oiliest, but his gearbox failed after 14 laps. Pedro, now a regular in the team, had to nurse a flat-sounding engine throughout the race after Giulio Alfieri had twiddled with it prior to the start and inadvertently turned it into F1's first V10. He brought his car home sixth behind Mike Spence's BRM H16, but was given fifth place by the organisers in a race in which Lorenzo Bandini's ultimately fatal accident overshadowed Denny Hulme's first victory.

On the way to the airport that evening Jochen and Roy had a huge argument after Salvadori told him he would never be World Champion unless he learned to treat his machinery with greater respect and mechanical sympathy.

The duo was well matched again in Zandvoort, Jochen qualifying fourth on 1m 26.5s and Pedro fifth on 1m 26.6s… But the Dutch Grand Prix marked the historic debut of the Lotus 49 and the Ford Cosworth DFV engine. At a stroke the combination rewrote the accepted parameters of Formula One design and rendered everything else virtually obsolete overnight.

Graham Hill took pole position in 1m 24.6s, and Jim Clark won the race going away. The Coopers ran well initially, with Jochen fourth and Pedro seventh, but this time Pedro's gearbox broke and Jochen suffered a problem with the front suspension.

Much was expected at Spa, where everyone remembered Jochen's fabulous performance the previous year. But after Clark had led and then stopped to have a broken spark plug replaced, Jackie Stewart drove heroically in the cumbersome BRM H16, holding it in gear and driving one-handed, until Dan Gurney overhauled him to score the sole Grand Prix victory for the beautiful Eagle-Weslake. Jochen had qualified fourth after some crafty slipstreaming but Pedro was way back on the fifth row, five seconds slower. He lost no time in the race slicing up to his team-mate, and for many laps they diced for fifth place with Chris Amon's Ferrari. In *Autosport* Gregor Grant described it as "a real get-stuffed match". At 14 laps, the half distance point, Pedro was running third behind Stewart and Gurney and ahead of Amon and Jochen. By lap 21, however, Chris had finally made a break, leaving the two Cooper pilots to continue slogging it out. In the end Jochen finished fourth behind the New Zealander, while Pedro was classified ninth after he'd retired after 25 laps when a piston broke. Jochen might not have liked the Mexican, but he respected him a lot more after their gripping encounter.

The French Grand Prix on the unpopular Bugatti circuit at Le Mans served only to show that the future belonged to powerful, lightweight cars such as the Lotus-Fords, which set the pace but each retired with crown-

OPPOSITE *The new Cooper T86 which appeared at the British GP was no Lotus 49, even when it later received a sleeker nose. The new 36-valve Maserati engine failed to go the distance.* (LAT)

LEFT *As Chris Amon drives by, Derrick White makes notes and Jochen prepares to step into the ugly new T86 at Silverstone, Ron Dennis stands to attention behind the left rear wheel.* (LAT)

wheel and pinion failures. In their place the Brabham-Repcos finished first and second, Jack leading Denny home. Jochen had a massive spin and then his Cooper broke a piston after 33 laps; Pedro limped his home sixth after a long pit stop to rectify a fuel pressure problem.

Roy Winkelmann remembered an incident as he and Jochen were driving to the Bugatti Circuit. "We were in his Peugeot going through this little village and a woman was teetering along on a bicycle overloaded with baskets of produce. She wobbled a bit and Jochen touched one of her baskets as we went past and it was enough to send produce everywhere. Fists were waved, and I told him, 'Jochen, we have to stop!' He said, 'Are you kidding, you wanna go to jail? I'm Austrian but they think I'm German; we won't get out for a week!'"

The new Cooper – Derrick White's "lightweight" T86 – arrived late for practice at Silverstone for the British Grand Prix, but it was an ugly duckling in comparison with the Lotuses, and its ungainly maw was evidence that it had been rushed to the race. It featured the long-awaited, heavily revised Maserati V12 which featured Heron cylinder heads with three valves per cylinder. The unit was said to be 30 pounds lighter than the 24-valver and to produce "over 400bhp", though there were many sceptics who smiled wryly at that claim.

Jochen qualified it eighth in 1m 27.4s, with Pedro ninth in the older car on 1m 27.9s. Cooper also entered a third car here, for Jochen's Winkelmann Racing team-mate Alan Rees, who had done a lot of testing for the team. He qualified 15th on 1m 30.3s. As Clark ran away to another trouble-free victory well ahead of Hulme and the duelling Amon and Brabham, Pedro finished fifth and Reesie ninth after obeying orders to take it easy. Jochen's new car leaked oil from an over-full catch tank and was thus accompanied by a smokescreen for the 26 laps it lasted in the midfield before consuming its new engine.

In 1966 the Cooper-Maseratis had been competitive round the Nürburgring in the German Grand Prix, but if ever proof were needed of how far the team had fallen behind, the 1967 race provided it. Clark took pole position by a mile from Hulme, Stewart (in a lighter but still heavy P115 version of the BRM H16) and Gurney. Jochen was ninth in the new car, less than two seconds ahead of Pedro.

He retired again, with either his third engine failure in a row or, as Salvadori suggested, with a loose steering rack, after four laps. Pedro was classified eighth after a pit stop to have a rear suspension balljoint replaced. After Clark's Lotus broke its suspension and Gurney's

Eagle broke a driveshaft with two laps to run, Hulme repeated his victory in Monaco to move closer to the World Championship.

Ron Dennis remembered Jochen mainly for what he perceived as arrogance, though his view is at odds with others who worked with him. In particular, Dennis remembered a moment before that Nürburgring race. "Salvadori came into the garage to get Jochen for the start and said, 'Time, Jochen'. And Jochen turned round

BELOW *Angelina Rodriguez times husband Pedro in the background, next to John Cooper, as Jochen shares a joke with new Formula 1 team-mate Alan Rees, who drove a Cooper T81 at Silverstone.* (LAT)

slowly, absolutely serious, and said: 'They'll never start the German Grand Prix without me'."

That may have had its roots in an incident in practice when he blew the new 36-valve Maserati and later had the flywheel detach itself on the spare T81B, creating a deep gash in the cockpit. He was subsequently accused by officials of having completed only four practice laps instead of the mandatory five, and therefore not being eligible to race. Having argued his cause successfully then, he may have been feeling invincible where petty bureaucracy was concerned.

"The relationships were pretty warm in our team in the sense that teams were teams in those days, we lived in each other's pockets, room sharing, anything to save money," Ron continued. "Physically the cars and mechanics went by road to events, so it built a different form of camaraderie in those days. The drivers were even more separated from the nucleus of the team, and they acted like superstars. And the lack of appreciation that the drivers had, which I experienced in the early days, was extreme. With the exception of Jack, who was reasonably friendly. But they were all so damned tight, they would never dream of buying a round of drinks for the boys. Nothing like that."

Perhaps it was a class thing?

"Absolutely. It's not like that at all now. Drivers have phenomenal respect for the brainpower of many of the people behind them, all of them are highly skilled individuals. And the cars are very sophisticated pieces of equipment. Just as you would respect a person taking apart a fighter aircraft, it's no different now with a racing car. But back then it wasn't like that.

"The night after a race there was still some pressure but you did most of the work back home and there was inevitably some sort of prize-giving, and that would be as good or as bad as the organisers. We went to most of them, though they are a pretty distant memory for me. The party atmosphere varied from country to country. Again, the drivers were relatively aloof. But some of them were far more a part of the team. Piers Courage was always very friendly and very correct and gentlemanly. Bonnier was always warm, a really nice guy. One time Jochen's manner annoyed one of the mechanics so much that the guy just turned and said to him, 'Why don't you just take off your helmet and fill it with ten pounds of spuds?'"

Jochen didn't have to tolerate Pedro Rodriguez's presence after that race, for the Mexican badly broke an ankle after sliding down the road in Enna when he crashed the wooden Protos Formula Two car a week later. In the inaugural Canadian Grand Prix which took place at Mosport Park on August 27, Jochen thus had British stalwart Richard Attwood as his team-mate, and he at last got his wish to take over Pedro's 1966 T81 chassis while Attwood took over Jochen's previous

T81B. Driving the wheels off the car, Jochen qualified eighth, two and a half seconds off Clark's pole time, but only after a nasty scare when the spare car threw its starter ring gear through the chassis after detaching itself as it had done at Nürburgring. But a rain-spoiled race saw fortunes seesaw among the leaders and Jochen retire early after a pit stop to investigate dire handling and then drowned electrics. Attwood was tenth. Clark led, Bruce McLaren impressed in his new BRM V12-engined McLaren M5A, but in the end Brabham came through to lead Hulme and Gurney home.

The T86 was back for the Italian Grand Prix at Monza, with a further modified 36-valve engine and a chin spoiler that cured a tendency for the now-sleek nose to lift at very high speed. And Jochen had another new team-mate, the upcoming Belgian Jacky Ickx. Again the Lotus-Fords and Eagle-Weslakes fought it out with the Brabham-Repcos, as Jochen was embroiled in a midfield dice with McLaren and Amon in a Ferrari whose new 48-valve engine had lost its edge after he over-revved it. John Surtees had also been part of that group in the new Lola-chassised Honda RA301, but the hugely popular Englishman had pulled away from the group. After mechanical problems had accounted for Hill, Gurney and Hulme, and Clark had been delayed by a puncture, made up a lost lap and retaken the lead only to fall back on the last lap with fuel feed problems, Surtees outfoxed Brabham on the run to the line to snatch victory. Clark finished third, while Jochen outlasted his group rivals to take fourth. Ickx was a commendable sixth in the T81B.

The US Grand Prix at Watkins Glen would be Jochen's last race with Cooper, and he left under a cloud. There had already been rumours that he would leave for Brabham, as Hulme was headed off to join fellow countryman Bruce McLaren in a two-car team of Cosworth-engined McLarens.

Hill took pole position ahead of Clark, with Gurney and Amon sharing row two ahead of the Brabhams in team order. Jochen was eighth, alongside talented Lotus guest driver Moises Solana in the third 49. Jochen had started out with the T86, which retained its 36 valves but now had 36 spark plugs as well. Studying the new powerplant, with all its untidy electrical leads and pipery, Cosworth DFV designer Keith Duckworth was moved to comment: "If you need more than one plug per cylinder there is something wrong with the design!" Jochen perhaps thought so too, for he raced the T81B earmarked for Ickx, leaving Jacky to qualify two seconds slower in the newer car, 16th in the line-up.

Under an arrangement between Ford's Walter Hayes, Clark, Hill and Colin Chapman, Hill was supposed to win this one, but once Amon had pushed the 48-valve Ferrari past Gurney's smoking Eagle, Clark was obliged to hurry up and pass his team-mate on the 41st lap as Graham struggled with a clutch problem. Then Amon

got horribly baulked by Jo Bonnier's tardy Cooper-Maserati, which gave the Lotuses some respite. Hill's clutch was getting worse, however, and by lap 65 Amon was up to second, intent of closing down Clark. But both Lotuses speeded up and broke the lap record, and Hill went back past the Ferrari. As the race moved into its final stages, and Hill started to experience gearbox problems and fading oil pressure, Chris repassed Graham, but then the Ferrari began to lose its own oil pressure and the New Zealander retired on lap 96. This was just as well for Jimmy, whose right rear suspension began to collapse with only a few laps to run. The Scot did his usual masterly job of nursing his equipment home, winning from Hill and Hulme.

That day the Lotus 49 fulfilled to the letter Colin Chapman's dictum that the perfect race car was one that was light and no stronger than it needed to be to break literally as it crossed the finish line…

By the time cigar-smoking, lavender-suited "Tex" Hopkins did his usual dance while flagging them home, Jochen's race – and his relationship with Cooper – was over. As he got to lap 34 he sensed that yet another Maserati V12 was about to fail behind him, and this time his frustration boiled over and he decided to help it on its way. These were the days before rev limiter tell-tales, and he happily dipped the clutch and gave the motor a bootful of revs to make sure it broke. It did that, all right, as the crankshaft snapped.

Jochen boasted about his indiscretion within Salvadori's hearing in the garage, and they decided that it was time to go their separate ways. Cooper would focus its efforts solely on the recovered Pedro Rodriguez in the final race in Mexico.

"I remember that incident," Ron Dennis said. "I mean, it was like a spoiled child mentality. I can remember tensions in the team. The important thing to remember is that Coopers really did commit to the 3-litre formula and came out with strong, safe cars. And they made cars not just for themselves but also for customers such as Guy Ligier, Jo Bonnier and Rob Walker. That was an unheard of starting point, to go with so many cars on the grid at the first Grand Prix of 1966. The car was relatively competitive until the Lotus 49 came along, which of course had the advantage of a custom-made engine from Cosworth. What Jochen did seemed disrespectful to a team that had put in so much effort."

Salvadori felt that he and Jochen largely got on together, though he conceded that they both had their moments and recalled one comment when Jochen said to him: "The best part of you is your wife…" He also remembered a time in late 1965 when he, Derrick White and Jochen drove down to Goodwood in Roy's BMW to test the prototype Cooper-Maserati, and what a terrible passenger Jochen was. It was raining, they were pushing on, and Roy was sliding the car through the corners.

Jochen and Derrick wanted Jochen to drive, but Salvadori knew Jochen's own reputation on the road and wasn't having that. Eventually, Roy was persuaded to stop for a cuppa, whereupon neither of his passengers would get back in with him until he let White take over as the optimum compromise. Derrick then drew the chorus of criticism. Subsequently they caught up with the transporter, Derrick pulled over, and he and Jochen travelled the rest of the way with the mechanics!

Looking back on that season, and the two drivers, Dennis compared Pedro with Jochen. "Pedro was a very nice guy. I remember he had a ruptured water pipe somewhere and he got his butt scalded, and how he wasn't properly looked after by the team. I remember

BELOW *After winner John Surtees pulled away from him, Jochen battled with Bruce McLaren at Monza. Ironically, the deformed spoiler on the T86's new nose helped reduce nose lift at 190mph.* (LAT)

that feeling, why don't they go and look after him? Pedro was quick, too.

"Jochen's English was okay, but I don't remember him as being a particularly friendly individual. I had a lot of respect for him because of his pace and because he was fearless. Absolutely fearless, especially in the wet. You could see that Jochen put in maximum effort, so you did too, you felt that way because of that, no question."

Michael Argetsinger only attended Watkins Glen in 1967, but said in 2008 that he was surprised Dennis felt Jochen was aloof. "Of course, Ron had his own perspective. Jochen wasn't 'one of the guys' like say, Mark Donohue was, or Bruce McLaren was, with the guys who worked with them. But he was friendly and got on well, as I saw it. What surprises me most about Ron's comment is that Jochen really made Ron's career. Apparently Ron doesn't choose to remember it that way, and I have no idea what ultimately transpired in that relationship. Ron is clearly a self-made man and there were many things that happened on his way up that I

have no knowledge of, nor do I pretend to be any kind of an expert on his life story."

Nina simply said, "I just can't figure out why Ron thought Jochen was arrogant."

For a long time, the friendship between Jochen and veteran Fleet Street writer Pat Mennem, doyen of the *Daily Mirror*, confused me, for on the surface they seemed unlikely chums. But the more I got to know Pat, a lovely, ruddy-faced bon viveur and gentleman who liked a drink and had olde worlde manners to spare, and the more I learned of Jochen's true character, the more natural it seemed. Neither of them put on a front; what you saw with each was exactly what you got.

"He and I were stuck in Geneva Airport on one occasion and we talked a lot," Pat told me back in 1990. "I went to see him in Switzerland and when he was in London I took him to lunch, introduced him to the *Mirror*'s editor. I liked him. He was not arrogant, but he was more intelligent than most of them, and much better read. He had a very rounded knowledge, of the environment, astronomy, government affairs. Quite astonishingly for someone whose parents were killed by the RAF, he had no hang-ups about the British at all. It didn't trouble him. He was very competitive, intensely so. Whatever you were doing he had to beat you, even if it was noughts and crosses, skiing, anything he had to do he had to win."

And Pat made one very interesting additional observation. "His most outstanding quality was that he never complained. When he was persevering with the Cooper-Maserati I used to say, 'What's the trouble?' and he'd just say: 'I've got cockpit trouble. I can't make it go fast enough'. He never went on about tyres, brakes, or whatever."

Jack Brabham was team-mate to both Roy and Jochen in his lengthy career, and in 2008 he observed, slightly tongue-in-cheek: "Jochen was unhappy at Coopers. I don't know why because I didn't go into it with him, but he was unhappy there. The car wasn't all that good anyway, and I don't think he got on all that well with Salvadori. You couldn't get anyone who knew less about a motor car than Roy did, and he was the team manager trying to teach somebody to drive… It couldn't work, could it?"

Though Watkins Glen had been his last race of 1967, Jochen went to Rockingham, North Carolina, on October 28 for a NASCAR race, the American 500, as his keenness to race anything surfaced to match Jimmy Clark's when Jackie Stewart was unable to accept an invitation from Bill France to accompany his fellow Scot.

"That race was another classic example of Jim's insatiable curiosity," said his biographer Graham Gauld, adding with a chuckle: "It was also a good example of the difference between Jackie and Jimmy. Jimmy was in Bermuda, and had invited Jackie and Helen and Jochen and Nina to his flat. Jimmy, Jackie and Jochen were there when the phone rang. It was Bill France, the big cheese of NASCAR. And Bill said to Jimmy, 'I believe you've got Jackie with you? I'd like you and Jackie to race stock cars at Rockingham'. Jimmy covered the phone and relayed the message to Jackie, who immediately went on the defensive. 'What kind of stock car? If I've got to race a stock car it's all got to be right, the best.' That sort of thing. And Jimmy told Bill that Jackie wouldn't be able to race, but said 'I've got Jochen here, I'll ask him.' And Jochen agreed and the two of them packed their bags and flew off the next morning."

Stewart told a slightly different version of the story. "We were all staying with Jimmy in Bermuda. His place was unfurnished, so we almost had to go and buy furniture before we could stay there. Helen was pregnant so she couldn't ride scooters and Jimmy got her to go out and buy all the furniture." Jackie broke off to chuckle. "And then he was worried about how much it all was costing. 'Och, I don't know if I want that at that price,' and it was already bought!" He laughed again at the memory, but there was a time in Bermuda when he wasn't laughing. Unknown to many he had broken the metatarsal in his right foot playing squash at night there on a concrete court in Hamilton, and the doctor who got called out to attend to him at the hospital was initially disgruntled.

"It was, 'Oh, he's a racing driver…' But he knew a little about racing and there was Jimmy and Jochen and me and he couldn't believe all this was on his pad! The three drivers that he knew about in the world from Formula One – and he must have been an odd one because he knew about Formula One – were all there. But he missed the break when he looked at the X-ray, and it was the girl who took the X-ray who found it. She said to him it was definitely a fifth metatarsal fracture. Later he married the girl!

"That's why I didn't do the NASCAR race. Jimmy was doing it, and then when they heard we were all together, Big Bill France called. We were supposed to go to Rockingham but I was in plaster; they got me wired up so that I was able to do the US Grand Prix, with the plaster off and everything taped up."

According to NASCAR lore, because their races were longer than Grands Prix Jimmy had Jochen there as a potential relief driver. Given that Jimmy in particular had raced at Indianapolis and finished the 500-miler there second in 1963, first in '65 and second in '66, had also finished at Le Mans in an Aston Martin, and in any case was not the kind of driver who ever needed relief, those facts seem a little shaky. It is more likely that France simply wanted a big bang for his buck by having them share the car.

Despite losing a wheel at one stage in practice Jimmy qualified the number 66 Holman & Moody Ford Fairlane 24 of the 44 runners. He impressed onlookers by moving smoothly up to 12th place by quarter distance, but when the engine broke on lap 144 Jochen didn't get his chance to show what he could do in the same car as a man he respected so much. Jimmy was classified 30th. Bobby Allison, newly installed in the retired Fred Lorenzen's Ford, won the race, while Lodovico Scarfiotti, the third member of the European party, failed to start Tom Friedkin's Plymouth after practice problems.

Michael Argetsinger was in Rockingham. "I didn't get there until that evening, in time to have dinner with Jochen, Jim, and Lodovico. Only Jim got to run on Sunday. He was brilliant and drove an impressive race until the car failed. What I remember most about the dinner is that Jochen and Jim were flabbergasted that we (my brother J.C. and his wife Joan were with me) had come all the way to the wilds of North Carolina to see them. What happened in truth is that J.C. was an infantry lieutenant stationed at nearby Fort Bragg. I was visiting prior to him shipping overseas. We read in the local paper that Jim and Jochen were racing there and we phoned Bill France. He arranged passes for the race Sunday and said, 'Why don't you come to the banquet tonight?' He seated us at the table with Jochen, Jim, and Lodovico. They seemed really pleased to see us. Of course, at Watkins Glen they were virtual gods, at Rockingham they were mostly a curiosity. So it may have been that they were just happy to see familiar faces – people who appreciated who they were. In any case, we had a great time."

Retrospectively, Argetsinger would also come to remember that happy dinner as the last time he ever saw or spoke to Jimmy.

At the end of the Formula One year Louis Stanley had dropped Jochen to ninth overall, behind Denny Hulme, Jim Clark, Jack Brabham, John Surtees, Graham Hill, Dan Gurney, Jackie Stewart and Chris Amon, and ahead of Jo Siffert, but said: "Another driver to have a frustrating season. Cooper-Maserati did not come up to expectations, the engine being down on power alongside the opposition. Only in Formula Two did Rindt show his ability. In more sophisticated machinery he was not outstanding. Nevertheless he has in abundance the attributes of a great driver, possibly without the basic quality necessary to be a brilliant one. He tends to be unpredictable. There are moments when it is sad to see such a plenitude of genius, so blithely treated as casual labour. Some of his drives are invigorating and exciting. Given a more balanced judgement under pressure, he could hold his own against anyone. That will come with experience. He should learn fast under Brabham. A refreshing feature of Rindt is his unsquashability. Few have such a healthy ego."

Salvadori believed that Jochen was leaving because John Cooper refused to countenance his demands for a salary of £25,000 (the equivalent of £340,000 today), but the truth was that he'd had enough of Cooper's way of going about Grand Prix racing. He really liked Jack Brabham, and the feeling was mutual. And Jack's cars were light, well engineered machines that had won the World Championships for Drivers and Constructors in 1966 and '67.

There had, however, been another opportunity that, curiously given its pedigree, Jochen turned down: to go F1 with Roy Winkelmann. Rumours were mentioned briefly in *Autosport* in October.

"What happened was this," Winkelmann explained. "I had a very generous offer from Firestone. It was an enormous offer, actually. It wasn't predicated on having Jochen but I wanted him, I felt we had bonded."

Winkelmann and his wife met with Jochen and Nina in a swanky restaurant in Paris. He remembers Nina chiding him and Jochen because they'd gone to such a cool, romantic place, and all they could do was talk about motor racing.

Winkelmann's plan was to build his own car. "Jo Marquart was going to design it. He had experience at McLaren and Lotus and was so good, he was definitely underrated. We would have had a good car."

But he said that two things militated against that. "I couldn't convince Jochen to join me," Winkelmann said, still sounding bemused more than four decades later. "He really wanted to drive for Brabham.

"And he wanted me to discharge Alan Rees. I told him I couldn't fire Alan, he was good in the office. I didn't know then that he would go off to found March a year later with Max Mosley, Robin Herd and Graham Coaker." Winkelmann believed that many of his personnel were lured to March, and added, "I thought that was pretty tawdry."

Jochen and Reesie were good friends, but Winkelmann disagreed and insisted: "There wasn't any love lost between them. I often broke up arguments between them, over silly things. Jochen would often call me to complain about things when I was doing my intelligence work abroad. And now he was adamant that he wanted Alan out. I really didn't feel I could fire him, so because of my loyalty to him I lost my chance to go F1…"

What Jochen particularly liked about Jack was the fact that he had not tried to pull rank over Denny in 1967 as they battled for the World Championship, but had let the cards fall as they would. He thought that was a key omen for 1968 when, he was sure, he would be given a competitive car to drive and have every chance, finally, of winning a Grand Prix.

He couldn't wait.

OPPOSITE *Maserati's 36-valve V12 engine was neither powerful nor reliable. The glum expressions of Ron Dennis, Mario Tozzi-Condivi and former team owner John Cooper tell their own story.* (LAT)

"I just don't think it was necessary for them to treat me like that. I'm not a kid, and even if they didn't like me wearing two-piece overalls they only had to say so – they didn't have to tear them off me. On top of this the car wasn't really competitive, so I didn't feel very happy.

"The trouble with Indianapolis is that the people there can't think of anything else. They don't know about anything except left turns and yellow lights and keeping women out of Gasoline Alley. They try to make up rules to cover all possible eventualities, and they act as if it is the world's one and only motor race. When I did my rookie driver's test they made me rest after every ten laps in case I got too tired, but when you get down to it you need less skill to drive at Indianapolis than on almost any road circuit; I would say it's about 85 per cent car and 15 per cent driver."

He hated the continual stoppages if it rained even slightly or there was debris on the track, and wondered aloud what would happen if there were as many pigeons in Indiana as there were in Trafalgar Square. He liked to refer to the USAC chief Steward Harlan Fengler as "Harlan Finger".

Small wonder that when, in 1990, Formula One refugee Eddie Cheever similarly questioned the rookie tests, old timers in USAC immediately cast their minds back to "That ornery Rindt guy!" "I'd had my run-ins with the FIA in my time in F1," Eddie admitted, "and when I went to Indy they obviously knew because they said they didn't want anyone behaving like Rindt did!"

"Jochen didn't like all that rookie stuff, oh no, no,"

BELOW *Jochen detested all the hype at Indianapolis Motor Speedway, especially the rookie tests, but found time to share humour with close friends Leo Mehl and Jimmy Clark in the 1967 build-up.* (Indianapolis Motor Speedway)

Stewart affirmed. "But you had to do it. We were all together out there, with Larry Truesdale, the Goodyear guy. We hung out at the track because that was the one thing about Indianapolis, it was all the waiting. You'd go out in the morning and then the temperature would go up so nobody would go any quicker, and then when the wind died down and the temperature was right you went out around five o'clock until the track closed at six and you had the Silly Hour. We hung out in Gasoline Alley, either in the Goodyear place or the Firestone place, underneath the steel grandstand."

While Jochen might not have won many friends among officialdom, it soon became clear that he was at home on the two and a half mile oval. "How we started it was that he did his rookie test, then I tested his car and established a lap time in it," Gurney remembered. "I made one tiny adjustment, as I recall. It was going slightly to oversteer mode so I changed the front anti-rollbar slider a quarter of an inch and that was the way that Jochen drove it. "Well, it didn't take him long to get to the same speed that I had done in the car, so I knew that he had to have been doing a very, very good job. It was a revelation to him that I could dial in the car and give him a target and that it could all turn out to be true! It established the relationship between us."

Later, in May 1967, came the shunt that would be the other reason Jochen came to be so well remembered at the Speedway, and one of the few things that distracted journalists from Parnelli Jones's controversial STP Paxton turbine car which had grabbed all the attention. It happened in qualifying as the throttle jammed at 160mph going into Turn One. Jochen steered into the concrete wall to try and scrub off speed, deliberately hit it at a shallow angle, and as it tore along the Eagle lost both right-hand wheels. As the left rear wheel also left the ground on impact, the Ford V8 over-revved wildly, hitting 12,000rpm and exploding immediately into a huge fireball.

"When Jochen decided to drive at Indy I had him view several accident incidents to show him that if he got into difficulties it was advisable to use the wall to assist in slowing down," Roy Winkelmann said. "Any other tactic could be disastrous. He did exactly that and took the right side of the car off, but only suffered a bruised little finger."

In the pits, the fire generated a huge scare thanks to its pall of black smoke, and Mehl, a close friend of Jochen's, remembered "the huge fireball that went round the corner and disappeared".

Gurney explained what had gone wrong. "Going into Turn One something happened with the throttle butterfly. It was held on by two screws. One fell out and the other worked loose and it kinda hung down from the shaft and kept the throttle open. Probably by as much as 50 per cent. Jochen had very little time to make a decision what

to do when he backed off and the engine didn't. He elected to move over towards the wall on his right and to hit it at an oblique angle instead of turning left and hanging on. He went right and relied on the centrifugal force carrying him around along the wall until the short chute that followed. Okay, the car was heavily damaged, but if he hadn't had that presence of mind…"

Jochen talked about how he and Winkelmann had figured out what to do if, for example, the throttle stuck open. "I don't know if I was lucky, but I had worked out beforehand that if I had trouble going into a corner it would be better to turn into the wall to avoid hitting it at too much of an angle," he told Phipps. "I hit the wall at about 20 degrees, which definitely lessened the impact. But it was a long time, over 600 yards, before the car stopped and while I was sliding along the wall I looked in

my mirror and saw that the engine was on fire..."

He was wearing seat belts for the first time in a racing car. He hated them, and was fearful that in just such an eventuality he might not be able to release himself quickly enough. He also knew full well that if he bailed out too soon, he would seriously hurt himself. Steering the Eagle with one hand on its crazy ride down the wall, he released his belts with the other and when he figured that the speed was right he prepared to emulate his Le Mans-winning co-driver Masten Gregory, and jump from a moving vehicle.

"My first instinct was to get out, but I realised that I would get hurt if I jumped out at that speed so I undid my belts, stood and then stepped out when the car finally stopped – by which time the fire trucks had almost caught up with me. You've got to have luck to be able to do things like this. But it helps if you figure out what to do beforehand."

Back then the Speedway was much more advanced in safety terms than the Formula One world, and within 15 seconds of the flaming Eagle coming to rest the fire trucks were there, and so was an ambulance. Within 24 seconds Jochen had distanced himself by 100 yards from the burning hulk. But the rules dictated that any driver who had been in a shunt had to be checked over in the medical centre.

BELOW *Jochen's first ride at Indianapolis came courtesy of Tom Friedkin and this Wagner Lockheed Brake Fluid Special Eagle. He crashed heavily when the throttle stuck open, but was unharmed.* (Indianapolis Motor Speedway)

The ambulance driver had been so shaken by the severity of the accident that he was quivering and Jochen, having closed the rear doors and elected to travel up front with him, had to steady the guy's hands and light the cigarette that he had offered him. He even opened the main gate for him.

In the medical centre, doctors were astonished to discover that Jochen's pulse rate had risen by only two beats, his blood pressure by only six per cent. Yet he'd slid along the wall for 1,800ft and was timed through an 1,100ft section at 150mph, with the engine afire! Small wonder that writer Eoin Young began calling him "Fearless Jo" in his *Straight from the Grid* column in *Autocar*...

In the press room journalists put a photo of the fiery accident on the wall, and written on it and underlined many times were the words "Rindt okay". They couldn't believe it either.

Jochen told Heinz Pruller that he had "a headache and a bit of a fright, that's all," when they met up after his medical check. And Heinz believed that the reality of the incident did not catch up with his friend for a while.

Meanwhile, there was still work to do. Jochen couldn't get Friedkin's back-up car going fast enough, and ironically a fast lap from Jackie bumped him from the traditional 33-car field that weekend. Now he would have to wait for the second qualifying session when, under Indy's arcane rules, anyone who qualified would have to start behind those who had qualified in the first, even if they had gone quicker.

Finally, he got in the field with a four-lap average of 163.05mph in All-American Racers' spare chassis, which Gurney himself had run at 163.7mph the previous day. This was 24th fastest overall, but under the rules that left him 32nd and in the middle of the back row. He had familiar company close at hand; Stewart's Lola was just ahead of him in 29th slot after a run at 164.099mph, and Hill's efforts in a Lotus 42 converted to take a Ford V8 instead of the stillborn BRM H16 engine had reaped only 163.317mph, leaving him 31st and to Jochen's left.

As an indication of what could have been for Jochen, who had quickly matched Dan's initial speeds in his primary car, Gurney qualified in the middle of the front row at 167.224mph, alongside polesitter Mario Andretti (168.892mph) and Gordon Johncock (166.559mph).

Jochen's mood had darkened since the accident, and his qualifying performance did little to lift his spirits. Pruller remembers the evening before the race was a sombre affair as he dined in a local steak house with Jochen and Nina, and Denny.

"Jochen would normally be full of joy and jokes, but he was depressed. 'All I am here for is the money,' he admitted. 'But if you haven't a chance of winning, the entire business is just senseless. It's dangerous, Indy frightens me. The Americans don't look in their mirrors, the officials think they know it all and the regulations are just childish. It's utterly boring to have to spend a whole month for just one three-hour race – and to get nowhere during the 30 days.'

"On race day we drove to the Speedway with the five of us squeezed into a small hire car," Pruller continued; "Jochen, Nina, Denny, Jackie and myself. The atmosphere was quite tense. Remember that it was only three years since the Macdonald/Sachs fireball. 'Every European driver,' Jochen observed quietly to me, 'must feel as if he is on his way to his own funeral.'"

To keep their minds off the challenge ahead, and to keep their spirits up, Jochen, Jackie and Denny decided their tactics together. "We'll try to stick together, to form our own group," Pruller remembered them saying. "That way we can minimise the risk and dangers of collisions."

As ever, the pomp and circumstance of Indianapolis consumed everyone soon afterwards, keying each driver up to a nervous pitch which was not helped when some inevitably dwelt on the multi-car shunt that had spoiled the start the previous year. Eddie Fisher, at that time the husband of actress Liz Taylor, gave his rendition of the Star Spangled Banner as his audience stood, and then came the classic command: "Gentlemen, start your engines".

Pruller stood by Jochen's car in the 11th and final row, and Jochen asked him nervously, "Heinz, what does Memorial Day mean?"

"I told him it's an American All Souls Day, like Armistice Day – a kind of hero's remembrance, especially for soldiers. Jochen looked at me and said: 'What an omen for the race...'"

This time everything went cleanly at the start, and Jochen soon settled into his run. There were no incidents, but after 108 laps his Ford V8 dropped a valve and that was it. If there was any consolation, Clark and Hill lasted only 35 and 23 laps respectively in their Lotuses before burned pistons sidelined them. But again there was a 'what might have been' for Jochen, as Denny drove his Eagle to a strong fourth place and a healthy pay cheque.

Afterwards, as Pruller tried vainly to smuggle Nina into Gasoline Alley, Jochen signed autographs for the Eagle mechanics and thanked them for their efforts.

The Great American Adventure was over, and he was richer not by the $1m (the equivalent of $6.45m today) he had seen as a carrot, but by a nevertheless useful $10,571 ($68,000). He used some of the money to buy furniture for his hitherto empty apartment in Paris.

"All the ballyhoo, the practising for a whole month; the pre-race activities and the publicity," Jochen said as he

OPPOSITE TOP *Jochen and Denny Hulme did their rookie tests together at Indianapolis, and were united in their dislike for the way their years of road racing experience counted for nothing with USAC.* (Indianapolis Motor Speedway)

OPPOSITE BOTTOM *Jochen was highly impressed when both he and team entrant Dan Gurney were able to hit the speeds that the Californian had promised him his Eagle Ford could achieve.* (Indianapolis Motor Speedway)

continued his anti-Indy rant to McNally the following year. "One of the big problems for a racing driver is autograph hunters and people who just want to talk to you. I think it is very important to be nice to them, but I don't want to talk to anybody just before a race – and afterwards I am usually too tired. It's very difficult. I am usually more nervous at the beginning of the season than at the end, and it's worse at some circuits than others. I feel worse at a Grand Prix than at a Formula Two race, because Formula Two is not so serious, not so important.

"In a race I never go faster than I want to, and I try to avoid getting too close to people unless I feel I can trust them. If I can, then it's okay. Last year, for instance, I had a big go with Jackie at Albi. Jackie is a very clean driver and we had equally matched cars, so we were able to pass each

other two or three times every lap. I could have stopped him overtaking and he could have stopped me, but then it would have been nasty business. It's the same with all the top Grand Prix drivers; you can rely on them not to do anything stupid. But it's entirely different at Indianapolis."

American hero A.J. Foyt, the winner in 1961, '64 and again in '67, had cautioned Jochen: "Never look back on Indy, otherwise you will be shaken and will swear to yourself that you will never come back!"

Betty Brabham had threatened Jack: "Whenever you dare to drive again at Indy, you will get a divorce!"

At that stage, Jochen had no intention of ever going back. But he did…

In 1968 Jack, perhaps mindful of Betty's ultimatum, entered a car for him, and Jochen would do anything for Jack. He had such a tight schedule that he had just one day in which to qualify, and the track was damp. He was allowed out, however, and despite some sideways motoring not usually seen at the Brickyard he qualified the blue monocoque Repco-powered BT25 16th at 164.144mph in a feat that both

BELOW *Jochen seems notably more relaxed before the start of the 1968 Indianapolis 500 than he had when he made his debut at the Speedway in 1967. Unfortunately his Brabham lasted only five laps.* (Indianapolis Motor Speedway)

staggered USAC officials but also pleased them as the fact that he went out meant they didn't have to reimburse the day's otherwise disappointed spectators. It was one of the few times the Jochen Rindt name was popular among Speedway officialdom! Ron Tauranac simply called it "Sensational!" But come the race Jochen finished only 32nd after a piston failure rendered him the second retirement after only five laps. "I wouldn't have gone back if Jack hadn't wanted me to," he grumbled. But even when he didn't like a track, Jochen never gave less than his best. He was a professional to the core.

There should have been one more shot left in his Indianapolis locker, but 1969 (when, incidentally, Jack disobeyed Betty and drove a modified BT25 with upcoming Peter Revson as his team-mate) could hardly have been less auspicious. Jochen was to have raced the innovative STP-backed four-wheel-drive Lotus 64 alongside Mario Andretti and Graham Hill.

Andretti proved the potential of the dramatic-looking car by lapping his at 170.179mph, and then boosting that to 171.789mph four days later. The following week, however, he had a massive accident when a rear wheel detached itself in Turn Four following hub failure. The

Lotus was wrecked, and Andretti suffered facial burns. Designer Maurice Philippe subsequently admitted that some parts from the unloved Lotus 63 four-wheel-drive Formula One car had been used on the 64, because of the serious time constraints, whereas it might have been wiser and safer to design bespoke components.

Jochen arrived the day before Andretti crashed, still recovering from his own massive accident in the Spanish Grand Prix at Montjuich Park. Team Lotus was in all sorts of trouble preparing its two late-arriving machines for him and Hill, and behind the scenes there were serious tensions in the relationship between Colin

Chapman and STP boss Andy Granatelli even though the colourful American entrepreneur did his best to keep things civil and sporting. Jochen figured things out almost as soon as he arrived at the Speedway on 19 May, the day before his first run, as mechanics were still frantically working to ready his car. And he quickly learned that, where Mario had been flying in his Clint Brawner-run machine, Graham had been struggling to get anywhere near 160mph in his. He would also have been furious if he had known that, in the 'equal number one' hierarchy, he would get only second dibs behind Graham and ahead of Mario if the spares situation got tricky. Or that Granatelli was giving Hill a fuel retainer worth six times what he would pay him. Granatelli, who would come to love Jochen, summed up the situation succinctly for team manager Andrew Ferguson: "When Jochin [sic] becomes World Champion, wins the '500' and speaks English adequately to be a good public relations man, I'll increase it".

On his first run in the third Lotus 64 to be built Jochen encountered the same engine misfiring and cutting out that was dogging Graham and, to his anger, a sticking throttle. That was the last thing he wanted after his experience in Turn One back in 1967. He reached 158.4mph, suffered more cutting out, but then managed 161mph before spinning. Altogether he managed 58 laps in which he still felt unwell after his dramas in Spain, while Graham attained a similar speed over 113 equally troubled laps.

As Mario switched to the back-up Hawk that would soon take him to the only Indy victory of his remarkable career, the sister Team Lotus entries for Hill and Rindt were withdrawn. There was no way, so soon after his trauma in the Spanish GP, that Jochen would ever have driven a questionable car at the Brickyard.

"It's not so nice if you are not sure that your car is fully tested and maybe not safe enough," he told Pruller, while explaining to fellow journalist Jabby Crombac: "The doctor forbade me to race at Monaco but on the day following I flew over to Indianapolis and arrived in time to see Mario Andretti lose a wheel. This crash convinced Colin of the danger and, despite opposition from his sponsors, he withdrew both his remaining cars when it became evident that there was not enough time to machine new hubs for Graham and me to test before qualifying. I was most relieved and fully agreed with Colin's decision."

Now his driving career at the Speedway really was over.

LEFT *Only days after his huge shunt at Montjuich Park, Jochen re-acclimatised to driving when he tried unsuccessfully to get the troubled Lotus 64 up to speed at Indianapolis in May 1969.* (Indianapolis Motor Speedway)

CHAPTER 9

Toe to toe with the best

Formula Two, 1966 and 1967

"Jochen was a hard driver but a clean driver. A lot of fun to drive with. You could really drive wheel-to-wheel with him in some absolutely unbelievable situations, and know you were okay. Incredible!"

Jack Brabham

LEFT *The king of F2 in his Winkelmann Brabham at Brands Hatch, 1967.* (LAT)

If 1965 had been a hard year for Jochen in Formula Two, life was about to get an awful lot worse in 1966 as the works Brabhams ran Honda's hitherto troublesome 1.6-litre motor. Cosworth's trusty SCA had a single camshaft and two valves per cylinder and generated 140 bhp; the Honda boasted twin cams and four valves per cylinder, and was good for another 10 bhp than the British motor could muster. In a category in which the chassis were so evenly matched, it was hardly a surprise that Jack Brabham and Denny Hulme wiped the floor with their breathless opposition.

But first, Jochen ventured to Sebring to take part in a 4 Hour TransAm saloon car race which supported the famed 12 Hour sportscar enduro. He drove an Alfa Romeo GTA for the Italian manufacturer's Autodelta sporting offshoot, and won from Bob Tullius's Dodge Dart and team-mate Andrea de Adamich. It was an impressive performance, especially as the car had to be rebuilt overnight after Roberto Businello pranged it in practice, and Jochen was a lap ahead by the finish. It was a good way to start the year.

Unfortunately, Brabham and Hulme started the way they intended to carry on in Formula Two by finishing 1-2 in the *Sunday Mirror* Trophy race at Goodwood on April 11, once they had disposed of Jackie Stewart's

OPPOSITE *The 1966 season started well as Jochen won the 4-Hour TransAm race for Autodelta at Sebring. He finished a lap ahead after the car had been rebuilt overnight when team-mate Robert Businello crashed it.* (LAT)

upstart Tyrrell Matra. Once Clark had dropped back with a puncture and Graham Hill had encountered valve problems in his Brabham-BRM, Jochen brought the lead Winkelmann Brabham-Cosworth home third, less than a second ahead of Rees. Best of the rest was better than nothing, but already the writing was on the wall.

Jack and Denny produced an encore the following weekend in the Grand Prix de Pau, and this time it was Graham who was best of the rest ahead of Stewart (who drove sensationally in his own Matra and then team-mate Jacky Ickx's when his car's throttle linkage fell apart) and Rees. Jochen had been only sixth in qualifying as Denny took pole again, and inadvertently clobbered

BELOW *This was how hard Jochen and Jimmy Clark had to drive in the* Sunday Mirror *Trophy race at Goodwood, in their fruitless attempts to keep the dominant Brabham Hondas in sight.* (LAT)

the delayed Stewart and damaged his Brabham's nose slightly just as he regained third place as Clark pitted with a flat battery. He was then overtaken by Hill when his engine failed.

A week later Jochen took pole and set fastest lap on his way to victory in the Eifelrennen at the Nürburgring, but it was something of a hollow victory as his main Formula Two rivals were racing in Barcelona, where, you guessed it, Brabham won in the rain with Stewart second and Hulme third.

The Formula One World Championship was very late starting that season, with the Monaco Grand Prix not taking place until May 22, so there was plenty of Formula Two to keep the drivers up to speed. The Grote Preis von Limbourg was next on the agenda at Zolder on May 8, and it proved to be a re-run of Goodwood, with Jack and Denny to the fore and Jochen third on aggregate after finishing third in both heats. The two Honda-engined cars were well ahead in the first heat, but in the second Jochen finished only four seconds behind Denny, who was right on Jack's tail. His refusal to give up, and the fact that he split the works Brabhams for a little while in heat two, drew significant praise.

After F1 interludes at Silverstone and Monaco it was back to Formula Two at Crystal Palace at the end of the month, where Jochen had high hopes of getting on terms with the Brabham-Hondas on the track where he had first made his reputation. But nothing had changed the 1966 status quo and this time the best he could do was fourth in both heats, and thus on aggregate, in the London Grand Prix. This time Rees got some revenge for 1964 by staying in front of him in both heats. After the first 30-lap race they were 20 seconds behind the Hondas; after the second 30 laps the gap was 26 seconds. The Honda engine was just too potent, and Jochen had a curiously off-form weekend even though he kept Rees honest to the flag each time.

A change of scene came with a return to the Nürburgring for the 1,000km sportscar race, where he shared a works flat-eight Porsche Carrera with Italian veteran Nino Vaccarella. Sportscar racing wasn't really Jochen's bag, but Porsche paid good money. Jochen provided full value in qualifying; John Surtees wheeled the 4-litre Ferrari P3 round in 8m 31.9s to take pole position ahead of Phil Hill and Jo Bonnier in the 5.4-litre Chevrolet-engined Chaparral 2D which the former champion took round in 8m 35.4s. Jochen was a sensation, lapping the 2.2-litre Porsche in 8m 44.1s. Unfortunately, the cars' reliability had yet to reach the

LEFT *Oops! Jochen drops a wheel in the dirt as he battles with Winkelmann Racing team-mate Alan Rees at Crystal Palace. In a curiously low-key weekend he took fourth, behind the Brabham Hondas and Rees.* (LAT)

ABOVE *No wonder Jochen smiled at the Nürburgring! While his main rivals were in Barcelona he took the Winkelmann Brabham to an easy pole position and victory in the ADAC Eifelrennen.* (LAT)

famed level that lay in the marque's future. After dropping to tenth after a mediocre start, he soon charged up to fourth behind Surtees, the Chaparral, and Lodovico Scarfiotti in the works Ferrari Dino. The car's chances evaporated, however, when shortly after the Surtees Ferrari hit trouble he needed a pit stop for a mechanical check over. Vaccarella could not maintain Jochen's pace during his stint. They were eighth by half distance, but thereafter the brakes went AWOL, forcing them into retirement.

After his fabulous drive in the Cooper at Spa, Jochen was back in an enclosed car for Le Mans in the middle of June, driving a Ford GT40 with the ebullient Scot Innes Ireland on behalf of Comstock-English. It was not a dissimilar pairing to Jochen and Masten Gregory the previous year, but this time around there would be no fairy tale ending; the engine blew up at Mulsanne around five o'clock on Saturday evening.

There was to be no repeat of Jochen's victory in the Rheims Formula Two race on July 2, either, the day before the French Grand Prix. The usual sweltering heat made life hard for everyone, and though Jochen started from the front row only a tenth of a second slower than Brabham, Hulme showed the true potential of the Honda-engined car on this very fast circuit by lapping a second and a half quicker than either of them. Jochen led several times in the usual dramatic slipstreamer, but soon he was in trouble with the fuel boiling in the heat. Brabham won easily, after no less a character than Honda's future boss Nobuhiko Kawamoto – "they used to call me Hong Kong mechanic!" – sorted out some practice gearbox problems. Denny dropped out with a broken rocker which punched a hole through the cam cover, so Reesie finished second for Winkelmann ahead of local hero Jean-Pierre Beltoise's Matra, but the Welshman was nine seconds behind Brabham – a huge margin by Rheims standards.

There was further bad luck when Formula Two headed for Rouen a week later. This time it was Denny Hulme's turn to win for Brabham-Honda as Jack Brabham's BT18 retired from the lead six laps from home when the gear lever broke off. Once again it was Jochen who had driven the wheels off his Cosworth-engined example in practice on Friday, but on Saturday Jack demoralised everyone when he was credited with a time of 2m 10.7s which nobody else believed, especially as Denny was next on 2m 12.7s and Jochen third on 1m 15.1s.

Jochen made a fabulous start, achieving the virtually impossible to decipher exactly what irascible starter Raymond 'Toto' Roche might do when he dropped the flag. He roared into the lead, but by Nouveau Monde Brabham was already ahead and he had opened a margin of three seconds by the end of the lap. Denny soon followed the boss through, leaving Jochen to focus on fighting for third with Surtees, Beltoise and Rees. Eventually he managed to work his way clear as the Hondas disappeared; by one third distance he was already 15 seconds down. Soon after half distance, however, his gearbox broke, leaving Reesie to finish best of the rest again ahead of Pedro Rodriguez's Lotus-Cosworth.

By the standards of Jochen's 1966 season Snetterton brought a little light belief as he raced for Autodelta again in the 500km touring car race at the end of July, after the British and Dutch Grands Prix. The Alfa GTAs of Rindt, de Adamich and Nanni Galli faced strong opposition from the BMW 2000TIs of Hubert Hahne and Dieter Glemser, and no less a face than Jackie Stewart in an Alan Mann Racing Lotus Cortina.

Stewart's team-mate Sir John Whitmore put his Lotus Cortina on pole ahead of Galli, de Adamich and Jochen. Whitmore led initially from Galli, Hahne and Jochen, as Stewart began moving up. Stewart quickly moved into the lead as Galli was delayed by problems with his rear brakes and then broken wheel studs, and Jochen suffered a leaking rear axle oil seal. Jochen's undoing came with rain after 44 laps; de Adamich moved into the lead as Jackie spun in the tricky conditions, and then Jochen dropped it at Riches and crashed into the bank. Andrea kept it on the island to score a solid victory ahead of Hahne, with Glemser a lap down.

It was back to serious business with the Cooper in the German Grand Prix, then it was a trip to Karlskoga in Sweden for the Kanonloppet on August 21 which saw Jochen's third Formula Two retirement in a row. As expected Brabham and Hulme ran away and hid as Clark battled home third. Jochen was well down the grid, lining up only eighth as Brabham, Hulme and Clark dominated.

Hulme led off the line but was momentarily overtaken by Frenchman Eric Offenstadt who was driving like a demon in his Lola-BRM. The Brabham-Hondas disposed of him after three laps and went their merry way, but an optimistically late bit of braking by Jochen saw him punt Offenstadt and break the Lola's fuel pump. The Winkelmann Brabham's steering arms were also bent in the impact, and the uncharacteristic misjudgement left Jochen on the sidelines too.

Curiously, when Finland's new Keimola circuit near Helsinki opened for racing during the following week it did so on the Wednesday. And, prefacing the trend of modern Grands Prix by more than 40 years, it was to be an evening race since it remained light until well after eight o'clock. Interestingly, Jochen's future father-in-law, former Formula Junior racer Curt Lincoln, had sold the television rights, and arranged for the highly impressive new facility to be marshalled by members of the local judo club…

Unfortunately for Jochen, the layout of the track was perfect for the Honda-powered cars as the uphill exit from the hairpin that led on to the main straight placed a premium on power and determined terminal velocity for the next third of the circuit, which comprised a long banked right-hander which then led via a flat-out left-hander on to the pit straight.

The Suomen Grand Prix was thus another cakewalk for Brabham and Hulme, who led Clark, Jochen and Peter Arundell home in the two, ten- and 25-lap, heats. Brabham and Clark had both missed the drivers' briefing – the Australian because he had flown his own plane home from Karlskoga and then returned to Helsinki by commercial jet and the Scot because he'd been testing for Lotus at Silverstone on the Tuesday before flying back to Finland. They consulted with their fellows before the start.

"You go when he raises the flag, don't you?" Jack asked Jimmy. And the Scot's reply demonstrated the superiority of the Japanese powerplant as he joked: "Okay, Jack, you go when he raises the flag, I don't mind. With that Honda you should be able to make up one minute's penalty in ten laps". Whatever happened, Jack and Denny made lousy starts as Jochen and Jimmy swept off to contest the lead of the first heat, but soon Honda power told, and then Jimmy put the Lotus ahead of the Winkelmann BT18.

One of the problems of televising the race, which took place in a holiday period, was that only 20,000 spectators turned out, so Lincoln asked the drivers to make a race of the second heat. Jochen and Jimmy did their best as Jack and Denny toyed with them for the first 20 laps, but then Jack and Denny got serious and preserved their two leading places even though they let Jimmy get a little under two seconds behind Denny by the flag. The result was exactly the same as the first heat, which left an identical result on aggregate: Brabham, Hulme, Clark, Rindt, Arundell.

Jochen was always keen to support the Austrian racing scene, and after the Italian Grand Prix at Monza he headed back home for the Austrian Grand Prix, which again would be run for sportscars. This time he was offered Colonel Ronnie Hoare's Ford GT40. He put this third on the grid in 1m 9.75s, right behind Innes Ireland's pole-winning Ford Advanced Vehicles version on 1m 9.6s and Jo Siffert's works flat-six Porsche Carrera on 1m 9.73s. Gerhard Mitter put another Carrera 6 on to the final front row slot with 1m 9.93s, so a tight encounter was on the cards.

The Porsches owned the race from the start, with Siffert sprinting into the lead from Mitter in the car he shared with Hans Hermann, and their team-mate Udo Schutz in the car he shared with Herbert Linge. Ireland

ABOVE *Jochen was back at the 'Ring for the 1,000kms race to share this Porsche Carrera 8 with Nino Vaccarella. He drove it to fourth place, but the pace took its toll on its brakes and forced retirement.* (Porsche)

initially held fourth from Jochen and privateer David Piper's Ferrari 250LM. Piper soon dropped back with a faulty wheel bearing. Jochen's GT40 was never fully on song, and as the Mitter car won from Siffert and the Schutz car, with Mike Salmon's GT40 disputing the result as his team believed him to have been third, Jochen had to be content with a distant ninth. It seemed that whenever he went back to the scene of a 1965 victory, the result was disastrous.

Two more retirements followed in Formula Two, which did little to improve his mood. The Trophée Craven at Le Mans, another of the French mini-series of rounds, very nearly fell to Jean-Pierre Beltoise's Matra-Cosworth after Jack Brabham suffered a rare retirement.

Jochen shared the front row with Jack and Denny, and jumped into the lead as Toto Roche performed his usual antics with the tricolor. He held on to it for the first lap, ahead of Brabham, Clark, Offenstadt (now partnering Jimmy in a Ron Harris Lotus-Cosworth), Stewart, Hulme and Beltoise. Brabham and Clark moved ahead of Jochen on the second lap, and Hulme began to move up rapidly, taking Beltoise with him. Jack's

retirement came on lap six as his engine seized, and three laps later Denny restored the status quo by taking over the lead from Jimmy. Beltoise had overtaken Jochen and moved up to hound Clark, and the three leaders then indulged in a fabulous dice that saw them changing places almost at will. Jochen could not stay with them, and was left to circulate in a lacklustre fourth place. On the 39th lap he retired with a broken throttle linkage clamp. When a similar problem stymied Clark, Hulme was left to lead Beltoise home by two seconds, with Offenstadt third a lap down.

Jochen headed for the Grand Prix d'Albi a week later hoping for better things, but it was another works Brabhamfest as Jack finished more than half a minute ahead of Jo Schlesser's Matra-Cosworth and Formula Three upcomer Chris Irwin who was entrusted with Hulme's Brabham-Honda as Denny was racing sportscars in the States.

Once again Beltoise starred, holding on to Brabham for 66 laps before his throttle cable broke, and once again Jochen was out of luck. He'd qualified only fifth, but as usual was in the thick of the battle in Brabham's wake, mixing it with Clark, Beltoise, Irwin and Schlesser. As Beltoise moved up to challenge Brabham's lead, Jochen ran third ahead of Clark. By lap 20 it was all over, however, as his engine blew up.

Never one to waste a weekend when he could be racing, Jochen headed back to Europe from the US

Grand Prix at Watkins Glen to drive a works flat-six Porsche Carrera to second place and fastest lap after starting from pole in the Prix du Tyrol in Innsbruck. He and winner Gerhard Mitter indulged in a race-long duel, which many observers believed to have been a neat bit of crowd-pleasing stage management in which the lead changed ten times in 25 laps. Later Jochen won the saloon car race in an Alfa Romeo GTA. It wasn't a bad weekend, as it was also confirmed that Cooper had taken up its option on him for 1967.

A week later there was another obscure outing, this time the Donaupokal sportscar and saloon car races in Aspern. He started from pole in the Carrera 6 and again finished second, this time to the similar car from Ben Pon's Racing Team Holland for Dutchman Gijs van Lennep who assuredly was not in his class as a driver. As van Lennep won easily, Jochen struggled with an incorrect rear axle ratio after the works team had made a late change for the worse, and had a spectacular spin which left him six seconds in arrears at the end of the 25 laps. He and Nanni Galli had a tight battle for the saloon car race, until Jochen retired his GTA with a broken gear lever.

Ironically, Jochen had enjoyed a somewhat better season in Formula One than he had in Formula Two, but fittingly he ended his season as he had begun it, with victory. It came at Brands Hatch at the end of October, a week after the Mexican Grand Prix had brought down the curtain on the first year of the new 3-litre formula. This was an important race, which attracted a huge crowd, and Jochen brought them to their feet time and again with a demonstration every bit as impressive as his breakthrough performance at Crystal Palace in 1964.

Things began badly for Brabham when fog prevented him getting to Sunday morning's practice session, which meant a start from the back of the grid. Brands, however, with its long back straight, was well suited to the Brabham-Honda, so he was confident that disadvantage could be overcome.

Jochen was easily fastest for the first heat, with a lap of 1m 37.0s compared to Chris Irwin's 1m 37.8s in the second Brabham-Honda and Beltoise's 1m 38.0s. Rees was fourth with 1m 38.2s in the second Winkelmann car, Clark fifth on 1m 38.8s after only just making it for similar reasons to Brabham.

Jochen blasted away from Beltoise and Clark at the start as Irwin's fuel injection faltered, while Jack made up six places over the first lap. By lap five he was up to second and the chase was on, but Jochen seemed able to preserve a seven second lead even when Jack put in the fastest lap of 1m 36.0s, six-tenths faster than Jochen's best, on the last lap. The second heat fell to Alan Rollinson from Trevor Taylor's similar Brabham-Cosworth, with Tony Lanfranchi's Lola-BRM third.

ABOVE *Le Mans 1966 brought no repeat of the previous year's fairy tale. The Ford GT40 entered by F.R. English and Charles Rathgeb's Comstock Racing team retired with engine failure on only the ninth lap.* (Ford)

Jochen thus started the 40-lap final from pole with Jack and Jimmy completing the front row, and Beltoise getting the second to himself after Irwin's fuel injection problems persisted.

Jack swept into the lead through Paddock Bend from Jochen, Jimmy and Jean-Pierre, and the quartet soon began to drop Peter Arundell as he ran fifth in his Lotus. Right from the start it was clear that Jochen had no intention of letting Jack get away, while Jimmy was shadowing them closely. And even though it was obvious that the Australian was pushing his car harder, and to more and more lurid angles, than he had ever had to in the whole season, he was not shaking off the Austrian or the Scot. It was pure racing, man to man, between three drivers who trusted one another implicitly.

It carried on this way until the 26th lap, when Jack and Jochen came up to lap upcoming Chris Lambert, a talented privateer who would lose his life two years later in a Formula Two race at Zandvoort following a clash with Swiss driver Clay Regazzoni. Forty years later Brabham still remembered Lambert as a "bloody nuisance" who got in his way, but Jochen's passing move

OPPOSITE *Jack Brabham loved racing with Jochen, especially in Formula 2, but was not so happy when he got beaten for the first time in 1966 in a gripping Motor Show 200 at Brands Hatch in October.* (LAT)

owed just as much to his ability to read a race, and an incident in the cockpit of Lambert's Cooper. Realising that Lambert was focused more on him than Brabham, who the Englishman had not spotted trying to slip through on the inside line, Jochen thrust boldly alongside the Cooper. At the very moment the two leaders came upon him, Lambert had also encountered his gear lever coming away in his hand and, not surprisingly, slowed as he missed the shift. That was all Jochen needed, and as Jack was momentarily hemmed in, he snatched the lead and the advantage of three or four car lengths. Jack was livid and launched a ferocious counter-attack over the remaining 14 laps. The pair of them threw their cars at the circuit, as Jack pushed back to within feet of the Winkelmann car that bore his name, but Jochen refused to get flustered and matched his rival's lurid driving inch for inch. The crowd lapped it up.

Over the final lap Jack gave it everything he had, harrying Jochen in the hope of forcing a mistake, but none came and as they burst through Clearways Jochen was still in front by two-tenths of a second after a fabulous duel that had left Clark another four seconds behind.

"It was undoubtedly one of the most difficult races I've been in," Jochen told Pruller, "but I was all the more delighted afterwards."

Just over a month later he had another victory, this time much easier, when he triumphed in a fun Formula Vee race at the Nassau Speed Week, having earlier tested the cars in Austria.

Expanding on his thoughts on racing, he continued: "It doesn't matter whether one is driving in a Grand Prix, in Formula Two or in long-distance events, there comes a point where one feels dead tired. But the more experience I get behind the wheel, the longer I can hold on; now I have little difficulty feeling in top form again right through the race."

These were not the days when drivers had to be the athletes they are today, with carefully calculated gymnastic routines and rigidly observed diets; Jochen was a brilliant skier and tennis player, but did not indulge in physical exercise to prepare himself for racing. Back then many drivers simply believed that 'doing' was the best way of honing their fitness.

It was also fashionable back then to suggest that Clark was happiest when he was out front, that he didn't like being in a bunch of cars. The truth was that he was

BELOW *As Jochen savours one of his greatest never-say-die victories, and the resultant hardware, Jack's face registers his great affection for the man he would soon employ to drive his Formula 1 cars.* (LAT)

ABOVE *Jochen shared the number 51 Porsche Carrera 6 with Gerhard Mitter in the 1967 Daytona 24 Hours. They retired, but Jochen enjoyed the trip after rekindling his relationship with Nina Lincoln.* (Porsche)

natural desire to make money – read, make a decent living – from it.

"If you only do Formula One you only have about ten races a year," he explained. "I love to drive, and Formula Two is very good because it's equal cars. Unfortunately some race organisers are spoiling it by taking a lot of ungraded drivers, who don't cost them anything; and having just a few big names to attract the public. I think they should have all the top drivers, or at least all of those who do Formula Two racing, or none at all. The French organisers have the best system; they only take 12 or 14 cars, but they are all potential winners."

To begin with, however, his first outing after the South African Grand Prix had kicked things off on January 2 was for Porsche in the Daytona 24 Hours at the beginning of February, where he shared a Carrera 6 with Gerhard Mitter. Ferrari's humiliation of Ford, with the new P4, grabbed most of the attention, when it wasn't focused on the dramatic new Chaparral 2F with its overhead rear wing, and the big-engined cars inevitably overshadowed the little cars on such a fast track. But though Jochen's car was surprisingly outqualified by Charlie Kolb's fleet 2-litre Ferrari Dino, he and Mitter took delight in being Porsche's fastest runner in a brand new, Goodyear-shod, chassis whose motor ran Bosch fuel injection. Their race was a disaster, however. Right from the start they experienced problems with out-of-balance wheels, stopping three times to have them changed. In the end, Mitter smacked a wall and broke a rear wishbone, forcing eventual retirement.

The Formula Two season kicked off at Snetterton on Good Friday in March, with the Guards Trophy race. The Winkelmann Racing team was equipped with the latest Brabham, the BT23, and now that Honda had withdrawn after achieving its aims in 1966 and because the formula had changed from 1-litre to 1.6-litre engines, the field was levelled again around Cosworth FVA power.

Jochen dominated practice by six-tenths of a second, leaving Graham Hill's works Lotus, Jackie Stewart's Tyrrell-Matra, team-mate Alan Rees, and Jack Brabham and Denny Hulme in the works Brabham-Cosworths to scrap over second place in heat one. Hill made the best start, but Jochen had displaced him by the end of the lap. As Graham and Jackie hit trouble, Jochen won by an easy four seconds from Jack and Denny. He started heat two from pole. This time Jack got the better start, but again the Winkelmann car was in front by the end of the lap. A lap later, however, Jochen's race was done as he coasted into the pits with electrical failure. Hulme went on to win from Brabham and Rees.

The scene was now set for a Rindt Special in the final. Starting from the back he was, incredibly, in the lead by

quite happy doing that with drivers he trusted, and that he simply didn't have to do it very often. Jochen felt the same, so long as those he was racing against knew where the limit was. If he had a problem at this stage, it was when he was running ahead of the pack, when he found his concentration wavering.

"Best of all I like to drive in a gaggle of cars, with at least one or two rivals whom I know I can beat; that doesn't put me under any strain. But if one is driving all on one's own, one is liable to stop concentrating and think of other matters, which can be dangerous."

As he looked forward to 1967, and what he hoped would be an improved Cooper-Maserati and an even more competitive Formula Two Brabham BT23, Jochen's spirits were high. It would be another busy racing year for him. He had a simple philosophy, part of which revolved around his pure love of racing and part his

the second lap, and started stretching it as early leader Brabham battled with Hulme, Frank Gardner (Brabham), Bruce McLaren (McLaren), Reesie and Hill. Graham, however, was also on a flier, storming through the field. First he disposed of Rees and McLaren. Then he passed Brabham on the eighth lap, and Hulme on the tenth. Jochen had a lead of more than two seconds, but Graham was charging and lap by lap that began to shrink. By lap 25 the Lotus had its nose alongside the Brabham all round the course as Graham tried everything to unsettle Jochen, and on lap 27 he succeeded in slipping ahead. Now the hunter became the hunted, and Jochen refused to give up. On lap 34 he saw his chance and snatched the lead back on the left-hand curve on the Norwich Straight. Incredibly, Graham repassed him on the 36th lap, but just when it all seemed over, Jochen found a way back to the front by outbraking Graham into the Esses on the penultimate lap. Through Coram on the final lap Graham drew alongside in the rush to Russell and they crossed the line side by side. They were so close that they were both given the same race time, but Jochen just got the verdict. They shared a new lap record.

Three days later he did it all again in the Wills Trophy at Silverstone on Easter Monday, winning both heats from pole and setting fastest lap, and taking overall victory on aggregate. He had staggered observers by setting the fastest qualifying time in 1m 29.2s, which was only a second off Denny Hulme's outright lap record set in the 5-litre Lola T70 and six-tenths faster than Jack Brabham's Formula One record. Once again Graham was his closest challenger, with 1m 29.8s in the Lotus. Rees and Stewart were next up, on 1m 30.0s.

Jochen put on another of his demonstrations in heat one, snatching the lead from Rees after a lap and then drawing away as Hill displaced the Welshman and set a new Formula Two lap record of 1m 29.4s that Jochen subsequently equalled. The Lotus wilted, however, the inner mounting points for its rear suspension breaking. So Jochen won that one from Reesie and John Surtees, who battled his Lola-Cosworth up to third place.

Jochen won the second heat too, as Hill staged another fighting drive from the back of the grid. He

battled up to second ahead of Surtees and Rees, and once again he and Jochen set a new lap record, this time in 1m 29.2s. Jochen won by four seconds, with Graham just snaffling second from John by two-tenths. On aggregate Jochen was the easy winner, 16 seconds ahead of Rees who in turn was eight ahead of Surtees. Yet again, it was another superb day for Winkelmann Racing, as Reesie moved into the lead of the European Formula Two Championship (for which graded drivers such as Jochen were not eligible).

The spree continued at the beginning of April when Pau surrendered to Jochen and the Winkelmann Brabham, and this time it was Jimmy Clark driving the Lotus that he vanquished. Clark owned practice, qualifying at 1m 20.8s, and with Stewart, Brabham and Hill next up, Jochen had to be content with a start from the outside of the second row after lapping in 1m 22.1. But he would make amends on race day. Clark led off the line, but as they sped past the pits Jochen slammed into the lead he would hold for the next 69 laps. As Jochen and Jimmy eased away, Brabham ran third ahead of Stewart, Jean-Pierre Beltoise in the works Matra, and Hulme. Brabham moved up to pass Clark, whose Lotus had the wrong gear ratios, and subsequently after a spin the Scot made two stops, for brake fluid as the pedal was going soft, and then to have a loose wheel tightened. Jack could make no impression on Jochen, and retired with engine failure, and it was Denny who came through to second place after Stewart had also hit trouble. Such was Jochen's domination that Hulme was 76 seconds behind and Reesie, in third place, had been lapped. It was a crushing performance, though a recovering Clark reminded everyone of his own talent by smashing the lap record with a time – 1m 20.4s – faster than his qualifying best.

The winning pattern was finally broken at Montjuich Park when Jimmy got his revenge to beat Jochen into second place in the Gran Premio Barcelona. Brabham took pole with a lap of 1m 34.7s which Jochen subsequently matched, ahead of Beltoise and Clark. For reasons best known to the organisers they imported the erratic 'Toto' Roche to start the race; the tubby, whipped cream-loving Frenchman strutted around the grid, pointed at drivers individually for a while, then suddenly dropped the flag and ran for it. Nobody ever really figured out how he survived such foolhardy antics, and there was more than one driver who dreamed of clipping him as they accelerated away. Clark pushed into the lead by the first left-hand hairpin, and just like Jochen at Pau, there he stayed for the duration. Brabham kept second,

and Jochen was third from Hulme, Hill and Beltoise. Jochen soon worked his way past Jack, but after ten laps Jimmy was 1.4s clear. Then Jochen made a mistake and spun on lap 11, dropping from second to seventh and losing whatever chance he might have had of winning. Brabham was also delayed as he just missed the gyrating Winkelmann BT23.

As Clark went super-smoothly about the business of winning, Jochen scurried back up the field, stealing the limelight as Clark had done at Pau as he chased after Brabham. Whether he would have caught the World Champion for second place proved a moot point, however, as Jack's engine broke on the 56th lap, four from home. By the flag, Jochen was 52 seconds behind, and just to rub it in, Clark had set fastest lap.

Jochen resumed his winning ways in the Eifelrennen at Nürburgring a fortnight later, when skis might have been more appropriate than race cars. This time his principal opposition was his 1966 F1 team-mate John Surtees, whose Lola T100 had been fitted with one of BMW's potent engines. Reversing the trend of the previous year's German Grand prix, Jochen beat Surtees with 2m 50.0s to 2m 52.9s, but both were upstaged by Clark's 2m 49.6s pole time.

On race day the drivers looked aghast at the snow that was falling hard. It had stopped by the time the race was due to start, but conditions were guaranteed to ensure low tyre temperatures. Clark was soon history, his engine faltering at the start with metering unit troubles, and lack of fourth gear stymied his attempts to recover ground. Jochen stormed into the lead from John, and nobody saw which way they went. Jochen soon dropped the Lola and went on to an 18sec victory, with leading ungraded driver Jacky Ickx half a minute further back.

What typified Jochen's racing life at this stage was the variety of races in which he competed, and nothing showcased that more than May and June that year. He raced a Porsche 910 in the Monza 1,000kms with Mitter, finishing third. Then it was Monaco at the beginning of May before he headed for the unloved Indianapolis Motor Speedway at the end of the month. Then came Zandvoort for the Dutch Grand Prix, followed by Le Mans in a works Porsche 907. Again he shared with Gerhard Mitter, and again La Sarthe was no longer benign. They retired with engine failure. Spa followed a week later, and he did not get back into the F2 Brabham until the Trophées de France race at Rheims the week before the French Grand Prix. On the flat-out roads through the champagne fields it was the familiar story: pole position, victory and fastest lap, but this was a super-close one.

"It was always a slipstreaming circuit – two long straights with a hairpin at each end – and all through the race there was a big bunch of cars fighting for the lead," Jochen recalled after a race-long duel with Hill, Surtees,

Stewart and Hulme. "As we came down to the last hairpin for the last time we all slowed down –nobody wanted to lead at the last corner because the leader at the last corner never wins the race and in fact it is usually best to be third or fourth at that stage.

"In the end it was Graham who came out of the corner first, with me second and Surtees third. On the way up to the finish line I pulled out and passed Graham, with Surtees trying to follow me through, but as Graham had helped me I felt it was only right to move back over and tow him through to second place, which I did. Jackie was fourth and Denny fifth, all of us only about 20 yards apart after 200 miles." They were separated by seven-tenths of a second.

Following the French Grand Prix at Le Mans, Jochen stayed in France for another Trophées de France F2 race, this time at Rouen where – no prizes for guessing it – he started from pole, won, and set fastest lap in an extraordinary race that saw both Jim Clark and Jackie Stewart crash. Jochen took pole from Jimmy and Jackie, their lap speeds massively undercutting previous F1 and F2 records. Jochen led away from Jackie, Jack and Jimmy, and soon the quartet was locked into a fabulous duel, each taking a turn in front. Soon, however, Jimmy's right rear tyre began to lose pressure, and the handling of the Lotus 48 became ever more lurid. In the cockpit, the Scot merely adjusted his style to cope, something which in later years brought criticism from Brabham.

"There we were racing, all having a real dice, passing one another," he recalled in 2008. "And the next thing we saw was Jimmy's tyre was gradually going down, you could see more of the rim each lap, and it was obviously going flat. I got up alongside him a couple of times and pointed at his tyre, and he didn't take any notice."

Clark's style was always to work around trouble and try to keep going, and he'd too many wind-ups from Jack on starting grids, where the Australian liked to point at his tyres as if there was a problem, to take too much notice now. But a wind-up on the grid and a wind-up in the race were two different things to Jack.

"It got to the stage where I thought 'There's no way that car's going to get to the bottom of the hill,' so I backed off and thought 'Let him have the accident on his own'."

Jimmy crashed on the downhill run to the hairpin at Nouveau Monde, and as Jochen went one side of the spinning Lotus and Jack the other, one World Champion tagged another.

"Sure enough," Brabham continued, "the very next corner he lost it, went off and hit the fence in a big way, bounced back out, and I took the whole nose of his car off." He laughed heartily at the recollection. "I shouldn't have backed off. If I hadn't backed off I'd have been all right!

"I'm still staggered that Jimmy didn't know when a bloody tyre was going down. Unbelievable. If I hadn't been there and seen it, nobody would have convinced me that he wouldn't know. But he just plain didn't know that the bloody tyre was going down."

Jochen still wasn't home and dry, for he had another playmate to cope with. He led laps 11 and 12, then Jackie too for 13 and 14 before Jochen moved back in front for two laps only to be displaced again. On the 22nd lap Jochen had a major moment at the Virage de la Scierie (Sawbench Corner) and dropped eight seconds behind the Matra. Bit by bit he began to claw it back, but Jackie had the race in the bag until he, too, got it wrong in the same corner with 11 laps left. He'd got on to the gravel, hit the straw bales, and vaulted into a ditch. Game over. So Jochen sped home to clinch the French Championship with yet another victory, which had come the hard way in a wonderful little formula in which the top guys raced with the utmost respect for one another.

"Jochen was a hard driver but a clean driver," Jack observed. "A lot of fun to drive with. You could really drive wheel-to-wheel with him in some absolutely unbelievable situations, and know you were okay. Incredible!"

Now Winkelmann Racing had found the sweet spot, and he seemed almost unbeatable in Formula Two. But not everyone regarded him as the next big thing, not everyone was a card-carrying Rindt fan who believed it was just a matter of time before he got his backside into a winning Formula One car. One of Jochen's sternest critics was diminutive writer Denis Jenkinson. 'Jenks' had earned his spurs as the sidecar passenger to 1949 World Champion Eric Oliver, and then by riding as navigator with Stirling Moss on the English star's famed run to victory in the 1955 Mille Miglia. Which makes it all the more incomprehensible that he should take against Jochen the way that he chose to.

Writing in the January 1967 issue of *Motor Sport* he had said: "With Surtees leaving Cooper-Maserati, young Jochen Rindt has returned to his position as number one, a place he relinquished to Surtees with splendid grace last July. A lot of up-and-coming drivers could well keep an eye on Rindt as an outstanding example of how to succeed if you have not got the outstanding natural ability of a Clark or a Stewart. I remember watching Rindt in the old Formula Junior in Europe, when he was just starting. Austria ran a Formula One race and he dearly wanted to drive in it, being his 'own' Grand Prix event, and he worked and got the loan of a 1.5-litre pushrod Ford engine, which was put in his Formula Junior. Against V8 BRM and Climax engines it was hopelessly outclassed, even if he could have driven as well as the factory drivers, but this did not trouble Rindt. He was in an F1 race, and he drove like a demon, thoroughly enjoying himself and putting up a performance that was no disgrace at all. He has kept his happy press-on characteristic all through his brief career, and it often carries him way ahead of better drivers who are busy grumbling and complaining."

Talk about damned with faint praise! Jenkinson's view did not appear to take any account of the progress Jochen had made since that race, in September 1963, when he was barely two years into his racing career. Nor of anything he had achieved in the meantime in Formula Two.

The new Cooper T86 did little to advance his cause in Formula One when it arrived in time for the British Grand Prix, but the day after Jochen hopped back home to Tulln-Langenlebarn for the Internationales Flugplatzrennen and won yet another F2 encounter on his home ground.

Jean-Pierre Beltoise set a time on the Saturday which none of the big boys – Jochen, Jimmy Clark, Graham Hill, Jack Brabham or Denny Hulme – could break when they practised after arriving on the Sunday morning. But Jack, Jimmy and Jochen joined the French upcomer on the front row. Jochen led, but just as Jimmy was shaping up to challenge him his Lotus whacked a loose chunk of asphalt and sustained a puncture, putting him out, Jack then took up the cudgels and hounded the Winkelmann car, but no matter what he tried nor how lurid the slides he threw his own BT23 into, Jochen could not be dislodged and ran out the winner by 1.4s as Beltoise took a distant third.

The Gran Premio de Madrid at Jarama a week later saw Jimmy lead Jackie Stewart home for a Scottish one-two, and a retirement for Jochen who, for once, had been struggling in practice. Hill took pole from Stewart and Clark. Jimmy and Jackie scrapped for the lead with Jochen after Graham made a slow start, and such was the pace that both Jimmy and Jochen spun and had to launch fierce recovery drives. Jochen had cut both of his rear tyres during his off, and on the twentieth lap he dropped from third place and retired with two punctured rears. Jimmy caught and passed Jackie, celebrating another victory with a stunning fastest lap, six-tenths quicker than Hill's pole time despite an oily track.

Jochen went back to Britain the following week for the inaugural BOAC 500 at Brands Hatch where, in a prelude to the 1969 season, he was due to share a works flat-eight Porsche 910 with Graham Hill. Interestingly, Graham lapped it in 1m 39.6s in the first practice session on Thursday, Jochen in 1m 40.2s. Graham eventually clocked 1m 38.2s for seventh fastest time on Friday, but after 27 laps he retired from a challenging fourth position in the race when a valve dropped after the car jumped out of gear. Porsche then hoicked Gerhard Koch out of the flat-six 910 he was due to share with Udo Schutz and popped Jochen aboard. They finished 11th, delayed by a persistent ignition problem.

Jochen got a bruising from his friend Jackie Stewart in a tough Kanonloppet at Karlskoga, where despite starting

BELOW *Jimmy Clark owned practice at Pau, but come the race nobody, not even the great Scot, could hold a candle to Jochen and the Winkelmann Brabham as he won by 76 seconds from Denny Hulme.* (LAT)

from pole and setting fastest lap he could not hold off the Scot's Tyrrell Matra-Cosworth in the week between the German and Austrian Grands Prix. The tight little track comprised 32 relatively slow corners linked by fast straights, and Jochen boiled into the lead from Jackie in the Matra MS7 and Jimmy Clark's Lotus 48. The first two had set the same time in practice, with the latter only a tenth slower, and they circulated as if tied together. Jochen led for six laps before Jackie pushed the hitherto disappointing Matra into first place in a duel that would see 10,000 rpm on both men's rev counters by the finish. Under braking for Troskurvan, the first corner after the pits, Jackie slipped inside Jochen to grab the initiative; inches further back Clark made it look easy while struggling with the handling of the Lotus. It was fabulous motor racing, all three running so close they were almost indistinguishable, yet giving one another the room they needed. Spectators knew they were watching the three best drivers in the world going at it.

Jochen got back in front on the 18th lap and held on until the 23rd, when Jackie got back past in the Velodromkurvan. Jimmy, meanwhile, was steadily losing ground as his rear Firestones were sliding helplessly on the now oily surface. Jochen thought he'd done it on the 29th lap, but Jackie popped back in front a lap later, and took the flag after 32 nail-biting laps just nine-tenths ahead of his friend. Jimmy had slipped back another 7.2s. Jochen had the consolation of fastest lap, quicker than they had gone in qualifying; perhaps that explained why his hard-used Cosworth FVA was boiling by the finish.

The Austrian Grand Prix was a sportscar race once again, and brought Jochen and co-driver Rolf Stommelen a disappointing tenth place finish in their works Porsche Carrera 6. Jochen always believed passionately in supporting national racing, and had worked tirelessly with the organisers to attract other drivers. The line-up included World Championship contender Denny Hulme in Charles Lucas's Ford GT40, tough Australian privateer Paul Hawkins in his own car, Jochen Neerpasch in Colin Crabbe's similar car, Scuderia Brescia's version for Nino Vaccarella and Umberto Maglioli, evergreen David Piper in his Ferrari 250LM, Jochen's works Porsche Carrera and one for Gerhard Mitter, and privateer Bill Bradley's own model. Jochen bent his in the first practice session when he tripped over a GT40 while trying to get down to the time Mitter had achieved the previous year, but made amends by achieving his goal with 1m 9.59s in the second.

The plan was that he'd do the first 100 laps, then hand over to Rolf who would complete the remaining 57. Jochen immediately became embroiled in a fight for the lead with Neerpasch and Hawkins, but it soon became clear that the Anglo-American cars had turned the tables on their German rivals since the 1966 race. When it began to rain after 40 laps Jochen pushed a mite too hard and

lost further time with a spin, then lost 16 minutes having a faulty left front damper replaced. To compound a miserable day, the right front needed replacing once Stommelen took over, and the disgruntled pair finished tenth and last, 17 laps behind the victorious Hawkins.

After the rain in the Canadian Grand Prix, Jochen flew to Europe and got straight back into the winning groove at Brands Hatch, where at the end of August he shredded his opposition in the Guards International Trophy race. This was another classic Rindt Formula Two job, and it came even though he, together with Jackie Stewart, Jack Brabham, Denny Hulme and Chris Irwin had had to hotfoot it back from Mosport Park at midnight on the Sunday, UK time, in order to make practice at the Kentish circuit. John Surtees, who had missed Canada because the finishing touches were still being put to the hybrid Lola-chassised RA301 with which he would soon win the upcoming Italian Grand Prix at Monza, dominated practice in his rivals' absence on Saturday, lapping in 1m 32.8s in his Lola-Cosworth. This was four seconds faster than the F2 lap record, and within two-tenths of Dan Gurney's F1 mark. The track was warmer and perhaps slightly slower on Monday, when Big John was again fastest with 1m 33.0s as Jochen lapped in 1m 33.2s.

As usual at Brands there were two ten-lap heats prior to the 40-lap final. The first heat was for Brabhams and Matras, and Jochen won comfortably. He was using a set of Firestone's new R Spec tyres, and he loved them. Jackie worked his way past Robin Widdows's private Brabham to take second and Jack recovered from practice troubles to snatch third from Jean-Pierre Beltoise on the final tour.

The second heat was for Lotuses, McLarens, Coopers, BMWs and Lolas. Surtees dominated until a faulty oil filter sealing ring prompted retirement, leaving victory to Graham Hill from the similar Lotus 48 of Jackie Oliver, Piers Courage's John Coombs McLaren and Brian Redman's Lola T100.

Not surprisingly, the first heat was the quicker, which put Jochen on pole for the final, with Stewart and Brabham alongside him. As Jochen led Jack into Paddock Bend it stirred memories of their fabulous duel the previous year, but soon Jackie overtook Jack and set out on a fruitless chase for the lead. This time out, there was simply no stopping Jochen, who sped into the distance to beat the Matra home by almost 20 seconds. It was his eighth victory of the season, and secured him the British Formula Two Championship in style.

OPPOSITE *Jochen's style could be boisterous and ebullient, but on his way to victory at Rouen he was smooth and limited himself to one spin on a day when both Jimmy Clark and Jackie Stewart crashed.* (LAT)

Such was the pace of F2 that season, Jochen's overall dominance notwithstanding, that one weekend's winner could find himself upstaged the next and that was the case when the series moved to Keimola in Finland where Jochen desperately wanted to show well. It wasn't just a case of him having family connections; he had worked hard with his father-in-law Curt Lincoln and Soini Kalpio of the Finnish AC to attract a topline field to both this race and to the follow-up at Hameenlinna later in the week. The start money was a deal that covered both events. But in the second Suomen Grand Prix Jochen had the unusual experience of being beaten in both his qualifying heat and the final as Jimmy Clark proved unbeatable.

The story of the race concerned some new Firestone tyres. On a fresh set of the experimental R Spec tyres that had served him so well at Brands Hatch, Jochen had lapped in 1m 16.54s. But Firestone rep Roy Foster had a problem: for some reason he was one front tyre short of four sets, and he had four contracted drivers: Rindt, Clark, Hill and Rees. None of them was prepared to be the guy who did without, so Foster did the only fair thing and withdrew the R Specs altogether and asked everyone to use the usual R125/108s. That didn't sit well with Jochen who had been seven-tenths faster than Jimmy on the same rubber so, in dudgeon, he went straight to Goodyear and ran a set of their tyres for the race.

Jimmy won the ten-lap qualifying race from Jochen and Graham, once Jack had led and then dropped back with fuel metering unit problems. And from that pole position for the final, Jimmy led briefly before Jochen squeezed ahead. The two of them then continued their great fight that left Hill a distant third. Jimmy gave Jochen absolutely no peace and slipped back in front on the 13th lap, the two of them sliding their cars at lurid angles out of the slow corners. Jochen returned the favour, nailing the Brabham to the Lotus's gearbox, but

BELOW *High-class front row at Tulln-Langenlebarn had Jochen on the pole in the Winkelmann BT23 from Jimmy Clark, Jack Brabham and Jean-Pierre Beltoise. Jochen won after Jimmy picked up a puncture.* (LAT)

gradually he began to lose ground until by half distance he was two seconds adrift. Jimmy eventually won by 3.3s, and had the satisfaction on beating Jochen's best of 1m 17.09s with the race's fastest lap of 1m 16.81s. There was a school of thought that inevitably wondered what Jochen would have done had they all run on the R Specs, since Jimmy's best on them had only been 1m 17.22s, but given the set-up progress Jimmy had made and the fact that his fastest lap in the race on R125/108s was only three-tenths slower than Jochen's 1m 16.64s on R Specs, they would have fought just as hard had there been sufficient experimental rubber.

There was some good news for the Rindt family: Curt Lincoln led home Freddy Kottulinsky and Ulf Svensson to win the Formula Three section of the race, and take sixth place overall. Interestingly, a kid called Ronnie Peterson was racing his ex-Kurt Ahrens Brabham BT18, and though he didn't feature he would later go on to assume the mantle as fastest and most spectacular man in F1 and F2 that Jochen would leave as his legacy…

Jochen got back down to business when he hit top form at the Hameenlinnan Ajot which was held in Finland two days later, on the Tuesday. The Ahvenisto circuit in the small town of Hameenlinna had been built in a disused sand quarry and, at 1.8 miles, was not entirely suited to the 1.6-litre Formula Two cars. But these were less militant days when teams and drivers were more prepared to go along to get along.

Jochen's FVA boasted a new injection system and many other engine accessories had also been replaced after he'd complained that the unit felt down on power at Keimola. Foster had not been able to locate a final R-spec front tyre so the newer Firestone rubber was not available; Jochen, however, had meekly gone back to the company's products, as part of his contract. Jimmy proved uncatchable in qualifying, lapping in 1m 24.54s to Jochen's 1m 25.22s, which was only achieved after two spins ruined other efforts. Brabham, with another new fuel metering unit, was third with 1m 25.27s.

In the Formula Three race that was run separately this time, and before the Formula Two cars, Lincoln had to give best to Kottulinsky, while Peterson distinguished himself with a strong run to fourth place.

The six-car F2 grid looked a trifle threadbare, but Jimmy and Jochen immediately engaged the spectators by launching into yet another duel. The Scot led for the first four of the 20 laps, but then Jochen slid ahead as the Lotus lost pace after overheating its rear Firestones. They actually touched lightly as Jochen pulled his move, in the uphill first right-hander on lap five. Thereafter he pulled away from the Lotus, but Brabham was having a much better race than he'd had of late and soon pulled right on to Jochen's gearbox despite a discharging battery that ultimately caused the fuel pressure to fluctuate and stymied his chances of challenging the Winkelmann car just after he'd set the fastest lap. So Jochen held on to take his ninth victory from 15 races, two seconds ahead of Jack. Jimmy nursed his 48 to the flag in third, nearly 25 seconds behind Jack, rueing his choice of Firestone's 115-compound tyres, which were finished long before the end.

The week after the Italian Grand Prix at Monza Jochen took the Winkelmann Brabham to seventh overall in the Oulton Park Gold Cup, fifth in the Formula Two section. As Jackie Stewart led initially in the F2 Tyrrell Matra, before being overhauled by Jack Brabham's F1 Brabham-Repco, Jochen indulged in a furious dice with F2 playmates Jacky Ickx, Jean-Pierre Beltoise, Jo Schlesser and Graham Hill. Jochen, however, was having a curiously offbeat weekend, and it was Hill who chased Stewart home in the F2 section to finish third on the road more than 40 seconds behind the Matra, with Schlesser and Beltoise next up. Jochen was classified seventh and fifth in class, but in reality everyone from Stewart downwards was a place higher as nobody took seriously the classification of George Pitt in second place to Brabham. He had qualified his 'F1' 2.5-litre Climax-engined Brabham BT23 slowest of the 18-car field and only completed 42 of the 45 laps.

Jochen was back on form for the Grand Prix d'Albi the following weekend, which saw him engaged in a fantastic dust-up with Jackie, and forced to settle for another second place to a Scot. Running the latest Dunlops, Jackie displaced Jim Clark from pole position, with Jochen third best, 1m 13.2s to 1m 13.7s and 1m 13.8s. Jimmy put himself out of contention for victory with a long sideways moment in the final left-hander on the fifth lap. For the rest of the race he would launch a fight back up from 13th place to an eventual third.

Jackie and Jochen launched into another of the duels each so loved, the Matra having a clear edge on the straight where it was doing more than 150mph. They swapped the lead countless times, again each giving the other room and putting on the perfect demonstration. This lasted until the fortieth lap when they came up to lap Schlesser, who inadvertently got in Jochen's way. He lost the Matra's tow, and thereafter began to fall back as the lap record-smashing Scot continued on his way. Jackie reached the flag after 75 laps almost 18 seconds ahead, with Jimmy another half minute down after his off-course adventure.

And so ended another frantic season of racing, in which Jochen's performances in Formula Two fulfilled all the promise he had shown at Mallory Park and Crystal Palace all those months ago in 1964. He got beaten at times by Jim Clark and Jackie Stewart, but he also beat them. In doing so he proved something that the Cooper-Maserati had denied him the chance to confirm in Formula One: he was without question one of the three best drivers in the world.

CHAPTER 10

Playing Black Jack

Formula One, 1968

"Every time I climbed in this car it was like Christmas."

Jochen Rindt

LEFT *Jochen in the Brabham BT26, at the British GP.* (LAT)

Jochen could hardly wait for the 1968 season to start such was his hunger to drive a competitive Formula One car, so he was gratified that the South African Grand Prix was held on 1 January. Jack Brabham was delighted to have secured his services to replace those of Denny Hulme. He liked his press-on driving style, was well aware of what he had been doing in one of his cars in Formula Two, and saw something of his youthful self in the Austrian.

"We'd seen what he did at Crystal Palace, although I wasn't there myself," he said, referring to that sensational day in 1964. "And of course he was always driving our Formula Two car. He really impressed me in 1966 when he had the Cosworth and we had the Honda. We won every race except one, and that one at Brands Hatch Jochen won because some bloody idiot I was lapping put me on the grass. I managed to get back on the track but they didn't wait, they just kept on going! I caught him right on the last lap, but not enough to get past him. We used to have some fantastic dices in Formula Two even before the Honda, when I drove the Cosworth."

Jochen, in turn, looked up to Jack. "He put his trust totally in Jack," Heinz Pruller said. "He wanted to be like him. He admired his attitude to motor racing, his dedicated professionalism. And because Jack drove the same car as his other driver, Jochen found driving for him reassuring. It was a relaxed, pleasant relationship."

"We got on very well together," Jack said, "and we had a lot of fun together as well! We used to have terrible dices on the track, and we'd laugh about it all night! How we almost put each other off! It was fantastic, we had a fantastic relationship. We went round Paddock Bend once with our wheels interlocked!" And Jack Brabham, so often portrayed as an interviewer's monosyllabic nightmare, actually broke off and giggled. "You couldn't do that with anyone else!"

The new Brabham BT26 was not ready for Kyalami, but the moment he drove the Championship-winning BT24 with its central-exhaust twin-cam motor, Jochen loved the machine that had taken Denny Hulme to the 1967 crown.

Few teams had their 1968 cars ready. Ken Tyrrell had the prototype Matra MS9 there with Cosworth DFV power, the pukka MS10 still being finished, so Jackie Stewart had an unusual green-primered machine with an ugly, truncated nose to drive. He didn't care, anything was better than a BRM H16.

BRM itself had one of those old tanks for the faithful Mike Spence to drag around, the supposedly 'lightweight'

RIGHT *Jochen loved the 1967 title-winning Brabham BT24, and took it to third place first time out at Kyalami in 1968, where he leads Surtees, team-mate Brabham, Amon, Hill, Gurney and Hulme.* (LAT)

ABOVE *Happy New Year! Left to right, Colin Chapman, Jochen, Graham Hill and Jackie Stewart tuck in as they celebrate the turn of the year in Kyalami, the day before the South African GP.* (LAT)

P115 that Stewart had driven for the second half of the previous season, while new team-mate Pedro Rodriguez was entrusted with the all-new V12-powered P126 chassis designed by former Lotus penman Len Terry.

McLaren's Cosworth-powered, Robin Herd-designed M7A wasn't ready, so the singleton BRM V12-propelled M5A was sent for Denny Hulme. Eagle and Honda likewise had single entries for Dan Gurney and John Surtees respectively.

Ferrari had Chris Amon, Jacky Ickx and Andrea de Adamich on hand, and Lotus brought regular 49s for Jimmy Clark and Graham Hill. Clark, predictably, set the pace in qualifying to annex pole position with 1m 21.6s from Hill, who was a whole second slower. Menacingly, Stewart put the Matra on the outside of the front row, a tenth of a second slower than Graham.

Jochen started gently, with 1m 29.3s to Jack Brabham's 1m 26.7s on Thursday; on Friday their respective times were 1m 25.2s and 1m 24.8s, but he made a very good impression on Saturday when he

lapped in 1m 23.0s to take fourth slot just ahead of the boss, who was two-tenths slower. Surtees, de Adamich and Amon completed the third row.

The insouciant Stewart served notice of what rivals could expect later in the year by snatching a big lead from Clark at the start, with Jochen jumping up to third as Hill slumped to seventh after making a poor getaway. Jimmy soon displaced his fellow Scot by the second lap and roared off to a record-setting 25th Grand Prix victory. Nobody knew that it would be his last.

Graham was still seventh at the end of the opening lap, but moved up to fifth as Jack took John for fourth on the second lap. On the seventh Jack moved ahead of Jochen temporarily, falling behind him and Graham three laps later when his engine suddenly lost power in a prelude to a pit stop and then retirement with a broken valve spring. Graham pushed Jochen back to fourth on lap 13, outpowering the Repco V8 as one would expect, and then caught and passed Stewart for second on lap 28.

Jochen was back in third on lap 44 when Jackie's engine threw a rod, and thereafter he kept in touch with Graham as he pushed as hard as his water temperature gauge advised him to, and drove like hell through Kyalami's numerous corners. In the closing laps he was catching the Lotuses at a second a lap, but only because Clark and Hill had eased off the pace. Jimmy won by

25.3s from Graham with Jochen the only other driver on the same lap, another 5.1s adrift.

It wasn't a bad start, especially taking into consideration the power boost that Brabham expected from the new quad-cam version of the Repco V8 that would power the forthcoming BT26.

Brabham elected to give the traditional non-championship races at Brands Hatch and Silverstone a miss as he focused on completing the first BT26 in time for the Spanish Grand Prix at Jarama on May 12. Before then, however, tragedy twice struck at the Formula One fraternity.

In the Formula Two race at Hockenheim on April 7 the incomparable Jimmy Clark was killed when his Lotus 48 sustained a rear tyre deflation and crashed into trackside trees. His fellow drivers were simply stunned, for they all believed him to be their yardstick, the man by whom they judged themselves.

"We all thought Jimmy was bulletproof," Chris Amon said. "And then we all felt very scared, because if it could happen to somebody as good as he was, we knew after all that it could happen to us." "It was," Jackie Stewart said, "motor racing's equivalent of the atomic bomb."

The tragedy hit Jochen hard, too. "Jimmy was my best friend in the racing world, as far as you can be a friend with a fellow driver," he said. "No one leaves the road in a gentle corner that is almost a straight, not even at 250 kilometres an hour in the wet. And Jimmy, who never made a mistake, is the last man who could do so. I am sure he was not killed because of a driver's error.

"What happened, I don't know. Why it happened, I don't know either. But it's always the same: whether Formula One, Formula Two or Indy, if somebody makes a mistake the result is the same. And this gives me a lot of thoughts."

A month later, to the day, BRM's Mike Spence was killed during testing at Indianapolis, when he was asked late in the day to test team-mate Greg Weld's turbine-engined Lotus 56. He and Graham Hill were about to leave for Spain. Mike had been flying on his first visit to the Brickyard, lapping at 169.555mph, while Weld had been struggling. In Weld's car Mike got out of the groove in slippery Turn One and experienced the same sort of impact that Jochen had the previous year. Like him, Mike tried to steer in at a shallow angle, but though the right front wheel was ripped off it remained attached by the steering tie-rod and swung back into the cockpit, inflicting fatal head injuries.

Jackie Stewart would also be absent. Two weeks earlier he had crashed during the Formula Two race at Jarama and was *hors de combat* after fracturing the scaphoid in his right arm.

It was a quiet, tense and deeply shaken fraternity that regrouped in Jarama, where the latest offering from Ron Tauranac duly made its debut. Jack would drive it, not because he was the type to pull rank on his other driver but because it made sense for the gaffer to bring all his considerable technical ability to bear in its on-track development.

"With Jochen, you put the car down and he just drove it," Jack said. "He didn't know anything about the development and he didn't want to know, either. He just had confidence in us, and the way the car was designed and set up. Some drivers always want to change something, but not Jochen... He would just get in and drive. And you'd soon know whether the car was any good or not, because he was gone like a rocket. He was a bloody great driver."

The BT26, however, did not make an auspicious debut. The new car was not fundamentally different from the old, though it was a bigger step over the BT24 than that had been over the BT20. It was an inch and a half longer in the wheelbase and had up to five and a half inches wider track. Tauranac had tried something new in the spaceframe technology to which he still remained faithful, by using alloy sheet panelling instead of tubular triangulation. This facilitated smaller-gauge, thinner-section tubes in the frame itself, thus minimising weight.

In the engine department, Repco had come up with a new unit which boasted twin overhead camshafts per cylinder bank in an effort to match the sort of 405bhp grunt that the Ford Cosworth DFV could muster at will. The best figure Repco saw from the 740 twin-cam engine was 330bhp, though in comparison with some power outputs claimed since the 3-litre formula had begun, they were pretty industrious horses.

The new engine was coded 860 and featured an aluminium block, four valves per cylinder, four camshafts and a worthwhile weight saving over the 740. Now the power output was around 370bhp at 9000rpm. Still less than the Cosworth, but a considerable advance over the old engine. Given how the BT24 had fared against its opposition in 1967, Jack, Repco and development engineer John Judd were confident that the BT26 could be competitive.

Unfortunately its race debut had to be delayed. It had only been completed on the Friday evening in Byfleet and was flown out on a chartered Douglas DC4 from Gatwick at 11.30 pm. The mechanics finished various detail jobs on it when it arrived in the paddock on Saturday, but when the new Repco engine dropped a valve insert after Jack had done only a handful of laps in the final practice session that afternoon, he was forced to non-start. The engine broke in the Nuvolari corner at the end of the pit straight, and Bruce McLaren was unfortunate to slide off and damage his M7A on Jack's liberated oil.

Jochen had a newly built BT24 similar to the one he had driven at Kyalami. He also missed Friday morning's

ABOVE *Jochen rounds La Source in practice at Spa, where Brabham's new BT26 was in the vanguard of wing development. Unfortunately, the Repco 860 engine ate a valve insert after five laps.* (LAT)

practice as Brabham had been busy building his car and the BT26 while also being preoccupied with testing of the BT25 at Indianapolis. The BT24 needed sorting and he lapped in only 1m 29.7s in the afternoon as it was troubled by overheating and problems with the oil breather. He could only match the time on Saturday in a car that should really have suited the sinuous little track, as the overheating persisted to such an extent that the engine had to be changed for the race after head gasket failure was diagnosed. He thus qualified only ninth in the meagre 13-car field, as Amon, Rodriguez and Hulme wrapped up the front row, with McLaren and Stewart's stand-in, Jean-Pierre Beltoise, on the second.

Prince Juan Carlos was the official starter and as Rodriguez burst into the lead from Beltoise and Amon,

Jochen was last away having been late getting to the grid. It was generally assumed at the time that the mechanics were still completing the engine change, and the car was still misbehaving on the warm-up lap. Jochen dived into the pits and got going half a lap in arrears. He soon got his head down and began to make rapid progress, only for the oil pressure to take a dive thanks to further overheating which forced him to quit after 11 laps. After Beltoise's engine suffered a faulty oil seal which forced a long pit stop shortly after he had taken the lead, Rodriguez had crashed while fighting Amon, and the New Zealander had lost a well deserved victory when a fuse in his Ferrari's fuel pump failed. Graham Hill thus scored an emotional win for the shattered Lotus team, which was racing in a Grand Prix for the first time in the red, white and gold colours of its sponsor, tobacco giant John Player's Gold Leaf brand. Hulme was second, and the fact that the underrated Brian Redman brought home the now BRM-engined Cooper to complete the podium was not lost on Jochen as he wondered whether his luck had changed at all.

Though the weekend had been a disaster for the team, Jochen's performance in those early laps had been scintillating. His opening lap occupied 1m 49.8s to leader Pedro Rodriguez's 1m 36.7s, but the second was 1m 29.3s; Piers Courage in Tim Parnell's BRM was the only driver to get anywhere close, with 1m 30.9s. All of the other quick guys were in the 1m 31s area. On the third tour leaders Rodriguez and Beltoise lapped in 1m 30.1s; Jochen's time was 1m 28.9s. When the car was working, before the overheating stymied him again, he was *flying*...

Jack had a little confession to make about the reason why Jochen was late joining the grid. "After Repco sent over a quadcam engine and all the valve inserts fell out of it, we couldn't race it. So we just had Jochen there with the old engine. Anyway, we were just sat there having a cup of tea and suddenly the bloody whistle went and they're all on the line ready to go while Jochen's having a cuppa! We ran down there and got him in the car and the rest of the bloody cars were all disappearing down the road on the warm-up lap! Then

he had to stop briefly to have the fuel filler closed properly, which meant lifting the bodywork. He must have been a good three-quarters of a lap behind to start with, but he caught a lot of them up! Unbelievable. God, he went like a *rocket*!"

Ron Tauranac chuckled when he remembered that story. "In the rush to get him out of the pits, the fuel was sloshed in that top tank and it went all over his bollocks!"

Both Jack and Jochen had BT26s at Spa, where the cars vied with the Ferraris as the first to wear front and rear wings. They had a torrid time with engine problems in qualifying, both ending up on the back row as Amon, Stewart and Ickx dominated the front, and Jochen retired after five laps when his engine dropped a valve insert.

Michael Argetsinger returned to Europe in 1968 when he got a job in Germany. "I was at most of the European Grands Prix that year although I was not working with any of the teams. I naturally spent a lot of time with Brabham just because Jochen was with them. A great memory came at Spa after the end of practice on Saturday. He had a Porsche 911 – I don't remember if it was his own car or one that someone had loaned him. He had been talking about giving me a lap of the circuit at some point and decided now was the best time. He was going to a private party at a home that was just off the track. It would have been only half a mile if we had driven the reverse way on the circuit. But we pulled out of the paddock and did 90 per cent of a full lap. It was pouring with rain and he was really on it. I remember looking out the back and seeing the enormous roostertail we were throwing up. It was a terrific ride. He had tremendous confidence on the road and I had the same in him. We did almost the full lap and then he pulled into the lane where the home was that he had been invited to. He turned to me and said, 'Take the car – I'll make my way back. Just be sure to have the car in the hotel parking lot tomorrow morning with the keys under the mat'. So I had Jochen's 911 for the evening! That was the kind of guy he was.

"Another thing I remember that weekend was Jochen introducing me to Piers Courage. Over the ensuing months I saw quite a bit of Piers and Sally. About the nicest people one could imagine. It makes me think of the two of them (Jochen and Piers) changing from their street clothes into their race suits as we talked before practice or a race. It was all very casually done in the back of the transporter. No special room or privacy. Pretty much the way we all did it over the years before motorhomes and hospitality suites. But here were these two great drivers and they were hanging their shirts and stuff over the ramps of the upper deck of the Brabham transporter. No doubt about it, it was a different time."

While the Repco engine would prove horribly unreliable, the BT26 was quick. At Zandvoort Amon again put the Ferrari on pole position, with a lap of 1m 23.54s, but Jochen was second on 1m 23.70s ahead of Graham Hill on 1m 23.84s and Jack on 1m 23.90s. And Jochen led the field away on a wet track. But because of trouble with their alternator bearings both he and Jack were forced to race without the electrical components being connected. By the end of the opening lap Hill and Stewart had pushed Jochen down to third, and gradually he fell further back until the drained battery ran

RIGHT *Jochen was mighty in qualifying at Rouen, taking his first of 10 Formula 1 pole positions. Unfortunately he was delayed by a puncture, and forced out when the fuel tank sprung a leak.* (LAT)

completely out of charge and he retired on the fortieth lap. Stewart won.

Like the BT24, Jochen loved the car even though it was so fragile mechanically. "I like the Brabham car, it suits my style. I don't think I am going to become rich with Brabhams, but Jack provides me with a car I can win the World Championship with, and this is much more worthwhile to me than everything else.

"Every time I climbed in this car it was like Christmas. With Jack, I always have the impression that he is driving the same car as I do, and therefore he gives all safety problems more thought than other constructors do."

He put the green and yellow car on pole at Rouen for the French Grand Prix, with 1m 56.1s to Stewart's 1m 57.3s and Ickx's 1m 57.7s, finding his feet more and more as the pacesetter. "You have to risk everything to climb up to the top, but once you are almost there, your experience does a lot for you," he said. "To drive beyond your limits doesn't necessarily make you go faster."

But more disappointment lurked in yet another of 1968's wet races. He got jumped by Stewart and Ickx at the start, moved back past Jackie, but then lost a lot of time after picking up a puncture from Jo Schlesser's fatal accident at the Nouveau Monde hairpin. Eventually a leaking fuel tank brought him to a halt on lap 46. This time Ickx scored his first Grand Prix victory.

In the aftermath of Schlesser's death, Jochen and Chris Amon walked through the paddock together. "We came face-to-face, and we both knew what was in the other's mind," Chris said. "We lit cigarettes, and I looked at him and said: 'I know what you're thinking'. And he looked back at me and said, very quietly:

BELOW *Driving the Brabham was like Christmas every day, according to Jochen, but the BT26's inherent unreliability bit him yet again at Brands Hatch when the fuel system short circuited.* (Roger Lane)

'Barbecue…'" Those were hard, brutal days to ply their trade.

The bad luck continued at Brands Hatch, after he had qualified a promising fifth behind the high-winged Lotus Fords of Hill and Jackie Oliver, Amon's Ferrari and Jo Siffert's Rob Walker Lotus. After the works Lotuses had retired, Siffert became the next man to break his duck with a stylish victory over Amon; Jochen dropped to eighth immediately thanks to the decision to run on rain tyres when, for once, it stayed dry, and retired on the 56th lap with a short circuit in the fuel system.

Nick Goozee was still working at Brabham by the time Jochen arrived in the Formula One team. "I got to know him better that year, when he raced for us alongside Jack," he recalled. "I'd finished my apprenticeship by then and was building the BT26 chassis, so I saw quite a bit of Jochen in the factory. He'd sit and chat, not just about racing but about his skiing and the other things he was interested in. He was a different person four years on, insofar as he had a lot more experience and his circumstances had changed, but in many ways his character hadn't changed at all. He would only open up to very few people, he was very introverted. He was always polite; there were so many drivers came through the workshops in those days but there weren't many I could say I really remembered, but Jochen was one of the ones you did. He was always courteous and would ask if there was anything he could do to help.

"I did a few of the shorter European Grands Prix that year, and he always said hello because he remembered people who'd worked with him in his early years. He was never arrogant with me, and having worked with Ron [Dennis] at Brabham between 1968 and '70 I know that

BELOW *Ready for the British GP cricket match (back row): Les Leston, Richard Attwood, Piers Courage, Jochen, Graham Hill, Pedro Rodriguez, Denny Hulme, unknown, Rob Widdows; (front row): Innes Ireland, Bruce McLaren, Chris Amon, Stirling Moss and Colin Chapman.* (LAT)

Ron could be… difficult. I think that part of the whole arrogant thing with Jochen was that he was reserved and aloof, and he looked like he might be arrogant, he looked imperial. And his language was not that great, his English. He was clearly from good stock, but he didn't have the verbal social skills to talk in English in that light-hearted manner that mechanics have."

Jochen's luck finally changed in the foulest possible conditions at the Nürburgring. Once again he qualified on the front row, alongside the Ferraris of Ickx and Amon. In the fog that was such a feature of race day, Stewart soon blasted his Tyrrell Matra into the lead on hand-cut Dunlop tyres and raced off to a stunning triumph. Hill and Amon ran second and third, but Jochen pushed into fourth ahead of Ickx and took the final podium slot when

Amon's differential malfunctioned and spun him off late in the race. Hill also spun, in a separate incident, so Jochen was only a few seconds behind the Lotus by the finish. To make it a good day for Brabham, Jack was fifth. The newfound reliability, however, did not last.

At Monza he could only qualify tenth, after dramas with a broken front wishbone mounting and then a valve failure in the spare BT26's engine. He ran no higher than tenth in the race, until another engine failure halted him after 33 laps.

The BT26 was beautifully suited to the twists and turns of Canada's St Jovite circuit in September, and once again Jochen claimed pole position. Amon later matched his 1m 33.8s lap, with Siffert third on 1m 34.5s. Chris and Seppi both beat him away, and the three of them outran their opposition. But soon the Lotus was smoking and the Brabham was losing water. Jochen bided his time as Seppi attacked Chris for the lead, and moved up to second when Siffert's engine quit on the 29th lap, but ten laps later the Repco expired yet again. Jochen was not alone in his disappointment; Amon should have won

ABOVE *The podium must have seemed an unfamiliar place as Jochen celebrated four more World Championship points with Graham Hill and his mate Jackie Stewart, who won by four minutes.* (LAT)

handsomely, but retired with transmission failure, leaving Denny Hulme to lead Bruce McLaren home in McLaren's first-ever one-two in a Grand Prix.

In America a faulty radiator pressure cap led to persistent overheating on Jochen's engine, then the biplane rear wing collapsed when a nut worked loose. Nevertheless he qualified sixth, six-tenths off surprise polesitter Mario Andretti in the third works Lotus. This time the engine lasted 73 laps before breaking when he was running fifth. That left just the Mexican Grand Prix, where he qualified tenth and retired after only three laps with ignition failure.

Inevitably, the unreliability of the BT26 had for some time given rise to speculation that Jochen would leave Brabham for 1969. He had turned down offers from every team for 1968, apart from Lotus. Now it was Colin Chapman who came knocking most heavily on his door. But Jochen didn't want to go.

"If I should leave Brabham, I would only do it with a broken heart," he said. "Jack, Ron and Leo (Mehl, still with Goodyear) are the nicest chaps in racing." Because of his admiration for Jack, he wanted in many ways to emulate his quiet character. "It's fantastic, how casual, how unaffected, how modest he is."

Jack had turned down a mid-season offer from Ford to switch motors, out of loyalty to Repco, and that also impressed Jochen. And despite all the disappointments with the Australian V8, he never lost patience. "We were hopeful all the time and convinced that everything must work out in the next race," he said.

The feeling at Brabham was mutual. Jack and Ron Tauranac loved Jochen. And they cared nothing for his reputation for complaining at Cooper, being something of a wild man…

"I don't think he was happy at Coopers, but I didn't have any problem with him at all," Jack said. "He never complained once about all the problems with the quadcam, and he liked the car, he liked the chassis."

They had few arguments, too. "Nothing I couldn't sort out," Jack confirmed. "You could have an argument with Jochen, it was always straightforward, and no problem when you were talking about something. I never had that problem where you'd have an argument with someone and you wouldn't know who was right and who was wrong. Jochen knew what he was doing and if you had an argument you could sort it out between you, no problem. He was a smart guy, with a good brain."

Tauranac told Alan Henry for his book *Brabham: The Grand Prix Cars*: "Jochen was always very pro us at Brabham. When he was offered the deal to go to Lotus he came to us, told us exactly what Chapman was offering, and said that he would stay with us for a fraction of the price.

"We got on really famously. We were watching our costs in those days and we used to share a room together for much of that season. He was a good bloke." And in Melbourne 2010 he added: "The real difference between Jochen and Jack was that Jochen was always on the rev limiter, whereas Jack would back off a little and look after the engine on downshifts before the corners. Jochen was harder on the car." "He was hard on the gearbox," Jack recalled.

"Very hard on the gearbox, actually. We had to replace it regularly! He didn't know what the clutch was for!"

Both men remember that Jochen once bought them skis as a present. "He got me some because I started skiing about that time," Jack said, "and I couldn't make out why when I put these bloody skis on I went twice as fast as anyone else downhill. It turned out they were bloody racing skis, they weren't proper skis like I should have had to start with…" Another big laugh. "Every time I pointed downhill I was passing people. Jochen probably got a big joke out of that!"

In the end, Chapman's financial blandishments swayed his thinking, and he told Jack that he was going to Lotus. "We didn't have an engine for him, really," Jack said. "The Repco engine was finished then, and there was no way that Repco was gonna compete from then on. We changed to the Ford, and had another bad year really because of that."

Jochen told Rob Walker: "Listen Rob, I want to win the World Championship so badly that I'm even prepared to drive for Colin to do so."

Bernie Ecclestone remembered the situation well. "At the end of '68 we had the choice for Jochen of the

RIGHT *At Monza, where he is seen leading Jacky Ickx's Ferrari, Jochen had a miserable time in qualifying and the race, which ended in engine failure. Already, he was pondering a move to Lotus for 1969.* (LAT)

Goodyear deal with Brabham, or the Firestone deal with Lotus. I said to him, 'If you want to win the World Championship, you've got more chance with Lotus than with Brabham. If you want to stay alive, you've got more chance with Brabham than with Lotus'.

"It wasn't a bad thing to say: it was a matter of fact. And I'm not saying it now because he got killed in a Lotus. That was what the pattern was, for whatever reason: people did get killed in Lotuses. Maybe Colin took things to the edge a bit – and anyone who drove for Lotus was prepared to go along with that…"

When asked when he actually started managing Jochen, Bernie gave a typically Ecclestone reply. "I never managed him but I always managed him. Nothing was ever official, we were just mates. When he did the contract with Lotus, for example, I did the deal for him. In those days that was the best deal there was. I reminded him again that perhaps the Lotus deal was the best because the car was quicker, but that there was a risk. But he said 'Let's do that'."

In the end, as he and Heinz Pruller walked back from a lengthy dinner at the Richlieu restaurant the evening

BELOW *So near, yet so far. At St Jovite in Canada Jochen claimed pole position together with Chris Amon, and was chasing the New Zealander for the victory when his engine blew up yet again.* (LAT)

before the race in Mexico, where everything was finally sorted out to go to Lotus, Jochen told him: "I can't afford to stay with Brabham and give away half the money. Lotus is going to be my third team now. One should not change too much, but if success doesn't come soon, I could be finished. Lotus produces the best car, the biggest sensations, there is nothing that Chapman can't realise technicalwise. To be really competitive there is not the smallest problem".

What could be difficult, he acknowledged even then, was the human side of the equation. Chapman was a mercurial man, not renowned for his people skills. Graham Hill was the reigning World Champion, and part of the furniture at Lotus as previously he had been with BRM. "But I am not number two," Jochen said firmly. A couple of days later he took Chapman by surprise, and perhaps gave him an indication of what lay in their future, when he said: "If I win the title next year, don't expect great speeches. I will go home to Geneva immediately".

The funny thing about the whole Lotus scenario was the initial conversation that team manager Andrew Ferguson recalled having with Jochen, after Chapman had instructed him to make the first approach for 1969. "With Colin's assurance that only constructive discussion with the Austrian was required, I went off to chat to Jochen during a tyre test," Ferguson wrote. "When he noticed my approach in the paddock he greeted me with an aggressively loud: 'Do you want to kill me, then?' When I

asked him to explain, he continued: 'You don't really expect me to get into a Lotus, do you? I don't want to die, so if you've come to see me you've wasted your journey'."

When Ferguson reported the conversation back to Chapman, the latter told him tersely, "Try Ickx". Ferguson found the upcoming Belgian star far easier to deal with and the basis for a drive at Lotus was agreed. A fortnight later Chapman chased him up demanding within the hour a statement about the team's new driver.

"You've spoken to Jacky, then?" Ferguson enquired.

"Jacky? Jacky who?" Chapman spluttered. "I'm talking about Jochen. He's just about to issue a press release in Vienna."

Ferguson had no time in which to contact Ickx, so the first time the Belgian learned that his drive had evaporated was when he heard the announcement about Jochen on the news…

Curiously, at the end of the year Louis Stanley dropped Jochen a further place, to tenth behind Graham Hill, Jackie Stewart, Denny Hulme, Jacky Ickx, Jo Siffert, Bruce McLaren, John Surtees, Chris Amon and Pedro Rodriguez, despite some stunning drives in the Brabham. But his summary of his future prospects showed remarkable foresight. "Jochen Rindt is a man of aggressive integrity, hot-tempered and warm-hearted," he wrote, "a natural driver of high ambitions and no pretensions. His stay with Jack Brabham must have been disappointing. Certainly as regards race results, things did not go well. It was therefore no surprise to see a switch to the Lotus ménage for 1969; no surprise that is from the engine point of view, but there must be reservations as to how the team as such will blend. An internal line-up that includes Walter Hayes, Colin Chapman, [Andy] Granatelli, Graham Hill, Mario Andretti and Jochen Rindt has enough pyrotechnic dynamite to upset any apple-cart. On paper the clash of driver temperament could make the memory of the Schell/Behra pairing seem a picnic, while a difference of opinion between the lot would be worth recording. The mixture could gell [sic], in which case Chapman will be collecting trophies and cheques. Whatever happens, Jochen Rindt will blithely go his way. He is there to get the best out of his car. If it holds together and he avoids spins, shunts, and blow-ups, his Championship points-tally could be impressive."

These were prophetic words. And like the situation regarding the announcement of the drive for 1969, it was an omen that nothing about the relationship between Team Lotus, Colin Chapman and Jochen Rindt would ever run smoothly.

BELOW *At Watkins Glen in October Jochen brings the Brabham into the pits with the rear wing at a perilous angle after failing at high speed. It wouldn't be his last experience of such incidents.* (LAT)

CHAPTER 11

The King of Formula Two

1968

"To say that Jochen was the King of Formula Two is to insult him, because that could indicate that there is no place for him on a higher platform."

Jacky Ickx

LEFT *Hotshots at Albi, 1968: Jochen, Beltoise and Pescarolo.* (LAT)

Another vintage season for Formula Two opened with the Gran Premio di Barcelona on March 31, but Jackie Stewart was on such hot form in Ken Tyrrell's Matra MS7 that neither Jochen nor Jimmy Clark got a look in. Jackie took pole with Jimmy and Jochen a tenth apiece adrift, and after the Scot from Dumbarton had lit into the lead Jimmy's pursuit was thwarted almost immediately when he was assaulted from behind at the hairpin on the second lap by an errant Jacky Ickx who inadvertently rammed the Gold Leaf Lotus 48 with his Ferrari. Jochen made a terrible start and spent the race clawing his way up to second place with his usual blend of aggression and derring-do. Sixteen laps from home he retired when a fuel line ruptured.

The sport was shattered a week later when Clark was killed in the first heat of the Deutschland Trophy Formula Two race at Hockenheim on April 7. A sudden rear tyre failure pitched him into the unforgiving pine trees on the run down to the first chicane, and motor racing went into shock. Jimmy was the giant, the man who had assumed the Fangio/Moss mantle. Those rare men – such as Jochen and Jackie – who could say that they had beaten the champion in a fair fight, truly knew that they had proved their own world-class talent.

Jochen was not at Hockenheim that black day. Instead he was at Brands Hatch, scheduled to drive the sleek but flawed Ford F3L coupé in the BOAC 500. Initially Clark should have been racing for Ford, but he was piqued by what he perceived as inefficient communication by the Alan Mann Racing team which was due to run the car and so he stuck to an earlier commitment to race in Germany for Colin Chapman. Graham Hill did likewise. Thus while one F3L was due to be handled by New Zealanders Denny Hulme and Bruce McLaren, the second would be shared by 1967 race winner Mike Spence, and Jack Brabham. When Jack was unimpressed with a test of the unsorted car at Goodwood the previous week, however, he withdrew, and Jochen was nominated instead as Spence's partner and thus switched from the works Porsche 907 which was taken over by Lodovico Scarfiotti.

McLaren practised his car minus its rear bodywork, which was late arriving, as the cars themselves had been that Friday. Jochen's car wouldn't start, and its tail could not be swapped over as that F3L had an inch and a half longer wheelbase.

On Saturday Bruce eventually worked down to 1m 35.6s to take second fastest time behind the Jo Siffert/Hans Hermann Porsche which had recorded 1m 34.6s. Jochen lapped the sister car, whose engine was overheating, in 1m 38.4s. When Mann subsequently decided that the engine was not in raceable condition he moved Spence into the McLaren car, leaving Jochen and Denny with nothing to do for the rest of the weekend.

The BARC's major opening race at Thruxton the following week, for Formula Two, was much more fruitful. The Hampshire track proved very popular with most of the drivers, and Jochen naturally loved its demanding and super-fast sweeps. The field was divided into odd and even numbers for two heats, each having separate practice sessions. Chris Irwin put his Surtees Lola on pole for the odd number heat in 1m 17.6s from Henri Pescarolo's works Matra on 1m 18.0s and Alan Rees's Winkelmann Brabham on 1m 18.4s. The even number heat contained the star drivers, and after Jean-Pierre Beltoise had set the initial pace in his works Matra, Jochen posted a devastating 1m 15.8s to unseat the Frenchman, whose 1m 16.2s held up for second place ahead of Piers Courage in 1m 16.8s in Frank Williams' BT23C. Pescarolo won the first heat comfortably from Jackie Oliver's Herts & Essex Aero Club Lotus 48, with Reesie third ahead of a rookie called Max Mosley, who would make a greater impression on the sport once he had hung up his helmet.

Jochen had a similarly easy ride in the second heat, leading home Courage and Beltoise. Thus he started from pole ahead of Piers and Jean-Pierre in the 54-lap final. It was the Frenchman who made the best start to boil into the lead from the Englishman and his compatriot Derek Bell in another BT23C, and then the Austrian. Jochen took 'Dinger' for third place on lap three, and moved in on the two leaders as Courage took the lead from Beltoise on lap four with some demon braking at the chicane. Two laps later, Jochen went round his friend, but it took him a while to open up any advantage as Piers kept pushing him with everything he had.

Eventually Beltoise got his second wind and moved in to challenge successfully for second place on the thirtieth lap, just as Jochen lost it completely at the Club Chicane at the end of the lap. As the tail of the Winkelmann BT23C came round on him he disappeared backwards through an advertising hoarding, behind a strip of barrier and into a ditch. Just as Jimmy Clark used to, and Gilles Villeneuve later would, he kept track of his position all through the incident and already had the car in first gear before it came momentarily to rest, then gave it a bootful of throttle, drove back round the ditch and rejoined the track through the hole he'd made in the hoarding. It was a classic piece of Rindt showmanship, and he sped back into the race just as Beltoise and Courage arrived hotfoot at the chicane.

The Brabham was now coated in dust and sported a bent exhaust pipe, but it was still healthy. As Piers's race ended when Beltoise's car threw a stone through his

OPPOSITE *Jochen put the Winkelmann Brabham off the road in the chicane partway through the Final of the Thruxton Trophy F2 race, but not even that could stop him winning as he pleased.* (LAT)

radiator, elevating Bell to a worthy third, Jochen opened up a 7.4s margin of victory after leaving the lap record at 1m 16.0s in a final spurt that demonstrated convincingly that his error had had zero effect on his ability to refocus. It was a fabulous display that suggested Jackie Stewart would have some very serious opposition as they sought to take up Jim Clark's mantle.

The Formula Vee race on the same day resulted in victory after a wheel-to-wheel dust-up for Gerold Pankl in his Bosch Racing Team Austro from Walter Reidl's similar Team Champion car and the Bosch Racing Team Kaimann driven by a third Austrian… Jochen's old friend from the wild days in Graz, Helmut Marko. He was delighted for him.

The mood was punctured a week later by retirement in the Grand Prix de Pau after starting from pole. Stewart led until Jochen passed him on the third lap, but when Jochen spun on the 15th Jackie moved back into a lead he was never to lose on his way to a victory that made up for a crunch he'd had at Virage du Buisson in practice. Jochen's indiscretion only dropped him down to second, clear of Beltoise, and by the twentieth lap he was again in a position to challenge. But on the 21st, as he came up to lap Chris Williams, Peter Gethin and Alex Soler-Roig at the Virage du Lycée, he misjudged the Spaniard's intentions, whacked the nose of the Winkelmann Brabham on the metal guard around the gearbox of the Lola, and spun. He had terminally damaged his own radiator hose, and pitted for good at the end of the lap. The fact that both he and Jackie had made a mistake over the weekend showed the pressure they were putting each other under.

Jochen took pole for the Gran Premio di Madrid at the end of April, having set fastest time on Friday and then sat out much of Saturday with a glum look on his face as a high wind militated against fast times. He miscalculated, for though he matched his Friday 1m 29.2s best, Stewart and Beltoise later clipped down to 1m 28.4s and 1m 28.7s respectively in their Matras. But Stewart was not destined to start. In an extra qualifying session held for some latecomers on Sunday morning, he lost control of the Tyrrell MS7 in the right-hander after the pits and slammed into the safety catchfencing. He damaged the scaphoid in his right wrist, and had to sit out the race. Instead, he was enrolled as honorary starter, and watched Jochen speed into the lead as a multi-car collision on the grid caused havoc. The Austrian might not have had his close friend to worry about, but JPB was well hooked up this weekend and they indulged in a furious scrap.

By lap 12 Jochen was three and a half seconds ahead and it seemed situation normal, but Beltoise got back in the groove and steadily closed the gap until he snatched the lead on lap 22. They passed and repassed for the next ten laps, before the blue Matra finally began to pull away from the green Brabham. The unthinkable was happening. Jochen kept pushing for all he was worth until the 44th lap, when he walloped a couple of marker cones, and after that he eased off a fraction and accepted the inevitable. Jean-Pierre could hardly believe it when he crossed the line 18.7s ahead of the King of Formula Two.

Jochen was swift to make amends, winning the first heat of the Limbourg Grand Prix at Zolder on May 5 with ease from Chris Amon and Chris Irwin, but he ran into a whole heap of trouble at the start of the second. The talented and underrated Englishman Brian Redman was shoved into him as they left the grid, and the Winkelmann Brabham spun for ages before Jochen was able to gather everything up and head after the departed field. He was up to seventh by the end of the lap, sixth after the second, and finished third behind the Ferraris of Ickx and Amon but close enough to take the victory on aggregate. If Ickx had obeyed pit signals to let Amon past, Chris would have won, but Jacky didn't think that way.

Until Monaco 1970 Jochen always said that Zolder was his greatest race. Everyone just assumed that he simply turned on the speed the moment he got into the cockpit, that the rage to win always burned. But in a comment that provided a remarkable insight into his mindset, he told Heinz Pruller: "I must have a Zolder race at the beginning of every season, a race that proves to me that I can manage to win even when things go wrong. I need that to be sure of myself and to be on top form."

After the adventures in Spain, Monaco and Indianapolis, Jochen went back to his old stomping ground at Crystal Palace for the Holts Trophy in June, where he won his heat – which ended in a dramatic cloudburst – and the final with insouciant ease. Piers chased him for a while in the latter until an injector nozzle broke, whereupon Redman took the place in David Bridges's private Lola. He was half a minute behind, and the only man Jochen had not lapped in a crushing performance that saw him set fastest lap in both of his races.

He was at it again the week after the Belgian Grand Prix as he won the Rhine Cup at Hockenheim. Traditionally races there were slipstream epics, and this one was no exception. But on the evening before the race Jochen sat down with Alan Rees and Roy Winkelmann and calculated just how he was going to win it. Because of his pace and flamboyance there were still some who believed him to be little more than a hothead on the perpetual verge of an accident, but he had everything carefully planned.

The teams were nervous initially returning for the first time to the scene of Jim Clark's fatal accident, but the practice times were as close as ever. Jochen was only sixth, behind the Matras of Pescarolo and Beltoise, and Frank Gardner who split the Ferraris of Ickx and Amon with his McLaren M4A.

For a time no fewer than 13 cars fought for the lead, and Jochen was content to run in the pack, keeping out of trouble, and only popping up as leader now and then. Otherwise he was content to let Gardner, Beltoise, Pescarolo, Pedro Rodriguez's Tecno, Chris Lambert's private Brabham or Jackie Oliver's Lotus 48 take their turns up front. It was wild, but the man in the dark green Brabham had things clearly figured out.

The prime requirements in the fight were courage and a strong engine, and entertaining though all the place changing was, all of the drivers knew they were just

practising for the final lap. There was one moment when Winkelmann and Rees felt disconcerted, when Jochen dropped to ninth on the 25th lap, as it was a place lower than it had been agreed that he should allow himself to fall, but they needn't have worried. Come the final lap, as spectators craned their necks to see who would come bursting out of the forest section and back into the stadium by the grandstands, Oliver was still leading as he had been on the 29th. Then suddenly there was Jochen, ducking out of Oliver's slipstream to push into the lead down the inside under braking. Oliver had his hands full fending off Kurt Ahrens too, and finished eight-tenths down on the victorious Winkelmann Brabham. From Jochen down to Richard Attwood in ninth place – Rindt, Oliver, Ahrens, Rodriguez, Ickx, Pescarolo, Courage, Amon, Attwood – there was a mere 4.8s after 200 kilometres of wheel-to-wheel racing.

It was one of Jochen's greatest races, and his coolness under intense pressure made it all look so easy. In reality, it was another demonstration of why he was the best man out there.

BELOW *Until Monaco 1970, Jochen said the Limbourg GP at Zolder in 1968 was his greatest drive, and that he needed a race like that each year to prove to himself that he could win even when in adversity.* (LAT)

After the Dutch and French Grands Prix he went home again to Tulln-Langenlebarn, where he had helped the organisers to assemble a very strong field of runners. The only notable absentees were Jackie Stewart, who still preferred to risk his injured wrist only in Grands Prix, Jacky Ickx who was racing the JW Ford GT40 at Watkins Glen, and the Ron Harris Tecnos of Rodriguez and Attwood. This was an important event for Jochen because of his personal involvement in the organisation, and he went to great lengths to make his fellow drivers and journalists feel at home by arranging hospitality for them at suitable eateries in Vienna in the evenings.

Former *Autosport* journalist Paddy McNally, now better known as the driving force behind F1's Paddock Club, wrote at the time: "Driving behind Jochen in Vienna is quite an experience, for everybody from paper-boy to policeman recognises him and one drives with the Viennese rule 'priorité à Rindt'."

"I was one of his biggest fans, and we sort of lived next door to each other in Switzerland," McNally told the author in 2010. "There was no bullshit about him. I never got the thing about him being arrogant. But then he was a hero for me. He was very kind and unassuming, and he picked me up at Vienna airport that time in this yellow Porsche 911 – I was just a humble journalist – and showed me the city. That was a great time to cover racing."

That 'priorité à Rindt' rule certainly applied on the track at the military airbase. Practice was a bit of a muddle as the first session wasn't timed and the third was wet, which meant that the lap times were taken from the second in which Jochen set the pace with 1m 3.27s, chased by Amon, Beltoise and Courage. His Winkelmann Brabham now wearing a rear wing, he won both 30 five-lap heats, demonstrating all his car control as he thrust the BT23C round. Beltoise, Pescarolo and Ahrens chased him in the first, and again in the second, and that was the order on aggregate as he headed the Frenchman by a mammoth 54 seconds.

The Gold Cup at Oulton Park followed the British and German Grands Prix in mid-August, after the European Championship round at Zandvoort (which Jochen had missed) saw the sad death of the upcoming Chris Lambert after a tangle with Clay Regazzoni. With Clark's death followed at monthly intervals by those of Mike Spence, Lodovico Scarfiotti and Jo Schlesser, and now Lambert, 1968 was indeed a tragic season.

A week later Jochen was back to his winning ways, this time at Enna-Pergusa. Yet again this was a brutal slipstreamer, but only after the organisers had rather ludicrously allowed only four cars out at a time for practice and made it clear that times gained with a tow might be discounted. There was another little wrinkle that cost Courage pole position; Pescarolo had equalled his 1m 13.7s best and the rules said that in such circumstances a driver must fall back on his next best time, which swapped their positions. Jochen started third. Just to make things even more ridiculous, the organisers spaced each grid row 75 metres apart, in the interests of safety.

All of that backfired in the race because it took only two laps for the six leading cars to be running nose to tail, as Courage, Rindt and Regazzoni took turns leading while Pescarolo, Beltoise and Ickx stayed right in there with them. 'Pepsi Cola' spun out of contention on the fifth lap, but Tino Brambilla came into the picture in his Ferrari, while Derek Bell and Brian Hart were getting in on the leading bunch's act and Pescarolo's recovery was taking Jonathan Williams towards the front, too.

Yet again Jochen was prepared to play it uber-cool, at one stage idling along in tenth place biding his time. Just to check things out he leapfrogged up to the lead on the 21st lap, before letting himself drift back again, to ninth. Brambilla came to the fore as the race moved past the 30-lap mark, then Jochen, having changed to his spare goggles, had another look-see up front. As the 45-lap mark approached and five remained, it was clear that the race would be between Jochen, Brambilla, Courage, Regazzoni, Ickx and Bell. Jochen led laps 41, 42 and 43, Brambilla 44 and 45, then Courage 46 and 47.

When it really mattered, however, it was Jochen whose nose broke the timing light a fraction before Courage's, with Brambilla, Regazzoni, Bell and Ickx all so close behind that the organisers were unable to issue race times for them all. There were some very tough fighters in that little group, and Jochen had outfoxed them all. He could do it so often in such awesome circumstances, that it clearly was not down to luck.

In the same issue of *Autosport* in which the Enna race was reported, Jochen told his friend and photo-journalist David Phipps: "When I started racing I drove as much as I could, just to get experience. In 1965 I did Formula One, Formula Two, sportscars, touring cars – anything I could get my hands on. Now I am concentrating on Formula One and Formula Two because I like them best." And he put the slipstreamers into perspective when he admitted: "A lot of people think I'm braver than Dick Tracy, but I can be just as scared as anybody."

Retirements then followed at the Trophée de France encounter at Rheims, which marked Stewart's return to Formula Two. Jochen took pole by a second from the Scot. Jackie sped to a fine win from Pescarolo, in another slipstreaming race in which the lead changed every lap, with Piers Courage third from Graham Hill. Jochen was in the fight and led for a while until pitting on the seventh lap with a fractured pipe pouring fuel all over one leg. He lost seven laps, rejoined intent on breaking the lap record, but called it a day when it started to rain.

That may have been the race at which Jochen learned

ABOVE *The Winkelmann Brabham was fitted with this ridiculous bi-plane rear wing in practice for the F2 race at Albi in October. It was hardly a surprise when it failed and was never seen again.* (LAT)

of Winkelmann's 'special powers'. Roy recalls that it was at an F2 race in France, but not which one.

"Jochen had given me his passport to look after while he was racing. There was a problem with the transporter rolling away in the paddock and people getting injured, and I was so annoyed by the lack of professionalism that allowed that to happen that I went straight back to the UK. With the passport.

"He called me and said, 'Hey, I'm stuck here with no papers. You've still got my passport! What am I going to do?'

"I told him I'd sort it out. 'Just go to the airport. Go to Orly and check in, it'll be okay. And when you get to Heathrow ask for a certain person… I'll get it sorted out.'" Winkelmann called on a few of the contacts he'd made in his intelligence roles, and had words in the right ears. Jochen made it home without a problem and duly

retrieved his passport. "After that he called me 'My friend, Mr Gestapo!'"

His second visit to Hockenheim for October's Preis von Wurttemberg saw the Winkelmann Brabham take a comfortable pole, and Jochen was again in the thick of things until the BT23C developed a vibration after 27 laps and he pulled in to retire. Tino Brambilla drove a wild race, which included taking to the grass in the stadium to snatch the lead from Henri Pescarolo, whom he beat to the finish line by two-tenths of a second to register Ferrari's first Formula Two win.

This was the race Winkelmann mechanic John Muller remembered in which Jochen had detected the clutch vibration problem. But while he might have been sensitive to such things, Jochen's understanding of chassis set-up was, at best, rudimentary. New Zealander John Martin came along after Muller (who would later become his brother-in-law), and told Paul Fearnley: "On the track we were lucky to have a thinking driver like Alan to set up the car, pick the gear ratios (both cars would be different) and plan the strategy. Jochen would not question the set-up, just get in and drive to win after win. He had a natural talent, the like of which we may never see again".

The next Formula Two race on the calendar was the Grand Prix d'Albi where the Winkelmann team tried the biggest rear wing ever seen on a racing car: a giant biplane device. Was it a serious development or just a joke to point out how ridiculous wings were becoming, journalist Mike Doodson asked him.

"This wing was a very serious development, designed by a well-known racing designer (who has aircraft experience)," Jochen said, referring to Robin Herd. "It wasn't made from the right material because there wasn't enough time for development and we couldn't spend a lot of money. But we also wanted to show how stupid the situation might become."

Jochen only ran the ridiculous device for three or four laps, and even though it had been designed to generate 300lb of downforce and to be stronger than F1 wings, in that time it began to fall apart. The upper section was removed, then the lower, and the Brabham was faster without it as he lapped in 1m 13.0s to take pole position from the Matras of Beltoise, Pescarolo and Stewart.

Jochen soon got the better of Beltoise, who'd made the best start, and with equal alacrity Stewart moved up to challenge the green Brabham. The pair of them then left the opposition behind as they re-enacted their 1967 duel until Jackie dropped away with a misfire. Now the race was Jochen's, and he had disappeared when the engine suddenly cut out and he coasted into the pits with suspected ignition failure. As Pescarolo won from Englishmen Peter Gethin and Piers Courage, all Jochen took home was a new lap record.

The 1968 racing season concluded with the Temporada series in Argentina, which took place over four races each a week apart in Buenos Aires, Cordoba, San Juan and Buenos Aires again. Curiously the Dino V6-engined Ferraris suddenly found such great pace in South America that even their use of Firestone's excellent YB11 tyre could not explain it all, and there were myriad queries about the capacity of their powerplants. Even Jochen was not able to come away with a victory as the red cars ran amok.

Tino Brambilla, the winner at Hockenheim in October and later in Vallelunga, won the first Buenos Aires race (on the Parc Almirante Brown's number nine circuit) by just two-tenths of a second from team-mate Andrea de Adamich, who had led until Brambilla passed him on the ninth lap. Jochen, who had beaten them to pole in sweltering conditions, had been the only man capable of getting anywhere near the flying red cars in the race but after leading briefly the Winkelmann Brabham was running third when its rear wing mounting wilted after 39 laps.

De Adamich was in control at the Oscar Cabalen Raceway in Cordoba, where it was a surprise to see Jochen qualify only fourth, behind the bespectacled law student, Clay Regazzoni's Tecno and Piers Courage in

BELOW *Ferrari staged a remarkable improvement in form in the Argentine Temporada F2 at the end of 1968, leaving Jochen to pick up only second and third places, and second overall in the title chase.* (LAT)

Frank Williams' BT23C. It was no surprise that Jochen grabbed the early lead, however, but subsequently Piers had a turn before Jochen went back ahead, but then Andrea went to the front on the 11th lap and stayed there to the flag. Jochen pushed him as hard as he could, but was still 4.4s adrift when the 70 laps were over. Brambilla had a miserable weekend, complaining of lack of power, so de Adamich now led the series with 21 points to Brambilla's 13 and Jochen's eight.

Indefatigable writer Andrew Marriott was covering the series for *Motoring News*. "We stayed in a big hotel in Cordoba, and I remember one night we played charades; Piers was there, and Jochen was really into it in a big way. And the following day he said: 'Piers and I are going to drive to San Juan,' which was a long way away across the pampas. They were going to borrow a car. 'Do you want to come?' And I said I had to write a lot of stuff for *MN* and of course in those days it was very difficult to file copy, and I had a plane ticket to San Juan, so I didn't go. And apparently it was an absolutely epic trip. Can you imagine? What an idiot! That was one

of the biggest regrets of my whole motor racing career, that I didn't go with them!"

This was where the friendship between Jochen and Piers really began to take off, and soon the two comrades would be inseparable. "When they finally got to San Juan I was already there and had been thrown in the swimming pool by Jackie Oliver," Marriott continued, "which ruined my watch and which I've never forgiven him for. I knew I'd been stupid, and all these years later it still rankles that I took a daft decision not to go!"

The Autodromo Zonda in San Juan was 3,500ft above sea level and laid out in the crater of an extinct volcano. De Adamich and Ferrari again proved unbeatable, his second victory being sufficient to clinch the title for him before he left the Scuderia to join Alfa Romeo for 1969. But it was Jo Siffert who took pole after the second session of practice on Saturday was literally blown away by a massive storm.

"The most fantastic thing at the San Juan race was that Jochen and Piers decided not to do the first practice and buggered off into the mountains to have a look," Marriott remembered. "Reesie gave him a real bollocking, and when it came to qualifying it was blowing a storm and Jochen did some absolutely phenomenal 'Jochen' laps to get the thing up the grid. I remember they were some of the greatest laps I've ever seen."

BELOW *On the Parc Almirante Brown's number nine circuit, Jochen was the only man capable of keeping the suddenly fleet Ferraris in sight in the opening round, until his rear wing collapsed under the strain.* (LAT)

The Ferrari drivers swept into the lead, with Brambilla shadowing de Adamich until his engine blew, whereupon Andrea had an easy run to the finish. Jochen was left to squabble over second with Beltoise and Siffert, the Frenchman getting the verdict but Jochen staying ahead of the Swiss.

The final round was held on the tortuous number-six circuit on the municipal autodrome in Buenos Aires on the Sunday before Christmas, and comprised a two-heat event. Brambilla and de Adamich were so superior in the first that they planned to stage a dead heat, but that plan backfired when Tino's engine quit on the last lap. Jochen, who had pushed them really hard in the opening laps before beginning an inevitable backward slide, finished second ahead of Jo and Piers.

Andrea's chances evaporated right at the start of the second heat when he discovered that he was in the wrong gear and the Ferrari was hit by Courage's Brabham and thrown into the pit lane, where it hit and injured several spectators.

"De Adamich got it all sideways and knocked down someone who was standing in the pit lane," Marriott recalled, "and a big American ambulance rushed up. They popped this guy, who was not badly injured, on to a stretcher, and put it into the back of this ambulance. And the guy driving it dropped the clutch, and the stretcher was on wheels and it came shooting straight

ABOVE Without any victories to celebrate, things were tense at times for Nina and Jochen as the Ferraris ran amok, but most of the time they made the best of all the travel opportunities that arose. (Grand Prix Photo)

out the back because they'd forgotten to close the doors. The guy broke his leg then!"

That pantomime allowed Jochen to build a comfortable lead over Piers. But then the Winkelmann car's fuel metering unit began to malfunction and he could not resist attacks from Courage, Oliver and Siffert. Right at the end Jochen salvaged something when Seppi slowed, believing he had taken the flag a lap sooner than it was actually due, so the Brabham pipped the Tecno for third place. On aggregate, Courage was classified first, and though the organisers put Siffert second on the podium from Jochen, the actual results correctly put the Swiss driver third behind the Austrian, with Oliver fourth and a recovered de Adamich fifth. Overall Andrea was champion with 36 points to Jochen's 21 and Piers's 14.

Marriott was a dyed-in-the-wool Rindt fan. "I thought Jochen was absolutely mega. While he was waiting for the right Formula One drive to come along, he was lucky that he had Formula Two to showcase what he could really do."

Yet again in 1968, he did that to perfection.

CHAPTER 12

Tasman triumphs and tribulations

January/February 1969

"*Most of the other drivers seemed to be tiptoeing whereas Jochen was dancing. He was unbelievable. The Lotus's body language was so different to any other car.*"

Peter Collins

LEFT *Jochen's first drive for Team Lotus came in the 1969 New Zealand GP.* (LAT)

The 1969 racing season started early for Jochen as he and new team-mate Graham Hill were to uphold Team Lotus honour in the Tasman Series, the annual championship Down Under that featured races in New Zealand and Australia for what were effectively 2.5-litre Formula One cars. He had big boots to fill, for Jim Clark had won the Tasman in 1965, '67 and '68 for Lotus and had scored a record 14 victories.

There was strong opposition, with Chris Amon running a satellite Ferrari operation with versions of the 166 Dino Formula Two car fitted with 2.4-litre V6 Dino engines, for himself and upcoming Formula Two racer Derek Bell. Frank Williams was also moving up, using the Tasman as a trial run for his forthcoming graduation to Formula One with his close friend Piers Courage. Frank, Jochen's 'number one fan', had purchased a Brabham BT24 from Jack Brabham and Kiwi mechanic John Muller had inserted a 2.5-litre version of the Ford Cosworth DFV engine called the DFW, the same as Jochen and Graham had. The most likely local challenger was the underrated Sydneysider Frank Gardner, a familiar face in European racing. He would drive a Len Bailey-designed machine that had been commissioned by respected entrant Alec Mildren, built in the UK by Alan Mann Racing and powered by a bored-out 2.5-litre version of Alfa Romeo's sportscar V8.

Jochen made his debut for Team Lotus in the New Zealand Grand Prix at Pukekohe, which kicked off the series on 4 January. And he immediately showed team-mate Graham Hill what he could expect for the remainder of his career as a works driver by lining up on the front row of the grid, two tenths of a second slower than poleman Amon despite gear selection problems which included two broken gear levers. Hill, after a troubled practice, took third ahead of Courage, four tenths down on Jochen. The Austrian had to have his rev counter replaced just before the start, in which Chris got the jump. Jochen moved ahead of him on the second lap, however, but under pressure from the New Zealander spun on oil at the hairpin on the 18th. Chris retook a lead he wasn't to lose, leaving Jochen to cope with a wing feathering mechanism that no longer worked. The clutch had also gone awol early on, obliging him to make tricky clutchless shifts with the synchronised ZF gearbox, and he finished second, 20 seconds in arrears.

The Lotus mechanics had learned that their driver was feisty and fallible, but that he had the speed and fighting spirit to set a new lap record; Jochen had learned that his Lotus was fragile and fallible, but fast enough. It wasn't a bad start to their relationship. And he had a better run than Hill, who had a torrid time driving in a bath of fuel after a bag tank leaked, before dropping out at quarter distance with a front suspension breakage.

Levin was next up a week later, for the Rothmans

International. Jochen didn't particularly like the tight little track. "After ten laps of going round and round I feel pretty dizzy," he joked. But he showed his class when he thwarted local hero Amon's pole position aspirations with a startling lap that was one second below Jimmy Clark's track record.

That wasn't the only wind-up Amon endured that weekend. Saloon car racer Dick Sellens was involved in shipping the race cars into and out of New Zealand and had acted for Frank Gardner for a couple of years getting his equipment and mechanics across from the North Island to the South Island at the height of the holiday season.

"FG and I were in the paddock earlier that day, clarifying his ferry bookings, and we were in the vicinity of the Shell/BP tent where Chris Amon and his engineer were gassing up the Dino. And Frank said with a wink and a nudge, "Jeez, Chris, you must have a problem with two and a half litre power and three litre gas consumption!" and then swaggered away. It was a wonderful wind-up. Chris and Frank were great friends, and the only one taken aback was the Ferrari engineer. It didn't stop Frank playing in the inevitable cricket match the next day at the Amon retreat."

Later that day, Sellens was to play a brief but crucial part in Jochen's career.

The Austrian got caught out at the start of the qualifying race when his pole position was wasted as the starter pulled a move that surprised several drivers.

"That was the only time I beat Jochen, my only claim to that fame," heat winner Derek Bell remembered, having led Amon, Hill and Rindt home. "I'd just read in the press about Jochen Rindt versus Graham Hill, their inter-team battle. Jochen was always quicker, and Graham was always slowest of the five of us. But I always used to wonder how seriously he took it. I didn't notice anything between him and Jochen at all, though I know Jochen was taking it all very seriously in his first time out against Graham as a team-mate. Naturally, he was *on* it."

New Zealand journalist Eoin Young noticed the aggro, however. Jochen had soon caught up with Graham after the snafu at the start, but the tight little track offered few passing opportunities, and neither did the reigning World Champion. Lap after lap Jochen would come steaming up the inside of Graham in the hairpin, only to have his advances rudely rebuffed. Eventually Graham proved his point once and for all by running over Jochen's left front wing with his right rear

OPPOSITE *As the Tasman series got underway, the sight of Jochen in a Gold Leaf Lotus cockpit was still unfamiliar, but as the races continued he would establish himself as the fastest man on the track.* (LAT)

wheel. Jochen had to settle for fourth as Graham took third behind the Ferraris of Amon and Bell, and he wasn't happy. He was not a believer in such robust tactics, and stormed from his car to let Hill know exactly what he thought.

This was interesting, because in 1968 Jochen had spoken about how safe he felt racing against Jimmy Clark, and had added: "The same goes for Graham Hill, though he is fighting wheel to wheel, but he would never put me in an embarrassing situation. His driving is very tough, but I am not different to him in that matter".

Graham was hardly going to make it easy for his new team-mate, but Jochen was adamant: he had been 1.12s faster round the 1.175 mile circuit and Graham should have let him by. Colin Chapman's two joint number ones were each keen to lay down their own marker...

A young Peter Windsor, later to become one of the great Formula One journalists, remembered another side of Graham that weekend. "I was talking the other day to my pal Rob Wilson, who was my counterpart in New Zealand back then, and he'd been sitting on the pit wall in Pukekohe watching the Lotus boys setting up Graham's car. And after a while Graham walked across from the paddock which is on the outside of the track there, and spent about five minutes walking around the car, squatting down looking at everything, and he went over to the chief mechanic Dougie Bridge and said, 'Who did the ride heights on this?' And Dougie said, 'Oh, John or Jim,' or whomever, and Graham said, 'Fire him'. Just like that. Rob was 16, 17 at that time, and was completely blown away by Graham's ruthlessness. But there was that side to him."

Jochen still had pole for the main race; at Hill's suggestion grid positions were calculated on fastest lap times from the preliminary race. Again, Amon got a better start, but this time Jochen found a way by before the lap was over and went past the pits with a one second lead. But this time he spun exiting the hairpin on the third lap, dropping down to sixth. He was still getting used to the Cosworth's peakiness. A few laps later he had a major shunt at Castrol Bend which was later attributed to unusual airflow over and through the nose sucking out the brake fluid. The 49 vaulted over a bank and overturned, and for desperate moments Jochen lay trapped in the upturned monocoque, fearing fire while awaiting rescue that was at best tardy. In the end, it was Sellens who helped to extract him.

"The paddock at Levin was on the outside of the circuit and Jochen went off in a big way, the car rolled and he was pinned under it," he recalled. "I was standing along with a mate, Len Vidgen, on the back of a truck which was backed up to the fence, which was about ten feet above the circuit and about five feet above the embankment that Jochen ploughed into. Without comment Len and I looked at each other and were over the barbed wire fence and sprinting about 20 yards to the wreck, before the dust had started to settle. Because I was kitted out in Nomex and Len was a lot stronger than me, it was unspoken that he would hold the car once we had lifted it and I would crawl under it so I could try and drag JR out.

"The car was a bit like a plate of Rice bubbles, crackling and spitting and there was a fair amount of petrol in the air. I recall Rindt could not get his hands to his harness buckle, even when the car was lifted, and that I knew enough to unlatch it and then grab him under the shoulders and kind of crawl backwards and drag him out.

"I don't recall his immediate reaction, as by then the crash crew – St John's ambulance guys – had managed to cross the track. There was no red flag, just a local yellow! I recall Jochen telling the St John's guys that he was fine and thanking me for pulling him out of the wreck, at which point the medics assailed me for acting in such an impetuous manner. After all, he could have damaged ribs and punctured a lung, and the wisest thing would have been to wait till they got there and had the expertise to remove him in a safe manner. But the silly buggers couldn't get across the track, and they did so only after we had him out!"

Sellens and Vidgen reacted with racers' instinct, but

Dick had another reason for the alacrity with which he launched the rescue.

"There was a very promising New Zealand driver called Kerry Grant who was a friend and associate back then, and he had been horrifically burnt when practising for the NZ GP the previous year. A mutual friend, Dr V. B. Cook, had commented that it was the quick

BELOW *Jochen had to wait until the third race before he won for Lotus, but when the victory came in the Lady Wigram Trophy at Christchurch in New Zealand, it was an emphatic triumph from pole position.* (Paul Cross)

discharging of fire extinguishers on him that had saved his life, and that when it came to injuries it was easier to mend a punctured lung than deal with a fried body. I think it was the recollection of that statement that impelled me to get Jochen away from the snap, crackle and popping that was going on.

"I think Jochen knew that the guys rescuing him were doing something that came naturally to those who had raced cars, or did what mere mortals would consider dangerous pursuits. I believe I was one of the first drivers in NZ to be fully kitted out in Nomex. Frank Gardner sent me a set when it first became in regular use in the UK, and I recall him saying how important it was not to breathe in the flames or smoke as you only had 20 seconds before your lungs were destroyed. Again, a thought that was probably tucked away with the urgency to get Jochen out."

Sellens said that there were no overwhelming accolades at the circuit. "The Porteous boys had arrived to take care of their man and the sorry Lotus, and casually commented on a job well done. And that was it. The real hero was Len Vidgen, who did the impossible in lifting and holding up the wreck. He had raced a 500cc car some years earlier and was a gun skier. He'd been a surf lifesaver and was very strong and athletic, and had a reputation as a skier of being always on the edge. "The other hero that day was Jochen and his no-panic cool in accepting the assistance he was being given."

Paul Radisich, who would go on to win the New Zealand Grand Prix in 1988, and to win FIA Touring Car Championships in 1993 and '94, was seven years old at that time. His father Frank raced a Lotus 22, and Paul was becoming increasingly hooked on the sport in which he would forge his own successful career. He was watching at the hairpin and saw Jochen's alarming accident and the Sellens/Vidgen rescue.

"I was standing right there, and saw the Lotus flip upside down and land over a ditch. It was a big shunt, and to be honest I thought Rindt must be dead. I remember that he was trapped upside down for a long time, and the other guys going over to help. Then finally this guy popped out from underneath the car. Of course, the danger side of it never even remotely occurred to me at that age; I just thought, 'That was pretty cool!'"

This time Graham retired with driveshaft failure, and it was beginning to dawn on the new boy that Team Lotus might not be the best organised team he had ever raced for. The cars and equipment were getting old, and while Colin Chapman did not bother to make the trip as he was busy supervising work on the forthcoming new 63 Formula One car and its 64 Indianapolis variant, the boss expected his hard-pressed mechanics to work miracles with what they had. They were beginning to realise that their new driver was very quick, for once again Jochen had claimed fastest lap.

He got a new car for the third round, the Lady Wigram Trophy at Christchurch. The 49 he had wrecked at Levin had been replaced by a 49B complete with the vented nose, the two-inch longer wheelbase and the Hewland gearbox. While dominating practice once a stiff steering rack had been sorted out, he wiped 1.1s off the 1m 19.6s lap record set jointly the previous year by Jim Clark and Amon.

Once again the two Lotus pilots went at it hammer and tongs in the preliminary race, after Jochen again made a bad start. Fourth initially, he fought his way past Courage and Amon, but though he briefly made it past Hill too, Graham repassed him and gave him another driving lesson for the remainder of the race. Jochen finished a tenth of a second adrift and once again they had harsh words when it was over.

"Jochen was one of those four or five greats that I raced against," said Bell. "He had an annoying level of talent! I think the great drivers, respectively in their careers, were Jimmy, Jochen, Ronnie Peterson, Alain Prost, Ayrton Senna, and Michael Schumacher... I can't remember exactly when we met. It would have been in the 1968 season, I guess, when I raced against him in Formula Two. We ran close at Thruxton, when he was in the Winkelmann Brabham. But it was in the Tasman that I got to know him well.

"And I don't think he was arrogant, like some people claimed. He just had that air about him, and that nose made him look it, like Michael Schumacher's chin maybe made him look it. Jochen just had an amazing ability and confidence. He was like lightning. He could miss Friday practice and run on Saturday only and still get the pole. I was on my way up back then, and he was the king and I was the dauphin – *Roi et Dauphin* – according to some of the French papers! As a driver he was so clean. He had his own way to drive, and to live."

That was part of the reason why Jochen did not condone Hill's forcefulness in defending his position. It was part of his code that you did not block faster drivers. But for all that such tactics might frustrate him, Bell remembered that Jochen never got desperate. "He always had a situation in hand. If you passed him, he knew he could repass you. He had that confidence. And a calm ability to storm off and leave everybody behind him."

That was exactly what Jochen did in the main race at Christchurch, to score his first win for Lotus at only the third attempt. Graham got a new engine in his car for the race, while Jochen got an adjustable rear wing that worked. Sellens made an interesting observation about the manner in which each of them used their wings.

"I was competing at Wigram; I can't remember if it was in a Mini or a Toyota Corolla, but I was in attendance. Because of the almost clubby arrangements of pit and paddock, and my association with Roger and

Dale Porteous at Lotus and that fact that I'd had a part in Jochen being available to race, I was introduced to the stunningly beautiful and elegant Nina. I recall that Rob Walker was also in the Lotus pit. I don't remember anything being said about the incident; those concerned had moved on. But I remember the initial observations of one of the Porteous brothers of the difference in the way that Hill and Rindt used the high-tech wing actuation. Hill would hang on in a lower gear and not flatten the wing going on to the short pit straight, whereas Rindt would noticeably flatten the wing on every opportunity and snatch a higher gear."

Sellens liked Jochen. "What do I remember of him as a man? From the few moments in his company I would say he was charming and gracious, thrilled that his wife was with him, and probably very private as he left it to Hill to attend the prizegiving and enthral the natives with one of his classic after-dinner speeches. And I do think he had a different appreciation of the work of the mechanics than Graham did. As for his driving, what can I add to the comments of his peers?"

Once again fastest laps in the preliminary counted towards grid positions for the final, and since Jochen lapped in 1m 18.8s to Graham's 1m 19.0s he started from pole after all with Hill and Piers Courage alongside. Amon and Bell shared the second row.

This time Jochen got his start just right and as he rocketed into the lead, Piers held off Graham, Chris and

BELOW *Only Englishman Derek Bell in his Ferrari Dino proved capable of keeping Jochen in sight in the rain at Warwick Farm, when the Lotus driver was in absolutely majestic form in the Tasman International 100.* (Paul Cross)

Derek. After 15 of the 44 laps he was 18 seconds ahead, and even when Graham finally moved past the Williams Brabham three laps later, it made no difference to the final result. Both Lotus drivers chipped wheel rims on the concrete kerbs, but after finishing 26 seconds ahead Jochen described his race as "Easy". The victory moved him into second place in the points, with 15 to Amon's 22. Things began to look promising. Subsequently, he gave the first trophy he ever won for Team Lotus to his friend and biographer, Heinz Pruller. Typical Jochen.

The final New Zealand round was held at Teretonga in Invercargill, celebrated as the southernmost race track in the world. A cold wind reminded everyone of the close proximity of the South Pole. This time Dunlop-shod Piers took pole position by a tenth from Firestone's three best runners, Jochen (who believed he'd been fastest), Graham (who now had a Hewland gearbox on his 49) and Chris.

"Piers in qualifying was just fantastic in Frank's BT24," remembered Windsor. "I think that was him absolutely reaching the next level of performance. He wasn't that far away from Jochen in terms of his car control and ability."

However, Jochen won the preliminary race easily from Piers and Chris, but at the start of the main event the Lotus broke its left driveshaft and as it lurched momentarily and then moved no further it was rammed, and then vaulted over, by the faster-starting Bell's Ferrari. Piers scored a memorable win for Frank Williams, with Graham passing Gardner and Amon to take second. Now Amon's tally was 26 points, with Courage second on 22 and Jochen third, still on 15.

While things might get a little fraught on the track between the Lotus drivers, everybody was relaxed off it, and several had their wives or girlfriends with them. They tended to hang out together, in a spirit of camaraderie that was a product of this special era of racing.

"We shared time together with Chris, Jochen, Graham and Piers," Bell recalled. "There was a comment one day. We were playing squash with Jochen in New Zealand and we got back to the hotel all sweaty and Chris was lounging in a chair in reception, smoking. Chris laughed and said, 'The day you can beat me is the day I'll get fit'. I was thinking, 'The day Chris is fit is the day he'll beat Jochen'. They were good races, the Tasman!"

Off-track it was a carefree lifestyle, as Jochen and Piers's friendship deepened and they spent all their action downtime playing gin rummy, just as Jochen would with Bernie. He found himself roaring with laughter on the occasion when Piers and Graham crashed a three-wheeled, tiller-steered, motorcycle-engined farm cart called a Gnat while negotiating a very steep hill. The three of them regularly skied, Jochen being particularly adept on only one.

Young was a central part of all the fun and had many tales of his time in the Tasman. One concerned Hill's efforts to expand his field of operation when it came to hobbies, from cricket and water-skiing to ski kiting. The moustachioed Englishman ski kited into the air and rose well above a lake in Sydney until the kite lost wind. "It felt like five thousand feet but I guess it was probably only 15," Graham admitted, after plunging back into the lake. "It started to sway around, letting all the wind out, and we had one hell of a shunt!" He bore a graze on his nose to attest to that, and when a Brisbane reporter happened to ask the drivers who was the best skier, Jochen replied: "For sure, Graham is the bravest!"

Graham, however, felt it was the other way around. Both he and Jochen found the front end of the Lotus 49 getting light in blustery conditions down the back straight at Christchurch while they were running with conventional front canard wings rather than the stilt-mounted front aerofoils, and they got starved of air while slipstreaming. Jochen didn't particularly care for wings even then, but he had not fully joined the anti-wing brigade. He was in favour of the high wings back and front, and Graham blanched visibly as he heard Jochen say: "Then I reckon the downforce on these cars would be so effective that Burnenville at Spa would be flat..."

Later there was the time when Graham flew Eoin, Piers and Jochen and Nina from Sydney to Brisbane in his twin-engined, six-seater Piper Aztec. Young remembered that it was a fairly bumpy ride. "For most of the three-hour trip we followed the coastline, flying low and looking for sharks. On the way up we had spotted a huge one basking just off the beach and suddenly everyone decided against going surfing. I asked Piers how fast we were going and he said, '190mph'.

"And how high?

"'The altimeter I can see says 26 feet – underground!' came the reply."

Interestingly Amon, one of the least political racers on the circuit, told Alan Henry that he hated the way in which Jochen and Piers behaved like a pair of elitist bores during their Tasman interlude, expressing the opinion that they would never have done so in Europe.

The racing resumed at Lakeside, for the 34th Australian Grand Prix on February 2. All of the cars were held up by bond problems in customs, and Team Lotus suffered the most as it lost a day of practice while the cars were ferried by road up to Brisbane. Hill's engine had been replaced after Teretonga, while the unit in Jochen's car was found to have sprung a water leak and required work on the head gaskets. Then, on start-up in the garage, Hill's new engine blew itself up, necessitating a plea to Frank Williams to borrow his spare. Hill then had his large rear wing sway sideways and collapse.

Amon, his Ferrari now equipped with correctly rated springs and an adjustable wing, headed Courage, Hill and Bell. Jochen was fifth, his new engine misfiring persistently. But since there was no spare engine left at Lotus, he was stuck with the apparently insurmountable problem for the race. It was a poor omen.

"Lakeside was a good example of how Jochen could just jump into a car and go fast," said Windsor. "He'd hardly done any practice, had never been to the circuit before and he just jumped in and raced."

Amon romped home an easy winner, leaving Hill and Courage to run second and third until they collided on the fifth lap. Piers spun and retired with a broken wishbone, and Graham's rear wing later collapsed again, on the fiftieth lap, possibly as a result of the Brabham going over the Lotus's rear wheels. That necessitated a lengthy stop to have it removed, which left him fourth. Bell backed Amon for a Ferrari one-two, with local racer Leo Geoghegan bringing his elderly Lotus home third. Jochen made a terrible start, dropping to seventh initially. Subsequently he worked past Geoghegan and Gardner to run fourth. To begin with he was closing on

Hill for third, until his own Lotus began to go slower and slower until it retired on the 43rd lap as his troubled engine showed signs of imminent failure.

Now Amon had the title in his sights, and Jochen needed several miracles to get back on terms in the remaining two races. He and Graham were joint third at this stage, with one decent engine between them. The situation was so desperate that, after he had been tracked down grouse shooting in Wales, Cosworth co-founder Mike Costin flew out to conduct emergency surgery in the paddock, building up a serviceable motor from the bits Team Shambles had left.

A miracle did happen at the penultimate round, the International 100 at Warwick Farm. And it was Jochen who provided it, not the gods. The meeting did not have a propitious start for him, however, as he missed Friday practice while Costin completed his own miracle on the engine front. Not that it mattered. As Bell said, he could miss sessions and still get right on it, and that was precisely what he did on Saturday. Within ten laps he had recorded 1m 28.8s on a track he'd never seen before, below the 1m 29s open-wheel lap record. In another ten he was down to 1m 26.6s, then took another second off that with more to come. The next day in final qualifying Amon dipped down to 1m 25.3s, before Jochen posted 1m 24.7s. Chris screwed 1m 24.5s out of the Ferrari, and that seemed to have settled the matter, until Jochen reeled off a fantastic 1m 23.8s to throw the issue beyond dispute. "Is that okay or would you like me to go quicker?" he beamed as he lit up a post-session cigarette.

This time there was no preliminary race, which was perhaps just as well as it was pouring down on the Sunday. "I have never liked driving in the rain," Jochen

BELOW *Jochen was so pumped after the Tasman International 100 that he had no need of an umbrella. His victory was without question the most dominant performance of the 1969 Tasman series.* (Paul Cross)

admitted cheerfully as he watched, clad in overcoat and hat. He looked over at Amon's Ferrari with a grin, and told the New Zealander: "You'll need bigger aerofoils than that!"

Amon led off the line, but by the end of the opening lap Jochen was 8.75s ahead. "I passed Chris on the first lap and had a lead of almost 12 seconds at the end of the second," he chuckled. "It's quite something to get a pit signal like that so early in a race!"

Nobody got near him for the rest of the afternoon, until they stood on the podium. Amon and Courage clashed and were forced into retirement, and that settled the title in Chris' favour since Piers was by then the only other driver who could have challenged his points tally. Graham rowed his 49B along in second place for a while before pitting with waterlogged electrics, and it was Bell who came through to take second place and his best Tasman result.

"That day I drove as hard as I could," 'Dinger' remembered. "Jochen would be exiting a corner just as I was coming into it. He finished first, me second. On the rostrum he turned and said to me: 'You shouldn't have kept the pressure up, you made me work very hard for it!' Why would he have said that if he was arrogant?

Now he didn't suffer fools, that's true, he had no time for them, and he had so many people in his life. But to have one of my idols say that to me was a great moment…" They had lapped everyone else, the rest being led home by Gardner in the Mildren-Alfa Romeo.

Peter Collins, who would later have spells managing the Lotus, Williams and Benetton teams in Formula One, was at Warwick Farm that day as a spectator. "They pushed on hard in the Tasman. People think it was a cakewalk, but I tell you, they pushed hard. I remember at the Farm in 1968 Jack [Brabham] was in a BT23 with a Repco V8 in the back, and he appeared over one of the crossings airborne, he was like six feet in the air. He got wide going in, slid out and the car was up here somewhere.

"I'd gone there in 1969 with some friends who weren't really motor racing enthusiasts and because we got there late and it was pissing with rain there wasn't really anything left anywhere under cover and very few places where you could actually see much. It was the first time in a long time that I hadn't actually been in the paddock, which had a fantastic view of what they called the Causeway. So we ended up at the horse track crossing after the first corner.

"The only place I could get to see anything was to sit on a fencepost. And I sat there for the whole race, an hour and 20 minutes, pissing rain, no umbrella, no raincoat, nothing. And it was just riveting, awe-inspiring.

"I was at the third corner after the start, maybe a quarter to half a mile from it, and Jochen already had three or four car lengths by the time he got there. It was just beyond belief. He was just phenomenal that day. Graham would get out of shape and looked edgy, but Jochen was just in one continual slide. The car was never, ever in a straight line because after he'd come through the first corner and then came into our view he was coming through a left-hander, so he would appear like this," – Collins broke off to indicate the sort of antics one would expect more from a sliding rally driver – "and then flick like this so he could go through the next right-hander. Most of the other drivers – Chris collided with Courage on the first lap and Bell was second – seemed to be tiptoeing whereas Jochen was dancing. He was unbelievable. The Lotus's body language was so different to any other car."

"When it was wet all bets were off, and Jochen just walked it," said Windsor, who also witnessed the miracle. "There's a shot of him coming out of Creek Corner – fantastic! I always remember Jochen getting out of the car and putting a fag in his mouth almost the millisecond he was out of it. And Nina was standing there as well, and everyone was soaking wet. It was just a fantastic performance. Everybody knew they had just seen a genius at work."

Sandown Park near Melbourne brought the curtain down on a great series, and after Costin had done more work on both Jochen's and Graham's engines, the former fought it out with Amon for pole position. Jochen just got it; Chris posted 1m 4.6s, Jochen pared that to 1m 4.3s, and Amon's reply came up short at 1m 4.5s. Graham was third, but the Englishman's engine then consumed itself.

Piers had collided with Hill and Amon in previous races and a joke went round that only Jochen and Derek Bell remained on his F1 driver hit list. Jochen had another at his friend's expense, when he ostentatiously tied Piers's Brabham to a tent post in the paddock.

In Adam Cooper's book *Piers Courage – Last of the Gentlemen Racers,* Sally Courage said: "Jochen and Piers had always been friendly. And then they became great, great friends. They'd known each other a long time, but they got very close in the Tasman series. We went on holiday together, we were always around each other, we tried to stay in the same hotels, things like that. Nina and I became very good friends."

In the race Graham was soon in trouble with the same throttle balljoint problem that had probably cost Jo Siffert the previous year's Mexican Grand Prix, while Courage broke a driveshaft. But in any case this was always going to be a two-horse race as Chris reprised the battle he'd had the previous year with Jimmy Clark. Jochen led away but Chris jumped him partway round the opening lap. They remained tied together for most of the race, but though Jochen had a few stabs at passing the Ferrari and actually got alongside more than once, he couldn't make any of them stick and Chris eventually avenged himself with a seven second victory to round out the most successful campaign of his frequently ill-starred career.

"I couldn't think of a nicer way to end the series," the new champion said. "Last year I finished second with a Lotus in front of me; this year it was a pleasure to see a Lotus just behind me."

Christopher Arthur Amon was the champion by 14 points from Jochen, but the Austrian had several consolations. He was far and away the fastest man in the series, and Amon was certainly no slouch. And his own team-mate, whom he had roundly outclassed, was the current World Champion. Had the Lotus been more reliable, there is no doubt that he could have posed a far greater challenge to Amon's success.

"Piers Courage has become increasingly competitive throughout the series," Chris said, "but without a doubt Jochen Rindt has been my greatest worry."

It was small wonder that Jochen thus approached the upcoming start of the Formula One season with great enthusiasm and expectation. But the tribulations of his Tasman adventure notwithstanding, there was no way he could have foreseen what drama and disappointment lay ahead in his last full season of competition.

CHAPTER 13

A foreigner in the camp

Formula One, March to May 1969

"It must have been quite difficult, because I think Chapman was quite used to people doing what he asked them to do or he got rid of them, whereas Jochen was good enough that he couldn't get rid of him."

Dick Scammell

RIGHT *Man on a mission: Jochen at Silverstone, March 1969.*
(LAT)

The 1969 season was to be one of chimeras for Jochen. Time and again he seemed to be on the brink of his elusive first Grand Prix victory only to have it snatched away by the unreliability of the Lotus that he had expected to take him to the World Championship title. What should have been a breakthrough season that finally cemented his status as the fastest man in Formula One while also making him the most successful, instead brought disappointment after heartbreaking disappointment with such monotonous regularity that for a long time it seemed inevitable that he would beat a hasty retreat back to Brabham for 1970. Without question, there were many times when he regretted having left.

After the tribulations of the Tasman Series he could be forgiven for heading to Kyalami at the end of February in a more optimistic frame of mind, believing that he had put his 'settling in' troubles behind him. But no sooner had he arrived in the paddock in South Africa than he discovered that Colin Chapman, who had not been present in Australia and New Zealand, had an unusual modus operandi. Straight away, Jochen was not amused to discover a third 49B on the entry list for Mario Andretti, whom he had not been aware would be doing occasional races for the team. Then he found that his own car was the only one without the more efficient four-into-one exhaust system. Rubbing salt into those admittedly relatively minor wounds, Jack Brabham put his eponymous car – now powered by the Ford Cosworth DFV in place of the horribly unreliable four-cam 860 Repco V8 – on pole position. Jack had problems in the race, however, which fell to Jackie Stewart who began the way he would continue by taking Ken Tyrrell's Matra MS10-Ford to an easy win. Jochen, who outqualified both Hill and Andretti to start alongside Brabham on the front row, ran third behind Stewart and Brabham in the opening stages, moved briefly to second when Jack hit trouble with his rear wing, but was then overtaken by Graham and then Denny Hulme's McLaren as his engine lost power. Eventually he retired from sixth place with a broken mechanical fuel pump on the 45th lap.

A fortnight later Graham upstaged Jochen in qualifying for the non-championship *Daily Mail* Race of Champions at Brands Hatch, taking pole with a lap of 1m 28.2s in a session notable for circuit manager John Webb's experimentation with Indy-style qualifying. Jackie was second in the bulbous new Matra MS80 on 1m 28.3s, and to put Jochen's nose further out of joint,

LEFT *Jochen was the fastest of Lotus's three drivers on his Grand Prix debut for the team in South Africa, but was unable to finish due to fuel pump failure. His great friend Jackie Stewart emerged victorious.* (LAT)

ABOVE *Jochen's drive from the back of the grid to second place in the Daily Express International Trophy race at Silverstone in March was the stuff of legends, convincing many that he was Jim Clark's heir.* (Roger Lane)

Jo Siffert took the final front row place with 1m 29.3s in Rob Walker's private Lotus 49B. All three of them ran after rain had stopped and the track had started to dry.

Jochen was fourth, on the inside of row two, on 1m 29.4s, a tenth ahead of Brabham. He'd had to rely on his Friday time, when his running was interrupted by the failure of the left-hand rear wing strut as he exited Clearways.

Stewart beat Hill in the race, after edging ahead of the Lotus at the start. Jochen squeezed ahead of Siffert on the opening lap, and had a fair old dust-up with Graham for second place as the two 49Bs ran round nose-to-tail. For a while Brabham started to haul them in, an indication of how much the obdurate Graham was holding up his team-mate. But after ignition trouble claimed the Brabham, Jochen got blocked by Jackie Oliver's BRM and dropped back a little before coming back at Graham in a rush after setting a stunning new lap record in 1m 26.8s. This time there was some fist-waving as he harried the Londoner, who was damned if he was going to make things easy for the Austrian, but then Jochen's oil pressure sagged just as it had on the latest Cosworth DFV in practice, and that was that. Graham finished second, seven seconds adrift of Jackie, and relations were a little strained between the Lotus drivers afterwards.

Next came the Silverstone *Daily Express* International Trophy non-championship race on March 30. When Jochen arrived on Friday he was astonished to find that Chapman had not sent any cars for the first

session of practice. As Stewart, Brabham and Chris Amon pounded round, he watched – and fumed. Then it rained on Saturday, when the Lotuses finally turned up. The rain stopped for the final practice session on Saturday afternoon, but the road was still wet, and grip limited. Out went Jochen, mouth set in a determined slit.

Writer Nigel Roebuck never forgot what he witnessed at Woodcote corner that day. "A string of cars – Brabham, Jo Siffert, Jacky Ickx – came through, slithering and twitching right out to the grass, and then Rindt appeared, the Lotus 49 travelling at a different sort of speed, and I knew, just knew, that this time he had overdone it, this time he wasn't going to make the corner. But always he did.

"Every 90 seconds there was an audible gasp from the grandstands as Jochen pointed that car at the apex, then a roar of relief as it hurtled off towards the *Motor* bridge, having beaten Woodcote again."

The outcome of this spectacular derring-do was eighth fastest time, good for the inside of the third row of the grid, among drivers who had qualified on a dry road... He won the two half-hourly awards of £100 for fastest time, and now he had a chance against the Brabhams and Stewarts, especially as on race morning Jackie had decided to forego the pole position he had won in the Matra MS80 in favour of his trusty old MS10 which proved better in the wet conditions that greeted the drivers. There were no narrow rims for the new car, so the Scot plumped for his South African Grand Prix winner and would thus start from the back of the grid.

Jochen, however, was immediately in trouble when the race began, his Cosworth DFV lapsing on to seven or fewer cylinders, its electronics drenched. And there was another problem, as if that wasn't bad enough.

"My tyres just wouldn't work in the early part of the race when the track was really wet, and after a few laps I was in 12th place, over a minute behind Jack Brabham who was in the lead," he reported. "But then the line began to dry out a little, the engine misfire cleared, and I was able to go faster and faster. The car was absolutely fantastic – I could do anything with it – and I was catching Brabham by two seconds or more each lap."

Now the Lotus – and the race – came alive. On lap 21 Jochen passed Stewart as if the Dunlop-shod Matra driver was tied to a post. Soon he was running fourth, with a trio of Brabhams ahead, Brabham leading team-mate Ickx and Piers Courage in Frank Williams's private BT26. As they reached Stowe, Ickx and Courage's battle was hampered by the lapped Lotus of Graham Hill and underpowered Parnell BRM of Pedro Rodriguez, who were also fighting one another.

"Already you had the ingredients for a perilous encounter at the end of the straight," Roebuck continued, "but there was more to come. Behind the quartet, looming out of the spray, was Rindt. As the five cars approached the corner Jochen was at the back. When they came out of it he was at the front... Confusing for the others."

It was Jochen at his finest, absolutely on the limit in a car that was handling just the way he wanted it to. The way so few of his F1 steeds ever had. Taking Woodcote at seemingly impossible angles, lap after lap, he hacked down Brabham's lead.

"At the finish I was only 2.2 seconds behind," he said, "but it should really have been about 11 seconds because Jack ran out of fuel on the last lap. That was a fantastic race; I never really expected to win it, but I just went as hard as I could and I really enjoyed it. Even though I only finished second it was definitely one of my most exciting moments." Once again, the growing legion of Rindt fans noted, he set fastest lap.

Before the Eifelrennen Formula Two race at the Nürburgring in May (see Chapter 16), the inestimable Mike Doodson, at that time *Motoring News*'s F2 reporter, conducted a remarkably prescient interview with Jochen on the subject of wings. And at that race he did another, with Graham Hill. Jochen's views were expressed, in his usual candid manner, in the May 1 issue of the paper that contained the Eifelrennen report. This made fascinating reading since it marked the first time that any driver had really stated the view that we have heard so often since the Eighties about the problems of running in aerodynamic turbulence...

Jochen, I understand that you do not like wings on racing cars. Why don't you like them?

"Well, first of all I don't think wings are part of a motor-car, and secondly, I think they have some very bad effects. One of the first is that they spoil racing to a great extent. To explain this – I don't want to mention any names – I was following another driver and found myself unable to pass him. The reason was that he had the full advantage of the wings, while the car behind had to stay in the turbulence of the car in front, so he doesn't have the full advantage of the wings. So if the man in front is going, say, 0.2s per lap slower, the man behind just doesn't have a chance of passing. This must be a bad thing because it spoils the dicing in the racing.

"Wings are also very dangerous because sooner or later, if wings get any bigger and the car happens to get in a spin, the air flow is reversed and the back of the car will lift off. You could say, of course, that a wheel might fall off, but I am sure that wings are going to get bigger and bigger, at the same time getting more and more effective, in fact ridiculous. If you're unlucky enough to hit a patch of oil, suddenly you find yourself sideways and you're in bigger trouble than ever before, because suddenly you are going to regret the speed advantage permitted by the wings."

If wings should be banned do you think that other major developments, like four-wheel-drive, should also be controlled, or even forbidden?

"No, not at all: I just think wings should be banned. One of the reasons that a bad car can handle well these days is because of wings. If you have a bad car, the design is really rather unimportant when you have the advantage of a big wing. In other words, wing development threatens to become much more important than chassis development as we have come to know it.

"I don't think in the normal course that anything should be forbidden. I think it's well enough known by now that I am against restrictions of any sort and I am only making an exception in the case of wings."

Do you see any possibility for wings being developed for use on road cars?

"I'm no designer or technician, so I can't say, but just to imagine a Mini with a big wing cruising down the road – it just doesn't make sense. If you want a wing effect on a road car, you'll have to build the feature into the shape of the body, and the wings as we know them on race cars are just not feasible."

The breakage of the wings on Jean-Pierre Beltoise's Matra at Pau was potentially one of the most dangerous incidents of its type that we have seen. Do you think the CSI should step in, even if the members are unwilling to ban wings, by setting some sort of international standards of design and construction?

"I don't think so, no. That was a very unfortunate incident when Beltoise's wing fell off, but lots of other things are falling off race cars, which can be even more dangerous. If wings are to be allowed to continue, I think they should be checked by the scrutineer and if everyone is sensible, they'll make their wings sufficiently strong. In any case, it would be very difficult to make regulations – you'd need one set for chassis-mounted wings and one for suspension-mounted wings."

Which do you think is the most important aspect of safety – circuit precautions, car design, or driver protection?

"I am assuming that in circuit precautions you are including spectator safety. I think that all have the same importance. Basically, you want a good car, healthy and strong, one which doesn't break. In the car itself, you want things like fire extinguishers and a rollover bar which is strong enough to protect the driver if he turns it over. The car mustn't crush if you hit something hard.

"Circuit safety is one of the most important aspects of this whole safety thing. We should do our utmost to make sure that circuits are made safer because it doesn't do the sport any good if too many people are killed."

Is it any easier to drive a car with a wing?

"Oh yes, driving a car with a wing is like driving on rails. A small wing can be quite nice in some circumstances, but at other times – for instance, as I've mentioned, when you're dicing – it can be unpleasant. I wouldn't say that wings make things any easier, but they certainly don't make it any more difficult, as long as you're not following anyone."

When you're following someone, does it ever feel as though the turbulence is going to throw the car off the road?

"It nearly happened to me as I was following Pedro Rodriguez through Abbey Curve during the International Trophy race at Silverstone this year. Obviously, the front wings lost all their negative lift, while the back one, out of the turbulence, was

working normally. Very suddenly I found that the car was in a state of monumental understeer – I had to tweak it viciously to correct and nearly found myself going off the road.

"It was one of the most frightening racing moments I've ever experienced."

The interview with Graham actually appeared in the following week's issue, dated May 8, which covered the fateful Spanish Grand Prix. He had some different views to his team-mate, and spoke more as befitted someone who understood the technicalities far better than Jochen did. And having spun at 150mph during a tyre test at Silverstone only weeks earlier, after a tyre lost air as he went through Abbey, he was able to report that there was no evidence that the rear of the car did try to lift when it was going backwards at speed. He also foresaw a point when the extra drag of really large wings would become self-limiting and that they could become similar to gear ratios, with a different set per circuit.

"The cars are getting faster, and there's no way of stopping this process," Graham said. "If you do try to stop it you are defeating the whole purpose of motor racing and you don't know what motor racing is all about. There's no way of stopping any kind of human achievement: at the moment we're on the point of landing men on the moon. You could say that this was a dangerous development, but I haven't heard loud cries from the papers that these astronauts should stay on the ground! This is progress, achievement, and ambition, determination, the will to win."

More than four decades later, Doodson provided the crucial background to this particular aspect of the story. "The important thing about the wing interviews was that I had unwittingly become involved in Lotus politics," he explained. "Jochen begged me to do the interview with him because he really was convinced that someone was going to get killed.

"Chapman was furious when he heard of the piece and called up Graham to put the other side of the argument. The next race was the Eifelrennen, so Hill summoned me to his room in the Sporthotel, where I interviewed him while he was in bed. If I remember correctly, you can read a rather unconvincing note in what he said. He was, in effect, spouting from Chapman's hymn sheet."

Doodson also attracted censure back in the *Motoring News* office. Part of Denis Jenkinson's dislike of Jochen stemmed from that interview and from the open letter that he later sent to the magazines, which Doodson managed to get into the paper but which sister monthly *Motor Sport* resolutely refused to publish. Jenkinson, curiously, did not believe that Jochen had a valid opinion on such matters, despite all his experience of wing failures and what he had just gone through, because he had not yet won a Grand Prix. Doodson had no doubt that *MN* and *Motor Sport* proprietor Wesley Tee, a prickly, often ignorant man, had been persuaded by Jenks that it was in nobody's best interest to publicise the Austrian's beliefs since they did not coincide with his. Doodson remembered getting a bollocking for his troubles in behaving like a proper journalist.

Ecclestone liked Jenkinson, but observed: "Denis would fall in love with somebody... But Jochen wouldn't kowtow to him."

The World Championship resumed at Montjuich Park on 4 May, and both of Doodson's interviewees could count themselves lucky to be around as events there materially affected the future for the strut-mounted aerofoil.

Jochen had been the GPDA member nominated to inspect the circuit at Montjuich Park, and found that the guardrails were far too low. The organisers told him they had been given the measurements by their counterparts at Monza. He suggested changes, and was promised they would be carried out. The Spaniards kept their word to install two-tier barriers, and it saved both his and Graham's lives.

Things started badly for Jochen during Thursday's practice. He damaged the front suspension after colliding with a stray dog which Ickx, whose Brabham had stopped with a blocked fuel relief valve, had been trying unsuccessfully to round up. The car still wasn't right on Friday due to a faulty damper, and on Saturday a cracked brake disc required replacement. But stunning form round the dauntingly fast and demanding street circuit earned him pole position in 1m 25.7s, from Chris Amon in the Ferrari on 1m 26.2s and Graham in the other Lotus on 1m 26.6s. Jochen was delighted to have overshadowed his team-mate so thoroughly, and also noted happily that Jackie was only fourth in the new Matra MS80, on 1m 26.9s. "I've never seen anyone go round Montjuich Park like he did," said *Daily Mirror* journalist Pat Mennem. "He used to *fly*. It was an unbelievable sight. He was really wound up..."

A chunk of Jochen's advantage lay in his sheer brio, but a significant part was due to the continual modifications Chapman made to the Lotuses' wings. The designer was all too aware that the 49 was two years old, but saw downforce as the key to greater performance and in a never-ending search for more kept adding wing area to the car. In Spain he had his hard-worked mechanics add six-inch wide riveted-on aluminium extensions to each outer edge of the high rear

RIGHT *The growth of the Lotus's rear wing is evident as Jochen leads Chris Amon round Montjuich Park. Failure of the support struts sent him careening into and along the barriers in an horrendous shunt.* (LAT)

wings. And as if they weren't sufficient he instructed the mechanics to deepen the chord and then had a huge Gurney flap adhesive-taped across at least 60 per cent of the width of the trailing edge. But these ungainly appendages were still mounted on the same spindly aerofoil-section struts which were lightly braced to the rollover hoop. Despite the increased wing size, and the extra downforce that would thus be exerted, Chapman did not employ any additional strengthening of the struts to take account of it. Struts which had already proved wanting on at least five previous occasions. Compounding all this, he ordered yet further work on the wings overnight. Mechanic Herbie Blash remembered

BELOW *The wreckage of Jochen's Lotus 49, stored behind the Armco barriers, gives graphic indication of just how violent the 150mph accident was, and how lucky he was to escape almost unharmed.* (LAT)

receiving a bollocking in front of everyone else for using up the last remaining sheet of aluminium to rework the front wings just when Chapman wanted it for the rears. And then Chapman taking him paternally to one side as if nothing had happened, and buying him a Coke.

"Chapman being Chapman, if you are on to a good thing and it keeps getting better, you just keep doing it, don't you?" chief mechanic Dick Scammell suggested. "We were out the back making wider and wider bits to tape on to the wings. And it just kept getting quicker all the time, of course. And that's what Jochen knew, he needed to drive a car he could win in.

"The cars were definitely built in that way [too light], that's why Colin made so much progress, Scammell continued. "That's the trouble with these things, isn't it? If you're going to make rapid progress you are probably going to be marginal on some things."

And his wife Frances, who went with him to many races back then, added: "The cars were fragile, Chapman

knew that, but they were making the speed… And it must have been a difficult mindset for him, too, because he knew he'd got people's lives in his hands." The undisciplined nature of the Lotus boss's ad hoc aerodynamic research would have potentially fatal consequences on raceday.

Jochen boiled into the lead at the start, from Amon, Siffert and Hill. Graham worked by the dark blue Lotus on lap seven, as Stewart moved ahead of Brabham for fifth. But it was Jochen's race to lose as even Amon could not keep up with him as he opened a lead of four seconds. Two laps later, however, Hill's Lotus swerved violently into the guardrails on the right-hand side of the road just past the pits, where the cars were running close to 150mph after negotiating a humpback. Graham was miraculously uninjured, considering the speed at which he had gone off and was soon joined by mechanics who had run down from the pits. He was adamant that something had broken. They were beginning to suspect

wing failure as Jochen completed his 18th lap and his mechanic Dave 'Beaky' Sims (who had also been Jim Clark's wrench) sprinted back to the pits to have Chapman call Jochen in. By the time he got there Jochen had completed his 19th lap and was eight seconds ahead. But he did not complete the twentieth.

"I was leading quite easily," he reported. "When the rear wing broke the rear wheels came off the ground and the car swerved into the guardrail on the left, bounced across the road into the opposite guardrail, hit the remains of Graham's car and overturned on top of me. Graham and the marshals got me out of the car very quickly, but my face was badly cut and I had a hairline

BELOW *Had Jochen not insisted that the organisers install two-tier barriers after a preliminary inspection on behalf of the GPDA, he and Graham Hill would probably not have survived their heavy impacts.* (LAT)

fracture of the skull." Again, considering the force of the impact, he'd been phenomenally lucky. Especially as the car had been rolling atop the guardrail at one point. No mistake, this was one of *the* big F1 accidents, with parts scattered all over like a plane crash.

Amon then led until his engine blew up, as had Siffert's, thus handing Jackie the luckiest of his 27 victories. Afterwards, Ken Tyrrell told him: "Jackie, that's the first race that you've won that the team would have won if I had been driving!" The Scot, the father of the sport's safety crusade, was most concerned for his friends, and his insistence on the use of metal guardrails had undoubtedly saved not just the drivers, but also spectators, from something far worse.

Jochen was taken to a private clinic run by Professor Soler-Roig, suffering concussion, a broken nose and a fractured jaw. According to his biographer Heinz Pruller, he promised Nina immediately that he would retire. When he then saw Bernie Ecclestone, he immediately asked him: "Did you pick up my start money?" That made Stewart, waiting outside for his turn to visit, laugh for the first time that traumatic evening.

Ecclestone recalled: "I went to the doctor afterwards and he said that he was quite impressed with Jochen's eyesight. He told me: 'This guy has got the perception of a bird'. You know when a bird can swoop down and pick a fish out of water? He said that Jochen's eyesight was exactly the same".

While he was recuperating in hospital in Barcelona, a drowsy Jochen told Nina: "I always wanted to know how Jimmy felt. I think I know it now: nothing, absolutely nothing. You watch what is going on from a neutral position, as if somebody else is going to crash. Without the double guardrails, there would be now two Grand Prix drivers less… Graham and myself."

"I only spent four days in the hospital but I felt pretty dizzy for the next week or so," he reported. Dizzy enough for the doctors to advise him to miss Monaco, but he went to Indianapolis to drive the Lotus 64 (see Chapter 8) and bounced back by winning the Formula Two race at Zolder (see Chapter 16) and was raring to go by the time the F1 circus rolled into Zandvoort for the Dutch Grand Prix. Outwardly he appeared to have no further ill effects from the accident (at least until he got to Clermont-Ferrand), though friends believe it took him a while before he was a 100 per cent fit again. What rankled with him for a long time was his feeling that Graham had not tried to slow him down. Ecclestone pointed out that was unreasonable, and that Jochen would have been highly unlikely to stop when he was on the verge of winning a Grand Prix for the first time just because his team-mate signalled him to, whereupon Jochen muttered that Chapman should have done so instead. It was just his way of venting. In fact, Graham had been a key player in his rescue.

Jochen would have been even less amused had he known the full story in the pits that day, however. "I remember Chapman sending Beaky and I down with a hacksaw to cut the rear wing off Graham's car because we could see that it had broken," Blash recalled. "We got there just as Jochen went off. He was very lucky to get out of that."

Subsequently Pruller did a radio interview with his friend. "At the very moment of impact one doesn't do anything," Jochen said. "One observes what is going on, rather like a third party. A broken off wheel, or even a collapsed suspension, would have given me more of a chance. And if they hadn't doubled the height of the guardrails, I wouldn't be alive now. I owe President Fabregas a debt of gratitude. I know they cost a fortune, but surely everyone will now realise that at certain places around any track there must be these barriers. Without them I feel certain… it's highly probable… there would be two fewer Grand Prix drivers."

When he got home to Lake Geneva at the end of that week, Jochen contacted his friend Gotfrid Koechert, the Viennese jeweller whose Ferrari 250LM he had taken to victory in the sportscar race at Zeltweg in 1965, and commissioned him to make a double-tier gold guardrail on a stone base. He sent it to the Automobil Club de Catalonia, with the inscription: '*With sincere thanks, Jochen Rindt.*'

While watching his team-mate win in Monaco, he told Pruller: "I am the Catastrophe Charlie of every team. I am always in the wrong car in the wrong races at the wrong time."

It was a changed Jochen Rindt who went out to Holland, however. The accident at Levin early in the year had concerned him, but he had truly been unsettled by the crash at Montjuich Park. It had given him a flash picture of his own mortality, and hardened his attitude to safety. Now he was even more aware of the fragility of both human life and his Lotus, which had suffered its third wing failure in four meetings. He had time to ponder the situation while he was recuperating in hospital, and spent some of it writing a letter to Chapman.

Dear Colin,

I just got back to Geneva and I am going to have a second opinion on the state of my head tomorrow. Personally I feel very weak and ill. I still have to lay down most of the day. After seeing the new Doktor [sic] and hearing his opinion we can make a final decision on Monaco and Indy. I got hold of this incredibly [sic] picture which pretty much explains the accident. I didn't know it would fly that high.

Now to our whole situation, Colin. I have been racing F1 for 5 years and I have made one mistake (I rammed Chris Amon at Clermont-Ferrand) and I had one accident at Zandvoort due to gearselektion [sic] failure otherwise I managed to stay out of trouble. This situation changed rapidly since I joined your team. Levin, Eifelrace F2 wishbones and now Barcelona.

Honestly your cars are so quick that we would still be competitive with a few extra pounds used to make the weakest parts stronger. On top of that I think you ought to spend some time checking what your different employees are doing. Please give my suggestions some thought. I can only drive a car in which I have some confidence and I feel the point of no confidence is quite near.
Jochen Rindt

He also wrote the open letter that was printed in publications such as *Motoring News, Autosport* and *Autocar,* the one that *Motor Sport* declined to print.

Jochen was now no fan of wings, since he believed they helped lesser drivers to overcome any shortcoming in their talent. And he particularly disliked high wings, especially when they broke. He had thus far in his career endured several failures prior to the final one in Spain. At Monza 1968 one of the wings on his Brabham BT26 had failed in practice; later that year at Albi the mounts for his Winkelmann Brabham's BT23C's biplane mounts broke, as they did again during the Argentinian Temporada series. Then the feathering mechanism broke on his Lotus 49 in the Tasman series opener at Pukekohe. There was another breakage at Kyalami, and one during practice at Brands Hatch at the Race of Champions. He could be forgiven long before the incident at Montjuich for believing that it was only a matter of time, as indeed he had intimated already to Doodson. Many other drivers had had similar experiences, among them team-mate Graham Hill and former Lotus driver Jack Oliver, and Brabham pilots Jack Brabham and Jacky Ickx... Thus his letter pulled no punches, as he made his points in his characteristically blunt manner:

Wings – Jochen Rindt's view:
This is an open letter to all people who are interested in Formula 1 racing. I want to demonstrate a few points about the aerofoils which at the moment are used on most of the F1 cars, in order to convince the so-called experts that they should be banned.

Basically I have two reasons why I am against them:
1. Wings have nothing to do with a motor car. They are completely out of place and will never be used on a road-going production car. Please note, I mean wings and not spoilers, which are incorporated into the bodywork. You can say they bring colour to racing, and I cannot argue against that; but after all F1 racing is meant to be a serious business and not a hot rod show.

2. Wings are dangerous, first to the driver, secondly to the spectators. When wings were first introduced to F1 racing at Spa last year they were tiny spoilers at the front and back of the Ferrari and Brabhams. They had very little effect except at high speed, when they were working as a sort of stabiliser. This was a very good effect and nobody thought any more about it until Lotus arrived for the French GP at Rouen a month later with the first proper wing. Suddenly everybody got the message about what could be done with the help of the air; but unfortunately nobody directly concerned gave much thought to what could happen if the wings went wrong; and what effect they would have on racing.

First of all, it is very difficult to design a wing which is going to stand up to all of the stresses, because who knows how big the forces are. If you make the wing stronger it is going to be heavier and therefore produce bigger forces on the construction; you make it lighter and it all goes the opposite way. This is not my wisdom, it all comes from one of the most successful racing car designers. Nevertheless I am sure that after some time – and a few more accidents because of wing failure – this problem could be solved.

Now some personal experience gained by racing with the wing: The wing obviously works via the airflow over it, and this situation changes rapidly if you happen to follow another competitor; he has the full use of the wing and you yourself have to put up with the turbulence created by his car. This could mean the man in front is actually going slower than you, but you cannot pass him because, after getting near to him, your wings stop working and you cannot go so quickly. This fact spoils racing to quite a large extent. On the other hand the turbulence can be so great that your car starts behaving very strangely and completely unpredictably.

This, I think, explains Oliver's accident at Rouen last year, and I personally have been in similar trouble very often, but luckily I have always managed so far. You will understand that these two facts stop close racing, which is one of the most exciting things to watch. Therefore it is in the interests of the spectators and the drivers to ban wings.

Let us have a look at the wing if something goes wrong with it, and they do go wrong quite often, but so far nobody has been severely hurt. My accident in the Spanish GP has been the biggest one so far and, through a lot of luck and the safety precautions taken by the Spanish organisers, nothing serious happened. Naturally I will always be grateful to the Automobile Club of Barcelona for lining the circuit with double guardrails and for providing such efficient marshals.

To explain the reason for my accident, I was

happily driving round the fastest bend on the track when my wing broke and changed its downthrust into reverse. The back end of my car started flying, and I nearly flew over the double guardrail on the left side of the track. Fortunately I was flying about ten inches too low and got bounced back into the road. I have got a picture to prove it. Can you imagine what would have happened if the car had flown into the crowd? By next year we will probably have wings big enough to do so, and all the owners of the circuits will have to think about new crowd protection. You can also get lift instead of down-pressure if you spin the car at high enough speed and start going backwards.

Altogether I have come to the conclusion that wings are very dangerous, and should therefore be banned.

Jochen Rindt
Begnins, Switzerland

In light of what would happen at the 1975 race at the same venue, when Rolf Stommelen's Embassy Hill crashed into spectators after its rear wing broke, Jochen's words were chilling. One point that he didn't make, and which many observers overlooked in the furore that followed Montjuich, however, was that Jim Hall had been running stilt-mounted wings on his Chaparrals in the US and Europe for many years, with an enviable safety record that said much about the engineering integrity of the innovative white sportscars from Texas in comparison with their F1 siblings.

Predictably, Chapman went ballistic about Jochen's letters. None of his drivers had ever had the temerity to offer such public criticism of him and his methods, and he didn't take to it kindly.

"Jochen was obviously quite able to stand up for himself," Scammell said. "Chapman was a very difficult person, but Jochen was equally determined and they used to have fairly beady-eyed set-tos about certain things, especially when we had the four wheel-drives. I've seen few people actually stand up against Chapman in that fashion. I've always seen Jochen as a very determined, pretty self-assured man." And, as far as Chapman was concerned, a very different character to Jimmy.

"It must have been quite difficult, because I think Chapman was quite used to people doing what he asked them to do or he got rid of them, whereas Jochen was good enough that he couldn't get rid of him, so he had to bend over a bit for him and allow him to do things. At Silverstone Chapman even got cars back for him, which was incredible! In my whole time at Lotus I never saw him do that for anyone."

"Colin was furious!" Jabby Crombac chuckled. "Jochen's letter was just what the CSI needed, in its wish to ban wings, and Colin was adamant that since the

British GP in 1968 Lotus had taken the lead in the development of them. Now his own driver was providing the governing body with the ammunition it needed to get rid of them!"

A ridiculous state of affairs then appertained in which neither Colin nor Jochen would speak directly to one another. Jochen resorted to using Bernie Ecclestone, his manager, as his mouthpiece, while Colin used Crombac as his go-between. "Colin used to phone me in my room, and would say, 'Tell Jochen this,'" Ecclestone chuckled. "And I would ring Jochen and say, 'Colin says this'. That's how the relationship was at that point."

Things might have been tense between his friend and Chapman, but Ecclestone clearly had a lot of time for the Lotus boss. Today, in the equivalent of a papal blessing, he simply says: "Colin was all right," meaning it in the most affirmative rather than the belittling, so-so, sense.

"It was a difficult situation all round," Crombac said. "Jochen I were close friends, but so were Colin and I. And Jochen could come across as very aggressive because of his Germanic manner of speaking. He was very blunt, but didn't always mean to be. Sometimes that was because he didn't always use quite the right English expression. He could be very blunt without realising that his precise phraseology exacerbated a problem where a milder form of speech could have alleviated it!"

More bad news awaited Chapman soon after the teams arrived in Monte Carlo for the Monaco GP, where Richard Attwood was to join Graham as Jochen's temporary replacement. An hour before Thursday's practice was due to begin, the Commission Sportif Internationale (the CSI which was at the time the name given to the sporting branch of the Federation Internationale de l'Automobile, or FIA) declared that wings had been banned as from this meeting. In the uproar that ensued, it was pointed out somewhat forcibly by the likes of Chapman that the governing body could not change the regulations in such a way without risking the championship status of the race. The CSI retreated for a while, and declared instead that it would meet to discuss the matter further after the session. Jackie Stewart lapped his high-winged Matra MS80 in 1m 24.9s, ahead of Graham Hill in the similarly equipped Lotus 49B on 1m 25.6s and Jacky Ickx's double-winged Brabham BT26 on 1m 26.0s.

A lengthy meeting then ensued, after which the CSI announced that stilt-mounted wings were banned in all categories of racing under its jurisdiction, but that body-mounted winglets were allowed ahead of the front wheels so long as they did not project beyond the inner edge of them, together with appurtenances at the rear so long as they did not protrude above the highest point of the coachwork. The situation would then be reviewed after the Dutch GP on 21 June. In the meantime, the practice session times were cancelled.

Chapman was furious, and so was Ken Tyrrell who pointed out that the Matra MS80 was the first F1 car to have been designed specifically around high-mounted wings. Their cries fell on deaf ears, however, as the CSI resorted to the dictum that would in later years become Max Mosley's mantra: safety. Soon everyone fell to bashing aluminium into upswept spoiler shapes of varying efficiency and with varying levels of good grace.

Chapman had the last laugh in the Principality as Hill took the final victory of his career after Stewart's Matra broke when leading. By Zandvoort many teams had a low-mounted rear wing with some bodywork, as their own interpretation of what the CSI really meant. McLaren and BRM read the wording differently, and retained crude upswept spoilers for the time being.

Jochen, back in action, went there determined to win.

BELOW *It wasn't always war between Colin Chapman and Jochen. There were times when the two men joined Nina Rindt in some light-hearted moments despite the underlying tensions in the relationship.* (LAT)

CHAPTER 14

Storm clouds gather

Formula One, June to July 1969

"Look, you've given me a car which, I know as I turn it into a corner, is going to go off the road on the way out. If I don't get it right on the way in, there's nothing I can do with it in the corner. I'm just waiting for the moment when I'm going to go off the circuit."

Jochen Rindt

LEFT *On the edge of adhesion, Zandvoort 1969.* (LAT)

The Dutch GP was not just the first event at which the teams had had a little time to ponder the ban on high wings, however. It was also the event at which the much-vaunted four-wheel-drive cars were finally to appear. Ever since the 3-litre formula had marked the return to power, pundits had suggested that ultimately all-wheel-drive would be essential to harness the 400+ bhp of the new breed of engines. That might have been the case had wings not appeared the previous season, and aerodynamic downforce provided an excellent solution to improved grip and thus transmission of horsepower. Even the low-mounted wings had proved, and would continue to prove, a better answer than cumbersome new transmission systems and by the time the new cars reached the resort on the North Sea, their time had already been and gone. It took the principal teams which had invested in them – Lotus and Matra – a while to acknowledge that, while Cosworth realised the moment its Robin Herd-designed contraption ran at Silverstone that it was a donkey, and

so would McLaren when its M9A was ready to make a hapless debut at Silverstone in July. Chapman in particular was loath to admit that he had blundered down a blind alley, and that would prove a further source of friction between the ebullient team boss and his number one driver. Jochen was adamant that he was not going to drive the 63, notwithstanding the evident frailty of the 49B. At least the latter was quick.

"Jochen started to get nervous about the cars after that big shunt in Montjuich, and then driving the four-wheel-drive car briefly," Herbie Blash said. "He didn't like the 63, not one little bit!"

Poor Jochen! He had had many misgivings about switching from Brabham, where he was happy, to Lotus, where things with Chapman seemed destined never to gel. The Tasman series had yielded two fine victories but many irritating – some dangerous – problems, and the F1 season had thus far been an unmitigated disaster. Here it was, nearly the end of June, and he was no closer to the Grand Prix victory he so desperately craved, let alone the World Championship that he wanted even more. He hadn't even scored a point!

His car was fast but fragile, two years old and running on what were effectively year-old Firestone tyres. Meanwhile, Jackie was in a brand-new Matra that was neither fragile nor unreliable, and whose Dunlop tyres were well up to the job. And on top of that Jochen had just had a major shunt that had frightened the hell out of him, and had upset his boss with his candour afterwards. He was the first foreign lead driver Lotus had ever employed, and though Jochen's English was good he did not feel he could always communicate the way he wanted to with a man who lacked patience and was driven by his own seemingly inexhaustible supply of genius and nervous energy. And as if all that wasn't bad enough, he was now involved in a fresh battle with him over a new car in which he had absolutely zero faith or interest. There were even rumours at this stage of the season, probably fired because Jochen made no secret of the fact that he still talked with Jack Brabham, of a possible immediate return to Black Jack's team. That would have been anathema to Jochen because he was not a man to break a contract, but it remained a definite possibility for 1970.

For his part, Chapman found himself with a driver who was totally different to the man who had preceded him, and whom Chapman had adored. Jim Clark had been quiet and introverted, and was prepared to let Chapman, his friend, make the technical calls. Towards the end of his life there were indications that Jimmy was becoming more cosmopolitan, however, and also that he was beginning to emerge from Chapman's shadow.

"Jimmy was a highly introverted man," Stewart recalled. "He ate his fingers, not just the nails but all the skin around them too. But living in Paris near the end changed his life quite a lot. He became more liberated, more worldly and rounded.

"Colin had protected Jimmy from everything. He could depend on Colin to do everything for him, to fix

LEFT *After some tense wheel-to-wheel racing reminiscent of the Tasman, Jochen opened out a lead over Lotus team-mate Graham Hill, who leads eventual winner Jackie Stewart at the start of the Dutch GP.* (LAT)

ABOVE *Jochen was never averse to lending a hand, even though Colin Chapman believed him to be aloof with his mechanics. Here at Zandvoort he helps designer Maurice Philippe to adjust the front wings.* (LAT)

his racing cars, to do his travel, because Lotus did that. Jabby was his racing and Chapman link, but a guy called Michel Finkel was another friend, a totally different animal. He opened the world to Jimmy. And suddenly Jimmy was not the border farmer depending on Colin.

"And you know I saw it, the change. I mean, he was a different man. He was more independent, more vocal about what he wanted. And I think Colin was going to have more and more trouble with him."

Photo-journalist David Phipps, a familiar figure on the F1 scene then and a close friend of Chapman's, Ecclestone's and Rindt's, also saw a sign of that. He was close with Clark and knew that the Scot had his reservations about the safety of the cars Chapman provided for him. "I remember Jimmy storming up to Colin following a component failure at Rouen," he said, "and shouting: 'You nearly killed me that time,' with the emphasis on 'that'."

Even so, a more assertive Clark would still have been a much less abrasive character than Rindt. Chapman, who was almost certainly still inwardly mourning the death of his great friend but perhaps not realising it as he immersed himself in racing as a means of escape from the tragedy, could not get his head round the fact that his new Austrian charge appeared to be so blunt. And, unfairly as we shall see given the strength of Jochen's relationships with the mechanics, Chapman believed that he preferred to surround himself with acolytes rather than immerse himself and become a true member of the team. Part of the truth, which Chapman was doubtless also struggling to reconcile himself to, was that Jimmy had not just been his number one driver but his best friend, and the relationship had been mutual; Jochen was just another employee, and an apparently disrespectful and intransigent one at that.

Herbie Blash disagreed. "Jochen was one of the most laid-back guys you could meet. I would say he was like a Fifties driver in the late Sixties. He wasn't hard on his people, even when the car went wrong.

"We socialised. Numerous times we went out to dinner. But Jochen wouldn't hang around the circuit. Graham would sit down and write from one to 20 and then he'd come up with 20 jobs. Chapman would list from one to 40. So we'd just sit there and keep working, working. And Jochen would say, maybe, 'Change the gear ratios,' and that was all! He would drive round problems. I can't think of one time when he was really technical at all. He was the kind of guy who would turn up, jump in the racing car, get the job done, and then disappear. Technically, *useless*.

"As far as being arrogant, well, that was more his looks than anything else. He wasn't that good looking, but he was a really nice guy to work with. He was a mate. He wasn't awed by Colin, but then nobody impressed him. He feared nobody. He was his own person and did what he wanted to do. He didn't really like Chapman."

Dick Scammell also disagreed that Jochen didn't bond with the mechanics. "The mechanics liked him. His manner seemed arrogant, like they said Michael Schumacher was arrogant. Well, Michael did come over as hugely arrogant, but if you were working with him he didn't come across as arrogant at all. I think Jochen may have had a touch of that about him.

"I think he was a very likeable person. He was very determined, but you've got to be that, they've all got to be that. He didn't suffer fools gladly, but if you're going to succeed you can't actually love everybody, can you? It's not possible to be reasonable all the time.

"Whether you liked him or not you had to respect Chapman for what he was able to do, and equally Chapman could see that he needed Jochen, and eventually they came to a bit of an understanding, albeit not a totally easy understanding, but a workable situation. Because it was going from bad to worse."

But that was still a while away.

The Lotus 63 looked quite elegant initially, before overheating issues saw the nose aperture cut back. It had a rakish wedge shape, and the Cosworth DFV was mounted back to front so that another driveshaft could be taken forwards to transmit power to the front wheels. Jochen was not at all happy about the manner in which his feet would be so close to all that equipment down in the footbox, which itself was ahead of the front axle line.

Pointedly he left Hill to get on sorting the new car, and focused all his efforts on a rebuilt 49B. "I was none too keen on this car," Jochen said of the 63 in conversation with Heinz Pruller, "because I was of the opinion that a brand-new model shouldn't be tested during official practice. McLaren, Stewart and Courage had already spent three days here, but not us. In Barcelona the Lotus 49 showed it was still capable of winning; why do we have to risk experimenting?"

It was Dick Scammell to whom Jochen turned as he attempted to explain his detestation for the 63. "I remember that he said: 'Look, you've given me a car which, I know as I turn it into a corner, is going to go off the road on the way out. If I don't get it right on the way in, there's nothing I can do with it in the corner. The throttle controls both ends and I can't work out what to do. So I know when I turn in, if I've got it wrong, I'm just waiting for the moment when I'm going to go off the circuit. That is not very pleasant!' And it was like, once you had chosen a trajectory, you couldn't alter it. That's why, in the end, they took all the torque to the back, and that made it all pointless, the four-wheel-drive, didn't it?"

Later that weekend Blash recalled: "We had the two 49s and two 63s, and Jochen said to Chapman, 'Why have you got those here?' And Colin said, 'Well, they're here for you to race.' Jochen said: 'I'm not racing one of them!' So Chapman said, 'Come over here,' and he took him round the corner, away from us, and as Jochen walked away I remember him turning round and waggling his finger, 'No way…' And then he came back and he'd got his way!"

Pruller remembered Jochen walking past a Volkswagen garage near the seafront and snaffling a *Bargain For Sale* sign, which he then put on the nose of his 63. Chapman was not amused.

On Friday Stewart dominated the first practice session with a lap of 1m 21.50s in the Matra MS80, with Hill second on 1m 22.01s in the Lotus 49. Jochen was only eighth in his 49 on 1m 24.21s, thanks to a gutless engine and spongy brakes. His Lotus equipped with a fresh motor and a neat new low-mounted rear wing, he hit back the following day, blasting round to a pole-winning lap of 1m 20.85s to Jackie's 1m 21.14s best (after an initial lap of 1m 20.41s had been corrected). In the 63, the obedient Hill lapped in 1m 25.75s, third slowest, while Stewart's best in Matra's MS84 was 1m 26.68s…

Under an overcast sky Jochen led the field round to the grid, for what seemed his best chance yet of breaking his Grand Prix duck. But it was Graham, who had finally qualified the other Lotus 49 third, who boiled into the lead, from Jochen who slipped ahead of Jackie going into Tarzan. There was some fairly tense motoring between the two Lotus drivers that evoked memories of their Tasman clashes, until Jochen outbraked his team-mate going into the same corner at the start of the third lap, and two laps later Jackie moved up to second.

"Obviously Graham being Graham you wanted to be number one all the time, regardless, and it must have been very difficult to swallow when Jochen was faster," Scammell observed. "Graham wouldn't have taken that very easily. He used to work and work and work and look at everything, and write it down in his book, and could be a pain in the arse. Jochen used to sort of arrive and get in it and go fast."

Jochen seemed to have this one covered and was in easy charge as he extended his lead from four seconds at the end of lap five to just under ten by the end of lap 16. Was his luck finally about to change?

On the exit to Tarzan on the 17th lap the answer came cruelly and clearly, as yet again the Lotus let him down. This time it was a driveshaft joint which had sheared. Another certain victory was gone, and once again Stewart was the beneficiary, heading Jo Siffert in Rob Walker's Lotus 49B and Chris Amon's Ferrari home. Jochen could barely believe it.

"We've lost two dead cert wins," he moaned to Pruller and, unable to suppress the note of defeatism in his voice which some observers took the wrong way, he added, "and things won't always go as smoothly in practice as they have done so far."

"Sorry," Chapman said.

Later that week Brabham crashed his BT26A heavily during a tyre test at Silverstone, and was fortunate to

escape with just a broken ankle from a very nasty accident in which he had been trapped for some time. He would be out of the cockpit until Monza at the earliest, but still Jochen would not be tempted to join Ickx while the veteran Australian recovered.

Stewart owned qualifying and the race at Clermont-Ferrand, winning the French GP by almost a minute as Matra team-mate Jean-Pierre Beltoise thrilled the home crowd by winning an epic battle for second with Ickx. Denny Hulme had beaten Jochen to the front of the two-by-two grid by a tenth, the pair of them two seconds adrift of the long-haired Scot. Still suffering from dizziness on the switchback track as a hangover from his Barcelona accident, Jochen changed from his new white full-face Bell helmet back to one of his friend Piers Courage's open-faced ones in practice and the race, but this time it was not the Lotus that let him down. A recurrence of the motion sickness obliged him to quit after 22 of the 38 laps when he had just dropped from fourth to fifth place. He was mortified.

"It only took five laps before I started to feel sick again," he revealed. "For as long as I felt reasonably fit I battled with Ickx, but then I had to let him

BELOW *Borrowing his friend Piers Courage's helmet after suffering motion sickness while wearing his own new full-face Bell Star, Jochen nevertheless had to retire after feeling ill during the French GP.* (LAT)

past – and Beltoise, too. For some time I managed to stay in fourth place. But from lap 12 onwards I wanted to give up.

"Increasingly I lost all feeling of balance, and I couldn't even go flat out on the straights. I reacted too late for the corners. I drove like a drunk, and I began to feel weaker and weaker… suddenly I had a mental picture of Bandini. He started to feel unwell during the race at Monaco. I felt unwell before I even started."

Bandini had kept going and then made the mistake that killed him. In such situations Jochen could show an uncharacteristic tendency to give in, and he did this now, before he too made what might be a fatal error. It was something that set him apart from his spiritual successors Gilles Villeneuve and Ayrton Senna, who did not know how to give up. When Jochen pulled into the pits and dragged himself out of the cockpit, it was his turn to give Chapman a dejected look and say simply: "I could kill myself… Sorry". To which Chapman sportingly replied: "That's all right".

To add insult to his injury, Jochen was sick during turbulence on the flight home to Geneva that evening. He was flying because there had been a problem while the Stewarts and the Rindts were driving from their neighbouring homes in Begnins to Clermont-Ferrand.

"Jochen had a Lotus Elan at the time and it was always breaking down," Jackie recalled. "I had this Granada because I was with Ford then. We were both going to drive to France. I was saying, 'Are you sure you want to do this? Why don't we all just go in my car?' 'No, no, I want my own car,' Jochen insisted. So we thought we'd at least run together. Anyway, we were going into some village halfway there and Nina was always going on about this Lotus being terrible, noisy, rattling, this, that and the next thing. And suddenly the door fell off it, Nina's door, going into this village. And it was fibreglass and it was bouncing along with fibreglass splitting off it. I'll never forget it! We put it in the Granada's boot and continued with Nina without a door!"

Helen Stewart remembered: "As soon as she got out

BELOW *Hanging out together at Clermont: McLaren and Hulme, Hill, 'Big Silv' Moser, Siffert, Stewart, Porsche's manager Huschke von Hanstein, Courage, Jochen, Elford, Beltoise, Ickx and Amon.* (LAT)

of the car, Nina said: 'I'm not driving with him'." So the Rindts flew home while the Lotus was taken off to be fixed.

Sadly, Nina did not remember the incident, but said: "They often 'raced' each other and I thought it was bloody dangerous. But I chuckled recently when I saw that film of Riccardo Patrese driving his wife around a circuit…".

She put down the strength of the relationships with Jackie and Helen, and Piers and Sally, to a couple of things. "I think it was because we were all the same age, and travelling together. And of course Jochen and I were neighbours to Jackie and Helen and saw a lot of them with our kids. It was the same with Piers and Sally; we went on a lot of holidays together. "Actually, I think that Piers and Jochen were closer than Jackie and Jochen, in some ways. Jochen had a name for Jackie: Mr Busy-Busy. He'd call him and say, 'Are you busy-busy, or can you come over to play tennis?'."

OPPOSITE *Wherever Jochen was racing around the world, Nina was usually there both to support him and to capture the events as an enthusiastic cine photographer.* (LAT)

Sally Courage remembered Nina once starting to read Piers's hand, and him pulling it away quickly when she saw something there that he didn't like. Nina didn't remember that, but did recall another time which put her off reading hands for good. "It was a silly thing to do anyway. There was this guy who was a sponsor, a bit older than me, and over dinner one night I read his hand. Why on earth I did, I don't remember. I saw something and I said, 'Oh my God, you've had a really bad accident!' And he said, 'Yeah, I've got a wooden leg!' I was *so* embarrassed!"

Now the sextet gathered to stay at Lord Alexander Hesketh's stately home in Towcester for the British Grand Prix, which would develop into a spectacular showdown between Jackie and Jochen, and one of the greatest races in F1 history.

Jackie had been one of the first to appreciate Jochen's qualities, right from the moment they began racing

BELOW *By 1969 Jochen and Jackie Stewart had become very close personal friends, and 'raced' down to Clermont-Ferrand together from Switzerland to attend the French GP. They frame Ickx in the background.* (LAT)

together, and their friendship had blossomed in 1965. But despite his performances in Formula Two, at times with the Cooper-Maserati in 1966, with the Brabham in 1968 and the Lotus in 1969, it took some others a while to realise that the Austrian with the boxer's nose was every bit as talented as the Scot. Jackie never had a doubt, while Jochen, in his blunt but honest manner, made no secret of the fact that the only drivers he regarded as true rivals were Jackie and the oft-underrated Chris Amon with whom he had enjoyed some close racing in F1 the previous year and again in the Tasman series earlier that season.

At Silverstone the show that Jochen put on, when he and Jackie went head to head and swapped the lead 30 times while running at lap record pace, was a sensational demonstration of his talent. And it left no doubt that he was a world-class contender right out of Jimmy Clark's mould. No wonder Jackie would remember the fantastic duel with his great friend as the most pleasurable battle of his career...

Stewart had walked on water thus far that year, winning in South Africa in Ken Tyrrell's old Matra MS10, then ruling the roost in Spain, Holland and France with the MS80. He was well on his way to the first of his three titles when the circus pulled into Silverstone. "Jochen and I were virtually identical in ability," Stewart said, "and the Matra and Lotus were so evenly matched, too."

In qualifying on Friday Stewart seemed set for pole position after lapping his Matra in 1m 20.6s. But Jochen had something of a scare earlier in the week when Chapman brought only four-wheel-drive Type 63s for him and Hill to drive, having sold the old 49Bs to privateers Jo Bonnier and John Love. Jochen was incensed, and was having none of that. Stone-faced, he declared trenchantly: "This is like a Barnum and Bailey circus – in two different rings".

Eventually Chapman saw common sense and embarrassingly was obliged to capitulate and borrow back a 49B from the Swede, whose dubious consolation was a run in a 63. Initially Jochen's 49B was given a 'practice only' pass by the stewards until narrower front wings were delivered, then he lost more time on Friday when the fuel tank in the seat sprang a leak. But eventually he confirmed the wisdom of driving the two-wheel-drive car by lapping in 1m 20.8s.

Drama befell Jackie when he clipped a damaged kerb at Woodcote, throwing up a chunk of concrete. "It came right over the front of the car, then hit the back of it," he remembered. The errant masonry punctured a rear tyre

RIGHT *Jochen and Jackie Stewart had plenty of heavy scraps together in Formula 2, but the British GP at Silverstone in July 1969 marked the first time they really slogged it out 'mano a mano' in Formula 1. (LAT)*

and spun the Matra into an earth bank. Jackie was unharmed and ran back to the pits, where team-mate Jean-Pierre Beltoise was called in to hand over his MS80. He had lapped it in 1m 22.1s, but despite his unfamiliarity with the Frenchman's settings, Stewart went out and worked down to 1m 21.2s to be sure of starting from the front row, his own pole time now history since the car in which he set that time could not be repaired for the race. Now Jochen had the pole.

Hulme was third for McLaren in 1m 21.7s, ahead of Ickx's Brabham on 1m 21.8s, Amon's Ferrari on 1m 21.9s and John Surtees in the revamped new BRM P139 on 1m 22.1s. Beltoise, of course, also lost his time, and was way down the grid in the four-wheel-drive Matra MS84 which he was now obliged to drive.

Jochen grabbed an immediate lead from Jackie, with Surtees boiling through from sixth to third place by Copse. But he only got as far as Stowe. Under braking for the corner the improperly welded front suspension of the dark green BRM wilted and he was the first retirement.

By the end of that opening lap the die was firmly cast. Jochen and Jackie were already miles ahead of Hulme, then there was a gap to Pedro Rodriguez, Bruce McLaren, Amon, Piers Courage in Frank Williams's Brabham BT26, Graham Hill in the second works 49B, Jo Siffert in Rob Walker's similar car, and Ickx. John Miles and Jo Bonnier were right at the back in the unloved Lotus 63s.

The lap charts record that Jochen led until lap five, Jackie took over from laps six to 15 after passing the Lotus under the brakes for Stowe. As early as the third lap Jochen had annexed a pair of gold cufflinks put up by the Hon Gerald Lascelles, president of the British Racing Drivers' Club, for the first 125mph lap. Jochen went back ahead on lap 16, at Stowe, by which time Denny was already 23 seconds in arrears. The Austrian then officially stayed in the lead until the end of lap 61, but the charts did not tell the whole tale by a long way.

"The fun we had!" Jackie recalled. "And we both drove with complete logic. People just wouldn't do it that way today. Jochen would be on my tail at Becketts and I knew he would slipstream by me before Stowe, but the last thing I would think of was moving over to the right to block him. That would just have slowed us both down. We each signalled the other where they could pass, and I'd probably close on him on the run from Club to Abbey, and he knew I would slipstream by at 150mph through Woodcote.

"There were more passes for the lead in that race than in the history of any other Formula One race, I would have thought. On a real circuit at any rate, as opposed to a slipstreamer. We would pass always on Hangar Straight, and coming through Abbey and then going to Woodcote. We would definitely have had more than 30 lead changes. And it was all intelligent stuff. That was the great thing we had. If somebody was going to pass you, you never blocked them. That was absolutely a no, no. Nobody moved over. There was none of this moving over to the right side of the track if you were going into a right-hand corner. That only really happened to me twice: at the Nürburgring in 1972 with Clay [Regazzoni], when he put me off the road; and the Swedish Grand Prix in 1973 with Ronnie [Peterson].

"You would come out of Becketts in a high second or a low third gear, and you would never think of overtaking because you would give each other all the room you needed because you would want to get out of there cleanly. One of the great keys to Silverstone was not suffocating the car in Becketts so you would get a clear run to get maximum power and maximum revs through Chapel and on to Hangar. So if anyone got it wrong in Becketts you would never try to do them between Becketts and Chapel, which you could, but you would never do that because you would draft them and then slingshot them. If somebody would come up to you too quickly coming out of Chapel, you would be on the right-hand side of the road. In the case of Jochen and I, I would know whether to point left or right because I would have seen how close he was before Becketts and how close he was after Becketts."

Such was their respect for one another, and the trust that each could put in the other, they fought for the lead yet still ran at lap record-breaking pace. For the first lap that still stood to Amon at 1m 25.1s from the *Daily Express* International Trophy race in April the previous year, but on the second lap the two leaders lapped in 1m 23.4s and 1m 23.6s respectively, and they continued to run way below that new mark lap after lap. For much of their battle each was circulating in the mid- to low-1m 22s. Eventually, Jackie would leave the new record at 1m 21.3s from laps 57 and 60. That represented 129.61mph…

The Lotus was a shade faster down the straights, the Matra more sure-footed in the high-speed corners. And Jackie was experiencing a problem with his clutch's free travel; eventually he stopped using the pedal, but the stickiness of getting out of gear caused him to miss the

shift to fourth coming on to the Hangar Straight which had helped Jochen to close up and pass on lap 16.

"There were definitely those 30 changes of lead," Jackie said, "but not all of them were over the start/finish line. We had complete trust and confidence in each other."

Approaching half distance Jochen got a clean run through traffic as they came up to lap the group battling for fifth. He got down the inside of Pedro Rodriguez's Ferrari at Copse, then Jo Siffert's Rob Walker Lotus on the run to Stowe. When Jackie towed up to the dark blue 49B, Jo lost fourth gear, got sideways and delayed the Matra enough for Jochen to build a two-second lead.

Jackie responded by breaking the lap record again and closed in once more on the Lotus, and the fabulous duel only ended when he signalled to the ever-unlucky Austrian on lap 59 that the left rear endplate on his rear wing had bent back and was fouling a rear tyre. "I passed him at Stowe and pointed to the rear wing, but I was in two minds how to tell him. I could not possibly *not* tell him, because if that endplate had punctured the tyre… And he would know that I was certainly not trying to sell him a pink elephant…"

At the end of lap 62 Jackie had opened a lead of five seconds, and the next lap Jochen roared into the pits, where the offending item was literally torn off by mechanic Herbie Blash. Jochen kept his second place ahead of McLaren, and for a while maintained the gap to Jackie at 34 seconds. But then the Matra's engine began to misfire as it cut out on left-handers. One of its fuel pumps had failed and Jochen started to pull back a second a lap. But whatever slim hopes he entertained disappeared on lap 78 of the 84 when his own Cosworth DFV began to hiccough as he ran short of fuel. Into the pits he shot again for a splash and dash, and this time that dropped him behind Bruce and Jacky.

"He was pissed off," Blash remembered. "*Really* pissed off! It was exactly the same problem that Jimmy had which lost him the race at Monza in 1967, when he had made up a lap after stopping to have a punctured tyre replaced, and retaken the lead. The 49 carried as much fuel as it could. We even had a special tank just behind the radiator for the longer races, and of course the hot air exiting the radiator used to heat the fuel. That really was Jochen's race…"

"Jimmy wasn't that pleased at Monza," Scammell recalled, "and now neither were Jochen or Chapman. Some cars'll run down to virtually nothing and some end up with fuel in them but they stop because they won't pick it up. The 49 was one of those.

"I think we were also a bit stupid back then because we didn't really realise that when you drove the car harder it would use more fuel. You actually see it all the time with the telemetry today. Back then you'd think, 'Oh, I wonder why it ran out of fuel?' Then you'd think,

'Oh, he was on full throttle a lot longer, therefore he used more fuel…'

"Chapman was always down to the limit, and we used to put more fuel in and he'd take some out and would get very stroppy about it. But I suppose you have to have people doing what you asked, not double-guessing."

"Jochen was driving beautifully," Jackie remembers. "Technically, he was driving superbly. No opposite locking, just driving by the book."

Indeed, McLaren said: "Most people believe Jochen is

on the ragged edge while Jackie drives coolly and calmly. Yet when they both lapped me, the reverse applied."

Rindt's other close friend, Alan Rees, agreed. "I would say he had quite a bit in hand then, maybe half a second a lap. He wouldn't drive it sideways if he was comfortable. He didn't need to."

Jackie's fifth victory of the season went a long way towards cementing his first title. "That was," he said 40 years later, his eyes sparkling, "the most enjoyable race of my career."

Jochen actually dropped to fifth on the 81st lap when he mistakenly thought that Piers Courage was a lap down; the Lotus team soon put him right and he was able to repass when Frank Williams put out a board telling Piers to slow and make sure of finishing as his engine had been misfiring for some time; the Old Etonian was *not* amused.

BELOW *Nina Rindt always embraced trendy fashion because of her modelling career. Her gamine looks and personality made her a popular figure in the paddock and the pit lane, where she timed her husband's laps.* (Roger Lane)

Many still believed that Courage was a playboy racer, not the real thing. But whenever he heard such opinions raised, Jochen was the first to leap to his friend's defence. "Piers is not any less professional than you," he insisted.

In the aftermath of a heady weekend, Jochen made the sage remark: "Jackie isn't just winning his races this year; he's winning mine."

Nevertheless, according to Ecclestone, he was not frustrated. "Jochen knew he had Jackie covered that day. He was that confident in himself that he didn't have to get angry. The good thing about him was that he knew he was so good. He never rammed it down people's throats. In himself he knew there wasn't anybody out there properly, in any other team, that he wouldn't be able to blow away."

The Nürburgring saw Ickx on pole from Stewart and Jochen, and the Belgian romped home the winner for Brabham as the Scot struggled without fourth gear. Jochen ran third behind them initially despite his engine sounding awful on the warm-up lap, but dropped back with increasing ignition problems before pitting at the end of the tenth lap.

The meeting was not a complete disaster, however, for it marked a turning point in his relationship with Colin Chapman. Before practice they finally sat down and had the heart-to-heart they should have had months earlier.

BELOW *With his tousled hair, flattened nose and clipped speech, Jochen could come across as arrogant, but those who knew him well spoke of a warm-hearted, humorous and utterly loyal character.* (Roger Lane)

CHAPTER 15

Late blossom at Lotus

Formula One, late 1969

"And we got to Watkins Glen and Jochen came to me and said, 'Colin wants me to drive for him for another year and has offered quite a bit of money...' So I said, 'Look, if that's what you want to do, that's fine'."

Jack Brabham

LEFT *At last! Tex Hopkins does his trademark leap as Jochen finally wins a GP.* (LAT)

Before he flew to Germany, Jochen told Heinz Pruller: "I feel my bad luck is destroying me. And Chapman and I only seem to argue with one another now." Things had got so bad, however, with the four-sided conversations from Holland continuing, that both men knew things could not go on as they were. They had to do something about the toxic atmosphere that was threatening to break Team Lotus apart.

Pruller remembered: "At the Nürburgring Jochen and Colin sat together in the transporter for three hours – there were no motorhomes in those days! – and even missed part of the first practice session. Colin had a photo of Jochen that had been published in England with the caption: 'Is this the perfect racing driver?'

"'Don't you believe it, Jochen, you're far from it,' he told him. 'You're fine in the car, but you're a bastard outside.'"

Jochen considered that, then replied: "Perhaps I shouldn't talk so much. Certain matters should be confined to the team. But when one suffers so much misfortune, hard words come easily."

In the burgeoning mood of reconciliation, Chapman agreed that selling the 49s had been daft, and that he worked the mechanics too hard, something Jochen had repeatedly been getting at him about.

While refusing to accept that the two cars he provided for Jochen and Graham were any different to those he had supplied to, say, Jimmy and Trevor Taylor, Chapman nevertheless offered Jochen unequivocal number one status for 1970, that Hill would be switched to Rob Walker's team though not kicked out completely after all the years of their relationship, and that he would get the full treatment and a clear number two driver. Chapman told him about an all-new two-wheel-drive car that was under development.

"His character is very complicated to describe," Jochen said of Chapman. "Obviously he wants to win, but the way he wants to win and I want to win are different, that's probably the reason for arguments."

The tension was certainly eased after their lengthy conversation, but no magic wand had been waved. "He only argued with Colin about the way the cars were built," Ecclestone pointed out. "Their frailty. I know they spoke at length at the Nürburgring but I don't know whether they ever got things out in the open. But things quietened down a bit."

Pruller remembers going to a party that Team Lotus held at Bernkastel on the Moselle that evening, though it was a sombre affair for Jochen after the death that

OPPOSITE *Eddie Dennis checks the time as Herbie Blash ponders form prior to the 1969 German GP, where Jochen and Colin Chapman finally sat down and tried to thrash out their differences.* (Grand Prix Photo)

afternoon of the promising young German driver Gerhard Mitter, whose Formula Two BMW had crashed. Chapman was the perfect host, full of bonhomie, glad-handing everyone and helping to serve them. "I turned to Jochen and said: 'In a year or two you'll both be saying we used to hate each other but now we're the best of friends,' but he almost shouted his reply. 'Me, stay at Lotus. I can't imagine that!'"

It was not just the idea of returning to Brabham that Jochen now had in mind. Behind the scenes he, Bernie Ecclestone and former McLaren designer Robin Herd had been dreaming up a grand new plan to start their own Formula One outfit. Herd, who had penned the unloved Cosworth four-wheel-drive car after leaving McLaren early in 1968 before his M7A design began winning races, would leave Cosworth to set up the new business. Wealthy Spanish racer Alex Soler-Roig, with whom Jochen had become friendly after his accident in Barcelona, was involved but would not be a financial contributor.

Later that weekend Jochen showed Heinz the initial brochures for the as-yet unnamed new venture, which would probably have borne the same Jochen Rindt Racing moniker as the Formula Two team that he and Ecclestone had set up that year. At that stage, according to Heinz, it called for Herd to design an advanced two-wheel-drive car and a four-wheel-drive machine, with the idea of Jochen choosing whichever was most suitable for prevailing conditions at any given race in 1970.

Jochen and Bernie would finance the enterprise and look for backers later, and the plan was for the three to share the profits equally until Ecclestone, according to Herd, insisted that Jochen and Robin should get 45 per cent each and that ten per cent would be sufficient for him.

"At that time we were talking to Robin about doing that," Ecclestone said. "Robin's right about the shareholdings. I did say that. I think it was quite close to coming off. I don't know why it didn't happen in the end. I don't remember… It looked like it was going to happen, but to be honest it was one of those things where we didn't care if it did or it didn't, you know?"

Little by little Jochen had begun to develop reservations about the project, as more people became involved. The way Pruller tells it, Herd was mandated to appoint a team manager and chose Alan Rees. That was no problem, but then Rees brought in Max Mosley, a failed Formula Two driver best known back then as the son of infamous World War Two Fascist politician Sir Oswald Mosley. Mosley really wanted to start his own race car manufacturing business, and brought with him businessman Graham Coaker as production manager. Mosley wanted Jochen as their driver, but Jochen felt that the original plan was being hijacked.

Herd tells a slightly different version. "The Cosworth programme was falling apart, and after Max had said to

ABOVE *Even before his Lotus 49 retired from the German GP with ignition failure, Jochen was busy contemplating forming his own team with Bernie Ecclestone and Robin Herd for the 1970 season.* (LAT)

me let's build our own car, Bernie came along and asked me to do a team with Jochen. He said, 'We'll form a company'. I was very tempted. What I really wanted to do was the car that became known as the March 711, which we eventually ran in 1971, with ground effects. We did a little bit of that with what became the 701, but we couldn't do it properly with the rear suspension arrangement that we plumped for in a hurry. I wanted a long wheelbase, the radiators and the oil tank in the middle of the car...

"It was a difficult decision. I don't remember there being a name for the car or the company, but contracts were there to be signed. I was living in Northampton and Jochen came to the house one day and said: 'Robin, you have to do this'. He was an arrogant bugger, but he was very quick and for sure I liked him. You know how you come across some sportsmen for the first time, and somehow they just have something about them? Jochen was like that."

In the end, according to Herd, the Ecclestone project

died, "Basically, because a) Max was very persuasive, and b) I knew Max and Alan Rees, and I didn't know Bernie."

Speaking of the deal around the time of his seventieth birthday in February 2009, Robin let out a guffaw and gave a rueful shrug of his shoulders as he added: "Looking back, it was a mistake. I lost the chance to do the one thing I regret not doing, which was to design an F1 car properly. Bernie, the money, Jochen, the time..."

And, with hindsight, he added of Ecclestone: "You know, Bernie is the most able person I have ever met. People criticise him in certain cases, but my God, his ability is beyond comprehension! He offered to buy Oxford United from me, and I turned him down. If I list my stupid mistakes in life, that was certainly one of them."

Thus March Engineering – Mosley, Rees, Coaker, Herd, with an added vowel – came into being instead for 1970 and a different chapter of F1 history was written. There were suggestions that the idea of a Herd/Rindt/Ecclestone project was nearly revived in 1970, but Robin denied that. "No, because I think by then Jochen had decided that everybody at March were a bunch of bastards! Beyond the pale!"

There was an amusing anecdote in all this. After Robin had opted to go the Mosley route, and was still trying to persuade Jochen to sign up, Jochen knew that the prototype Formula Three car that March was building was being put together in Coaker's garage because they had yet to find premises. And he let it be known that he had no interest in driving for a company whose sole product thus far was being put together in "Graham's shack". Except that with his heavy accent this came out as "Grem's shek," and with typical ironic humour Herd and Mosley initially christened their nascent business Gremshek Engineering.

There was another little financial matter that Jochen had to resolve at that time. "1969 was pretty much the same thing for me as 1968," Michael Argetsinger said. "I got to most of the Formula One races although my own racing was picking up a bit so I missed a couple. I had Jochen's phone number at his home, but I only remember having occasion to phone him a few times. The time I remember most was in the summer of 1969. I was living in Bremen. I had a call from Mal Currie, who was the Press Director at Watkins Glen, and he wanted me to get Jochen to agree to speak at something we called 'Inside Track Seminar' over the US Grand Prix weekend. He said the fee was $500 [the equivalent of $2950 today]. I called Jochen and we had a nice chat. I told him what the deal was and what we could pay. He said, 'Oh, Mike, it's a problem. I'd like to do it but Bernie says I can't do anything any more for less than a thousand dollars.'

"I said I understood and was sorry, but that the budget wouldn't go over 500. Without any argument Jochen then said, 'Okay, for your family, I'll do it this time.' There was a pause. And then he said. 'Just don't tell Bernie!'" Told the story in 2010, Ecclestone chuckled and said: "Those were good days..."

Later that summer, as his interest in the Herd project faded, Jochen had brief talks with McLaren about joining as Denny's partner, since Bruce was looking to retire from Formula One and spend more time on the Canadian American Challenge Cup series. Jochen discussed things with Bruce's business manager Teddy Mayer, and his old friend Leo Mehl of Goodyear, but McLaren's unwillingness to open up a slot for him in the lucrative CanAm series ultimately stymied that avenue too.

There were brief approaches from Matra, which would return with its own V12 engine and a works team run from France rather than by Ken Tyrrell in 1970, and from Ferrari, but the possibility that interested Jochen much more was an offer to return to Brabham. Like Bruce McLaren, Jack, who had turned 40 in 1966, wanted to retire from driving.

"When I was going to give it all up and go back to Australia," Brabham explained, "I thought that the best man to have in our bloody team would be Jochen."

Roy Winkelmann remembered having a coffee with Jochen at Heathrow that September, as Jochen prepared to fly to Monza for the Italian Grand Prix. "He said to me, 'Am I brave or stupid, driving a Lotus?' And I said, 'Colin always makes his cars light and they break. You understand that. And it's your choice. But you are also very brave'."

Things had begun to reach fever pitch by then, but in the month-long break in the World Championship since Nürburgring, Jochen and Colin had started to get on better. And as other avenues closed to him, Jochen began to consider rather more seriously the possibility of staying with Lotus after all. It boiled down to a simple choice in the end: Lotus or Brabham.

One day at the Hotel de la Ville, where Team Lotus always stayed, Pruller realised how much things were changing when Chapman said to him: "Jochen made it very difficult for me to get to know him, it took me almost a year. But once I knew him I discovered that he had a heart of gold. He is so very, very blunt, but sincere and honest in all his opinions, and I have learned to respect this".

Part of the reconciliation had occurred at Oulton Park, when Jochen agreed to drive the hated Lotus 63 in the non-championship Gold Cup. It was still uncompetitive, but by spread-eagling himself on the ground at selected corners, Chapman was able to watch Jochen extracting everything the car had to give, and later declared that he had learned more about four-wheel-drive then than during thousands of miles of testing. Enough, it transpired, to steer well clear of it while working with designer Maurice Philippe on the new car for 1970 which would use two-wheel-drive only and be called the 72. The car that would take Jochen to the pinnacle of the World Championship one year hence...

Jochen dragged the 63 home second to Ickx's Brabham in Cheshire, and told Crombac afterwards: "Very soon after the beginning of practice I realised that the distribution of power between the front and the back had to be modified; a long-winded operation as one needs about a month to cut the necessary gears!"

Back on the championship trail for the Italian Grand Prix at Monza, his luck began to improve. Canny slipstreaming with his mate Piers Courage helped both until the McLaren drivers got in on the act too, which left the grid Jochen and Denny; Jackie and Piers; Bruce and Jean-Pierre Beltoise. And with the exception of Hulme, who dropped back with mechanical trouble, the other five would fight out a dramatic race which saw Stewart clinch his World Championship with a finely judged victory that yet again denied Jochen by the tiny margin of eight frustrating hundredths of a second.

OVERLEAF *Jochen hated the Lotus 63, but as part of his rapprochement with Colin Chapman agreed to drive the four-wheel-drive car in Oulton Park's Gold Cup, where he finished a distant second to Ickx.* (Nick Loudon)

ABOVE *One of the things Jochen hated most about the 63 was the way in which it had a mind of its own going into and out of corners, unless you got the line absolutely correct as you lined up on entry.* (LAT)

Wings were still relatively new technology, and several drivers elected to race without them. Jochen, Stewart and Siffert were among them, but Beltoise, Hulme, McLaren and Courage elected to keep theirs.

Back then Monza had yet to be ruined by chicanes, and slipstreaming was the name of the game as gaggles of cars ran together. Jochen led Denny off the line, and the New Zealander buckled his left front wing against Jackie's Matra as they sped away and Jackie dived between the McLaren and the Lotus before they reached the first corner.

Stewart led Rindt, McLaren, Siffert, Courage, Beltoise, Hulme, Jack Brabham and Graham Hill at the end of the first lap and stayed in front until the seventh, when Jochen took a brief turn. Then it was Hulme for a lap, until Stewart went ahead from the ninth to the 25th, whereupon Jochen had another three laps out front. Jackie had the blue Matra in the lead again on laps 28 to 30, before Piers led a Grand Prix for the first and only time. Then it was Stewart again on lap 33, Jochen on 34, Stewart on 35 and 36, Jochen on 37, then Stewart all the way from lap 38 to 68. It was not, however, as straightforward as mere words make it seem. Lap after lap positions behind the leader changed as the leading bunch – Stewart, Jochen, McLaren, Beltoise, Hill, Siffert, Hulme and Courage – drafted by one another. It was like Jackie and Jochen's battle at Silverstone all over again,

with interlopers. Whenever the Scot led, the others were never far behind and were content to bide their time.

Hill had chased after and caught the bunch by lap 20 after losing ground initially, but as he closed up Hulme began to drift back with clutch and brake problems. Then Siffert began to lose ground as half distance approached, his Rob Walker Lotus showing the first signs of the engine problems that would end its race.

McLaren was content to ride along at the back of the six-car group that was left, but set a new lap record on the 37th tour. Subsequently Beltoise, who was also content not to be the leader, bettered that on the 64th, leaving it at 1m 25.2s or 150.96mph. Nobody was hanging around.

Courage was the next to strike trouble. With 12 laps left his Cosworth DFV began to cut out at high revs, so gradually he began to lose the tow. Now there were five cars left, and Hill asserted himself in second place from the 46th to the 62nd lap as a mere two seconds covered them all. But then the reigning World Champion dropped a place to Jochen on lap 63, and suffered a broken driveshaft on lap 64, only four laps from home.

So now there were four, as Rindt, McLaren and Beltoise planned how they would unseat Stewart when it really mattered. What they didn't realise was that Jackie had A Plan…

Jochen led through the Lesmos on the final lap, but as they stormed towards Parabolica here came Jean-Pierre, leaving his braking impossibly late in the bewinged MS80. Jackie had also got past Jochen, preventing him from taking the optimal line, so momentarily it was a Matra one-two. But the Frenchman simply went in too deep and scythed across his team-mate and the Lotus driver's bows, and as he began to understeer wide they nipped back inside him on the sprint to the finish line. And that was where the canniness of Jackie Stewart and Ken Tyrrell paid off.

They had invested a lot of time in practice on Saturday painstakingly choosing the right gear ratios. "It was an idea that Ken and I had," Jackie reiterated at Monza, 40 years on, "and we spent endless laps getting it just right. I figured that if all I had to do was change from third to fourth coming out of Parabolica, rather than changing up to fifth gear as well, the saving of that gearchange could give me a crucial advantage. So I had quite a high third gear and a very long fourth".

But it went deeper than that. He and Tyrrell also carefully calculated the fuel weight the car would likely have at the end of the race, so that they got the ratios spot-on.

"It might have seemed a lot of work for such a tiny advantage," Jackie continued, "but back then every time you changed gear you risked making a mistake. At the sort of speeds we were doing, any momentary loss of momentum could translate to 40 or 50 metres.

"I got through the Parabolica quite well, but I was hoping that I hadn't got through *too* well, because then you might carry a few too many revs and need to make that extra gearchange.

"In such a tight finish, that apparently insignificant attention to detail gave me those few extra inches, and that proved the difference between winning and losing because I won by a distance of just 12 inches."

Stewart made it to the line eight-hundredths of a second before Jochen, whose momentum swept the Lotus ahead of the Matra just after the finish. Beltoise was nine-hundredths adrift of Jochen, and two-hundredths ahead of McLaren. Bruce thought he had beaten Jean-Pierre; Jochen said he didn't realise it was the last lap. He had seen neither the official scoreboard

BELOW *Side by side going into the Parabolica ahead of Piers Courage, Jo Siffert and Bruce McLaren, Jackie and Jochen duked it out for the whole race at Monza, before victory sealed the Scot's first title.* (LAT)

nor Lotus's pit signal. "That's what Jochen said," 70-year-old Stewart scoffed good-naturedly in 2009. "But Colin was never very accurate…"

Jackie and Ken knew all too well that it was the last lap. They won more money as lap leaders than anyone else, and they won the race. But even more importantly, they clinched their first World Championship together. And they did it in style. Only 0.19sec covered the top four in their dramatic blanket finish, Jochen to Jackie's right, Jean-Pierre coming up on their left with Bruce on his tail.

But Jackie had to be convinced by Tyrrell that he had really done enough to win the title.

"There's no doubt. You're the World Champion," the hatchet-faced entrant told him.

"Ken, listen to me. Are you absolutely sure?"

"Yes."

So what was that all about? "It was no good thinking I was World Champion unless we were absolutely sure of it," Jackie subsequently revealed years later. "I wanted to be absolutely sure Ken had got it right, because there were dropped scores to be taken into account back then. I was so conscious of the fact that he might have thought we'd done it, when we hadn't quite."

Eventually, the Scot was convinced and finally allowed himself to celebrate his first World Championship. Later, he and his wife Helen had to escape the frantic Monza crowd via a window in the administration block's toilet. Momentarily they took refuge in the Dunlop transporter before they were spotted again – Stewart was already an icon with his long hair, sideburns and black Beatle cap – and were finally rescued by their friend Phillip Martyn who whisked them away to the Ville d'Este in his 6.9-litre Mercedes.

Jackie remembered that things really sunk in the following day when he overheard the concierge trying to reschedule his flights. "This is important. It's for Jackie Stewart. He is the new World Champion, you know." That was when he finally began to savour the moment, after what he described as "one of the most important races of my life".

Sadly, when Jochen's crown was confirmed a year hence, he would no longer be around to savour a similar moment.

In Canada Ickx won from the returned Jack Brabham, after the Belgian had inadvertently turfed Stewart off the road. The Lotus's Firestone tyres were no match for the Matra's Dunlops or the Brabhams' Goodyears round Mosport, and after leading initially Jochen dropped back to finish a nevertheless happy third, delighted that his car was finally reliable.

Motor Sport's Denis Jenkinson had never been a Jochen Rindt fan, as we have seen, and somewhat petulantly declared that he would never win a Grand Prix. He was so certain of himself that in Monaco he had bet that should Jochen actually win in 1969 he would shave off his famous beard.

He had done this once before, when he bet that Sydney Allard's dragster would not get below a certain elapsed time for the standing quarter mile. When it did, he saved his hirsute appendage by performing well in the car himself. But this time he would be held to account as *Motoring News* scribe Andrew Marriott was present when the comment about Jochen and victory was made, and challenged him once again to bet his beard. Commentator Robin Richards drafted a pledge on a table napkin and handed it to Brands Hatch supremo John Webb for safe keeping, once Jenks had signed it in front of witnesses Pat Mennem of the *Daily Mirror*, Anne Hope of the *Sun*, and John Langley of the *Daily Telegraph*.

"I was sitting at a street café having a meal," Jenkinson told writer Alan Henry. "To be honest, I was a little bored with the way it had suddenly become fashionable to be a Rindt fan and we got into a bit of an argument about it."

In the October 1969 issue of *Motor Sport* Jenkinson had even likened Jochen to Mercedes's second-rank inter-war driver Manfred von Brauchitsch, knowing the latter assuredly not to have been in the league of the great Rudolf Caracciola or upcoming Hermann Lang.

"Rindt would seem to be the re-incarnation of von Brauchitsch," he wrote. "A good, fast driver who seldom won GP races. If anything was to go wrong it seemed to happen to von Brauchitsch, such as tyre treads coming off while leading, his car catching fire at the pits when refuelling, spinning off and being disqualified for receiving outside assistance. He also drove in great opposite lock power slides when Caracciola and [Dick] Seaman drove just as fast without any tail sliding. Even if Rindt does *not* make excuses for being beaten, there are those who are only too ready to do so for him! Is he really the unlucky one, or is something missing from his physical and mental make-up? Does he lack that difficult-to-define 'something' that Stewart has got, and Clark and Moss had before him?"

There was no love lost between driver and writer. Jochen detested Jenks, and was oblivious to any embarrassment he might cause to third parties by steadfastly refusing to acknowledge the little writer's presence if they all happened to be in the same group. Jochen would talk with those he liked, and simply ignore those he didn't. Since Jenkinson would later revere Ayrton Senna, who demonstrated so many of Jochen's greatest characteristics, a cynic or somebody who knew Jenks's character well might assume that ranking him on a par with von Brauchitsch was a calculated insult born of the curmudgeonly writer's famed orneriness.

As he headed to Watkins Glen for what would be his 50th Grand Prix start, however, Jochen would finally have the perfect riposte. And unfortunately for

Jenkinson, it would come while that issue of *Motor Sport* was still on the shelves.

It happened like this. Jochen took pole position with 1m 03.62s despite a persistent misfire, which just beat Denny Hulme's 1m 03.65s for McLaren, with Jackie Stewart a tenth slower and Graham Hill another three tenths further back. That pleased Jochen no end as there was a $1,000 (the equivalent of $5900 today) prize for the polesitter, and because the Lotus mechanics gave him a fresh engine for the race since the cause of the irritating misfire could not be located.

After the drivers were taken round the circuit in open Chevrolet Sting Rays so that the 100,000 spectators could get a look at them, the grid formed in almost perfect Glen autumn weather. But the warm-up laps had effectively accounted for both McLarens, Bruce's

blowing its engine, Denny's suffering top gear selection dramas. Then there were interminable delays, with cars held on the grid until some began to boil while the local cops followed up a reported spectator trespass on to the track. When finally the race got under way, Denny faltered immediately and nearly stalled as Jochen swept into the lead from Jackie and Graham. The McLaren was clearly history, and soon Jochen and Jackie left Graham and Jo Siffert to themselves as they resumed their Silverstone duel.

BELOW *At last, on October 5 1969 at Watkins Glen, Jochen finally broke through to score the first, and long overdue, Grand Prix victory of his career. And when it came, he made the success look easy.* (LAT)

When Jackie took over the lead on the 12th lap, courtesy of a small error from Jochen, they were already 20 seconds clear of Piers Courage who was into a terrific scrap with the works Brabhams. The Matra led for nine laps before Jochen pushed the Lotus back in front on the 21st lap as it was Stewart's turn to make a small mistake. Despite Jackie's best efforts, Jochen was to stay there until the end. As the Scot's engine note changed very slightly, Jochen edged gently away, so after 30 laps he was two seconds clear and in control. He was also about to lap seventh-placed Hill, who was rueing a different choice of Firestone tyre that had necessitated suspension changes that had upset his 49B's handling.

As he went into lap 36 a telltale plume of oil smoke emanated from Stewart's left-hand exhaust pipe, and the writing was on the wall for the Scot. He crept into the pits as the engine had blown an oil seal, and suddenly Jochen was holding a commanding lead of more than half a minute over his great friend Courage, with no prospect of anyone challenging him but the gods who had so often tricked him. There were still 72 laps to go, and in some ways they were agony for him, as he pondered everything that was likely to go wrong. But nothing did. Lap after lap the red, white and gold Lotus sped past the pits, and interest centred on the increasingly fraught battle between the three Brabhams for second spot, which Courage showed no inclination to surrender. Innes Ireland wrote in *Autocar*'s race report: "As Stirling Moss said, the only way to slow Rindt down would be to dig a ditch across the track!"

With 18 laps left, Team Lotus's great moment was soured when ill fortune struck Hill. The veteran spun as he got on to oil and his almost treadless left rear tyre gave up the fight to grip. The starter motor failed to fire up the stalled engine, so Hill undid his belts, leapt out, and bump-started the car down a slight slope. Jumping back in he intended to head back to the pits to have his belts retightened. He never made it. The left rear lost its air suddenly at the end of the main straight on the 91st lap, and as the car spun and overturned several times the hapless Hill was thrown out and suffered a broken right leg and a dislocated left.

There were concerns for Jochen too, in the closing laps, as his engine sounded less crisp and mechanics waited on tenterhooks for him to dive in for fuel in a notoriously long race which played havoc with fuel consumption. He had broken the lap record three times – 1m 04.40s on lap 24, 1m 04.044s on lap 54, and 1m 04.34s or 128.69mph on lap 69 – but had then eased back from 9,800 to 9,500rpm, and he stayed out. He had judged it perfectly, having at one stage let Brabham unlap himself so he could slipstream Jack's delayed BT26A. There was to be no repeat of the Monza or Silverstone fuel pick-up dramas. Finally, Karl Jochen Rindt, from Mainz, crossed the finish line first to be greeted by the acrobatic Tex Hopkins. It was surely the sweetest sight he had encountered to that point in his career.

He had won a Grand Prix.

Actually, he had won the world's *richest* Grand Prix. He trousered $50,000 (the equivalent of $295,000 today) for winning and a further $2,000 ($11,800) and the Lentheric Trophy for setting the fastest lap, to go with $1,000 ($5,900) he'd won for pole position. And as Piers, himself $5,000 ($29,500) better off after being voted BOC Driver of the Day, led John Surtees home, he could be forgiven for feeling that the podium made it the happiest day of his racing life. Graham's accident apart, the only fly in the ointment was that Nina had stayed at home because of the expense of travelling to the US.

"I could not believe that I was going to win until I started my last lap," Jochen admitted, "and even then I was not sure what was going to break in the last few yards. I was happy, but it was odd because I had waited for this too long."

Subsequently, Jenkinson temporarily lost his beard. Half of the shavings remained for years, embalmed in plastic in a special position in the clubhouse at Brands Hatch. The other half was mounted and subsequently auctioned in the Doghouse Club (for racing drivers' wives).

Of all the people around Jochen, Jackie Stewart possibly best understood the frustration he had felt for so long in not being able to win a Grand Prix. "I always thought he was gonna win one and I always told him that," Stewart said. "I won a Grand Prix in 1965, at Monza, and another in 1966, in Monte Carlo, and I had also won the *Daily Express* International Trophy race at Silverstone, so I had won three Formula One events early on. Jochen was winning regularly in Formula Two, and I was winning occasionally in Formula Two and so was Jimmy. So it was more than obvious that he was gonna win in Formula One if he could do that, but it was a question of going with the right team and the right people. And if there was anything lacking with his decision-making process, it was with whom you go and when you go with them.

"I went to BRM and it was the right move because the logic was that I would learn more from Graham Hill than I would from Jim Clark. I knew that Jim was linked very closely to Colin Chapman, without any fear of contradiction; ask Peter Arundell or Trevor Taylor, who were both very good racing drivers. But they were never going to do anything as number two drivers to Jimmy at Lotus because, albeit for different reasons, it was like

OPPOSITE *Jochen's sole regret in Watkins Glen was that to save money Nina hadn't come. Having his great friend Piers Courage alongside him on the podium just added a cherry to the long-awaited cake.* (LAT)

racing at Ferrari when Michael Schumacher was there; it just wasn't gonna happen. So there wasn't a lot left.

"Jochen didn't have easy access to what I would call a top team. For whatever reasons Ferrari, I don't think, were in the loop for him somehow, despite the win at Le Mans in 1965. I had a big advantage, because for me to go with Ken Tyrrell in 1968 it was because I had done Formula Three and Formula Two with him and his preparation was faultless and his choice of mechanics and engineers was the best. He was very demanding, but he was incredibly good to people. Ken's people all had pensions. In those days that didn't happen. So I knew that the integrity of Ken Tyrrell for me would be so much better than anyone else. I was able to see that. And that's one of the missing links that some of the drivers didn't have who could easily have won as many Grands Prix as I did and as many World Championships and maybe they would have gone on a lot longer than I did.

"I'm not sure that Jochen had that thread early enough in his career. He got stuck at Cooper for a long time, and I think he could have done better. Everyone knew by 1964 that he was a hotshot about to happen. I have to say that I was delighted when he finally made that breakthrough, because he totally deserved it."

The final race of the F1 year was held in Mexico City on October 19. As in 1965 it was a Goodyear benefit, thanks to the latest G20 tyre, but this time it provided a runaway victory for Denny Hulme and McLaren, with Jacky Ickx and Jack Brabham endorsing the result with second and third places in their Brabhams. The new World Champion was fourth in his Dunlop-shod Matra. Jochen, having been narrowly outqualified for fifth place on the grid by Jo Siffert in Rob Walker's similar Lotus, ran fourth initially behind fast-starting Stewart, Ickx and Brabham, after Hulme's car wouldn't go into first gear.

But Denny soon hit his stride, and as the orange car worked its way towards the front of the field, Jochen set about hounding Jackie after both Brabhams had passed the Matra by the ninth lap. The two friends were mere tenths apart until the Lotus's upper left-hand front suspension wishbone wilted on the 21st lap. Quite possibly the component had succumbed to pounding over the kerbs in the chicanes, in which case the Brabhams were markedly stronger as Ickx in particular used more kerb than anyone else, throughout the race.

So Jochen's run of points was over, but he ended the year in much happier frame of mind than he had been in at the midpoint. The arguments with Colin Chapman

OPPOSITE *Jochen always had to be moving very quickly. He was an expert skier, and once delighted in giving novice Jack Brabham a pair of racing skis as a joke, to the Australian's surprise and discomfort.* (Grand Prix Photo)

were largely over, and they had patched up a lot of their differences. There was much more respect between them, and they could see a point to a future together. And Jochen, at long last, was a Grand Prix winner! If Jackie Stewart had stepped forward to inherit Jimmy Clark's mantle as the yardstick, Jochen had proved that on his day, when everything was right, he had the speed and the talent to take on the Scot and beat him. Stewart might be the *best*, but Rindt was acknowledged as the *fastest* man in F1. And as he had shown since Silverstone, he had learned how to keep it smooth.

And he was going to stick with Chapman and Lotus after all. In Canada Alan Rees had made a fantastic offer on behalf of March Engineering, to sign as its number one driver. If the deal with Ecclestone to take Jochen Rindt Racing into F1 had gone through, Jochen stood to make £35,000 (the equivalent of £405,000 today). Now Reesie offered him £100,000 (£1.15m), a huge sum at the time for an F1 driver and one which gave the lie to Jochen's comment to Pruller back at Indianapolis in 1967: "If there is one driver who can manage to become a dollar millionaire through the sport, then it's Jackie. I can't".

Pruller believed that if the money had actually been there, Jochen would have accepted. But of course it was conditional. That amount of money always had to be. Rees had yet to source the funding that would enable March to pay him so much. As things turned out, that would have bankrupted a team that would sail very close to the financial edge in its early years.

"All the hints Max dropped at the launch about big secret sponsors was all smoke and mirrors," Herd admitted years later. Jochen's £100,000 would never have materialised.

Meanwhile, Jack Brabham had become utterly focused on the idea of Jochen being his team's number one driver, in a new monocoque BT33 that would use the same Cosworth DFV that had transformed Brabham's fortunes after the appalling reliability of the four-cam Repco V8 in 1968. At one stage the deal was all done verbally, until Chapman pulled out a second trump card: he would help Jochen to run his own Formula Two team, which would be overseen by Bernie. Jochen loved F2, and found that aspect of Chapman's deal most attractive. Ecclestone flew to Canada to handle the negotiations on Jochen's behalf, on the understanding that if Brabham could make an offer that amounted to 75 per cent of what Chapman had put on the table, then he would sign for Jack. Ecclestone spoke with Goodyear, but ultimately Jack had to concede that he could not raise more than 50 per cent of the Lotus offer.

Leo Mehl recalled being so cowed by a brutal approach from Chapman at one race, where he told him with steely eyes that no matter how much Goodyear stumped up he would beat it, that he didn't bother pushing the issue any further with his management.

"As far as my personal observations, it was clear that Jochen was happier in the Brabham set-up than he was at Cooper," Michael Argetsinger remembered. "It's a shame really that Brabham was in a transitional year in 1968 because Jochen should have had great results there. It was an example of bad timing. Along with many others, I wish he had gone back there in 1970 but I have no unique insight on the matter. If it is true, as I have heard and read, that Chapman trumped Brabham's offer with a very substantial amount of money, then I would find it very believable.

"Jochen very much wanted to get out of racing with some real money. He was just pragmatic in that way. I don't mean to say that he was cold-blooded and calculating, because he wasn't. He was foremost a sportsman and loved the racing for itself. But he was also very practical and expressed the view to me – and to others – 'There should be a way to make some real

BELOW *Jochen was often a more than snappy dresser, with a preference for pink shirts and white trousers in his days in Formula Junior, and later Davy Crockett jackets or this bearskin coat in 1969.* (Grand Prix Photo)

money at this'. He was always interested in finding a way to make some decent money in racing."

Just before the US GP, Jochen and Bernie agreed to Chapman's terms. "Jochen knew that driving for Lotus, the chance of having a serious shunt was a lot more than they were with Jack," Ecclestone said, adding after a pause: "I ...I suppose in a way I wanted to put him off, but he wanted to win the Championship, and he thought that was the best chance." Ironically, it was.

Now Jochen had to go and see Jack. "I had a contract with him, he was going to drive for me and I'd retire out of it," Jack said. "And we got to Watkins Glen and Chapman offered Rindt a lot more money. So Jochen came to me and said, 'Colin wants me to drive for him for another year and has offered quite a bit of money...' So I said, 'Look, if that's what you want to do, that's fine. You go ahead and do that and I'll drive for another year with Ron,' which I did. We didn't have the money to do it with Jochen, and I thought bugger it, if he wants to go and drive for Colin, that's fine."

Many people misunderstood Jochen not just because of his curt and candid manner of speech, but because he had that Austrian pragmatism that we still see today in Helmut Marko and Niki Lauda. If some thought that Jochen's first words of English were 'start money', a standing joke of the era, it was because he was totally pragmatic and honest about wanting to make money from practising such a dangerous profession. Who could possibly argue with that?

So Jochen signed a one-year extension to his Lotus contract, with the proviso that, whatever he might do if successful in his quest for the World Championship, he would undertake six months' worth of promotional and public relations activity on behalf of the team.

"I could've held him to it, our contract," Jack said in 2008. "And he said to me, 'If you really want me and you want to hold me to that contract, just say so.'" There was an air of regret still evident in the great triple champion's tone because he still felt slightly guilty not to have held Jochen to that contract, even though nobody could ever have foreseen the turn events would take. What he did was an honourable act between one friend and another. "It was his decision in the end," he said, and there you had it.

At the end of the season, *Autocourse* editor David Phipps rated Jochen second behind Jackie in his Top 10, and ahead of Ickx, Brabham, Hulme and Amon. "With a little luck Jochen Rindt might have made Jackie Stewart work even harder for the World Championship this year," he summarised. "He was robbed of two races by wing failure, and of another by driveshaft trouble, and was always remarkably fast for someone in a two year-old car running on one year-old tyres. Next year, in a new Lotus, he must be one of the favourites for the Championship."

In November 1969 Jochen and Heinz went out for the evening to a small tavern in Vienna, where they talked all night. "In 1970 I want to be World Champion and the biggest name in motor racing," Jochen said, without braggadocio. "But racing will only be a part of my life. When I have the title, I am going to retire immediately. I just don't want to be finished and exhausted before I am 30 and just carry on racing because there is nothing else I want, can do – or am interested in. There are so many things which I would like to do. Time is the most valuable thing you can have. And listen: I will be living another, say, 50 years. But I have taken out from 28 years more than you can usually gain. Isn't that simple to understand?"

"I asked him," Heinz recalled: 'All right, you get the title. But then, wouldn't you like the idea of becoming one of the all-time greats, maybe equalling Jimmy Clark's world record of 25 grand prix wins?'"

Jochen was always very Austrian in his views – forthright, devoid of romanticism. And Heinz always remembered that he had replied slowly, "Look where Jimmy is".

But equally his single victory was not enough. He still needed to prove something; that he was the best in the world. "Because today there are only two real top professionals. Jackie Stewart and myself. Because we drive with our heads."

Jochen was a supremely intelligent man, educated, well-read, who saw a bigger picture to his world than just motor racing. And the 1969 season had made him brutally aware of the risks.

"The possibility of getting killed is a big one," he said that evening. "It's just luck, good luck or bad luck, whether you can manage to survive. I have been racing for eight years now; no one can understand what it means. Eight years of racing! You know, my racing car show alone can earn me my living."

That he was determined to quit if he won the title in 1970 was beyond question at that moment. The decision to stay with Team Lotus would ultimately enable Jochen to pursue and, ultimately, realise his cherished dream. But it would also cost him his life.

BELOW *Jochen and Nina enjoyed their last Christmas together in 1969, at the home they rented from boxer Ingemar Johansson in Begnins, Switzerland, while plans progressed for their own bespoke house.* (Anon)

CHAPTER 16

No sign of abdication

Formula Two, 1969

"I think that anyone who goes to take part in the F2 race is sticking a knife in the back of those of us who want to make racing safer. The race itself will just turn into a big slipstreaming drag like Enna."

Jochen Rindt

RIGHT *The king still reigns, Thruxton 1969.* (LAT)

Formula Two was generally deemed to lack a little sparkle in 1969, despite the usual slipstreaming epics at Rheims, Enna and Hockenheim. And Motor Circuit Developments' introduction of Formula 5000 limited the category to only one race in England, the season opener at Thruxton.

Jochen's switch from Brabham to Lotus affected his F2 ride, and part of his deal with Colin Chapman allowed for a square-tube framed Lotus 59 designed by Dave Baldwin and powered by the venerable Cosworth FVA, which would be run by now-retired Alan Rees via Roy Winkelmann Racing. In Rees's place, Graham Hill stepped in as Jochen's regular team-mate, with guest appearances by Lotus F1 racer John Miles, and

BELOW The move to Lotus prompted the need for a new Formula 2 car. Dave Baldwin's neat and attractive 59B was as much a winner in Jochen's hands as various small-bore Brabhams had been. (Roger Lane)

upcomers Rolf Stommelen, Gerhard Mitter, Alan Rollinson, Andrea de Adamich, Hans Hermann and Roy Pike.

There were 15 races overall; Jochen entered eight and won four, his principal opposition coming from the Matra-Cosworths of Jackie Stewart, who also entered eight and won two; Jean-Pierre Beltoise who entered nine and won one; Johnny Servoz-Gavin, who entered 12 and won one; and Piers Courage in Frank Williams's Brabham and the works de Tomaso who entered nine and won one. They finished in that order, with 40, 33, 32, 31 and 29 points respectively, Servoz-Gavin scoring 37 in the European Trophy points for which the others, as Graded drivers, were not eligible.

Jochen's winning spree began at Thruxton. Jackie won the first heat from Beltoise and Hill, and the remarkable motorcyclist Bill Ivy who was slower only than Stewart in practice and recovered to fourth after a bad start. His performance put many in mind of Jochen's back at Mallory Park in 1964. Jochen led the second heat for six

RIGHT *Compared to 1968, the trophy seemed to have shrunk at Thruxton, but after another supremely dominant performance Jochen was just as happy to sip the victory champagne.* (Roger Lane)

laps before picking up a puncture, whereupon Courage triumphed from Henri Pescarolo and Tino Brambilla. The lamentable performance of the Italian's Ferrari inevitably raised even more questions over the marque's dominant form in the previous year's Temporada series.

Jochen started the final from the back row but was in the lead after 19 laps following yet another sensational performance, setting a new lap record as he

BELOW *Nina Rindt met with the enthusiastic approval of Jochen's new Winkelmann Racing team-mate Graham Hill, as her fashion sense again drew favourable comment from race fans.* (Roger Lane)

vanquished the Matras of Stewart, Beltoise, Pescarolo and Servoz-Gavin.

It was a similar story in the Grand Prix de Pau, two weeks later. He started from pole, set fastest lap and led throughout, with Jackie chasing until he retired with a broken universal joint on the 46th lap.

Graham Hill led away in the Nürburgring's Eifelrennen on 27 April, but was soon overhauled by Stewart and Jochen. Jackie won easily as the two Lotuses pulled up with cracks in the welds on their lower front left wishbones.

That weekend *Motoring News* journalist Mike Doodson interviewed Jochen for the paper on the subjects of wings (see Chapter 13), but also asked him a couple of other interesting questions. One was how the Lotus 59 compared with the trusty Brabham BT23C he'd driven in the Temporada.

"I think they're both very good, in fact there's not much in it," Jochen replied. "The Lotus has its front wing low and the Brabham has the front wing high – each system has its own disadvantages and advantages. "The Lotus does seem to put the power on the road better and it's not so ready to slide. The Brabham is perhaps a more controllable car and it's easier to go quick with it."

Doodson also asked him if he was prepared to take part in a projected F2 race at Spa, which was intended to take the place of the cancelled Belgian Grand Prix on June 8.

"You must be joking!" Jochen scoffed immediately. "All we're trying to do is making racing safe. Here is a track that is so dangerous that you can hardly imagine it. The organisers don't want to do anything in the event of rain in a Formula One Grand Prix and they don't want to make even the slightest improvement in safety precautions. How on earth can they run a Formula Two race and expect everyone to come just because they've changed the formula? I think that anyone who goes to take part in the F2 race is sticking a knife in the back of those of us who want to make racing safer. The race itself will just turn into a big slipstreaming drag like Enna."

Days later Jochen had that massive shunt in the Lotus 49B at Montjuich Park, and the Grand Prix du Limbourg at Zolder on June 8 was the first race for which he was fit. The Spanish accident had shaken him up, as his letters on the subject of wings confirmed, but it didn't affect his driving even remotely. Piers now had Frank Williams's new Brabham BT30, and Jacky Ickx made an appearance in Frank's old BT23C now owned by privateer Alistair Walker. Jochen won the first heat

LEFT *Yet again at Pau, Jochen proved totally uncatchable, setting pole position and fastest lap on his way to another dominant victory that further underlined his untouchable status in the category.* (LAT)

ABOVE *Victories in both heats of the OAMTC Flugplatzrennen at Tulln-Langenlebarn naturally brought Jochen the aggregate victory. He always worked tirelessly to attract a competitive field for the races.* (LAT)

Cevert won in a Tecno, but was back on form for the Flugplatzrennen at his local track, Tulln-Langenlebarn near Vienna. Jochen won the first heat from Jackie by 2.3s, with Graham third; and the second by only 0.32s from the aggressive Scot, with the Englishman again completing the podium. All of them got a huge shock from upcomer Peter Westbury, however, who stayed with Jochen and Jackie all through the second heat, after passing and repassing Graham with his FIRST Brabham before his FVA exploded.

Doodson chuckled as he remembered that race in 2008. "I first met Jochen at Thruxton in 1968, in Formula Two, but I didn't really get to know him until the middle of 1969, when his style had started to calm down a bit. And I think he was a slightly different person in the last two years of his life. He didn't show the arrogance which was the characteristic that the people who didn't take to him seemed to find objectionable in him.

"In Formula Two he was very friendly and helpful and he even found me some work. He asked me if I'd like to help him with some publicity for Sebring, the exhaust pipe company. And I did the work but I never did get paid, so that's the only complaint I had!

"I went to that race at Tulln-Langenlebarn, which was on the border with the Czech Republic, and I was on the same plane as Brian Hart. We arrived at Vienna airport and we'd both got hire cars organised, but when we came through customs there was Jochen waiting for us.

"'Ah, hello boys,' he said. 'Do you have a car?' We said we had hire cars. 'Forget that,' he said, 'I have a car for you outside'. He had prevailed upon Ford Austria to provide a number of new Escorts and he'd parked them in the flower beds outside the airport. And he said, 'What are you doing for dinner tonight?' And I said that I didn't have any plans. 'Okay, I send my driver for you. Be in the lobby of your hotel at 7.30.'

"I came down the stairs into the lobby of my hotel at 7.30 that night, and there was one person there, and it was Jackie Stewart. He looked at me and said, 'Are you having dinner with Jochen tonight?' I said, 'Yes, I am actually.' And he laughed and said, 'Och, the little bugger. He told me to pick up a VIP!'

"So Brian and I spent a very enjoyable evening in Grensing, a suburb of Vienna, dining with Jochen and Jackie. They were always in competition with each other and I remember one of them had a new Rolex watch, almost certainly Jackie, and Jochen was saying 'Oh, I got a new Mercedes for Nina...' It was like a competition.

"That was my experience with Jochen. He was never arrogant with me, because he didn't have to be. And I wasn't conscious of being submitted to any tests that he might have set, before deciding whether he liked you. He was always extremely tolerant and kind to me."

Next up came the Nordic Cup at Keimola on August 24, where Jochen and friend Alex Soler-Roig shared the

from Ickx and Hill, and in the second he beat Ickx and Courage, to take the win on aggregate.

"I first met Jochen in Formula Two in 1966, and then in 1967 when he was driving for Winkelmann in a Brabham, with huge success and a lot of skill. He was outstanding," Ickx said. "In F2 everyone already was saying at the time he is the real talent coming. We had a hell of a race that time in Zolder, when I had the Brabham for Alistair Walker. A private car, purple. He won the race and I finished second."

Jochen crashed at Rheims, where upcomer Francois

Spaniard's Porsche 908. They started from pole, set fastest lap – and won.

Back on the Formula Two trail in the Grand Prix d'Albi between the Italian and Canadian Grands Prix in September, however, he could only manage third. Jackie waltzed away until his Matra's engine failed, but Jochen had trouble bedding in new brake pads and spun regularly. Graham came through to win with Servoz-Gavin slipping between the two green Winkelmann cars.

"This explains how talented Jochen was as a gifted race car driver," Roy Winkelmann said. "Graham was so obsessed with the correct anti-roll bar setting on his car that at one race he spent considerable time making finite adjustments down to a millimetre. Jochen started from pole position and led the race. During the race his anti-roll bar broke. He still won the race without the benefit of it. He later said that he didn't notice any difference in

ABOVE Back in a Porsche at Keimola, Jochen and his good friend Alex Soler-Roig paired together to steer the Spaniard's short-tailed 908 to pole position, victory and fastest lap in the Nordic Cup. (Porsche)

the handling." It was like Jimmy at Monaco in 1964; Jochen simply adjusted his style instinctively and drove around problems.

The week after he'd won his first Grand Prix at Watkins Glen, Jochen was crashing out of the first heat of the Gran Premio di Roma, at Vallelunga, following brake failure, and that was how his Formula Two season ended. He was still the king, still the man to beat, and just to finish the season on a high he and Soler-Roig were victorious again in the Madrid Six Hours at Jarama, once again taking pole and setting fastest lap.

CHAPTER 17

Magic in Monte Carlo

January to June 1970

*"The thing that'll always stick out in my mind is that he didn't even realise he'd won. When he came back to the pits, I remember the smile on his face. He couldn't **believe** it…!"*

Herbie Blash

LEFT *Jochen's greatest drive, to victory in Monaco.*
(Grand Prix Photo)

The 1970 season began with a decent second place for Jochen and his chum Alex Soler-Roig in the Buenos Aires 1000kms in the Porsche 908 with which they had won in Jarama the previous year. Up against works Matra and Alfa Romeo opposition and David Piper's Porsche 917 they qualified fourth and ran in the top six the whole time. As the 917 chunked its tyres, and the Alfas suffered suspension and engine problems, they moved up to second but lacked the sheer grunt to get on terms with the Matra 630/650 piloted by Jean-Pierre Beltoise and Henri Pescarolo. There was excitement when the two cars made late fuel stops and the gap between them shrank to 40 seconds, but by the flag the blue car was 77 ahead.

But his Formula One campaign got off to a less than happy start as the South African Grand Prix early in March kicked off the World Championship. He believed the year offered him his best-ever chance of winning the title, and said: "All I need is the right car and a little bit of luck, though it does not necessarily indicate that you are the best driver in the world when you are the World Champion." But Lotus did not have its new 72 ready for Kyalami.

Jackie Stewart and Chris Amon set joint fastest lap, in the hated March 701s from 'Gremshek Racing'. Jochen used the ageing Lotus 49 which had been mildly warmed over in C-spec with modified front suspension to take 13-inch front wheels, and was fourth after setting the fastest time in Friday's practice. He was separated from them by Jack Brabham in the new monocoque BT33 that he could have been driving had he not been swayed by Colin Chapman's blandishments.

He fudged his start, and after tangling with Brabham and Amon in the first corner and then slithering over the

OPPOSITE *Even though Bernie Ecclestone remembers that the new Lotus 69 was still being finished off in the paddock at Thruxton, Jochen had no trouble dominating the 1970 Formula 2 season opener.* (LAT)

BT33 and on to the grass, he dropped to 17th but steadily fought his way back up the order. He was running fifth with eight of the 80 laps to go when his engine broke, and he watched as Brabham won first time out in his quick new car, from Denny Hulme in the new McLaren and Stewart in the March, two other cars he *could* have been piloting.

Jackie and Jack were fast again at Brands Hatch in the Race of Champions on 22 March, setting the fastest practice times ahead of Jackie Oliver in the new BRM P153, another of the fast new breed of Formula One cars with which Jochen still had to contend as Chapman's Lotus 72 was being completed back at Hethel. He qualified fourth, only four-tenths off Stewart's 1m 25.8s pole time.

Oliver led the opening laps from Stewart and Brabham, who passed the Scot on the eighth lap. Jack then deposed Jackie O the next lap, the BT33 loving the Kentish circuit's notorious bumps as much as Stewart's March hated them. But Black Jack's ignition went on the blink after 47 laps, leaving Jackie to victory after Oliver had retired with a broken driveshaft on the 13th lap.

BELOW *Jochen Rindt, team owner. As an indication of where his aspirations for the future lay, Jochen started his own team with Bernie Ecclestone in Formula 2 in what would be his final season.* (LAT)

After an unusually unobtrusive drive Jochen brought the 49C home second ahead of Hulme and Brabham.

In the Wills Trophy Formula Two race at Thruxton Jochen celebrated the formation of a new racing team with Bernie Ecclestone in the best possible way. Roy Winkelmann had retired, so Jochen and Bernie had created Jochen Rindt Racing. He won his heat and the final in the new Lotus 69 after starting from pole in each and setting fastest laps, thus securing victory at the Hampshire circuit for the third successive year. He was so dominant in his new car, as he beat Stewart's John Coombs Brabham BT30 by 12 seconds, that the one significant problem he encountered all weekend was a raging toothache which affected his concentration as Stewart set the fastest practice

time. When somebody mentioned his plight over the public address system, Hungerford dentist George Dunbar stepped forward, took him back to his surgery and removed the offending molar that evening. Jochen rewarded him with a pit pass for Sunday, and invited him on to the rostrum after the race to pour him a glass of champagne.

"We had to build the thing from bits, and at Thruxton we were putting the thing together on the startline," Ecclestone remembered, then laughed as he added: "I used to look after everything financially for him, and we ran the Lotus Formula Two team together as partners. I used to do the deals and Jochen used to collect the money and drive the car."

Next Jochen won the Grand Prix de Pau for the second year running, but only after Goodyear-shod Jack Brabham had led him for 21 laps in the Coombs Brabham until its fuel metering unit packed up.

Nick Loudon remembers taking a photograph of Jochen there, which he presented to him later, at Crystal Palace. "He was very pleased with it and said in his inimitable English 'We wish to use this.' Naturally I was in agreement. I asked him at the British GP meeting if he had yet used it, while giving him another photograph. His answer, 'No, but you will be paid.' I said, 'I know that.' I again asked him at the Oulton Park Gold Cup and he reiterated that I would be paid. I said again, 'I know

that Jochen, but I would like a copy of whatever you use it for.' He said that he would arrange that.

"The following year I was talking to writer Mike Doodson and he asked if I had given Jochen a copy of the photo. I said that I had, and he replied: 'Well, you know that a week after Oulton he ran a Formula Two race in Austria and the photo was used as a poster all over Austria. I assume that as he was killed you were not paid?' I said that was the case and Mike said that Jochen was the sort of chap who would have come up to me later, had he lived, tapped me on the shoulder and given me a fistful of money. I completely agreed, as I considered him totally trustworthy and reliable."

After starting from pole in the Deutschland Trophy at Hockenheim Jochen's luck deserted him when rookie Carlos Reutemann's ambitious bid for early glory resulted in his YPF Brabham punting the Lotus off. He rejoined but could only finish 14th as the car would not select fourth gear. He contemplated going out for heat two in team-mate John Miles's car, but left the decision too late for it to be refuelled in time.

The long-awaited Lotus 72 was introduced before the Spanish Grand Prix at the twisty Jarama circuit on 19 April, and it created a sensation. Chapman and designer Maurice Philippe had come up with something truly revolutionary that bristled with innovation. Gone was the front-mounted water radiator; instead there was a small radiator either side of the cockpit, mounted far back,

ABOVE The 72 certainly looked the part, with its sleek chisel lines, but partly because of its unseen anti-squat and anti-dive suspension geometry it would take months before Lotus sorted it fully. (LAT)

facilitating the same dramatic wedge shape of the 1968 turbine-engined Type 56 Indy cars. But that was just the start of the novelties. The wedge shape was complemented by a three-tier rear wing and only small nose fins. And to reduce unsprung weight, something on which everybody had been focusing with inboard-mounted rear brakes, the front discs were also thus mounted, having their own shafts to transmit braking torque to the wheels. And the suspension was all new too, activated by longitudinally-mounted torsion bars designed to enable the car to run the softest tyre compounds possible. The suspension also incorporated geometry to limit dive under heavy retardation and squat under hard acceleration. It looked every inch a champion's car, and just like the 49 that preceded it, rewrote the rule book.

There was only one problem. In its original guise the 72 simply didn't work. As Brabham snatched a rare pole position with 1m 23.9s, Hulme lapped in 1m 24.1s and Stewart 1m 24.2s to settle the front row of the grid. Jochen, who had driven the 72 briefly at Lotus's Hethel track, posted 1m 24.8s which left him only eighth, with Jean-Pierre Beltoise's V12 Matra, Pedro Rodriguez's V12

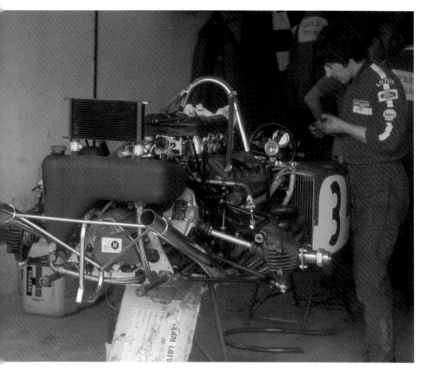

ABOVE *On its Grand Prix debut in Jarama, Spain, mechanic Herbie Blash found that Colin Chapman's new supercar required an awful lot of work just to qualify in eighth place.* (Grand Prix Photo)

BRM, Amon's March and Jacky Ickx's developing flat-12 Ferrari ahead of him.

The biggest problem with the 72 was that it just lacked any kind of feel, which made it spookily uncommunicative under braking. "It was an horrendous car to begin with," chief mechanic Dick Scammell admitted, "with that anti-squat and anti-dive on it. No feel on it at all. We'd tried anti-dive on the Lotus 18 and Innes [Ireland] had been driving it at Brands Hatch. He said: 'I can't drive this. It doesn't do anything. I put the brakes on and it just sits there'. Jochen said the same things to me. The drivers needed the feel, for the car to move a bit.

"The radius arm mountings on the 72 weren't very good, either, and you got toe-in on the rear wheels because of them flexing. It took a major, major rebuild, with virtually nothing really left of the original car, just the seat back!"

To make matters worse, Jochen had a big scare when a front brake failure sent him off the road at 175mph at

RIGHT *In a car that gave him no feel or feedback, Jochen struggled to stay ahead of John Surtees' McLaren and the Marches of Mario Andretti and Johnny Servoz-Gavin before ignition failure.* (LAT)

the end of the main straight and the spinning Lotus stopped a few inches from the barriers. Failure of the heat insulating material at the inboard end of the brakeshaft had caused its bolts to shear. He was extremely lucky to escape uninjured and stalked back to the pits, white-faced. His new car wasn't just uncompetitive, it was fragile, too. Rob Walker's team had the pit next door to Team Lotus, and Rob overheard the conversation between Jochen and Chapman. His first words to the team boss were: "I'll never sit in that f---ing car again as long as I live!"

Rob remembered asking Graham Hill, who had been transferred to his team and had driven to an heroic sixth at Kyalami after a breathtaking recovery from his accident at Watkins Glen the previous autumn: "What happens now?" And Graham replied: "Oh well, Colin will let him cool down for a bit and then he'll get him in a quiet corner and talk to him for ten minutes or so, and then he'll get back in the car and drive".

"And that," Rob marvelled, "was exactly what happened."

Soon after the start a broken stub axle sent Jackie Oliver's BRM careening into Ickx's Ferrari in a downhill left-hander, both cars being burned out in the ensuing inferno from which both drivers were fortunate to escape virtually unharmed. Stewart went on to score his sole Grand Prix success of the season, helped by a crankshaft breakage for a closing Brabham, but an ignition failure brought the Lotus's unhappy debut to an inglorious end after only nine laps when Jochen was fighting for sixth place.

There was no visible improvement in the 72's form in the *Daily Express* International Trophy race at Silverstone. As Amon aced Stewart for pole with a lap of 1m 21.4s to 1m 22.1s, Jochen's best in his red, white and gold machine was 1m 32.3s. Incredibly, Lotus turned up late for practice again and Jochen missed most of the dry running and was left an angry 16th in the line-up, behind not just F1 rivals but also ten of the 5-litre stockblock Chevrolet-powered Formula 5000 cars that were running concurrently. At the end of a trying day he got out of the car and told Chapman and the mechanics, "I'm going for a cuppa. Don't touch anything on the car. *Anything.* You can't possibly make it any worse!"

In the wet on Saturday his own excellence shone through, however, as he and Jackie battled over the *Daily Express*'s £400 (the equivalent of £4,640 today) prize. In the least-worst conditions the Scot lapped the Dunlop-shod March in 1m 37.2s; as conditions worsened Jochen took the honours with 1m 42.1s. In the wet afternoon he again aced Jackie with 1m 42.7s.

He fought through to finish fifth on a dry road in heat one behind Amon, Stewart, Piers Courage in Frank Williams's de Tomaso and Bruce McLaren in his M14, unable to fend off Piers. Both Jochen and his close friend were incensed when grid positions for damp heat two were decided upon original qualifying times rather than heat one results as normal. Piers drove a feisty race to third again, but it was all academic for Jochen as he retired on the seventh lap with more ignition problems. For once the ever-unlucky Amon triumphed ahead of Stewart and Courage, all of them in conventional cars that, on paper, should never have been a match for Chapman's wonder wedge.

He kept his spirits up by winning the ADAC's Eifelrennen F2 race a week later, leading all the way from the middle of the front row after the underrated privateer Peter Westbury had remarkably beaten him to pole in his Brabham. Derek Bell was third, with F2 rookie Emerson Fittipaldi fourth. A friendship was burgeoning between the Brazilian tyro and the Austrian star.

"When I went to Switzerland I went to Jack's house," Emerson said, in his distinctive way of referring to Jackie Stewart, "but Jochen was always around too and he was very good to me. One of the funny stories of Jochen: The first time in Nürburgring for the Formula Two race; I was in a Lotus Seven to learn the circuit, because of the car's height from the ground. I stayed a whole week, driving from eight o'clock to five, paying every lap. And I say, 'Now I know the way.'

"The weekend comes, and the race. In qualifying I was fourth. And I went to Jochen and said, 'Jochen, if I get into second at the start can I follow you?' Jochen say, 'Sure, Emerson.' And I did get into second and I did follow Jochen, and the first lap everything Jochen was doing, I was doing. And I was thinking, 'Great! The first lap and I am second, running behind Jochen!' And then we were behind the pits, the first downhill, and it was like he just waved, 'Bye, Emerson!'" He laughed heartily. "I lost the compass, I lost the GPS! He just disappeared. And I only saw Jochen afterwards, when he was on the podium and I had finished fourth. And I said to him, 'Jochen, I still have to learn a lot!'"

"Jochen was good with everybody. He wasn't bad," Ecclestone said. "Arrogant? No. When we did that film, *Grand Prix*... You can see him joking in the background... In Formula Two he used to collect the starting money, use it to keep the team going. Where I used to live he had a key to my house, he'd come back maybe three o'clock at night after a race. He'd knock on the bedroom door." He laughed. "I'd go down to the kitchen, and we'd end up playing gin rummy."

They played that all the time, for money – in airports, on aeroplanes, in the paddock. Who was the better player? "I think we were about as good as one another."

OPPOSITE *Despite the tireless ministrations of his chief mechanic Eddie Dennis, Jochen steadfastly avoided racing the Lotus 72 after Jarama, preferring the feel and raceability of the trusty 49C despite its age.* (Grand Prix Photo)

Such was the ongoing poor performance of Chapman's new 72 that Jochen flat-out refused even to consider racing it at Monaco, and while only one car was brought along as a spare and the other was being upgraded back at the factory with a stronger monocoque and without the trick suspension geometry, he appeared to be in a sulk for much of the weekend.

That didn't stop him from enjoying himself in a speedboat that came with the yacht *Crest Cutter* on which he was staying in the harbour with Bernie and Chapman. When the first officer warned him the sea was much too rough, Jochen grinned and said, "That's exactly why I want to go out!"

Jochen had already inadvertently broken the leg of Bernie's pilot, after the unfortunate individual fell over during a rough ride, but that didn't discourage Piers or Heinz Pruller, who took a beating for 15 minutes as Jochen slammed the hull from wave to wave.

Stewart and Amon Marched on to the front row of the grid, with 1m 24.0s and 1m 24.6s respectively, from Hulme, Brabham, Ickx, Beltoise and the latter's team-mate Henri Pescarolo. Jochen was again only eighth, with 1m 25.9s. But this would turn into perhaps his greatest race, on the weekend that kick-started his World Championship challenge.

Before the start, he was offered some words of advice. Bernie told him: "Whatever happens, don't come back to the pits today, except walking". Chapman said: "You always have a chance in racing, put on the pressure, carry on, you don't have to win races from the lead, especially at Monaco".

Bernie remembered that conversation, and an incident just before the start. "I can see him now. We were sitting on the counter in the pits, with Colin, and we all used to have those leather armbands as credentials. Jochen had his tucked in here," – he indicated the front of his shirt – "and this policeman came up. Here he is, in his racing suit, everyone knows who he is. And the policeman started on to him, about his credential. So Jochen took his armband out of the front of his overalls and put it round his ankle. And when the policeman grabbed his leg and made as if to remove it, Jochen kicked him in the face!

"It was just before the start of the race, so we all jumped off the counter and hopped over to the car, Jochen, me, Colin and all the guys, just strong-armed the police out of the way…"

Stewart led the first 27 laps until his March's Cosworth V8 expired, but Jochen got away only seventh,

RIGHT *Jochen accelerates out of the hairpin at Monaco during the chase after Jack Brabham's leading BT33 which would have such dramatic consequences on the very last corner of the race.* (Grand Prix Photo)

dropped to eighth on the third lap after Pescarolo outfoxed him, and only moved back to seventh on lap 12 when Ickx broke a driveshaft. He remained seventh until the 22nd lap when Beltoise's transmission failed. Still Jochen seemed mesmerised by the other Matra, and remained behind it as Stewart's demise elevated everyone a place.

Jochen admitted that he drove the first half like a taxi driver, but then, as Pruller put it, suddenly the dynamo within him began to work. He couldn't understand why so many people followed racing, because he himself found watching it rather boring, "but in Monaco for the first time I got excited".

It was not until the 36th lap that he finally outfumbled Pescarolo, and now the order read: Brabham, Amon, Hulme, Rindt, Pescarolo, Jo Siffert (in the second works March).

Some of Jochen's early laps had been within tenths of Stewart's; their sixth was actually identical in 1m 27.2s. But now he finally had clear road and soon he was up with Hulme, whom he slipped by on the 41st lap. Amon now got the hurry-up signs, and was still lapping slightly quicker. The times of the three leaders fluctuated as they hit traffic, and as Jack nursed a three-second margin over Chris, Jochen was still between 11 and 13 seconds adrift of the March. Then Amon's rear suspension broke on the 61st lap, and now only Brabham stood between Jochen and victory. There were 20 laps left, and Jack had a cushion of 13.5 seconds. It seemed that it was all over; Jochen would kickstart his World Championship campaign with six points. The gap even grew to 15 seconds by lap 63.

On the 70th lap Jack was baulked and the gap came down below 12 seconds for the first time. But still the former champion seemed to have it covered. Then he got baulked again on the 77th lap, which took him 1m 29.3s, when he came upon Siffert's March moving slowly with fuel starvation. Jochen's lap occupied 1m 24.7s. From 8.9s on the 76th, the gap was now suddenly only 4.4s. Jochen scented blood. The Monaco Grand Prix had come alive.

Lap 78, 2.4s; lap 79, 1.3s as Jochen's penultimate lap took him only 1m 23.3s, faster by far than *anyone* had gone in qualifying. Halfway round the final lap Brabham was still a second ahead, but approaching the final corner

he pushed inside Piers Courage, who kept his de Tomaso well to the right. Jack felt he lost a little more time there, and was anxiously watching for Jochen in his mirrors while also monitoring Denny Hulme's McLaren, just ahead to his left, which he was about to lap. In that crucial moment he overshot his braking point by a fraction, and just missed the turning-in Hulme as the Brabham's front tyres lost traction on the marbles of rubber that lay just off the ideal line. Suddenly the turquoise and yellow car understeered helplessly into the barrier on the outside of the corner. It was a sensational development that caught many unawares as Jochen dived through on the inside and accelerated away to the greatest victory of his life. Brabham, the nose of his car battered first by the impact and then a marshal falling on to it as he pushed the car backwards, finished a chastened second, 23.1s behind.

The Clerk of the Course was so surprised when only one car sped for the line that he forgot to wave off the winner. It remains to this day one of the most extraordinary and dramatic final laps of a Grand Prix. As testimony to the manner in which Jochen had suddenly awoken, he had shattered the lap record on his last lap, leaving it at 1m 23.2s. That was eight-tenths faster than Stewart had gone to claim pole position...

Looking slightly bemused, yet exhilarated by his astonishing success, Jochen headed to the winner's meeting with Prince Rainier. "The thing that'll always stick out in my mind," mechanic Herbie Blash said, "is that he didn't even realise he'd won. When he came back to the pits, I remember the smile on his face. He couldn't *believe* it!"

Meanwhile, Chapman shouldered his way angrily through the police who had formed a protective barricade around his driver on the start/finish line. Jochen ran up the red-carpeted stairs to be presented with his trophy by Prince Rainier and Princess Grace, and a young Princess Caroline. Blinking tears, he stood to the right-hand side of the stairs as the British national anthem was played.

He went back down the stairs and was hugged by Chapman as he was handed the laurels, then went back up for more photos and smiles. Now he looked momentarily very solemn again as the Austrian anthem was played, and the magnitude of his achievement began to sink in. He had pushed his old boss into a hugely embarrassing and public error. He had led only 400 yards of the race, but they were the 400 that counted. He had won the Monaco Grand Prix! It was, perhaps, his finest hour.

Jochen might still hate his precious Lotus 72, but right then Chapman loved him.

Now Brabham held the lead in the World Championship with 15 points to Stewart's 13, but Jochen and Hulme had nine each. The race was on.

The winning streak continued at Zolder, where on the Sunday he once again won the Grand Prix du Limbourg in what was to be a busy weekend. Taking pole easily from rising star Tim Schenken and Jacky Ickx, in Brabham and BMW respectively, he saw the fast-starting Belgian blow his engine after missing a gearshift on the first lap of the first heat, then breezed past the Australian on the third lap and was never thereafter challenged. It was Rolf Stommelen's turn to lead in the second heat, but Jochen made short work of the German and raced to another easy win, taking the aggregate victory from Bell and Pescarolo.

Then he won yet again at Crystal Palace the next day, Bank Holiday Monday, but only in his heat. Stewart had won his heat, the first, at a faster speed, leaving the Scot on pole from Jochen and Clay Regazzoni's Tecno. The three indulged in a fabulous crowd-pleasing battle in the final of the Alcoa Trophy, but Jackie went on to win from Regga and Fittipaldi after Jochen's Lotus had led but retired at the half distance point with a faulty battery terminal.

Days after Crystal Palace the motor racing fraternity was shattered when Bruce McLaren was killed testing one of his new McLaren M8D CanAm cars at Goodwood. The tail section blew off, and the big papaya orange car spun and crashed into a marshal's post. "That it happened to him, who was probably the last man to have an accident, indicates that this can happen to everyone," Jochen said of his former team-mate.

It was a saddened circus that headed to Spa-Francorchamps for the Belgian Grand Prix at Spa, where Lotus came even further down to earth. Chapman brought two revised Lotus 72s, one with the anti-dive removed, the other without anti-dive. Jochen had another scare in first practice on Friday evening when 72-1's left rear hub seized, thankfully at the La Source hairpin, one of the slowest parts of the circuit, and thereafter he refused to drive the new car again and took over team-mate John Miles's 49C. He was more comfortable with it and sat it between the Stewart and Amon Marches on the front row, even though the car was now four years old. He led initially, too, but the more slippery Marches were ahead of him at the end of the opening lap, and he was powerless to resist Rodriguez's BRM as the Mexican swept by on the third lap. As Pedro went on to pass Stewart and Amon to score the Bourne marque's first Grand Prix win since Monaco 1966, Jochen lasted only ten laps before his engine broke.

There were slim pickings back at Hockenheim for the Rhine Cup, where he qualified third behind Reutemann and Fittipaldi, led initially, but retired early with a broken driveshaft.

But things were about to change.

OPPOSITE *Through the sweep of Stavelot corner at Spa Jochen hurls the old reliable Lotus 49C, which he used in preference to the new 72. He led initially but was running fourth when the engine broke.* (LAT)

CHAPTER 18

The winning streak at last

June to August 1970

"Jochen said that he would only do one more year of racing when he was World Champion, and that would be it. But that he would have to do that last year because he would make so much money out of it."

Frances Scammell

RIGHT *A victory without joy: Jochen at Zandvoort, 1970.* (LAT)

It was the Dutch Grand Prix at Zandvoort on 21 June that changed everything for Jochen. It was the race where the Lotus 72 finally came good, and where the death of his close friend Piers Courage made him question the very reason why he did what he did. And how much longer he wanted to do it. Coming so soon after Bruce's death, it was a reminder of his own mortality, of the heavily loaded risks of his profession. Piers's death revived and magnified Jochen's insecurities about the structural integrity of his Lotus, made him ever more aware of the danger that stalked Grand Prix drivers in that era. He would never feel quite the same way about racing again.

Chapman brought along another iteration of the 72, effectively the 72C, for him to drive which featured a much stiffer monocoque and standard suspension without anti-dive or anti-squat, and they went testing at Zandvoort before the race. When Jochen lapped it in 1m 17.6s, hopes suddenly rose dramatically. That was *seven* seconds faster than Stewart's 1969 lap record! Now that the basic platform of the 72 was correct Jochen found that he had a sensitive, responsive car that he could *really* drive. He didn't get near that time in qualifying, but 1m 18.50s was enough to beat Stewart to pole position, as they were chased by Ickx, Amon and Oliver.

That evening Jochen and Nina dined in Bloemendaal, a small village to the north of Zandvoort, with Piers and Sally Courage, Ed and Sally Swart (*née* Sally Stokes, Jimmy's former girlfriend), and Frank Williams. "It was just a merry dinner, lots of laughter," Sally Swart told Adam Cooper. "I don't remember anyone saying anything memorable – we were just having a jolly time." The following day, everything changed.

Though Ickx led initially, Jochen swept majestically past the Ferrari going into Tarzan corner after two laps and thereafter owned the race. Ickx lost time with a puncture, finishing third behind Stewart. Jacky set fastest lap in his recovery, but the truth is that once he got into the lead Jochen never remotely had to extend the 72. But even before the race was over the drivers knew that another tragedy had befallen one of their brothers. Courage had been battling for seventh place with Jochen's team-mate John Miles when his de Tomaso left the road on the 23rd lap, crashed and caught fire. The Old Etonian perished in the flames.

"I saw the burning car and I saw Piers's helmet very near to it," Jochen said. "For some laps I desperately hoped that he had climbed out and thrown away his helmet, but then I realised that Piers, if he had come out, would never have put his helmet down so near to the car."

Jochen and Piers were so close that his death hit Jochen very hard. They and their wives had had so many adventures. Nina left the circuit with Sally long before Jochen took the chequered flag, and admits that she was angry with him for winning. "I rushed off immediately to see Sally," Nina said. "She was sitting in the car with Frank Williams. You knew immediately. Sally was very, very upset. She said, 'Say it's not true, say it's not true'. But I knew. I think Frank told me.

"It was odd, but I was angry that Jochen won. It was sort of, 'How *could* he win the race in which Piers was killed?' It was all just so horrific, so disgusting. I was very angry, though not really at Jochen. I was just angry at the whole thing."

Jochen's expression on the podium betrayed his own anguish, and the realisation that he had finally got his hands on a car that could take him to the world title rendered the whole weekend bitter-sweet. Yet he still had the moxie to do an interview with Heinz Pruller for Austrian television. They did it up on the roof of the pits. "That somebody is lost in this sport is nothing new," he said. "But it is bitter indeed when it happens to be your friend."

On the way to the airport Jochen discussed his future long and hard with Bernie. In the end he decided that you finished what you had begun. Perhaps, had he not won Monaco and Zandvoort, it might have been easier to stop there and then. Nina pointed out that the Tyrrell driver Johnny Servoz-Gavin had been able to do just that earlier that very season, though it would later transpire that the Frenchman had done so because he had suffered an eye injury he had tried to keep secret. Bernie said if he was minded to stop, he should do it straight away. But Jochen told them both: "If I want to keep my self-respect, I can't quit during the season".

"It was a bit of a bad time, obviously," Ecclestone said with the deliberate understatement of a racer. "I brought Sally and Nina back in the plane to London, and Jochen was just terribly upset about the whole thing. He was talking about quitting immediately afterwards, sure, but I didn't think he would ever have stopped. And he didn't."

Jochen left Zandvoort traumatised and deeply saddened. It was his third Grand Prix success and gave him 18 points to Stewart's 19 and Brabham's 15. But it was victory without joy. Pruller remembered that the first time he ever saw his friend in tears was at Piers's funeral. The tragedy triggered the toughest time in Jochen and Nina's marriage, as each coped with their own grief while spending endless hours helping Sally in her darkest hours.

"I guess the thing was that Piers dying showed that it *could* happen," Nina said. "When Jimmy died Jochen

OPPOSITE *Designer Maurice Philippe (background) looks on thoughtfully as Graham Bartells, Colin Chapman, Eddie Dennis and Jochen discuss the 72's revitalised form in practice at Zandvoort.* (LAT)

was shattered. But I sort of pushed it away. I told myself it was a fluke, it couldn't happen to Jochen. I was brought up with racing because of my father, and I never regarded it as dangerous. When you are a young person, you just push danger away, don't you? Or you couldn't survive.

"When it was Piers, when I saw Sally and the kids, I realised that it was really serious. We took her home in Bernie's plane, and then Jochen and I stayed with Bernie and Kwana at his place. I completely collapsed when we got there. Jochen was angry with me. 'You have to come down for dinner!' But I just lay there. How could anyone care about dinner?"

Meanwhile, a thought kept tormenting Jochen. At Christmas they had spent time with the Courages skiing in Zurs, together with a friend called Ernst Moosbrucker, who was the nephew of the people who ran the hotel and whom they'd met when skiing there previously. "He was such a nice young man, and he died very quickly of cancer," Nina said.

Now Jochen would wonder, over and again, "Is it better to die the way Ernst did, or to die instantly, like Piers?" "It was awful," Nina said. "Jochen would ask that question, and he thought perhaps it was better to go like Piers. We lost all three of them that year…"

Piers's death was the most traumatic thing Jochen had ever had to face in his young life. "He was hit hard by Jimmy's death," Nina said. "We'd spent a lot of time with him in Paris, a lot of time. Jimmy was a great guy, but stingy! Jochen was completely shattered then because that was the first time for him… But, yes, Piers was more traumatic for him, emotionally worse, because they were *such* close friends."

And it set Jochen worrying that he might be the next green bottle to fall from the wall. "He was always worried about the car, especially the brakes. He was always fighting with Colin, every race. He kept asking him to build the car stronger."

The Thursday of that bloody week after Zandvoort they journeyed to England, to see Piers laid to rest in the Chapel of St Mary the Virgin, in Shenfield. Later that sad day they flew to Rouen with Jack Brabham, for a Formula Two race. Nina remembered that flight to France, the terrible strain. "We were all dressed in black, and I went and changed into jeans."

The men at least had the distraction and the adrenalin rush of driving again during practice, of losing themselves for a time in what they were there to do, what they were so good at. Nina had no such distraction, any more than the other wives or girlfriends did. All they had to do was to sit, and to worry. And try to forget what *could* happen. What *had* happened.

"It was so awful. I was sick to my stomach. I didn't want to move, I didn't want to go anywhere. It was terrible. I just sat in the car and read my book."

And then something extraordinary happened, which darkened Nina's mood further, if that was possible. "Jean-Pierre Beltoise came and sat next to me. I have never forgotten what he said. It was so stupid. For some reason he reminded me that Jochen had won that race in Zandvoort, and that there had been the smell of burning every lap they drove past the place where Piers had crashed. Beltoise had been through an awful lot of

hardships in his own career, but what on earth possessed him to say such a thing to me that day?"

She was 26 years old, bereft, scared witless for the safety of her husband. Totally lost. And, as if her worst feelings needed to be compounded, two upcoming young Frenchmen, Jean-Luc Salamon (who was due to drive alongside Jochen in a third Lotus in the French Grand Prix) and Denis Dayan, were killed in separate

BELOW *Despite their rapprochement in Germany the previous year, and the stunning form of the redesigned Lotus 72 at Zandvoort, Jochen and Chapman continued to have their differences.* (LAT)

accidents in the Formula Three race that supported the main event.

Jochen was second in his heat, having qualified only fourth. And as the weekend progressed it became apparent that he had little taste for racing. Initially he ran strongly in the final, third behind the duelling Jo Siffert and Henri Pescarolo, in BMW and Matra respectively, but gradually he fell back and after rookie Ronnie Peterson made an error that cost him his first F2 victory for March, Siffert won from Regazzoni and Fittipaldi. Jochen finished a lacklustre ninth, just ahead of Peter Westbury.

Better things came a week later in France, however, where his F1 luck continued and his spirits were better. He was pleased to find that he suffered much less nausea than he had in 1969 as he slid the 72 to its second consecutive victory after qualifying sixth behind polesitter Ickx, local hero Beltoise, Amon, Stewart and Brabham. But there had been a nasty incident in practice shortly after he had swapped his full-face Bell helmet for his trusty open-face headgear. In an unpleasant preview to what would befall his friend Helmut Marko there two years later, he was hit on the right cheek by one of the numerous trackside stones. He was pressing on in second gear at the time and was lucky not to suffer concussion from the impact, and the stone opened a nasty cut and loosened a couple of teeth. That evening Alex Soler-Roig took him down to the Grand Prix Medical Unit. The 39-year-old Spaniard had studied surgery for four years with his illustrious father, before going racing, and neatly put in three stitches to help the wound heal.

Ickx and Beltoise surged into a private duel for victory the moment the race began, but Jochen was content to take things easy to avoid nausea. Ickx lasted 16 laps before his engine failed, whereupon Beltoise was set to grab the honours in front of his countrymen until he was slowed first by a puncture and later by fuel starvation. Jochen had earlier got the jump on Amon and controlled the margin to the flag to head the March home by just under eight seconds.

He could barely put a wheel wrong, and now he had an eight-point lead over Stewart in the World Championship, 27 to 19, with Brabham matching the Scot's tally. The luck was running his way. He hardly dared to believe it.

It continued to hold at Brands Hatch for the British Grand Prix later in July, when yet again Jack Brabham was unfortunate. Jochen and Jack shared pole position in 1m 24.8s, with Ickx taking the final front row slot on 1m 25.1s ahead of Oliver and Hulme. After the first practice session Jochen had made good after his bitter comments at the International Trophy at Silverstone, when he told his crew: "It's absolutely perfect! Don't touch the car, don't alter anything, it's bloody marvellous!"

Jack led initially until Ickx squeezed by at Druids. But going into Paddock Bend at the start of the seventh lap the Ferrari suddenly slowed with a broken differential. As Jack moved out to go around him Jochen seized his chance and squeaked down the inside of the BT33 in a beautiful move that left a cigarette paper's width between the Brabham's and the Lotus's rear wheels. No wonder Jack so loved dicing with Jochen! So now Jochen had the lead and seemed set for his third win on the trot. But Jack stayed with him all the way, and for the next 62 laps never gave him a moment's peace in a duel that evoked memories of the 1966 Motor Show 200. Whenever the vagaries of traffic separated them, it was noticeable that the Australian could close the gap at will as his Goodyears worked better than Jochen's Firestones on the increasingly greasy surface, and the *coup de grâce* came as he swept into the lead again on the 69th of the 80 laps when Jochen missed a shift. Within four laps Jack had streaked away to the tune of two and a half seconds a lap, and he began his last 13.3s seconds clear of the man who had vanquished him at Monaco. But...

Jack had been aware all through that his engine was running rich, and knew that this meant that one of his mechanics had omitted to return the fuel mixture to its normal position after richening it while the engine was being warmed up before the race. This time he was two corners from the flag when drama struck, as the BT33 sputtered and ran out of fuel.

For many years he would mentally berate the unfortunate Ron Dennis, who had switched to working on Jack's cars when Jochen left at the end of 1968. Subsequently, however, Nick Goozee, who had helped Jochen at Mallory Park and Crystal Palace back in 1964, put his hand up to the error that cost the boss yet another win as Jochen swept to the line more than half a minute ahead and Jack rolled silently across in second place. He nearly didn't lose, however.

After the traditional victory parade lap with the winning car on the back of a trailer, it was discovered in post-race scrutineering that the Lotus's rear wing support stays were bent and chief mechanic Dick Scammell was told to straighten them. He refused to do so without first consulting Chapman, and the car was promptly disqualified by autocratic Clerk of the Course Dean Delamont of the RAC. Chapman appealed immediately, and once the stays had been judiciously straightened and refitted, in all of their possible positions, the wing was found to be of legal height from the measurement plane.

OPPOSITE *In practice at Brands Hatch for the British GP, Jochen shared pole position with his old friend Jack Brabham. Here he leads the man who would inherit his mantle in F1 and F2: rookie Ronnie Peterson. (LAT)*

"The wing *was* too high," Herbie Blash said. "We got the car in the transporter and we knew it was too high. They had two stays supporting it at the back and we had to lean on these stays and push the wing down, like we'd done on the victory trailer. Chapman was there urging us to do it. The only problem was we leaned too hard and the stays buckled and dropped the wing something like six inches! While that was going on, waiting to see if we'd won or not, I remember Jochen was sitting with Twiggy – she and Justin de Villeneuve were mates of Bernie's."

Three and a half hours later, the RAC finally confirmed that the Lotus conformed to the rules. "When it was announced that he'd won Jochen was just delighted!" Blash said. It transpired in later years that Chapman had deliberately raised the wing almost half an inch because it made the car handle better, and that the mechanics, knowing this, had taken it upon themselves to lean on the wing to help out after the race.

In an amusing aside, Scammell remembered that when the officials weighed the car afterwards they failed completely to see that he had inadvertently left his brief case in the cockpit... Afterwards, Jochen said to Pruller as they sat in the Lotus caravan: "My luck now really starts worrying me. I know how fast good luck can turn back on you, bringing bad luck with it. And I have had some good fortune during this summer."

The Trophées de France Formula Two race at Paul Ricard brought none. He qualified only ninth as several Cosworth runners encountered weak engines. He was bouncing the 69 over kerbs trying to make up places in the race, but never got higher than seventh before the treatment damaged the fuel tank and he dropped out as the cockpit filled with petrol. Regazzoni won from Schenken and Cevert.

The German Grand Prix had moved late to Hockenheim that August as the drivers unanimously decided to boycott the Nürburgring while modifications were made, and now the Ferraris were really beginning to hit their stride. Jacky Ickx put his on pole with a lap of 59.5s, with rookie team-mate Clay Regazzoni third on 59.8s. Jochen's 59.7s split them and left him alongside the Belgian on the front row of the two-by-two grid. Hockenheim was a pressure cooker, with a huge crowd there to cheer on their German-born champion-in-waiting. Going into the race Jochen had 36 points to Jack's 25, Jackie's 19, Denny's 16, Chris's 14 and Pedro's 10. Jacky seemed out of it completely, with just four.

LEFT *Yet again the luck ran with Jochen during the race. As Ickx's Ferrari retired suddenly at Paddock Bend, Jochen took the lead from Brabham, lost it after 69 laps, and regained it when Jack faltered on the last lap.* (LAT)

Regazzoni got away first, with Amon, Ickx and Beltoise pushing ahead of the Lotus going into the tight first right-hander. But Jochen got the Matra before the first chicane, as Ickx passed Amon. Jochen did the March by the second chicane, so as the crowd cheered them to the echo as they entered the stadium for the first time, it was Ickx, Rindt, Regazzoni.

A classic duel ensued: Ickx led laps one to six; Jochen seven to nine; Ickx 10 to 21; Regazzoni 22 and 23; Jochen 24 and 25; Ickx 26 to 31; Jochen 32 to 35; Ickx 36 to 43; Jochen 44; Ickx 45 and 46; Jochen 47; Ickx 48; then Jochen 49 to 50. He got those last two laps perfectly right and led Ickx across the line by seven controlled tenths of a second. He played down his part in the result, giving all the credit to Chapman's once

BELOW *Chased by a lapped Peterson, Jochen takes the chequered flag for the fourth time overall and the third successively in 1970, while out of shot Jack Brabham trails home a distant second, out of fuel.* (LAT)

unloved wondercar. "A monkey could have won in my car," he said. "Thank you Colin."

He didn't like Ickx, and privately took great pleasure in beating him, but on the podium he offered him the champagne-filled trophy to sup from. "Jochen was a great character," Ickx said in 2008. "Like Jackie Stewart, one of the first real professionals entering in a new era. They were both turning the page of the Sixties with all the philosophy about racing, security, sponsoring, the basic idea to make money out of racing and not only being a sport or chivalry from the old times. They were going on very well, I must say."

And he fondly remembered his duel that day with Jochen. "At the time the cars were not really suffering from aerodynamic turbulence when you were behind another. Back then the focus was on maximum speed, but downforce was important in those early days, the wings were there to stabilise and stop the cars lifting. Hockenheim was based then on slipstreaming, so it was easy to overtake. The idea back then to touch the wheels and all these things was hardly acceptable, because if

you had any kind of problem like that…" He mimed running over another car's wheels and taking off… "If you go up… you never know which shape you were coming back on the asphalt. So when you were on a race course like Hockenheim you had to give a sign to the other where you are expecting to come. And after 50 laps together you know where he is going to pass. Look on your right… Look on your left… And then you know. Basically it was a gentleman's approach of racing. Changing your line to make sure they don't overtake you, these things were not existing at the time."

Formula One writer Gregor Messer remembers that race like it was yesterday. "August 2 1970 – that was when I went to my first Grand Prix. I grew up in a bad area of Wiesbaden, near a place for homeless women, a slaughterhouse and a scrapyard, and there was a petrol station nearby which had posters for the races. There was a poster for the German Grand Prix at the Nürburgring. Then three weeks before the race the poster changed: the German Grand Prix at *Hockenheim*. There had been a change of venue.

"I had been to the Nations Cup Formula 5000 race at Hockenheim with my brother Thomas the previous year, so we knew the distance from where we lived. I was 10, Thomas was 12. It was a very hot summer and when our dad came home, tired from work, we were on our knees begging him to take us to Hockenheim to see this race. We had tears in our eyes! He agreed, and straight away our mother started boiling eggs and making us wienerschnitzel to take the next day!

"I had just started reading newspapers, and remembered the day early in June when Bruce McLaren was killed. I remember feeling shocked. Now I read about Jochen Rindt, who had been born in Mainz, which was not even five kilometres from our home! He became our instant hero!

BELOW *Jochen had a succession of Lotus road cars, including this Elan presented to him by Chapman at Hockenheim in 1970. Its predecessor famously lost a door en route to Clermont-Ferrand in 1969.* (LAT)

"Race day was amazingly hot and we arrived late so we didn't even see the supporting races. We ate our eggs and wienerschnitzel and then took our seats in the grandstand. Because we'd got there so late we weren't even sitting together, but that didn't matter. We were in a stand on the outside of the left-hander that followed the right-hander that brought the cars back into the stadium at the end of the lap. We couldn't see the cars coming down the straight leading into the stadium, but we could hear them.

"The 50 laps were full of tension, with Jochen fighting Jacky Ickx, and Clay Regazzoni and Chris Amon also in there for a while. It was a real race. When it was over we were really glad that Jochen – *our hero!* – had won.

"Then a friend suggested we go to the paddock, which was just behind our grandstand. I didn't even know what the paddock was. And there was this huge crowd around the Gold Leaf Team Lotus truck. Jochen was still in his overalls, with a cigarette dangling from his lips, wearing sunglasses. He had a lot of patience and was sitting in the cab of the truck signing autograph after autograph while answering Pruller's questions. I still have the picture on the page that my brother tore from the programme, which we got Jochen to sign. There were two big photos in it, one of Jochen and one of Jackie Stewart. After we'd got Jochen's autograph my brother forged Jackie's on the other photo!

"After that great day I never missed watching a Grand Prix, it ignited my passion for racing. I started to buy the monthly magazine *Sport Auto*, by collecting glass bottles to get back the deposit on them until I had the three Deutschemarks I needed. Then that Christmas my aunt Gertrud bought me a subscription."

Jochen's custom was to give his laurel to the mechanics. Beaky Sims took it and laid it at the spot where Jimmy had perished. Jochen would have appreciated that, no question.

So now he had 45 points to Brabham's 25, Hulme's 20 and Stewart's 19. Nobody could ever have known it that day, but Jochen had scored the final World Championship points of his life. Had done enough to secure the title. Normally he was a happy-go-lucky individual, but the wing failures of 1969, and the deaths of Gerhard Mitter at the Nürburgring that year and sportscar racer Hans Laine there in 1970, and of McLaren and, especially, Courage, weighed heavily upon him. It was almost as if he felt that he was living on borrowed time.

Chris Amon recalled a conversation he'd had with Jochen shortly after Zandvoort, when the immediate pain of Piers Courage's death had yet to start receding. "We had lunch in London and he told me he wanted to stop. He was frightened of the Lotus's fragility. A month later he'd won some more Grands Prix, he was going to

win the title, and he told me he'd decided to do one more year."

Dan Gurney was himself feeling lonely and isolated, driving for McLaren alongside Denny in the terrible aftermath of Bruce's death and contemplating his own future in a sport in which he'd lost too many friends. He'd finished sixth in the French Grand Prix but dropped out of the British with an overheating engine. He and his wife had also talked to Jochen after Zandvoort, when the Austrian had suggested to them that he could be the next one.

"I remember Evi and I were talking to him about Lotus," Dan said. "He said it was so easy to win races like this, that he was going to hang in there even though the cars were an unknown entity as far as reliability was concerned, and that if he made it to win the World Championship he was going to retire and concentrate on his other businesses."

And there was no respite at home, either. Jochen and Nina continued to argue, surrounded by pressures on their marriage. She had spent a lot of the summer with Sally Courage, looking after her, and inevitably it all weighed heavily on a young wife who had now seen, in the most brutal detail imaginable, just what could happen on the race track.

There was even talk that Jochen had promised her £10,000 (the equivalent of £115,000 today) if he should keep racing in 1971. "That wasn't really true," Nina disclosed. "But I desperately wanted him to stop, and I told him that Johnny Servoz-Gavin had stopped mid-season. I told him that if he didn't stop I would go home, and take Natasha with me. That I would still come and see him now and then. That I would come back when he stopped racing. It was blackmail, of course.

"And he looked at me and said, 'If you really love me, you won't do that'. And of course, I didn't leave. I understood that he didn't want to stop. But at least I thought I could try to persuade him. It was always so difficult for the women. If you made the men stop doing what they loved doing, they would always hold that against you… Jochen told me, 'I need you'. And I stayed. He didn't have to promise me money. My father loved racing, and I remember that my mother always wanted

him to stop and that I used to think she was very silly... You learn as you grow older."

Sally visited the Rindts regularly, and told Adam Cooper of her final trip in Jochen's lifetime. "When I said goodbye I looked at him, and he looked so sad. He could hardly say goodbye. And I thought, 'I'm never going to see you again'. Then I thought I was just being silly."

Michael Argetsinger went to the Osterreichring that year, for the Austrian Grand Prix in the middle of August, but had only a brief chat with Jochen. "It wasn't a conversation that lent itself to any kind of depth. We did not touch on the subject of Bruce or Piers, for example, but it was not a situation where we would have. Jochen was under a lot of pressure and demands on his time that weekend. It was his home Grand Prix, and he'd won the four previous Grands Prix and everyone wanted a piece of him. We talked for maybe ten minutes in the paddock and it wasn't a private environment. He asked if I would be at Monza and I told him no. We agreed to spend some time together at Watkins Glen.

"I do remember what he said when I told him I had driven down from Bremen in my Lotus Europa. 'I assume you brought a mechanic along,' he said. It was a typically funny and insightful Jochen thing to say and, of course – also typically – it had an edge to it." It was their last conversation.

Jochen almost welcomed the return of adversity at the Osterreichring, which was to host the Austrian Grand Prix for the first time, as if he felt that he had ridden his luck too far. If Hockenheim had been a pressure cooker, it was nothing compared to Osterreichring where *everybody* wanted to talk to their champion-elect. His face was everywhere, and Heinz Pruller interviewed both him and Jackie together.

The Ferraris were in their element on the majestic track's fast sweeps, and Regazzoni was fastest in two of the three practice sessions. But to the delight of the locals Jochen topped the timesheets in the second with 1m 39.23s which beat the Swiss to pole position by half a second. Ickx and Stewart were third and fourth, chased by Giunti and Amon, Beltoise and Brabham.

At the start Regazzoni got the jump from Ickx, Amon, Jochen and Giunti. Jochen soon passed Chris. Then he began to catch the Ferraris quite easily, and looked a good bet for victory as Ickx swept by Regga into the lead when the Ferrari rookie got sideways on oil from Francois Cevert's engine which had blown on the

LEFT *The Ferraris of Regazzoni and Ickx beat Jochen away at the start in Austria and finished in a reverse order 1-2. Jochen was superstitiously pleased that a broken engine ended his spate of good luck.* (Toni Temburg)

first lap. Then JPB came up on the Lotus's tail, and after Jochen had slowed for the oil flags the Frenchman slipped ahead followed by Giunti and Amon. Now the leaders had split into two groups of three – Ickx, Regazzoni, Beltoise, then, further back, Giunti, Amon and Jochen, who repassed the works March on lap six. He began to stage a recovery, pushing back past Giunti four laps later. But he'd kept the engine with which he'd run at Hockenheim, and he was still six seconds adrift of the top trio when that gamble failed and, on lap 22, the Cosworth DFV broke. Ickx won.

Perhaps confirming that he was almost relieved to have been the beneficiary of bad luck again, and that the failure was a sop to the gods who had been smiling on him almost since Monaco, he was in good spirits as he headed back to the pits and lit up the inevitable cigarette. He did not seem remotely upset as he smiled at his journalistic friends Pruller and Zwickl, and cheerfully informed them: "Motor kaput!"

Chapman watched all this with an almost paternal expression, clad, like Nina, in a Jochen Rindt tee-shirt. Later, as Jochen stood atop the pits, the crowd screamed themselves hoarse chanting his name as he reached down and signed autographs.

He retained 45 points, Brabham had 25, Hulme 20 and Stewart 19, and the man on the move was Ickx, now with an equal score to the Scot's. But Jochen was so far ahead that he could afford to feel relaxed about the situation. He might not be home and dry, but he could see the promised land ahead and it was no mirage. He might have retired from the race, but he was almost at the top of the world. One more victory, at Monza, could cement the title.

But first there was one more non-championship race to run, the Gold Cup at Oulton Park. It took the form of two 20-lap heats, with the result to be aggregated. John Surtees took pole position comfortably in his eponymous new Surtees TS7, from Jackie Oliver's Yardley BRM and Frank Gardner's F5000 Lola T190 after rain had disrupted both Friday sessions of practice. Jochen didn't get out in time and was stuck down in tenth, while the other point of interest was Stewart's decision to forego fifth place on the grid in his regular March 701 to start from the back of the grid in Ken Tyrrell's hitherto top secret new Tyrrell 001.

Surtees won the first heat quite easily from Oliver, with Jochen third after regretting a change of top gear ratio that limited his straightline speed. Surtees finished 6.6s ahead of the BRM, and 12.8s ahead of the

LEFT *In his last-ever Formula 1 race, Jochen took the Lotus 72 to second place behind John Surtees in his eponymous TS7, before departing post-haste to the International Stainzer Bergrennen in Austria.* (Nick Loudon)

Lotus, as Stewart set fastest lap after a pit stop to cure a stuck throttle.

Jochen made no mistake about the second heat, which he won after fighting his way first past the Surtees and then the BRM. Surtees later also passed Oliver, and Jochen could only open a gap of 9.4s on the little red car, leaving Big John the winner on aggregate over him by 3.4s.

Immediately after getting out of the car Jochen hightailed it to a waiting helicopter en route to Vienna, after parking the Lotus at Old Hall and grabbing his case from a marshal's post. He had driven his last Formula One race, taken his final F1 chequered flag, though there was still the Formula Two race at Salzburgring upcoming.

He had prevaricated all season about possible retirement. But in August 1970 as he realised that, barring disaster, he was going to be crowned World Champion, the business side of his mentality kicked in. And he *had* changed his mind. That weekend at Oulton Park, August 22, Frances Scammell remembered sitting in his car as they chatted while keeping out of the rain during practice. Given the timing of what Jochen told her at that moment, it was a definitive expression of his intentions for the future.

"He was such a gentleman, and such a gentleman to *me*, really," she said. "There were a lot of drivers where a mechanic's wife wasn't far enough up the tree, whereas Jochen was always very polite. If he'd got his car there he'd always say, 'Oh, come and sit in the warm'. Because there was nowhere to sit in those days, it was either the transporter or whatever cars were around.

"If you just looked at him he could give the impression, very much, of being arrogant. But in my experience he wasn't. Jochen was always very straight with me, and so was Mario. "Jochen and I sat in his car that weekend and he said that he would only do one more year of racing when he was World Champion, and that would be it. But that he would have to do that last year because he would make so much money out of it. It was a financial decision that he would do that. I don't think he ever intended to make old bones in motor racing…"

Jochen had hightailed out of Oulton because he had to get back to Vienna by Sunday for the fifth International Stainzer Bergrennen at Stainz, not far away. He was to be paid 20,000 schillings (around £3,000 then, the equivalent of £35,000 today) to run the Jochen Rindt Racing Lotus 69 in this popular hill-climb event. He cut a hugely popular figure, in shades and tassled Davy Crockett jacket, but in the wet conditions he lost out to Austrian privateer Klaus Riesch's more powerful Alfa Romeo T33 sportscar.

The spectators once again turned out in their droves to fête their hero at the Preis von Salzburg at the Salzburgring, where the indefatigable organiser Willy Lowinger promised him 200,000 schillings start money (£30,000 then, around £350,000 today), considerably more than his rivals.

The crowd was to witness one of Jochen's finest drives, on a weekend when the luck ran against him. Things began to go wrong in practice. The BMWs of Ickx, Siffert and Dieter Quester were fastest in the morning session, the Belgian's 1m 15.0s in the car with a new, more powerful engine eclipsing his team-mates by half a second. Jochen managed 1m 16.2s which was fifth fastest. In the afternoon, however, as Tino Brambilla brought his Brabham up to equal fastest with Ickx on 1m 14.2s, a tenth ahead of Siffert, Jochen's car again filled its cockpit with fuel due to a lose union, and he lost the session while things were sorted out. That left him ninth on the 19-car grid, but to the intense consternation of the organisers, who had seen 30,000 people flock into the track, he ground to a halt on the grid lap with what mechanic Terry Day quickly identified as a blown head gasket. To keep the punters happy Jochen made a staged start from the back of the grid, which predictably lasted only as long as it took him to creep into the paddock for an engine change. A frenetic race was won by Ickx from Brambilla's brother Vittorio and Fittipaldi.

While that was going on there was another race taking place in the paddock as mechanics, including Jochen himself, worked feverishly to change his FVA. It was not a quick job at the best of times, and the Lotus 69's rear-mounted oil tank made it trickier still, but with help from the organisers, who delayed the second start, they got it done and the national hero started from the back of the grid once more. Since the race result was to be the aggregate of two heats Jochen had no chance of overall victory, but he went out in the second determined to entertain the crowd.

As Quester led the first lap, Jochen made spectacular progress; fourth on the opening lap, he was leading by the second. The crowd went crazy. His new engine was a really strong one, and even the BMWs were struggling to stay with the dark green Lotus despite the Brambilla brothers' best efforts to gang up on it. Halfway round lap 22, with three to run, it nearly all fell apart for Jochen as the leaders came up to lap backmarker Giancarlo Gagliardi whose Jolly Club Brabham was being pressured by local boy Hans Binder's Tecno. Ickx and Tino Brambilla were able to get around them, but as he saw the leaders come by Gagliardi moved over, right into Jochen's path. Jochen kept his foot in it and still went around him, losing places to Quester, Vittorio Brambilla and Graham Hill in the second Jochen Rindt Racing Lotus.

The incident was the cue for another of Jochen's unique demonstrations of the art of slipstreaming, for which he had become so famed. Clinically he picked off Vittorio B, Quester, Hill and Ickx on the penultimate lap, so that only Tino B remained. And he dealt with him with disdain on the final lap to take the last chequered flag of his life seven-tenths ahead of the Italian.

As Ickx won overall from Vittorio B and Quester, Jochen was classified only 13th overall. But it will stand for all time that in his last-ever race he won in the finest, bravest style against all the odds and shattered the lap record, after a drive that left his rivals gasping. If epitaph there had to be, that was the best there could possibly have been. His eyes shining, Jochen had demanded of Mike Doodson after that final victory: "Well, what did you think of that, then?"

But this was also race in which Doodson witnessed something altogether extraordinary. "There was a huge crowd which had come to see him win the race. I don't know why, but Jochen had a thing about Jacky Ickx." Doodson is adamant that he watched Jochen cutting Ickx up mercilessly in the second heat, in a manner that seems completely out of character and the way in which other competitors described his immaculate driving ethics. "Jochen actually tried to push Ickx off the track. I saw it. It was childish, and the Salzburgring was a flat-out track. I don't think there was a corner in anything less than fifth gear there and it was narrow, with barriers on either side. It was that weekend that I actually asked him what was wrong with Jacky, because of what I'd seen him do to him. 'I just don't know,' Jochen said. 'He's a little **** with big balls!' That's how he described him."

Writer Gerhard Kuntschik recalled another important event at the track, which received little publicity. "That weekend was when Jochen and Manfred Kessler set up the CDSF, the club of the Salzburgring track marshals. It was something he believed in passionately." He also remembered that Lowinger could only pay Jochen a portion of his earnings straight away, with the rest to come later. "Jochen told him that was no problem. It was typical of him to be that way with a man he trusted. Willy was always familiar and called him Jochen, but Jochen was deferential and would always call him Mr Race Director…"

Helmut Marko also had cause to remember that weekend. "Of course, Jochen and I kept in touch, and I was at that race. We had some discussions because he wanted to do his Formula Two team again in 1971, together with Ecclestone. The other driver was Emerson and I was supposed to be involved as well. He had already developed a very, very good business sense.

"The strange thing was that Jochen never was scared. He was the one, you know, that kept his foot down. But we had a long conversation and for the first time he was really worried. He said he wanted to stop, he didn't trust Chapman any more. He was *scared*,

something I had never seen with him before, not even really at Indy.

"Then Chapman came around him with all his talk of his fantastic new car for 1971, four-wheel-drive, the turbine engine… Just half throttle and you are winning everything. Of course one reason was to cash in, but what really made him thinking was this new type of car, because it looked so revolutionary. And that made Jochen consider to continue racing the next year. But… he just didn't believe in Colin like he would have done two years ago."

There was another factor, too. Jochen was once again considering going it alone, with Bernie. "We would have done our own thing," Ecclestone insists. "Probably it would have been Jochen Rindt Racing, revived around something else. In those days it was easier and quicker to do things, as March showed, even if we had bought cars." He says that they never got as far as discussing a possible purchase with anyone, or talking with potential designers. "Because we knew full well that if we wanted to, we could do it." So Jochen could have 'done a Fittipaldi', five years before Emerson quit McLaren for his own set-up at the end of 1975. And yet…

In 2010 Roy Winkelmann revealed an extraordinary story. And it had nothing to do with Formula One. "I did Jochen's business management, and he was going to quit F1 at the end of 1970 if he was World Champion," he insisted. And then came his bombshell. "And we had gone to Daytona together to see Bill France to talk about Jochen doing NASCAR in 1971. We negotiated a huge deal with the Ford team. He didn't think he'd been paid enough for the risks he had to take in F1, and teams such as Richard Petty's could pull in big money in those days. Up to a million dollars. And he wanted some of it."

Winkelmann was adamant that it was going to happen, notwithstanding Jochen's comments to Bernie after his experiences at Rockingham in 1967. Bernie remembered them clearly, only days before Winkelmann told his story. "He used to ring me up when he was away, and after driving in practice in Rockingham he said: 'These guys are bloody mad, they've got their door handles under mine. They're crazy!' He wasn't very excited by that experience. He thought they [the cars] were terrible, he didn't like it at all! He was a pure open-wheeler guy."

"Believe me," Winkelmann insisted, "the deal was cut to go NASCAR. I went with him to see Bill, and he stayed in my house in Sarasota. It was going to be NASCAR after he'd become World Champion. That was the plan."

Neither Bernie nor Nina knew anything about that, but in any case it was academic. Monza was next on the calendar, and there was still a World Championship to win. And there Jochen's dramatic story came to its end.

CHAPTER 19

So near, yet so far

Monza, 4/5 September 1970

"I feel wonderful."

Jochen Rindt

LEFT *Monza, Friday September 3, 1970.* (LAT)

Jochen had just turned 28 and was so close to realising his dream of winning the World Championship that, as he checked into the Hotel de la Ville in Monza, opposite the Villa Real, he could almost touch the World Champion's trophy. The Ferraris were hitting their stride and, particularly at such a fast track, their flat-12 engines' horsepower advantage over the Ford Cosworth V8s would be more pronounced. But he knew that he no longer had to win. He held the view that he had ridden his streak of luck for all it was worth, and he was now ready to drive for podium places where necessary. He had a 20-point advantage over his closest challenger and the odds were totally in his favour so long as he just kept scoring points in the remaining four races and none of them really got a run going.

He was no longer threshing over the dilemma whether to retire at the end of the season, or to exploit the success as champion for another year, either. That decision had pretty much been made. Racing for a season as the World Champion made a lot of financial sense, and he was feeling more relaxed than he had been now that he had acknowledged that to himself. Even if he wasn't sure whether he'd be driving for Team Lotus, his own set-up or anything else.

On the way to the track that Friday morning, as he drove down in his BMW 2800 from Begnins with Nina and Bernie, he told her the news she dreaded. "He said, 'I can't stop. I want to go on. If I win the World Championship, I want to go on; this is the time I can make the big money'."

There were two practice sessions on Friday, and drama befell the Team Lotus squad in the afternoon's. For the first time that season Chapman intended to run three 72s. But Nina says there was a story even behind that. "Jochen initially said he wanted to drive the 49 at Monza. That he didn't think the 72 was safe there," she revealed. "Colin just said, 'Yeah, yeah,' and when we got there, there were only the three 72s. Colin made it clear it was drive the 72, or don't drive at all. It was like blackmail."

Jochen was expected to race the latest chassis, 72/5, which had just been completed and would be shaken down that day by Brazilian rookie Emerson Fittipaldi before he switched for the remainder of the weekend to chassis 72/2, which Jochen had used since Zandvoort. John Miles would drive his regular car, 72/1.

"Monza was the first time I was driving the 72," Emerson said reflectively. "Colin asked me to do a few laps in 72/5, it was brand new, on the Friday. Make sure all the systems were working. Jochen was going to drive that car on Saturday and Sunday. And then I destroyed it…" Years after the event he still sounded utterly crestfallen about the mistake that he made on the approach to the Parabolica, one day before Jochen's fatal crash there.

"I was watching the mirrors because I was not going fast. I mean, I was going fast on the straight but I was backing off very early for the corners. Not pushing at all. Just doing those few laps to scrub in the car. I looked in the mirror and Jack Brabham was coming up on me fast. That was my last good view. The next one was the back of Ignazio Giunti's Ferrari when I looked ahead again. He had overtaken me earlier and there was his car right in front of me at Parabolica and no way could I avoid it.

"I was 100 metres deeper into the corner than I should have been. We were running without wings, looking for better straight-line speed. I just locked up and hit Giunti. I had to be honest, and say that I just screwed up.

"I went over the Ferrari, over the bank, and then landed on a nice strong tree outside of the track! I had two high risks. One was to survive and the next one was to face Colin after going back to the pits. I survived the first one, and in the second one he nearly killed me. 'Emerson, what happened? You destroyed my brand new 72!' I say, 'Well, Colin, I misjudged it. I look in the mirror and I was 100 metres deeper in the braking than I should be, and that's it'. Lack of experience…"

Such are the vagaries of fate. But for that rookie driver's moment of inattention, Emerson would have been driving Lotus 72/2 instead of Jochen the following afternoon. It was a chilling thought that the Brazilian preferred not to dwell upon.

While this was going on, Jochen and John were lapping in the other 72s. Jochen had the idea of trying his without the wings, having run his 49 naked in the previous year's race when Stewart had beaten him so narrowly to the chequered flag. "I remember taking the wings off the car," chief mechanic Dick Scammell said. "I think Jochen sort of started with that idea and Colin carried it on. I don't think the cars were particularly nice to drive like that. John hated his that way. I think you had to be the sort of person who could take it by the scruff of the neck and live with the situation, because it made it quicker."

"I think it was one of those things that happened, and it wasn't a decision," Ecclestone thought. "Sort of shall we, shan't we, maybe we could, maybe we couldn't, shall we try without them, whatever. That's the sort of thing that happened. I think generally it was felt it would be better to run without them."

Jochen reported that he picked up another 800rpm without the drag of the rear wing, and that was enough to convince Chapman it was the way to go, regardless of

OPPOSITE *On the Friday at Monza, the atmosphere was relatively calm as teams began to ready themselves for the first practice sessions, blissfully unaware of what the next day would bring.* (Grand Prix Photo)

how evil it made the handling. There had never been any question about the size of Jochen's cojones, notwithstanding that he had admitted being scared to Marko at the Salzburgring. If taking the wings off made the car twitchy but quicker, he'd give it a go.

John Miles admits that his confidence had been shot to hell by a front brakeshaft failure in Austria, and he was unhappy when Chapman insisted that he drive his 72 without wings when he thought it better to run with the front wings trimmed out and the middle plane of the rear removed to reduce drag. "One lap was enough to convince me that my car was undriveable," he wrote. "It snapped into oversteer at the slightest provocation."

Ecclestone says he doesn't remember whether Jochen mentioned the car's behaviour to him, but that it looked a handful when you watched it. But he stressed the point: "It wasn't spooky for *him*."

That afternoon, Nina recalled to Heinz Pruller something unusual that her husband said during the session. "Jochen turned to me, apropos nothing in particular, and said: 'I feel wonderful, Nina.' He had never previously said anything like that before a race. He felt wonderful and I could understand why. He was just about to reach for the stars."

The following day they had a leisurely breakfast and then lunch with Jackie and Lynn Oliver at the Hotel de la Ville where, earlier that morning, Chapman had signed Emerson to drive one of his cars in 1971. Jochen and Bernie had also gone through all the formalities with the Brazilian to drive for their Formula Two team. "The other driver was still all a bit up in the air," Ecclestone reported.

"Jochen had been urging me to sign with the Lotus F3 team, so then, he said, I would eventually wind up driving for him in F2," racer Howden Ganley revealed. "However, I had just been adopted as a Bruce McLaren protégé, so I was going along with whatever Bruce wanted me to do. Which didn't include me driving for Jochen. Bruce had a guy wanted to support a young upcoming driver, so he was talking to me about a Formula 5000 season. I did that with Barry Newman financing what was really a works car."

Helmut Marko was still a possibility.

Jochen and Nina then drove to the track together, enjoying the sunshine as they went through the park. As he headed off at 2.15 to sort final details with the team prior to practice at 3.00, Nina watched him at work for a moment. She considered seeking shade in the Goodyear Pavilion, but changed her mind and headed to the pits to

get ready to time his runs. "Someone gave me a magazine and I shoved it under the lap times list, to look through later in peace and quiet," she recalled. She still missed Sally Courage, from whom she often had had to be separated when they liked to sit together lap timing on the pit roof. Their husbands insisted that they really ought to sit on their respective pit counters.

Beautifully dressed as ever, in a white lace top and broad white sun hat, she duly took up her position sitting in the Lotus garage with her stopwatch, and ate an ice cream as practice started.

The previous day the Ferraris had been as fast as expected, with Jacky Ickx lapping his in 1m 24.14s in the second of the day's sessions. Jochen wasn't really on it, and had lapped the Lotus in 1m 25.71s with clearly much more to come. But after he had suggested the idea of running without wings, Chapman took it up like a religion, and with a fresh 'super-Cosworth' motor installed the number 22 Lotus was loaded with a 205mph top gear for qualifying. Jochen and Bernie, however, weren't all that bothered about going for the pole. This would be another Monza slipstreaming epic and they could afford to start from the third or fourth row and still have an excellent chance of victory. And as Jochen had proved countless times in those Formula Two epics at Rheims, Enna-Pergusa and Hockenheim, he was the master of slipstreaming tactics. In his own environment, he missed Piers, from whom he'd got a great tow the previous year.

As the engines began to fire and warm up for the start of practice, he signed an autograph for the 14-year-old daughter of Austrian radio sports director Edi Finger, then spent a little time filming the introduction for the motorsport television show he had started doing that year for producer Lucky Schmidtleitner, telling the crew he'd reshoot after practice if the noise of the engines had spoiled it. Then he wandered down to the March pit to see his faithful Formula Two mechanic, Pete Kerr, who had joined 'Gremshek Racing' from Winkelmann Racing at the end of 1969.

Jochen would never forget anyone who had helped him, and Kerr had been a cornerstone of much of his success in F2. "As he approached me I had the impression he wanted me to be around, now that he was winning the World Championship," Kerr told Heinz Pruller. Kerr said to Jochen: "Well, you've got your title now". And Jochen replied: "You know, you can never be sure of that".

"I was near to telling him 'Be careful,'" Kerr admitted to Pruller. "I suppose I thought he might break his leg or something similar, but I couldn't quite bring myself to tell him that."

"The last words Jochen ever spoke were in English," Heinz said: "'I must go.'" Then he climbed into the cockpit of the Lotus, left foot first as was his

OPPOSITE *Colin Chapman is occupied, but Jochen makes conversation in the pits on Friday afternoon with Hazel Chapman and her two daughters prior to the start of the first official practice session.* (LAT)

unbreakable habit, and soon he was out on the track. It was warm and sunny, a perfect day to go fast.

His out lap occupied 1m 40.78s, and as he passed the pits for the first time he was nicely placed to pick up a tow from Denny Hulme's McLaren. Three more laps, during which he overtook Denny: 1m 27.59s, 1m 27.24s, and 1m 26.75s. Still warming up. The plan only really called for a fast lap, good enough for the first three or four rows of the grid, right at the end of the session. Then the red, white and gold Lotus failed to come round on its fifth lap, and eventually Hulme's orange car trickled slowly into the pits. There was widespread unease as the New Zealander headed straight for the Lotus pit, not his own.

Denny had been following Jochen down to the Parabolica, the place where Wolfgang von Trips had been killed nine years earlier, and reported that under heavy braking the Lotus had momentarily bobbed uncomfortably, left then right, before suddenly veering sharply to the left. The chisel nose dug under and slid along beneath the steel barrier and then, as it reached the next stanchion securing it, the car spun violently in an anti-clockwise direction around its own axis as its frontal acceleration was halted, tearing off the whole front end and shedding components explosively all over the track.

It was 3.35 European summer time, Frank Williams noted; exactly the same time it had been when Piers went missing from the lap charts in Zandvoort three months earlier.

Hulme took sharp avoiding action, and was very lucky not to be hit by the Lotus's left front wheel and suspension, but still struck some small pieces of debris. He told Chapman that it had been a big shunt, but that he thought Jochen was okay.

Jackie Stewart had been in the pits having an oil leak attended to on his Tyrrell March when Jochen's car went beyond his control. "I knew that something had happened. You always do. Cars started coming back into the pits. When that happens you know something is going on. Denny came in and called me over. He told me that Jochen had had a very big shunt. I immediately asked if he was okay. Whenever there was a big accident that is the first question I always asked: Is he okay? He said it looked bad, so I went to race control. They told me Jochen was out of the car. I asked *them* if he was okay, but I couldn't get a straight answer. I left the tower and was then told that Jochen had been taken to the medical centre. I had to go through a series of gates to get there and access wasn't easy, but at that time everybody knew who I was."

Jochen was out of the car, but only because he had been thrown out through the shattered front end. He hated wearing crutch straps, and though they were always installed in the Lotus he habitually refused to have them done up. "I think he just felt uncomfortable

with them, it had nothing to do with very much else," Dick Scammell said. "All you can say is that maybe if he'd had them on, he'd have stayed in the car. When the front of the car was torn out and then the car spun, and of course it spun round the engine and the heavy end of the car, very quickly, the rate it spun at was huge, and it just centrifuged him down under the belts."

That movement inflicted fatal injuries to Jochen's aorta and thorax.

When he got to the medical centre, the first thing that Jackie saw was Jochen alone and abandoned, lying prone on the back of a pick-up truck. And in that moment he *knew*. His best friend in racing was dead.

"Jochen was just lying there, on his own. I will never forget that. There was nobody else there. I could immediately see that his ankles were very badly damaged, but there was no bleeding. If there is no bleeding it means the heart is not pumping. A priest came to give him the last rites while I was still there. I walked away knowing for myself that Jochen was not coming back. Nina, Helen, Bernie and Colin went to the hospital, each at that point believing that he was still alive. In Italy they never pronounced a driver dead at the scene of an accident, otherwise they would have had to call off the event. Always they would say that they died on the way to the hospital, but I had seen Jochen's feet. I *knew*."

After the silence as the session was stopped, Nina saw Denny say something to Chapman that she didn't catch.

"What's up?" she asked.

"Nothing," Chapman responded. "Jochen's spun, that's all."

Racing cars often spun, and Nina was well aware of that. It was a driver's occupational hazard. At that moment, despite everything they had gone through that edgy summer, she didn't feel alarm. If anything, she remembered that she felt a moment of release from the task of clocking her husband's lap times. "I thought I now had a bit of time to take a break and could have a look at the magazine."

But then somebody rushed up to her and said, "I'll come with you, Nina."

"Why?" she asked. "Where?"

"They've taken Jochen to the medical centre."

Again, she asked: "Why have they done that?"

"You know the Italians, Nina. They take you to the medical centre for the slightest little scratch."

She, Chapman, Helen Stewart, Bette Hill and Lynn Oliver ran there. It seemed like thousands of people were already waiting. They met Jackie there.

OPPOSITE *As Nina (in the green hat) sits with Bette Hill in the background on the pit counter, Eddie Dennis prepares to strap Jochen in for the last time as he pulls on his helmet ready for the final battle.* (LAT)

"Where's Jochen?" Nina asked him.

"In there," Jackie replied, gesturing.

"Can I see him?"

Stewart shook his head. "No," he replied.

"Why not?"

"He's okay," Jackie said. But Nina noticed that his whole body was trembling.

"It's only a broken leg," he insisted, "nothing more than that."

"Then why can't I see him?" Nina persisted, putting him on the spot.

"I promise you," Jackie repeated, "it's nothing, absolutely nothing."

"I remember that Jackie was shaking," she said. "They wouldn't let me in the ambulance with Jochen. 'Why won't they let me go with him?'"

The people around them pressed closer, and Nina could feel them watching her as the tension mounted within her. "They were all looking at me," she remembered. "It was awful."

A priest emerged from the medical centre and she shouted, "What was a priest doing in there?"

Jackie implored her to calm down, and said that they always fetch a priest straight away in Italy. But then the priest stopped in front of her and said: "Have courage, Mrs Rindt!" She asked herself, "Why courage?"

Then they took Jochen away in the ambulance, and suddenly the memory came surging back of Piers's death at Zandvoort, "and I knew that something very bad indeed had happened. I could see that from the faces all around me."

And yet, incredibly, she was numbed rather than shocked.

"It sounds really weird, but I was less shocked by Jochen's death than I was Piers'," she admitted. "They were so close together. I wasn't surprised any more. I had lived through so much by then. The first time it was really, 'My God, it can actually happen'. You're so young, so stupid, you have this defence and you don't think about it. And I don't think Sally did, either. I was in shock, but maybe not as much as I would have been if Piers had not died."

Jabby Crombac drove Nina, Helen and Bette in his hire car to the Niguarda Clinic in Milan, but the ambulance with Jochen in it had got lost and initially headed instead to the local hospital in Monza.

"Colin was there," Nina recalled when the ambulance finally got to Milan. "Bernie went into the room, and the doctors told him what had happened. It was like people

didn't want to give me the bad news. They told Bernie, 'Don't tell her'. He said, 'What do you want me to do, tell her tomorrow, the day after?' It's funny how people react; it was like nobody wanted me to know. In the end it was Bernie who told me. He came out and approached me and said simply: 'Jochen is dead'."

Scammell recalled: "I went off to Parabolica to try and find out what went wrong and I discovered Jochen in a sort of typical Italian ambulance with all these people jumping up and down on his chest, and that was that really." And he noticed what Jackie had seen: "There was no bleeding at all… Once I saw what they were up to, I just thought to myself, 'We can forget that, can't we'."

Words on a page which, read bluntly and without context, could seem callous, something which Scammell and his genre assuredly never are. They are the technical doctors of the sport, the mechanics, dedicated to preserving lives with the preparation effected by their skilled hands and their consciences. But in such moments a coping mechanism kicks in that can often seem uncaring to outsiders unused to the fraternity to which they belong. You keep going, keep doing something, because there is nothing else you can do.

"I went back to the pits and did the only thing I knew, which was carry on. We'd had all this before with Jimmy and the accident with von Trips in 1961, which was very difficult, so now I just said to the other guys, 'Right, get this lot loaded up. Forget the car. And get to the Swiss border as quick as you possibly can, because otherwise we were all going to be in trouble'. I was especially aware that it was the same team, a second time.

"In 1961, the first time around, we all said, 'Oh dear, oh dear, oh dear,' and then it all started getting very fraught. So this time we knew not to do that any more. I know some people will think that was very hard, but it was the only way to deal with it. You had to go and get on with *something*. And whether you like it or not, life carries on. It was an awful thing, but that was the way I dealt with it, always. It gave all the mechanics something to do, too. Just put everything in the truck and let's get out of here. We weren't going to get the car."

Eventually they would retrieve the engine and gearbox after getting permission to go into one of the lock-ups at Monza to remove it. There was a story that Maurice Philippe disguised himself as a mechanic so he could at least get a look at some of the damaged parts, but Scammell said: "Later we got the engine and box, and Maurice did come with us. I don't know if he disguised himself; I wasn't aware of that if he did."

Formula One writer Pino Allievi, yet to establish his career, was in the pits at Monza that day with his friend Enrico Benzing. "This was in the days when I was just starting out as a journalist, before I started with *Gazetta dello Sport*. We usually went to Parabolica to watch. In those days they were braking at 150 metres, and we

OPPOSITE *Nina did everything she could in that terrible summer of 1970 to persuade her husband to give up his dream of the World Championship, especially after the death of their dear friend Piers Courage.* (LAT)

wanted to watch the Lotus without its wings. We were beginning to head down there when suddenly we saw lots of people running and the ambulance, and then they started blocking the access to get down there. We knew something had happened. And we were obliged to go back.

"I remember seeing Jackie Stewart, who went straight to Nina. He said something to her and they disappeared. Then I spoke with Gianni Restelli, the director of the Monza autodromo, and he said to me, 'The condition of Jochen Rindt is desperate.'

"I can remember it like it was yesterday. But only that episode. It's strange, I remember nothing else of that day. It was like all my day was just those five or ten minutes."

Frank Williams's memory was similarly telescoped by events. "The thing I can still see is Bernie, jogging down to the Parabolica," he said in 2010. Ecclestone had sprinted down to the accident scene before access was closed off, getting there before mechanic Eddie Dennis even though the latter was younger. There, Bernie picked up Jochen's white Bell Star, a driving boot, and from the opposite side of the road, the left front wheel which still had suspension and brake parts attached. He handed that to Dennis.

BELOW *As the wreckage of Lotus number 22 is trucked away from the accident scene at Parabolica, the ambulance carrying Jochen's body is getting lost in Monza instead of heading to Milan's Niguarda Clinic.* (LAT)

David Phipps, close with Ecclestone, remembered: "Bernie looked a very sad, slight figure as he walked back from the Parabolica that Saturday carrying Jochen's helmet."

"He was missing and somebody said there'd been an accident at Parabolica, so I ran to the corner," Bernie recalled. "It's not a nice thing, but I remember carrying his helmet back. I didn't see him in the car or in the ambulance because by the time I'd got there, to the corner, he'd gone.

"When I got back to the paddock, I said, 'Where's he gone?' and they told me where, so I jumped in the car – I forget who I was with – and he'd gone to the wrong place. I arrived at the hospital in Milan. Whether he was dead at the scene or died on the journey, I don't know. He was certainly dead when I saw him in the hospital.

"I was told by people there that he'd been in the medical centre and they'd tried to revive him, banging on his chest. That was the root of his problems, the chest injuries from the seat belt. He wasn't dead for sure when they first put him in the ambulance."

Like Scammell, Ecclestone's need for action kicked in. "We had the problem that they wanted to impound the car so I told Colin they needed to get the hell out of there, and I stayed there with him and one or two of the others." But not before he had arranged for Nina to be flown home in his private jet.

Was it helpful, that he had something to do to distract him?

"They were going to arrest Colin... Somebody had to do something."

Shortly after the ambulance had left the circuit, practice resumed. Stewart let himself be strapped back into Ken Tyrrell's unloved March 701, still in a state of shock, his thoughts in turmoil. He was still being emotional as the mechanics fastened his belts, only his tinted visor protecting his dignity by hiding the tears that he could not hold back.

"Ken told me I had better get back in the car. I was really, really upset. I remember getting in the cockpit then bursting into tears because I knew Jochen was dead. I had tears in my eyes when I put my helmet on. I don't suppose anyone would have known. Ken maybe. I remember the sensation of salt in my eyes."

Moments later he left the pits, and in an act of remarkable self-possession and cold professional courage he drove two stunning laps which momentarily put the blue car on pole position. The minute the engine had fired, his racer's instincts had kicked in and had guided him while he was out on the track. The man who had always prepared himself for high-speed motoring by deliberately seeking to be like a deflated rubber balloon, had put his emotions aside long enough to get the job done.

"I drove out, put the visor down and did a slow warm-up lap," he said. "I got to the Parabolica, had a look to see where Jochen had hit the barrier on the left-hand side. By doing that I had made my commitment to the Parabolica. I did two laps clean as a whistle and put it on provisional pole. I was not in any way distracted. They were the cleanest laps I had done that weekend, clinical. I was fine until I got round the Parabolica again on my in lap. I came into the pits and burst into tears again. I had somehow managed to tuck the incident away to another part of my mind. You close the visor and the lights go out. When I got out of the car I came back down to reality. I had been in a fantasy during those two laps.

"My best friend, John Lindsay, handed me a bottle of Coca-Cola. I was staying out of the way of people, photographers, etc. At this point no one knew that Jochen was dead. I had not shared what I had seen. I was so angry at the stupidity of his death, that his life had been taken just like that, I threw the bottle against the back wall of the pit garage. It smashed into a million pieces.

"Clay Regazzoni ended up with pole, but those two laps are the best example I can give of a racing driver compartmentalising the mind."

The following day Stewart would cry again before the start, then finish a superb second as Regazzoni scored his first Grand Prix triumph. The crowd's savage pleasure in a Ferrari victory was devoid of any shred of sentimentality for another hero's passing.

"I felt completely empty, drained and exhausted,"

Stewart said, when it was over. "I felt capable of nothing, and absolutely lost."

As the sun began to set on the Parco Monza that sad Saturday, desultory groups of spectators gathered at the scene of the accident at Parabolica, conversing quietly, studying the guardrail, kicking the sand in the limited run-off area, offering their own theories on yet another tragedy that had shaken the Formula One fraternity to the core for the third time that season.

For this book Ecclestone looked back on that bittersweet weekend.

"The night before we went to Monza I'd gone to Jochen's house in Begnins and we were going to drive down with Nina. We had a guy we were trying to get to do some sponsorship. We got in the sauna, and the guy said he didn't want to be in there. We insisted, and I said to Jochen, 'Bring him in.' And I could see him sat there, and Jochen, and I was pretty fit back in those days and we sat there and it was getting hotter and hotter, and we'd ladle some more water on, and we were talking to this guy about this deal. He was a big guy and he'd be saying, 'Yes, yes,' while he just got hotter and hotter and sweated. And I'd say, 'Well, we ought to do something. Can we do a deal?' 'Yes, yes.' 'Okay, then, let's shake hands.' The guy would have given us his factory just to leave the sauna!

"The next day we jumped in the car and headed to Monza, and we laughed about that. We rarely had the chance to be as relaxed as we were then...

"I'll tell you what happens, I think," he continued. "The shock at the time doesn't hurt you as much as afterwards, because there's so much going on, you have to do so much... You just get swept along."

He'd gone through it all with his friend Stuart Lewis-Evans who crashed and sustained the burns that would ultimately kill him in the Moroccan Grand Prix in Ain Diab in 1958. More than half a century later, he spoke for the first time about how the tragedies changed the way he looked at racing.

"They were both very close with me, those guys. That's when I decided that maybe I would take a bit of a break. I did try to distance myself from getting close to drivers after that, but there was Carlos Pace, and Reutemann. It's difficult, when you are with nice people and they are friends. It's hard, then. All my drivers, I've been good friends with, you know? Still today, all of them are very close. It's hard to distance yourself, much as perhaps you'd want to.

"It's funny, I was lucky to know good people, like Stuart, Jochen, Pedro Rodriguez... Ayrton, too. Friends, very good friends."

He acknowledged that racers sometimes have to pay a heavy price for that closeness – too often back then. And he quietly offered up the words so many have found comfort in since: "Thank God it doesn't happen now."

CHAPTER 20

Aftermath

Post-Monza, September 1970

'We grieve deeply for Jochen Rindt'

Stickers on taxis in Graz

LEFT *Jochen and the Lotus 72, iconic images of 1970.* (Grand Prix Photo)

Nina flew straight to Begnins from Linate, on the flight arranged by Bernie Ecclestone. When she reached home, Sally Courage was already there, sitting on a bench at Geneva airport, waiting for her.

Herbie Blash recalled: "Chapman shot off immediately. Just went." Bernie had advised him to get out of the country very quickly, given the need under Italian law to find somebody responsible for such deaths and to place them under arrest.

"Nina had flown home to Switzerland," Blash continued, "so we had to get Jochen's belongings from the Hotel de la Ville. Bernie arranged everything. I had to take Jochen's BMW 2800 back up to Begnins. When I arrived in Geneva there were all sorts of banner headlines in German: 'Jochen Rindt killed'. As I drove up to the house Nina was at the bedroom window and waved like mad. I can imagine now that it was as if it was Jochen returning home, although of course it couldn't have been. There was nobody in the house, just Sally and Nina. And there I was… what? Twenty-one years old? Sitting there on the settee between these two women, both of whom had lost their husbands in racing that year. What can you say in a situation like that?

"All of a sudden Natasha, who was two and upstairs, cried out, 'Papa, Papa!' Both girls burst into tears, and there I am, not knowing what life's about, with one arm round Sally Courage and the other round Nina Rindt."

"Yes! I remember that," Nina said. "Poor guy!"

Tim Schenken was also a young man then, 27 years old, and at Monza he had been readying for only his second Grand Prix. A phenomenon in Formula Ford and Formula Three, the Australian was on the verge of the big time. What he said spoke for the majority of the drivers of that era.

"I took a deep breath because I felt so awkward going along and asking Frank Williams for a ride," he confessed, "after what had happened to Piers Courage. Would he consider me to drive the last races? He agreed. That was a tough thing, or naïve, I don't know what you'd call it really. I was just so desperate to get into Formula One. The first Grand Prix I did was in Austria in 1970, the second was Monza.

"Jochen was a big hero of mine. I had been doing Formula Two that year and in those days you had Formula One drivers doing it too, so you had Graham Hill, Jacky Ickx, Jackie Stewart, and of course, Jochen. Jo Siffert was in the BMW. And then there were all of us young guys, Emerson Fittipaldi and Ronnie Peterson and myself. So I sort of knew Jochen through that, though I didn't know him well. We didn't talk much, he was just one of the guys.

"But there was something special about Jochen. There was an expression: we used to talk about Clay Regazzoni looking like pole position just standing around in the paddock. Well, that was Jochen too. Pole position, standing still. Absolutely, that was Jochen."

Schenken was stunned by the events at Monza. "All I remember is that after Jochen was killed I was a very confused young man, because you really had no one to turn to about it. In today's Formula One the drivers have their managers and close friends and lots of hangers-on, but back then we had none of that. I wasn't even married then. I just kept to myself and was very, very confused. Because here was something I wanted to do more than anything else, to race in Formula One, and one of my heroes was killed.

"The thing that happened in motor racing in those days, that was amazing, was that you had a fatality and then you had a funeral. And that was so depressing and heavy. And yet the following weekend there would be a race somewhere, and nothing's changed, everyone seems back to their normal self. I think you just naturally put things like that to the back of your mind, and you can't afford to dwell on that sort of thing when you're driving. You've heard that expression and it's exactly true, you never think it's going to happen to you."

Visibly affected as he spoke, in Melbourne in 2008, Schenken recalled the day many years after Monza 1970 when he'd been forcibly reminded of Jochen. "It was in Austria, must have been one of the last races at Osterreichring. I can't remember if it was dinner or we just went out for a drink. Paddy McNally said that Natasha Rindt was going to come along and join us. Well, when she walked in it was Jochen all over, and I mean that in a nice way. And I felt this big lump in my throat…"

Mike Doodson was appalled by the scenes he witnessed on raceday at Monza. "It horrified me to see the crowd chanting 'Re-ga-zzo-ni' as their new Ferrari idol sped towards his first-ever F1 victory, apparently ignorant of the fact that my friend had perished less than 24 hours before."

Emerson Fittipaldi was also struggling in the aftermath. He had yet to turn 24 and stood on the threshold of his F1 career. Jochen had been his team-mate and idol. "Emotionally, it was devastating," he said. "Very tough. Was my first year in F1, and I quickly began to realize just how fragile life was. The odds on getting killed were so high back then. I'm so happy to have survived. After Jochen's death, Jack [Stewart] gave me lots of advice, helped me move to Switzerland and everything.

"This is Fate, you cannot dwell on it. I didn't feel any guilt for crashing the car, and what happened

OPPOSITE *In 1974 Natasha Rindt and her mother visited the Austrian GP at Osterreichring, the circuit that Jochen had done so much to publicise, to unveil a monument to the nation's first World Champion.* (Grand Prix Photo)

JOCHEN
RINDT
GRAND PRIX
WELTMEISTER
1970

subsequently, because I could have got killed myself. What happened was just a mistake. But I ate with Jochen on Saturday morning, in the Hotel de la Ville. He had a Formula Two team with Bernie at that time, and he said, 'Emerson, I'm too tired to drive Formula One and Formula Two. Can you drive for me and Bernie in Formula Two next year?' I said, 'Sure, I would be honoured to drive for you next year.' He said, 'Okay, well, we'll do the contracts later.' Only hours later, he was killed...

"Eight months I raced together with Jochen, Formula Two and Formula One, and I always fitted in because he was a fantastic guy. Took me by the hand, and showed to me what to do.

"When I first tested the Lotus 49C, at Silverstone, Colin asked him to test my car. Jochen at that time was thinking every moment to test the 72, but he tested my car. Three or four laps he comes in, says, 'The car is fine for Emerson to drive'.

"I jump in the car, I went out, after four or five laps the car was understeering and I came in. Colin said how was the car and I said it was understeering. Typical Colin, you could see his mind start thinking. Then Jochen said, 'Colin, don't change anything on the car'. And then he turns to me and says quietly, 'Emerson, you know the car is understeering... Well you have to use the throttle, and the understeers go away!'" He laughed. "Typical Jochen! I said, 'OK, OK,' and I went out and I started driving harder and it was so good. And then Jochen came with the sign board. He was so enthusiastic that he came with the sign board to the pit wall, because I was doing a good job and he was happy. He was one of my heroes of the track. He was fantastic, and very good to me."

Looking back, years later, Chris Amon spoke for many of his fellow racers when he admitted: "I don't know how I coped with all that. I think there was a lot of stuff being pushed into the back of my mind".

"Jochen was a very special guy," his Lotus team-mate Mario Andretti said, and coming from arguably the most charismatic and versatile race driver ever put on earth the words had even greater impact. "Very professional. No nonsense and very serious. And he was always so relaxed before a race. He'd be reading a book or something. He was a good team-mate. And he was a good man all round. A guy you respected immediately."

Others had their own memories of the moment they heard the news. "I was in the UK and had to go to hospital to see an employee who had had a bad accident;

OPPOSITE *Jochen's headstone, in Graz's Zentralfriedhof, is still beautifully maintained, and parties of schoolchildren still regularly make visits to light candles at the grave of a great sporting hero.* (Gerald Pototschnig)

they'd broken their back," Roy Winkelmann said. "There was a television screen in their room, and Jochen's image came up. 'Ah, fastest time, pole position,' I assumed. There was no sound, and of course no closed caption in those days. It was only later that I realised the truth."

"I was out with a falconer, in Chertsey," Nick Goozee said. "We went out to fly his bird. When we got back to his home, his wife said, 'There was something on the news about an Austrian driver in a Lotus who was killed today'... That was how I found out."

Franz Tost, today the team principal at Toro Rosso on the Formula One trail, was a boy the day that his hero died, and his enthusiasm for him encapsulates so much of what made Jochen such a star around the globe. "He had this special charisma. He was so fast! And his car control was unbelievable! The drifts, and the angle of the wheels. This natural speed and control. Nobody could understand how he did it. Unbelievable!

"I was a kid of 13, 14 years old, and he was simply my hero. I never met him personally, just saw him on the television, driving and doing interviews or whatever. But there was a special atmosphere and a special message in what he was saying. Here was this person who was taking so many risks but so enjoying his racing, with no fear.

"I started reading racing books, like *Powerslide*. Jochen was my first and only hero. To put that into context I was half a child still, and no other driver ever made such an impact.

"I went to every Jochen Rindt Show, first in Vienna and then in Essen. It was like Mecca, a must. Seeing the Lotus 72 there was so special it was like it released a special energy out of me. It was such a special feeling. Seeing those brakeshafts, seeing this wonderful car. No other racing car ever had such an emotional impact for me.

"At school I had this collage on the wall, which featured just pictures of Jochen racing. I was totally shocked when I heard that he had been killed. We had a restaurant, and I was in front of the radio when I heard the news. There had been this very bad accident. This can't be! Never in my life since have I ever felt so shocked."

Photo-journalist Gerald Pototschnig understood that totally. "You know, 90 per cent of Austrian people remember what they were doing the day Jochen died. I was just over eight years old at the time and I'm just over 48 now, and I know exactly what I was doing on 5 September 1970. I was coming home late on the Saturday evening. We lived in an apartment on the first floor and my grandmother lived in the basement. She had a black and white television. As we arrived home she came out and said: 'Have you heard? Jochen Rindt died'.

"One week later we were all in the mountains, in a cabin, for a holiday, my grandmother and my family, and we all sat around another black and white TV watching the funeral in Graz."

Jochen was buried in the Zentralfriedhof there on Friday, 11 September 1970. It was a hot and humid day, just as Monza had been. Poignantly, local taxis bore stickers which said reverentially: 'Wir trauern um Jochen Rindt – We grieve deeply for Jochen Rindt'.

Thirty-four private planes packed into the small local airport, and 30,000 people went to bid farewell to their fallen hero. Among them were so many of Jochen's comrades from racing: Bernie Ecclestone; Jackie and Helen Stewart, Jack and Betty Brabham; Graham and Bette Hill; Colin and Hazel Chapman; Jo and Marianne Bonnier; Alan Rees; John Miles; Rolf Stommelen; Jo Siffert; Chris Amon; Derek Bell; Ken Tyrrell; Stuart Turner; Peter Warr; Maurice Philippe; Leo Mehl; Udo Poschmann. His friends from Graz: Helmut Marko and the gang from Bad Aussee. Austrian politicians and local dignitaries; celebrities from other walks of life.

"I was sitting in Graz," Marko said, recalling when he heard the news of his friend's death. "There was Stefan Pachanek, another friend, I think there was some TV and radio, but not the full coverage, and then we got this message which we couldn't believe, you know? Because it was so unreal. We just got the message: 'Horrible accident,' and I think it was half an hour, an hour later, we learned what had happened. We couldn't believe it, you know? We were hanging round, and we got drunk in the end.

"And then at the funeral, with at the end a trumpet solo, it didn't fit the image that Jochen had at the beginning. He had a change, maybe because of Natasha he saw the value of life…"

"At least Jochen attained what he wanted, to be World Champion," his Le Mans co-winner Masten Gregory said at the graveside.

"Jochen will for all of us be the one and only true 1970 World Champion," Bonnier said in a moving eulogy.

Eddie Dennis particularly remembered how nervous he felt about seeing Nina for the first time since the accident, as did all the Team Lotus mechanics, and how she had graciously lifted the weight of the world from the shoulders of the men whose lives had revolved around giving her husband the best machinery, when she embraced them all warmly.

In particular, she was kind to Chapman. "In his own way he only wanted the best for Jochen," she told Heinz Pruller. And to Chapman himself she said: "Don't worry on my account, Colin. I'm not against you".

"I could imagine how Colin felt, but I wasn't *that* kind," Nina said in 2010. "I hated Colin, but why show it? He had dropped me in Geneva after Monza, and I

couldn't tell him to go away at the funeral… As for the mechanics, it wasn't their fault. They just did what they were told. And nothing could bring Jochen back."

Chapman himself was shattered. The accident followed so soon after the deaths of Jim Clark and Mike Spence and, as we have observed, such was the pressure of the Formula One scene that he had probably never mourned these two lost friends fully. Not for the first time he seriously considered whether he should stop racing, going through the angst that all team owners know who have faced similar tragedy. "When I lost Jimmy I thought nothing worse could happen," he said. "That it should happen again with Jochen, with whom I had started to be friends, is more than I can bear."

Even today, parties of schoolchildren are taken on bus trips to Jochen's grave. "It's a bit weird. I'm not sure that's what you should do with children," Nina observed. "They light candles on November 1, the Day of the Dead in Austria."

Years later, she was acquainted with a remarkable discovery. Her Protestant husband had been buried in a Catholic grave. "The city of Graz wanted to handle the funeral, and I said 'Yes, that's wonderful,' because I was so shattered I was really in no fit state to organise such a thing myself. Nobody asked what religion Jochen was. I had no idea about the Catholic thing until it was in the papers recently, but I was criticised for it. It wasn't my fault!" Nina paused, then smiled. "Jochen would have laughed about that!"

Karl Jochen Rindt: the man who wanted to retire before he reached 30; who wanted to pursue so many other interests in his life. Who wanted to get old looking after business interests and watching his baby daughter growing up.

Pruller said that he often imagined his friend in later life: "A Jochen who had escaped to a safe career and a fantastic business life. And Colin Chapman commenting: 'His natural ability would have given him the world title for years and years – but he didn't want it, because he discovered racing to be boring.' How I wish that vision had become reality."

Gradually, various parties began to try to put together what had happened to the Lotus. There were two distinct schools of thought. One suggested that the right front brakeshaft had sheared under heavy braking from 200mph as Jochen slowed for the Parabolica. The other that removal of the wings had left a car designed around the aerodynamic appendages, and running different compound tyres on each side, to

OPPOSITE *"Colin was all right," Bernie Ecclestone said warmly in 2010. Despite the spells when Jochen would only speak to Chapman via his very close friend, Bernie and Colin had a strong relationship.* (LAT)

become violently unstable under braking, with resultant loss of control.

In 1972 the *Grand Prix Accident Survey 1966-72*, created by respected PR men/journalists Adrian Bell, Ray Crowther, Eric Dymock, Ray Hutton and Michael Kettlewell and published by the Jim Clark Foundation, contained a lengthy report on Jochen's accident.

After describing the factors that led up to the crash, it continued: "The car hit the barrier on the left-hand side of the track at an angle of about 20 degrees, and the barrier broke at a joint. These are of the butt type, the sections of the barrier do not overlap.

"The car carried on, hitting the next upright, which was bent backwards and prised upwards by the nose of the car, which then dug underneath the rail, while the rear of the car started to pivot outwards, i.e. to the right. The right front wheel hooked on to the barrier's upright, but the momentum of the rear of the car carried it on spinning. The entire front assembly, comprising the box fabrication carrying the front suspension, the brake discs, and driveshafts, steering, pedals, and the front bulkhead, was wrenched off from the front part of the monocoque.

"Thus far the driver was probably relatively safe, retained in the car by the cockpit sides, which were still intact, and the seat harness. But with no front of the car there was insufficient restraint on him from being thrown forwards and downwards, still within his harness when the momentum of the heavy engine and gearbox end of the car spun it round again. This was the movement that inflicted some of his worst chest, throat and body injuries. The buckle of the harness caught him under the chin, preventing him from being fully ejected by centrifugal force in the spin. It is likely that some of these injuries would have been prevented had Rindt worn crutch straps as well as the four-point fixed belts. Had the crutch straps been fixed, the terrible leg injuries Rindt suffered might also have been avoided, although it is not clear at what stage of the accident they occurred.

"The right front wheel was wedged under the barrier at the second impact point, i.e. where the front of the car broke off. The front sub-frame was also here, although largely disintegrated. The left wheel was the one Hulme saw coming out of the dust and it was picked up on the other side of the road.

"Writing afterwards, the Italian technical journalist Giuliano Orzali, who attended the preliminary examination of the wreck, wrote, 'Both assemblies of these units (the brakeshafts) had been shattered, together

with the whole front suspension. One of the calipers was still clinging to its disc, this bearing a nearly complete shaft that was broken near its outer end. This was thought to be the right-hand unit. The right wheel was still bearing its upright complete with wheel hub and, protruding from this was a short stub of shaft. Looking closely at the point where the shaft sheared off, it seems that some wrenching action took place on the material as the fracture line was askew.'

"Orzali concluded: 'that the front brakeshaft sheared so near to the right front wheel, meant that the Lotus was left with an unbalanced braking action at a very critical point at very high speed and pointing to the left'.

"The possibility that the accident was initiated by the failure of the brakeshaft carrying the braking torque to the front wheel from the inboard disc was freely discussed after the accident. Until a detailed examination of the brake is made, however, it is not possible to determine with certainty whether the break was caused by fatigue or snapped by torque. On the evidence available, it is possible that the break occurred when the right front wheel slid under the barrier, and the front axle sub-assembly was broken off the car. Indeed, the eye-witness description of the break which is 'askew' in Orzali's words would suggest that this is when it broke. On the other hand, the behaviour of the car prior to the impact does suggest that the shaft broke under braking torque.

"Immediately after the accident, the wreckage was impounded by the Italian authorities, and only the engine returned. Accordingly, it is not possible to carry out the examination that would clear up the mystery".

Chapman took a leaf from Jochen's book by writing an open letter to the press a few weeks after the accident, presenting his view of the cause(s):

It is alleged...

1... that the car lost a wheel before impact. This is disproved because there are photographs in the Press of the car actually on the point of impact with the barrier where all four wheels are intact, and one can see black marks on the road and across the verge from the effect of heavy braking.

2... It is alleged that parts of the front suspension and brakes were made from... presumably dangerous materials (Chapman here answers critics of the lightweight construction of his cars and describes the material he uses).

3... It has been stated that there was a failure in the seat belt attachment points in the monocoque. Subsequent inspection... showed that all four seat belts used were still firmly attached. Unfortunately, the two additional crutch straps which were fitted and still in place in the car had not been fastened, and it had been Jochen's habit never to fasten these crutch

OPPOSITE *Nina and Jochen, in a beautiful photograph taken at Le Mans in 1967, the year in which they resolved their differences when she realised how much he had matured, and married in March.* (Porsche)

straps since about mid-1969 although they were always provided in the cars.

4… Other journalists have alleged other mechanical failures, variously quoted as a) front universal joint, place unspecified; b) front driveshaft at Zandvoort; c) front driveshaft at Osterreichring; d) brake failure at Monza on Jochen's car causing the accident.

[Interestingly, Chapman made no mention of the brakeshaft failure at Jarama.]

We would reply that, since the inception of the Lotus 72 which involved many new design concepts and two subsequent major detailed design revisions, there had only been one previous case of structural failure, and this concerned a front driveshaft on car number 72-1 driven by John Miles at the Osterreichring.

A final investigation on this failure is still being carried out by English Steel in their research laboratories in Sheffield, but first inspections have shown that the design, materials, manufacture and heat treatment, etc, of the shaft was entirely to requirements. The failure which occurred in Austria was a relatively straight transverse shear failure consistent with a fatigue crack emanating from the inside skin of the shaft on its parallel section towards one end. The shaft is from thick wall tubular construction machined from the solid. It is most unusual for fatigue failures to originate from the inside skin such as this because the stresses here are considerably lower than those on the outside skin. Because of this factor, English Steel are pursuing a much more detailed investigation as to a possible reason for the failure.

At present (September 1970) it is thought that this crack must have started from a minute flaw or surface defect on the inside wall of the shaft, which would not have been revealed by the normal crack detection process carried out during manufacture – nor during the subsequent routine Magnaflux inspections carried out by the Team personnel regularly all season.

Realising the critically important function they perform, all the remaining shafts were removed from the cars after the Austrian Grand Prix and, together with the spares, they were subjected to the most stringent further tests we could devise. Further, more detailed Magnaflux tests were carried out, and sample X-ray photographs were taken, but these were not considered adequate to guarantee the condition of the inner surfaces. As a better test, all shafts were then tested by ultrasonic crack detection ion equipment at Bix Limited of Lowestoft. This process has been shown in other tests to reveal even the minutest flaw on an inner surface and would certainly have revealed any faults had they existed. All the remaining shafts were free of defects.

The design calculations were further checked by our own staff and Mr J.E. Russell, the liaison and Special Projects Manager of the British Steel Corporation at Moorgate, Rotherham, and confirmed to provide an adequate reserve factor of strength over any load likely to be produced under operation on the race track.

An inspection of the damage after the Monza accident showed that the front end of the car had suffered almost total demolition on impact with the Armco barrier, and this was more severe than might have been the case, because a joint in the barrier immediately ahead of the impact point had parted, allowing the car to impale itself virtually head-on to the projecting end of the next length of rail which was bent back in the process. The force of the impact must therefore have been exceptionally severe because, instead of sliding along the barrier, and bouncing off as is the intention with these Armco barriers, the car was arrested almost instantly.

There was a great deal of damage to the mechanical components of the front suspension and forward monocoque suspension frame, and the right front driveshaft was seen to be broken. The fracture of this shaft was, however, of an entirely different nature from the previous clean transverse fatigue rupture as on number 72-1 at the Osterreichring and was a jagged bird's-mouth type of fracture more consistent with torsional failure due to extreme overload than fatigue. Just how this fracture came about it is impossible to say with any degree of credibility at present. Whether this shaft broke under braking, which seems unlikely because it had only completed 15 laps' running since its detailed inspections previously described or whether with the brakes locked on it received an additional to normal maximum torque, it is impossible to say.

Further detailed examination of the shaft itself when it becomes available to us from the Italian authorities may help, but until then, it is impossible for us to comment further…

Chapman raised some strong points, not the least that the history of each shaft was logged.

Peter Warr, who joined Team Lotus as team manager in October 1969, offered an alternative view of what went wrong. In 2008 he told writer Simon Taylor, in a

OPPOSITE *Jochen as he will always be remembered, the victor at Hockenheim, scene of the final Grand Prix triumph that would give him enough points to become the sport's only posthumous World Champion.* (LAT)

ABOVE *Jochen, his unpainted helmet bearing allegiance to his Jochen Rindt Show in Vienna, prepares to go out on to the Monza track for the last time, Saturday, September 5, 1970.* (LAT)

story published in *Motor Sport*: "In Austria John Miles drove the other 72 slowly back to the pits after an inboard front brakeshaft broke. I think it was a one-off manufacturing fault, but it was a failure that was to come back and haunt us. When we got to Monza the 72 wasn't that quick in a straight line, mainly because it had such wonderful downforce. Jochen said he wanted the rear wing taken off. It had never been run in that configuration and Colin was against it, but Jochen insisted he wanted the wing off and a 204mph top gear, for ultimate straight-line speed. But he didn't adjust the brake balance, and without the downforce of the rear wing it would have had too much braking on the rear. Firestone had a hard rear tyre for the left side and a softer one for the right, because Monza is mainly right-hand corners: the harder tyre took longer to come in. If you add all those things together you've got the ingredients for an accident.

"I think quite simply when he got to the Parabolica, with too much braking on the rear and the left rear tyre not fully warmed up, he hit the brakes and the car started to fishtail. It went one way, he caught it, it went the other way, and barrelled into the Armco and the car swapped ends, and went along it backwards. That tore the front pedal box off, which dragged him down the cockpit because he wasn't wearing his crutch straps – he never liked them – and the lap belts broke his neck. I'm convinced that the front brakeshaft was broken by the impact with the barrier, and did not break before the accident and cause it. We went to on to use the same shafts on the 72 for six seasons."

Rob Walker, who also withdrew the Lotus 72 he had entered for Graham Hill, disagreed. "I guessed immediately what had happened and, sure enough, when Colin examined the wreckage of Jochen's car he found that left-hand front brakeshaft was broken which, although this could have happened in the crash, was all the confirmation I needed to withdraw our car at once. Graham initially was very unhappy about this decision, but he saw the wisdom of it when Team Lotus also decided to withdraw John Miles and Emerson Fittipaldi. Later, when we got back to the racing shop, I had the brakeshafts taken off our car and sent to Vickers Armstrong, who did all our crack testing in those days, and their report described the shafts as 'shattered'. I rang them up to ask what this meant in layman's terms and they told me it means that the shafts could have broken at any time in the next half-dozen laps at Monza. I reckon Graham had a very lucky escape." Walker raced his car in Canada, but only after Lotus had supplied some much stronger, solid, brakeshafts.

Interestingly, Fittipaldi spoke of the time he tested a 72 without wings, at Silverstone in 1971. "It was awful under braking. Very unstable. As soon as I started braking heavily it began weaving so badly that I nearly crashed, and by now I was well used to the car. Perhaps that played a part in Jochen's accident, I don't know."

In a story he wrote on working for Colin Chapman for *Vehicle Dynamics International* magazine in March 2003, Miles said: "For me, the final confidence breaker was when a front brakeshaft snapped, nearly sending me into the trees at the Austrian GP.

"What was going to fall off next? Deep down my tolerance level for breakages was being tested to the limit. There was an air of unreality at Monza. The cars arrived late because mechanics had been working all-nighters. The arguments will continue as to what made Jochen turn sharp left at the end of the straight. It was he who asked for the wings to be removed. His car looked dreadful in the corners, but with suitable gearing it would attain more than 200mph on the straight.

"Colin ordered me to take the wings off my car for the final day of qualifying. I argued, but to no avail. Jochen died in the first few minutes of qualifying. Thankfully I never got out. The violence of his departure from the straight still inclines me to think that a brakeshaft broke. We shall never know for sure."

Dick Scammell agreed. "The aerodynamics were different between the 72 and the 49, which we'd run without wings there the year before. I think this time it unsettled the car more. But I don't think it was anything to do with that, I'm afraid. Everything leads you in the direction of a brakeshaft failure, doesn't it? It was like the Jarama and Osterreichring failures. I think you come down on the probability that it was. I can't see otherwise why it should turn sharp left."

"The general feeling was that it was the right front brakeshaft that broke," Ecclestone said. "I don't know. But if the car was getting out of control, for want of a better word, because of the aerodynamics, Jochen would have been able to control it." His inference was simple: easy for a guy who could spin nine times on the Masta Straight at Spa and get away with it.

Peter Warr also concurred with the views of Jackie Stewart and Dick Scammell, that Jochen died in the accident. "Jochen must have been dead within seconds of the impact," he told Taylor, "but they went through the performance of getting him out of the car, taking him to the medical centre, putting him in the ambulance, and then saying he died on the way to hospital.

"I took Colin and Nina straight to the private terminal at Linate and went back to sort out what was left. I had to get a lawyer, I had to identify him, I had to deal with the undertakers, and I bought a scarf from somewhere to cover up Jochen's neck."

Eventually, in May 1976, the Italian authorities acknowledged that, regardless of what might have caused Lotus 72/2 to go beyond its driver's control and crash at Monza on September 5, 1970, it was an incorrectly fitted guardrail that allowed the car to dig beneath the barrier rather than deflecting it, and thus caused Jochen's death. Colin Chapman and Team Lotus were finally absolved of all blame.

Comfort was in short supply as the Formula One circus sought to regroup yet again in the aftermath of sadness, that September in 1970. But there was a shred in an official communication from Paris in the days after Monza. There had been suggestions that a departed driver should not be eligible for the World Championship, as if because he no longer existed his results should not either. But fortunately common sense and decency soon prevailed and the CSI quickly made it clear that Jochen would justly be crowned World Champion... If nobody beat his score.

CHAPTER 21

Miracle at Watkins Glen

4 October 1970

"When I got back to the pits after the slow-down lap, I couldn't remember a word of English! Was a fantastic time of my career!"

Emerson Fittipaldi

LEFT *Emerson Fittipaldi, Watkins Glen 1970, victor and saviour.* (LAT)

Colin Chapman not only withdrew the surviving Lotuses from the race at Monza but had no stomach to run them in Canada, either. But Jochen's tragic demise paved the way for Emerson Fittipaldi's subsequent success at Watkins Glen, such are the vagaries of fate. The next time he sat in a 72, the Brazilian ended up driving it to victory as Lotus returned for the US GP on 4 October.

"After Monza, there was a month with a lot of pressure," he remembered. "First, Colin didn't know if we were going to the States or not. I was very anxious because of what happened in Monza, who was going to be number one. I never expected Colin to call me. Then he said, 'I want you to be number one at Lotus,' and I said I thought he was going to get somebody experienced. For me that was a big surprise. I hadn't been expecting that at all. So there was tremendous pressure, going to the Glen. These were two huge pressures, you know? Back again driving after a very tough weekend, and being number one driver after only three Grands Prix. I had read all the stories about Jim Clark and Team Lotus, and suddenly it hit me: 'Shit, I'm their number one driver!'

"From the tragedy weekend, and then going to such an incredible weekend of opposites for Team Lotus... We were in God's hands, to make that happen. Sunday happened the way it had to happen, and it was fantastic."

There were two key changes to the Lotus 72 he drove at Watkins Glen. First it was fitted, like team-mate Reine Wisell's, with solid brakeshafts; second, it used the development DFV that Jochen was using that tragic afternoon at Monza. Emerson qualified strongly, third on the grid behind Jacky Ickx, who was half a second faster than Jackie Stewart in the Tyrrell-Ford.

"I had a high fever Saturday night, Colin came up with an American doctor to my room and I was sweating like crazy. Ferrari was fast enough to take away the points that Jochen needed to win the Championship. Colin said to me, 'Emerson, whatever you do you must finish in front of Ickx because of the Championship'.

"Well, I had this fever, and I always knew my limits. I was never a kamikaze driver. I told him I would do everything I could. You can imagine the responsibility I felt..."

Perhaps because of that he made a terrible start. As Jackie beat Jacky off the line, Rodriguez moved up to second, leaving Ickx third. Emerson had to start fighting back from only eighth place at the end of the first lap,

OPPOSITE *When he started the British GP in 1970, Fittipaldi said he could have died happy to have achieved his ambition of being on the same grid as his heroes. He finished eighth on his Formula 1 debut.* (LAT)

separated from Ickx by Clay Regazzoni in the second Ferrari, Chris Amon's March, John Surtees's TS7 and Jackie Oliver's BRM.

There was an added edge to Stewart's performance. He passionately believed that Jochen should be the 1970 World Champion, and was another who was hell bent on preventing Ickx from winning and taking the title away from his fallen friend.

He summarised his feelings in the introduction to Heinz Pruller's excellent biography when he said: "The thing I wanted most, after Jochen died, was to be sure that he won the World Championship. At one time there was a doubt whether it would be awarded to him, even if nobody else surpassed his points total. I felt very strongly that it should be awarded to him; I really could not imagine anyone taking this honour away; it really would have been a terrible thing".

He soon opened up a healthy lead, even when Ickx moved past Rodriguez on the 16th lap. Emerson was also making gradual progress. Surtees and Oliver hit trouble early, with engine failures. Then Regazzoni needed a fresh Firestone and later had a problem with the ignition black box, and Amon needed a new Firestone too. So by lap 50 the lead Lotus was up to fourth. That became third when Ickx pitted on lap 57. The Ferrari had ruptured a fuel pipe along one of its flanks, spraying fuel everywhere, and whatever happened the Belgian's title hopes were now over. He rejoined in 12th place, and even if he were to win in Mexico, he could not now beat Jochen's points tally.

Stewart eased back a little, apparently home and dry, but on lap 75 his Ford engine began smoking badly and he finally quit on the 83rd with a suspected piston failure.

That left only Pedro in the Spa-winning BRM ahead of Emerson. But there was to be no second victory for the team from Bourne; the P153 was marginal on fuel capacity and in this longer than usual race where the track's characteristics imposed a heavy toll, the Mexican had to make a late pit stop on lap 101 to top up. Now, with only seven laps left, Emerson found himself running in the lead of the season's richest, $50,000 (the equivalent of $277,000 today), race.

"I never saw Pedro go into the pits, but then I got a signal that said I was P1. I couldn't believe it. I looked behind me because I thought it must be for someone else!" Emerson remembered. "Then they gave me P1 again. All the lap I had been thinking they must have made the mistake. But I was first! I was leading the race! I could win my first Grand Prix!

"Then my mind started working overtime. I thought about the fuel. Did I have enough? I thought about what might break. The last laps went on forever, and the last one was the longest of my career. The finish line was at the bottom of a hill, and when I came through the last

corner I saw Colin Chapman jump the barrier and throw the hat to me. I saw that image so many times with Clark and Graham Hill. But this was for me.

"When I got back to the pits after the slow-down lap, I couldn't remember a word of English! Was a fantastic time of my career!"

It was only Fittipaldi's fourth Grand Prix, and his success had cemented Jochen's title. There was another poignant postscript: 12 months earlier it had been Jochen who was celebrating *his* maiden triumph. Chapman was in tears.

To make things even better, Wisell brought his 72 home behind the recovered Rodriguez, and ahead of Ickx, who broke the lap record in his gallant comeback drive.

Subsequently Nina sent a letter to Jacky Ickx. "First of all, I want to congratulate you on your win in Canada. To be honest, I was a little worried that you might win Watkins Glen and Mexico City as well, which would have meant that Jochen had lost the Championship. I am very happy that Jochen managed it after all; it was his only burning wish."

And in his turn, Ickx wrote: "I consider it important that Jochen Rindt died a happy man. When, after four years of courage and disappointment, success in Grand Prix racing finally came to him, he became a different person. At the moment when he climbed into his car for the last time, he was particularly happy. He had the looks and manners of a contented man.

"There can be little doubt that he remained happy until the very moment of his accident, for we drivers are always happy behind the wheel.

"And even if one can talk of untimely death, all I can say is that the duration of life should not be measured in days or hours, but by that which we achieve during the time given to us. There isn't a single one of us who hasn't left his hotel room in the morning well aware that he may not return, but this does not prevent us from achieving complete happiness.

"On the contrary, perhaps it enables us to be all the more so. The knowledge that everything could finish before the end of the day enables us to enjoy the wonders of life and all that surrounds it all the more."

For many years a story did the rounds that the Belgian had 'created' the fuel line problem, so that he would not *have* to win the title. Speaking at Spa in 2008 he smiled at the suggestion, and said: "No, we really *did* have a fuel problem. And that was a lucky moment in the race. Such a *release*. Because being in front, in a Championship, with a man who was not on earth any more, doesn't bring me any satisfaction.

"Frankly, I am glad Jochen won the World Championship. It was 40 years ago and I am still thinking the same way today. To win without glory is not interesting, and winning in front of Rindt that year would not have been interesting. At all. Yes, it would have been in the records, ah, Jacky Ickx won in 1970. But what poor satisfaction! There was a justice there. If God exists, he made the right decision."

So Karl Jochen Rindt, the orphan from Mainz, became Formula One's only posthumous World Champion.

Later that devastating year, in a magazine interview, Nina said: "Now and again Sally comes to visit us here at Le Muids. Jackie and Helen Stewart also come with their children. Sometimes I think it must be really strange for Jackie and Helen, when they see Sally and I, to be the only ones left of the happy and merry crowd of those early days".

On November 17, a Tuesday, many drivers gathered in London for the annual Champion luncheon, where the spark plug manufacturer's World Champion trophy was handed over to Nina by Jackie Stewart, who had jetted in from New York before they hot-footed over to Vienna for the Jochen Rindt Show. Attendees included past champions Graham Hill, John Surtees, Jack Brabham and Denny Hulme, plus racers Jo Bonnier, Pedro Rodriguez, Jo Siffert, John Miles, Jackie Oliver and Francois Cevert. The teams were represented by Colin Chapman, Louis Stanley, Rob Walker, Ken Tyrrell, Frank Williams, Colin Crabbe, Ron Tauranac and Tim Parnell.

On Saturday 12 December Nina was in Paris where, amid great emotion, she accepted the FIA World Champion's trophy from Prince Alfons Metternich, the new president of the CSI.

"I spent that Christmas with Sally and her boys, and some of Jochen's friends, at home," she said. "But Jackie and Helen came over too. Helen came to see us all the

BELOW *Even Jacky Ickx, seen here at Watkins Glen in his Ferrari 312B, admitted his relief that a fuel leak sidelined him there and prevented him from amassing sufficient points to supplant Jochen as champion.* (LAT)

LEFT *Jochen did not like Ickx, for a variety of reasons now largely lost in the mists of time and wholly irrelevant, but here they share the victory champagne after Jochen's victory at Hockenheim.* (LAT)

time. She used to come over every day. How awful it must have been for her... She was a nervous wreck.

"Jochen and I were young and in love, and I always have a very strong impression of him," Nina says today. "I think of him when I'm with Natasha and the children, and I have photos of him in certain places. I think of him quite a lot, actually...

"He was such good company, great to have around. Very easy to live with, always satisfied with everything, never criticising. As long as I was ready in time, he was such an easygoing sort of guy."

BELOW AND RIGHT *Bernie Ecclestone and John Cooper (in hat) share a joke in 1974. Cooper gave Jochen his first works ride in Formula 1, while Ecclestone was Jochen's closest friend within the sport.* (LAT)

POSTSCRIPT

"Because none of us knows how long we will be alive, we have to pack into our lives as much as we can and use our time to the limit."

Jochen Rindt

Forty years after Jochen's death, the fortunes of so many of his fellows merely serve to highlight the cruelty of his youthful passing.

Jackie Stewart, the great survivor, won the World Championship again in 1971 and 1973, when he retired with a record 27 Grand Prix victories against his name, and was a 28th as a team owner between 1997 and 1999. He was knighted in 2001, and turned 70 in 2009.

Jackie was one of the few people consulted for this book who was sure Jochen would stop racing at the end of 1970. "He had got quite nervous at Lotus. Nina still has letters that Jochen wrote to Colin. He talked to me about it. He was going to retire. I really think he was. He was getting excited about business. I think he would have gone into business with Bernie. I don't know that he would have got the extra money from Colin that he would have needed to make that decision. And I think he was getting so nervous about the mechanical breakages. And that [Monza] was a mechanical breakage. That was what his great fear was. He talked about it a number of times.

"He and Piers were very close. He had a big thing about riding his luck, that's why I think he would have retired. That's why I genuinely believe he would have been out. And the house, and the baby, Natasha. And he was getting interested in business and Bernie was there. They were going to do things together, and they might have had a racing team. I couldn't see the logic of that, at that time. Like Emerson subsequently doing his own thing. There was nobody making that kind of money. Nowadays if you get it right…"

He described as "hideously dangerous" the era in which he and Jochen raced, when it seemed so random whom the gods chose to leave and whom they chose to take. "The statistics were that if you raced for five years,

OPPOSITE *Karl Jochen Rindt, in thoughtful mode in the summer of 1970 just before he turned 28 and while he was on the wave of luck that seemed destined to sweep him effortlessly to the title he so coveted.* (LAT)

there was a two out of three chance that you were going to die. I saw too many friends killed and it is the most horrible thing you can imagine. First you see the destruction of the car and the man's body. Then you see the hopeless tearing of the heart in his family and friends and the way they are invaded by despondency about their future. You see how the fans and your own family view what is happening and how bad it is for them, and yet you go out and do it again."

The Stewarts became used to clearing hotel rooms for their departed friends. "Helen has cleared up more rooms of more dead people than I care to remember," Jackie said. "It's not a nice thing to have to go into the room of a friend who has just died and see the impression of his head still there in the pillow, to pack his suitcase with his belongings."

Stewart says that the best racing driver he ever raced against was Jim Clark. "But Jochen was of that calibre and that generation where – and this sounds very old-fashioned and some of the people who don't know enough about it will immediately poo-pooh it as times gone by – he had impeccable manners on the race track. And there weren't many, even at the time that I raced, there were few people you could race wheel-to-wheel with, who had etiquette. Jim Clark was one of them and unquestionably Jochen was another. He was a seriously good racing driver. Some had similar talent but not the other chemistry that made victories come. Jochen had that.

"Not a month goes by that I don't have some thought of people such as Jochen. It's more often than that. Sometimes it's every day. I still think the spirit is still living, and you can say what you like about it, you can think it's just memory lane, but I still think that the spirit does live. It happens too often for me.

"He was always relaxed. The way he walked was relaxed… Serious, and funny. There was a serious side, where he was quite intense, but he could also be funny."

Dan Gurney retired after the British GP in 1970, aware perhaps that he had pushed things as far as it was wise to push them in a great career in which James Clark informed him at Jimmy's graveside that he was the only racer his son genuinely feared.

"If I had to think of somebody from the modern era that Jochen reminded me of, I would have to say Ayrton Senna," Dan said. "He had that intense kind of talent. He and Nina had a healthy marriage from what I saw, and he was an Austrian who was trying to do separate things, away from racing. Like his Jochen Rindt Show. He was willing to take that on. He was like Niki Lauda in that sense, there was something else there.

"I'm not sure, looking back, that Jochen and I ever really raced that closely together, but of course the cars I saw him drive essentially weren't – I won't say inferior – but they weren't front runners. And he was extracting 100 per cent of their potential. I could tell that it was only a matter of time if he got a front-running car that that was where he would be running. He was just a gifted athlete driver, oozing talent."

Jack Brabham retired from driving at the end of 1970, the oldest man in the game at 44 and still a potential winner. And still full of regrets that he had not, after all, kept Jochen to their verbal agreement to race together that season.

Chris Amon never did win a Grand Prix and was undoubtedly the greatest of his ilk never to achieve that, but while the gods denied him such success, they spared him the fate of many of his contemporaries. He finally quit racing in 1976 to return to his native Bulls in New Zealand, from whence he stayed involved in development work for Toyota for many years.

Jacky Ickx, too, made it through. When we talked about Jochen at Spa in 2008, he made a poignant comment that put so much into its proper perspective as the discussion turned to his arguments over safety with Stewart. Like his peers, Ickx raced to be the best; giving his all was at least as important to him as the end result. He was a racer. Just like Jochen. Just like Jackie.

"When the things go by with time, everybody progresses, you have different thoughts," he said. "Each time I see Jackie today I have a lot of positive feelings and we have a lot of pleasure to cuddle together. And most of the time probably we don't even remember why we had disagreements. The only thing we know is that – him with all his talent at the time, three World Championships and so on – the only thing that we know is that we are members of the few survivors of that era that was so difficult, and when to survive was only a matter of luck. And frankly, we both think it's a privilege."

And so does Emerson Fittipaldi, the man who should have been driving the Lotus 72 in which Jochen was killed that day at Monza. He went on to win the World Championship with the Lotus 72 in 1972 and again with McLaren in 1974, before wasting the rest of his F1 career at his brother's eponymous team until retirement in 1980. He then rebuilt his reputation in IndyCars, winning the series title in 1989, and the Indianapolis 500 twice before retiring for good, bar a brief return in GP Masters, in 1997.

After his spell with March, Alan Rees moved on to operate Shadow and then Arrows with partner Jackie Oliver before retiring in 1996. "In Formula Two Jochen invariably won races, even against Jimmy and Jackie, but he had a better car," he said. "Don't misunderstand me, I think Jochen was just as quick a driver as Jimmy, which is saying a lot. It's very difficult to draw a difference between them. The only difference I would say is in the way they looked on the track. Jochen would perhaps be a little more flamboyant than Jimmy, but they had exactly the same sort of skill. It just came out a little different on the track. Jimmy looked a little bit more organised and under control, but the skill was almost identical, I would say, between the two of them. The Brabham made the difference, I think."

Alan and Debbie Rees's marriage did not go the distance, but they take pride in watching their son Paul racing. He moved up to Formula Two in 2010. That was a year after Jochen's old team-mate and sparring partner John Surtees, who had retired from driving in 1972 to focus on running his F1 team that lasted until 1978, went through the anguish of watching his 19-year-old racing son Henry killed in a freak accident at an F2 meeting at Brands Hatch in July 2009.

Against the expectations of many, especially himself, Masten Gregory also survived despite a philosophy in which he admitted: "Frankly, if I couldn't go motor racing I would have to do something else involving hazard because it is the moment of risk that makes the rest of life bearable, valuable or delightful."

And he also confessed: "When I was about 33 years old, it came to me that up until that point in my life I had never believed I would live to be 30. I hadn't made any plans because it didn't seem worthwhile. Stirling Moss told me flatly that I was going to kill myself soon after I got to Europe. Everybody thought I'd kill myself, and looking back I'm surprised that I didn't."

He told his brother Riddelle: "If I should die, just bury me wherever. Along the side of the road would be fine". But despite his penchant for leaping from crashing race cars, the 'Kansas City Flash' did cheat death on the track, and died in his sleep of a heart attack at his winter home in Porto Ercole, Italy on November 8 1985. He was 53.

Helmut Marko took on Jochen's mantle for Austria, together with Niki Lauda, joining the F1 circus in 1971, the year in which he and Dutchman Gijs van Lennep won Le Mans for Porsche, and quickly showing with BRM in 1972 the speed of a future winner. Sadly, on his first run in a P160 at Clermont-Ferrand he qualified and ran in the top six, and was fighting over fourth place with aces Emerson Fittipaldi and Ronnie Peterson when a stone thrown up by the Brazilian penetrated his visor and blinded him in one eye. His racing career was over. He went on to run his own teams in F3 and F3000, however, and today takes charge of Red Bull's driver programme as a consultant to team owner Dietrich Mateschitz in F1.

"Jochen did his racing car show and was aware that he needed to keep all that alive, that it needed someone in Austria who is doing some international racing and is successful," he said. "So he was already planning, and I think if he would have survived and stopped racing, he would have been part of something with Ecclestone. They were so similar, they liked playing cards and gambling and all that and it would have been an ideal combination. Definitely.

"I would say, in his appearance, in his character and personality, for sure in this German-speaking area, Jochen was a decade ahead. He immediately acknowledged the value of television, he made his own commentary, everything was perfect. When we were 18 we had been the bad boys in Graz, we only could come to the back door and the girls could not tell their parents if they were going out with us. And as soon as he got some success, there was the red carpet. And also his face, with his broken nose or whatever it was, it was a very characteristic face.

"He was an outstanding personality of racing. Austria wouldn't be where it is now without him. At some stage we had two race circuits… No Lauda, no Berger, no Pruller or Zwickl would have made it without Jochen, because he was the pioneer. I live in Graz, and if you go to his grave it's always fresh flowers and fresh candles, and that's 40 years on. Of course the younger ones, they know nothing; so maybe if it was a computer game they would know him. But if you ask people my age who have seen him, yes, Jochen is The One."

Many of Jochen's friends, rivals and spiritual successors did not survive. Too many joined racing's roll of honour. Pedro and Seppi, and Ignazio Giunti in 1971. Jo Bonnier in 1972. Roger Williamson and Francois Cevert in 1973. Peter Revson in 1974. Mark Donohue and Graham Hill and Tony Brise in 1975. Ronnie Peterson in 1978.

Roy Winkelmann quit racing at the end of 1969, and went on to work in intelligence for Saddam Hussein and then the Royal Family in Riyadh. A period of intelligence work for the Iraqi government had direct sanction from both the UK and USA state departments, and he did four tours as a technical counter-espionage field specialist during the Iraq-Iran conflict. Today, Winkelmann remains a topline paralegal investigator and his intelligence agency in Florida operates globally, backed by 40 years' experience. And he still waxes lyrical about Jochen.

ABOVE *Jackie Stewart, aged 70, prepares to drive his Tyrrell in Bahrain in 2010. The Scot said that never a week goes by without something stirring a memory of one of his closest friends in the sport.* (LAT)

"He just wanted to get in a car and race, and of course back then it was a really risky business. He was absolutely an easygoing guy if he liked you, but if he didn't, forget it! I've seen him in a rage… But he was so talented. Better than Ayrton Senna, and he'd have given Michael Schumacher a run for his money, too. He just had this natural ability…"

Robin Herd prospered with March, as did his partner

ABOVE *Two years after Jochen's death at Monza Emerson Fittipaldi, the man who cemented his World Championship with victory at Watkins Glen, celebrates his own title success at the Italian track.* (sutton-images.com)

Max Mosley. Robin left the sport, came back again with Leyton House, then switched to running Oxford United football club and also entering the lucrative world of waste disposal. He turned 70 in 2009.

Mosley acted as Bernie Ecclestone's lawyer during the critical FISA/FOCA war for control of F1 in 1980/81, then succeeded Jean-Marie Balestre as president of the FIA in October 1991. He became the most controversial figure the sport has ever encountered during a reign that successfully steered it through the trauma of the deaths of Roland Ratzenberger and Ayrton Senna at Imola in 1994, before finally standing down after an embarrassing sex scandal and further acrimonious arguments with the teams late in 2009.

At his fourth try Ron Dennis finally made it as a team owner, then was part of the shotgun marriage between Marlboro and McLaren that resulted in the formation of McLaren International in 1980. From then until 2009 Dennis presided over what arguably became the greatest-ever British race team, winning championships in 1984, '85, '86, '88, '89, '90, '91, '97, '98, '99 and '08 and making champions of Niki Lauda (again), Alain Prost, Ayrton Senna, Mika Hakkinen and Lewis Hamilton.

Frank Williams likewise prospered after years of struggle, losing his team to Walter Wolf in 1977 and setting up again in partnership with Patrick Head to form the team that won championships in 1980, '81, '82, '86, '87, '92, '93, '94, '96 and '97 and made champions of Alan Jones, Keke Rosberg, Nelson Piquet (again), Nigel Mansell, Alain Prost (again), Damon Hill and Jacques Villeneuve.

Peter Collins headed for Europe at the end of the Seventies and eventually worked in team management with Colin Chapman at Team Lotus, then Williams and Benetton. In 1991 he and designer Peter Wright fought a noble battle to re-energise Team Lotus until the financial climate finally overwhelmed them in 1994. In his time Collins, who had so admired Jochen's scintillating performance at Warwick Farm in February 1969, brought on greats such as Nigel Mansell, Johnny Herbert, Mika Hakkinen, Alex Zanardi and Kimi Raikkonen, and today oversees the burgeoning career of his latest protégé, Tonio Liuzzi, with the Force India Formula One team.

Jabby Crombac died as he had lived, with a strong heart and no regrets. He was the doyen of Formula One writers, whose career embraced not just outstanding

ABOVE *What might have been? In 1971 would Jochen really have driven a similar Mercury to Donnie Allison's, seen here in the Winston 500 at Talladega, as Roy Winkelmann was so adamant?* (Getty Images)

journalism and the co-founding of the monthly *Sport Auto* magazine in France, but spells as a representative of the FIA, as manager of Matra, as a driver manager and as Lotus chief Colin Chapman's European agent.

Just weeks before his death in November 2005, he spoke cheerfully from his bed in a hospice where he was being treated for incurable cancer. A man not overburdened by ego, he was known respectfully in the press room as 'Legend' and his fund of anecdotes was a testament to the time he had spent in the sport. He was touched when friends communicated their feelings for him in his final days, but urged them to be happy. "I have had a wonderful life. Who else can say that they saw the eras of Ascari, Fangio, Moss, Clark, Lauda, Prost, Senna and Schumacher?" he asked.

Jochen's journalistic friends Heinz Pruller and Helmut Zwickl continued to cover Formula One through the turn of the century, faithfully recording its history for posterity. Helmut retired in 2008, to focus on his highly successful Ennstal Classic historic event each summer, while Heinz, Jochen's biographer, eased off after a stroke early in 2010.

Peter Windsor moved to Europe in the Seventies and, via *Autocar*, became one of the most respected Formula One writers, moving in to re-establish himself at *F1 Racing* after a spell as team manager for Williams in the early Nineties. In 2010 he came close to achieving one of his dearest ambitions, setting up his own Formula One team, USF1, in conjunction with designer Ken Anderson.

After his start covering Formula Two races for *Motoring News*, Mike Doodson moved into Formula One in 1969 and later became sports editor of *Motor* before a spell in public relations with John Player led him to set up as a freelance journalist. He remains part of the F1 scene today, and is still happy to discuss the career of a man he greatly admired.

Andrew Marriott moved on from *Motoring News* to set up in public relations and television presentation, areas in which he remains energetically active.

Alan Henry became one of the most prolific F1 writers the world has seen, and still has his finger firmly on the pulse of the sport.

Herbie Blash moved from Lotus to Brabham, forging a strong relationship with owner Bernie Ecclestone. In the Nineties he moved to an administrative role with the FIA and remains a key figure on the race management side in F1.

"A guy who loved racing, but wasn't in love with it? I'd agree with that," he said of Jochen. "He had a sense of perspective on it. Right at the end, it was just the start of the big money for the drivers, and I think he suddenly realised there was a lot of money to be made, and he became very money orientated.

"At the end of 1970 there was a lot of talk of Jackie and Jochen actually driving together. Either with Roy Winkelmann or maybe Bernie, because Bernie was running his Formula Two team, Jochen Rindt Racing. Jochen would have liked it to go into Formula One.

"I'm sure Jochen would have carried on for another year or so. But I think he'd have left Colin. I think eventually there would have been a Superteam, with

Jochen and Jackie. Who they were going to drive for, I don't know, but the two of them were very close, and they wanted to drive together."

Dick Scammell rose through the ranks to manage Cosworth, before retiring at the turn of the 21st century. "The car had to be designed right for Jochen, I think," he suggested, when asked the difference between Jochen and Jimmy. "And if it was designed right he didn't really make a mess of it, but if it came to trying to put it right I don't think he had the ability that Graham did.

"I think possibly Jimmy was more sympathetic on the machinery, which was a plus. Again, I think Jimmy had the attribute, with Chapman, to be able to sort the car out, where I don't know that Jochen really had that ability. He was hugely quick, and just a natural talent. I think they had similar speed."

Nick Goozee went on to an illustrious career working in the UK for Roger Penske, overseeing the build operation of the cars that would win so many IndyCar races and Indianapolis 500s, until he retired in March

BELOW *Ron Dennis went on to take McLaren to the highest level within the sport. Here at Monaco in 2008 he celebrates Lewis Hamilton's triumph in the year the Englishman was crowned World Champion.* (LAT)

2009 after 46 years in the sport. Today, he works for Lord March at the Festival of Speed, giving guests invaluable insight into the cars and drivers they encounter.

"It was more black and white back then," he says of the era in which Jochen raced. "There was, for want of a better word, more of a temporariness about things. So many people weren't going to last. It's hard to describe, but there was an unspoken inevitability – at least until Jackie, and later Jochen, began to speak out about safety – that some people weren't going to be coming back.

"People today don't understand that the drivers really did face fear; they were generally scared when they got into the cars. There was death, or serious injury, all around them. They were in their own zone, psyching themselves up to get into the cars. They weren't aware of the effect they had at the time."

Michael Argetsinger raced in Europe for about ten years, mostly on the Continent and, despite Jochen's insistence, in Formula Ford. His biography of Mark Donohue met wide acclaim in 2009.

Dick Sellens, one of the New Zealanders who rescued Jochen from his upturned Lotus 49 at Levin back in 1969, continued to race in saloon cars of various capacities. "Besides the customs and shipping agency I was building up I had a motor accessory shop and a small workshop where we did some race preparation. It was a nice tax write-off to cover my expensive hobby!" He now lives in retirement in Eugene, Oregon.
And Jochen's loved ones...

Uwe Eisleben graduated as a Doctor of Engineering from the Technical High School in Braunschweig in 1971, the year after he had read of his brother's death in the newspapers. Circumstances in their very different lives had kept them from meeting one another since that drive in the Simca, but they kept in regular touch via letter.

"It was not our intention not to meet, but that was life," Uwe said in 2010. "And neither of us had thought at any time of Jochen's early death ten years later. Jochen consequently was building up his career and I was busy studying for my graduation as engineer at the university.

LEFT AND BELOW *Jackie and Jochen at the Jochen Rindt Show in Vienna in 1969. A huge event in Vienna and a crucial part of Jochen's business life and future, it is still organised annually as an automotive show.* (Archive Erich Walitsch)

ABOVE *Bernie Ecclestone remains the prime mover in F1 circles after steering it into the commercial age, and still believes that his great friend was one of the five best drivers he ever saw in racing.* (LAT)

Each of us more or less thought there would be time enough later.

"At the beginning of 1970 Jochen wrote me a letter suggesting we should perhaps work together in the racing business in some future days. As I understood it, he had the intention to build up his own racing business. My answer was that we should see, because I also wanted to get my doctorate in engineering in production techniques."

"When he had his accident, I read it in a newspaper at the university. At first I could not believe it, perhaps I would not believe it. Then I was very, very sad, that I could not see him again and make some plans for the future, whatever that might have been.

"My uncle and aunt lived in Graz and we went together to the funeral. Jochen's world was quite different from mine. There were of course a lot of people of his world. As we, my uncle, my aunt and I, were the next relations of Jochen, we went directly behind his

coffin. During all the ceremony I was not very present there with my mind; I more thought about the time of our youth we had spent together at our vacations in summer and winter, and what nice times we had together. All was so sad."

Uwe worked initially as assistant to the director of production in a company producing high-voltage switches, then moved on to manage a small firm that produced precision winding machines for the textile industry. After four years and up until his retirement in 1997 he managed the maintenance and buildings in a large printing and publishing company headquartered in Germany, with offices in France and the US.

He and his wife Jutta live in Offenburg and have two sons, Marc and Falk who were born in 1969 and 1970 respectively. Falk and his wife Jola made Uwe and Jutta grandparents when Leo was born on 2 May 2010 .

"Jochen in his last years was a cool, calculating sports-businessman, and with good reason," Uwe said. "His job had high risks and he knew that very well. In my last letter to him, I wished him luck to drive round all the risks. It was his fate, that this should not become true.

"My overriding memory of Jochen in our young years was that he was a very vivid young boy. He liked to play matches with other boys, and of course there must be always some action. He was a very friendly playmate, who liked jokes."

Bernie Ecclestone bought Brabham at the end of 1971, and ran the team until 1990. At the same time he moved into control of F1 via his FOCA and later FOM enterprises, securing the rights to the commercial side of the sport in the FISA/FOCA war and later buying the commercial rights outright from the FIA for £360m for 100 years. He remains the prime mover behind the sport that he dragged screaming into the age of commercial sponsorship and investment four decades ago.

Nina slowly rebuilt her life. "I was fumbling in the dark," she admits of the months after Jochen's death. "I don't remember much. I was very busy moving home, from the place we rented to the house at Le Muids that Jochen and I had been building. And I had to devote a lot of time to Natasha, who was only two."

She married international gambler Philip Martyn in 1972 and they had a daughter, Tamara. "We didn't last long but we are still very good friends," she said. "Natasha calls him Daddy."

She married Alex, Viscount Bridport, in 1979, and they had a son, Anthony, in 1983. When the time came, Anthony wanted to go racing himself. "You can't stop people," Nina said. "I hated the idea of my son racing. I wasn't going to be a karting chauffeur. But I said he could go to Silverstone when he had finished school. He did quite well when he went through the course there, he won his race. He said it was like Christmas! And that he wanted to start seriously. So I said speak to your father, he will sponsor you with a loan, but you have to do every single thing by yourself. And he never did that. He wasn't hungry enough." It was a clever way to handle a difficult situation, and relief for a woman who had lost so much to racing.

She and Alex also divorced. "We are still friends, and he and Philip share the same birthday, though they are ten years apart," she said. "I guess nobody could live up to Jochen…"

Like her father, Natasha became a highly accomplished skier. She inherited not only his looks but also many of his mannerisms, according to her mother, including the way she walks and her posture and poise on skis. She once trained intensively with the Austrian national team before she gave up dreams of becoming a ski racer to take up flying. After a spell with FOCA TV in the Nineties she flew her godfather Bernie Ecclestone's private jet before marrying Gayer Ridgway, another of his pilots. They have two daughters, three year-old India who Nina says with a smile in her voice is "a troublemaker who skis with absolutely no fear!" And Sophia who was born early in 2010. They live in Switzerland near Nina.

And Jochen himself? What might he have become, given a kinder fate?

F1 writer Gerhard Kuntschik revealed that Nina was surprised when she went to Magny-Cours a couple of times in the Nineties to find that so many people were still interested in her first husband

"He was a very bright fella," Dick Scammell said. "He wasn't going to be this retired racing driver. He would have moved on to something else."

The Jochen Rindt Show was enormously important to him, and there is no doubt that he would have put even more time into that once he had stopped driving. He started it in Vienna in 1965, investing £10,000 and signing five-year deals with Formula One teams who agreed to send cars for display. In 1969 he brought Art Arfons and his famed Green Monster land speed record car over from Akron, Ohio. Juan Manuel Fangio was another guest; Jackie Stewart was a regular habitué.

He ran the Show in partnership with Austrian jeweller Gotfrid Koechert, whose Ferrari 250LM he once raced, and his right-hand man was Udo Poschmann, who had organised the speed event at Innsbruck airport at which 'The toff from Graz' had officially begun his competition career.

Jochen was so into it that he made himself ill with gastritis in 1969, when he missed the annual Team Lotus dinner dance in London because the Show took priority. Colin Chapman bypassed the fact that both of his drivers were missing by organising a telephone hook-up between Jochen and the injured Graham Hill, who was hospitalised in London and dosed with heroin because morphine wasn't strong enough to help him through the pain of his leg injuries.

Jochen told him: "Pity you can't be here in Vienna to open the Show for me, but I can't afford you, Graham."

The Show was important for other reasons, too, beyond business. Jochen had a strong sense of giving something back to the community. One year he allowed blind and partially sighted visitors to run their hands over the cars, so they could gain a greater insight into their dramatic shapes. Parties of schoolchildren were always welcome.

"He loved it," Winkelmann said. "He wanted me to go international with it. It was very well supported and everyone enjoyed it. Motor racing was his first love, and I couldn't see him doing anything but race cars, but he had big plans for the Show.

"I was a little disappointed with him once there. I'd become his business manager and we were at the Show one year and Nina was very ill. She is such a lovely lady. So much class, poise and charm, a beautiful woman and a lovely person. She had a high temperature, fever; I thought she should be in hospital, but Jochen continued at the Show. I told Jochen that I had mislaid my car keys and could not return to the Show, he was very displeased. I explained that Nina was very ill and needed someone to care for her. I was very disappointed at his lack of concern for her. But we had a good relationship, all of us."

In 1970 Nina bravely helped the Show to continue. "I was convinced by the people who were involved in its organisation to do it in Jochen's name. It was terrible. I was on tranquillisers. I wasn't coping very well. There were photos of Jochen everywhere, and people wanting my autograph. Like I was the star… What had I ever done? I kept asking myself, 'What do these people want from me?' It was absolutely awful, just too much. I completely broke down, but behind closed doors…

"But Jochen loved the Show, and I'm sure it would have done a lot better if he had lived. After a couple of years I redid my contract and just had a retainer. Eventually it became the Essen Motor Show, because what did the Jochen Rindt bit mean?" It continues as that today, albeit focused much more on the automotive rather than racing side of the industry.

Then there was Jochen's television and radio work. Kuntschik put him into greater perspective from a nationalistic point of view when he said: "He was one of the first analysts of Formula One for a TV/radio station's show. ORF did this programme every Monday, called 'An den boxen' – 'In the pits' – which was produced by Lucky Schmidtleitner, the famous sports director. It was about motor racing and boxing, with the play on words with boxen. The motor racing was on first and Jochen would work with Heinz Pruller and Helmut Zwickl to do a review of one race and a preview of the next. He'd be there with his microphone and the cameras. It started in 1970 and was very popular because it was authentic. One of the stars of the track was one of its presenters…

"He really blazed a trail, helped to build racing in Austria. There was Jochen, Pruller and Zwickl, and Dieter Stappert and Rico Steinemann at *Powerslide* in Switzerland. Then the Salzburgring and the Osterreichring were opened in 1969 by famous politicians, after Jochen had helped to make racing so popular in Austria. He really made the difference, and even after he was killed his success and popularity had paved the way for Helmut Marko and Niki Lauda, and later Gerhard Berger."

On July 30 2009, the Salzburg Rallye Club and the artists' network Lawine Torrèn premiered an opera at the Salzburgring, using the original location and some historic cars and an international cast of dancers, singers and actors to reconstruct Jochen's last days.

"As tragic as the end of this hero of the pop-era was, we remember him with the sentiment that he did not die for nothing," said director Hubert Lepka. "Often, the triteness of his accidental death flagrantly contradicts the myths of heroism and redemption following him. Accommodating both at the same time, the simplicity and the uniqueness of this hero and his time, is our very concern."

In 1968 Jochen told writer and presenter Barrie Gill that he didn't see himself racing beyond 30. Ecclestone, who knew him better than most, didn't buy the retirement bit. "You know how people say these things. But Jochen would have raced as long as he could have, as long as he was competitive."

Almost certainly, the two of them would have entered into some sort of business enterprise together, quite likely running Formula One. They spoke the same language and thought the same way, understood and respected one another. Though that didn't stop Bernie coming out the better side of a deal when the opportunity arose. David Phipps recalled: "Jochen was a very positive person and he was never in awe of Bernie. I remember him coming to my home in Bromley in a white Rolls-Royce with white carpets and whitewall tyres – which had very little tread on them.

"'Wherever did you get the car?' I asked.

"'Where do you think?' Jochen replied. 'It was in Bernie's showroom.'"

Ecclestone doesn't remember that deal, but laughed at the story. "We had a good understanding together, a good sense of humour. We had a super friendship outside of racing. And he was one of the best friends I ever had in racing."

Nina remains convinced he would be working with Bernie. "They had great respect for each other. Jochen thought that Bernie was the best thing ever. They just clicked. When Jochen was 28 he was as mature as a 40-year-old, and that's maybe why, because Bernie was 40. Jochen used to say that he learned so much more from him than he did from his young friends."

"The only person that Jochen used to look up to was

Bernie," Herbie Blash said. "He thought Bernie was the greatest thing since sliced bread, because Bernie was serious, and because Bernie was also very funny. Jochen used to like to gamble, used to like to play, and Bernie was that type of person. Bernie was really his best mate."

"We'd have been together, for sure," Ecclestone said in 2010, breaking into a laugh. "I don't know *what* we'd have been doing, but we'd have been together, for sure."

Asked for an overriding memory of his friend, he came up with this anecdote: "In the early days with Cooper we went to Mexico. I got there first and he arrived later. I went to the hotel and the air-conditioning wasn't working. So we pulled the beds out into the hall where it *was* working...

"The guys had said to me that down by the swimming pool there were some girls, for a massage. I think in my life I've only ever had two massages because I don't like anybody massaging me. So I went downstairs and one of the girls, nice looking, a nice girl, asked me if I wanted one and I said, 'No, that's all right, thank you very much indeed.' And we talked, and then Jochen arrived from Germany or somewhere just after I'd gone back to the pool again. And I said, 'Why don't you go and have a massage?' I told him I could show him where, and this girl had told me her name. So I went down the steps with him and introduced them, whatever her name was. And she didn't know who Jochen Rindt was, and probably didn't care. In went Jochen for his massage, and I went back to where the pool was, probably sitting in my suit because I never had anything else but a suit. And then Jochen came back and said, 'Not good.' I said, 'What do you mean, not good?' And he insisted, 'Not good!' I said, 'Look, I don't understand, what do you mean, not good?'"

At this point Ecclestone burst out laughing. "Jochen replied: 'She said to me, "Naughty boy!"'

"That *was* Jochen, a naughty boy."

For Bernie, Jochen will always be in the top five best he ever saw, including Ayrton Senna and Jimmy Clark. "I wish he was around now, same age as he was then," he said wistfully. "He'd give these guys something to think about, I tell you!"

The casual fans, reared on the heroes of the moment, may not remember him. But wherever racing aficionados gather to talk about the sport they love, whenever their conversations turn to the great question of who were the fastest men of their era, there will always be just one name that they conjure up for that period of Formula One from 1968 to 1970, the immediate post-Clark era.

One name, in italics.

Jochen Rindt!

OPPOSITE *Jochen as he will also be remembered, looking reflective in the cockpit of the Lotus 72 that took him so close to the World Championship in his lifetime, when he was the fastest man in Grand Prix racing.* (LAT)

RACE RESULTS

Compiled by David Hayhoe (Grand Prix Data Book)

Date	Country/ event	Circuit	No	Car	Model	Engine	Configuration	Notes	Result
1961									
	Steirische Bergwertung	Strassenrennen	109	Simca	Montlhéry	Simca	4		
	Flugplatzrennen Innsbruck	Innsbruck		Simca	Montlhéry	Simca	4		6
1962									
	Flugplatzrennen Aspern	Aspern	118	Alfa Romeo	Giulietta TI	Alfa Romeo	4		1
	Gaisbergrennen (hill climb)	Salzburg		Alfa Romeo	Giulietta TI	Alfa Romeo	4		
	Timmelsjoch (hill climb)	Südtirol		Alfa Romeo	Giulietta TI	Alfa Romeo	4		1
	Semperit-Rallye	Waidhofen	72	Alfa Romeo	Giulietta TI	Alfa Romeo	4		4
	Italienische Bergrennen (hill climb)	Italy		Alfa Romeo	Giulietta TI	Alfa Romeo	4		2
	Triest-Opicina (hill climb)	Italy		Alfa Romeo	Giulietta TI	Alfa Romeo	4		1
	Martha-Gold-Pokal-Rallye			Alfa Romeo	Giulietta TI	Alfa Romeo	4		
	Flugplatzrennen Innsbruck	Innsbruck	140	Alfa Romeo	Giulietta TI	Alfa Romeo	4	engine	DNF
1963									
07/04	Gran Premio Caltex (It Formula Junior)	Vallelunga	25	Cooper	T59	Ford	4	11th (heat 1), pole/starter failed	DNS
14/04	Circuito Int Riviera do Cesenatico (It FJ)	Cesenatico	21	Cooper	T59	Ford	4	2nd (heat 1)	1
28/04	Internationales ADAC-Eifelrennen (Ger FJ)	Nürburgring	11	Cooper	T59	Ford	4	clutch	DNF
05/05	Trofeo Bruno e Fofi Vigorelli (It FJ)	Monza	21	Cooper	T59	Ford	4		3
25/05	Grand Prix de Monaco (non-ch FJ)	Monte-Carlo	34	Cooper	T59	Ford	4	4th (heat 1), driveshaft (final)	DNF
09/06	Budapest (non-ch FJ)	Budapest		Cooper	T59	Ford	4	accident	DNF
13/06	Preis von Wien (non-ch FJ)	Aspern	6	Cooper	T59	Ford	4		DNF
30/06	Gran Premio della Lotteria di Monza (It FJ)	Monza	41	Cooper	T59	Ford	4	driveshaft (heat 2)	DNQ
14/07	Gran Premio Cidonio L'Aquila (It FJ)	Collemaggio		Cooper	T59	Ford	4	6th (heat 1), half shaft (final)	DNF
25/08	Race for Friendship of Nations (non-ch FJ)	Brno	21	Cooper	T59	Ford	4		2
01/09	Austrian GP (non-ch F1)	Zeltweg	15	Cooper	T67	Ford	4	connecting rod	DNF
08/09	Grand Prix Portoroz (non-ch FJ)	Portoroz	97	Cooper	T59	Ford	4		2
15/09	Internationales Flugplatzrennen (Ger FJ)	Achum	41	Cooper	T59	Ford	4		4
29/09	ADAC-Eifel-Pokal-Rennen (Ger FJ)	Nürburgring	12	Cooper	T59	Ford	4		DNS
06/10	Preis von Tirol (non-ch FJ)	Innsbruck	8	Cooper	T59	Ford	4		DNS
1964									
12/04	Preis von Wien (F2)	Aspern	10	Brabham	BT10	Ford Cosworth	4	carburettor (heat 1), retired (heat 2)	NC
26/04	ADAC-Eifelrennen (F2)	Nürburgring	19	Brabham	BT10	Ford Cosworth	4	front row	4
17/05	Grovewood Trophy (Brit F2)	Mallory Park	10	Brabham	BT10	Ford Cosworth	4	pole	3
18/05	London Trophy (Brit F2)	Crystal Palace	21	Brabham	BT10	Ford Cosworth	4	f lap/1st (heat 2), front row/f lap (final)	1
24/05	Grosser Preis von Berlin (French F2)	AVUS	12	Brabham	BT10	Ford Cosworth	4	front row/suspension (heat 1)	NC
31/05	ADAC 1000 km-Rennen (World Sports)	Nürburgring	137	Ferrari	250LM	Ferrari	V12	with Umberto Maglioli/accident	DNF
20-21/06	24 Heures du Mans (World Sports)	Le Mans	58	Ferrari	250LM	Ferrari	V12	with David Piper/oil pipe (Rindt did not drive)	DNF
05/07	Grand Prix de Reims (Trophées/Fra)	Reims	56	Brabham	BT10	Ford Cosworth	4	accident	DNF
19/07	Trophée d'Auvergne (Trophées/Fra)	Clermont-Ferrand	5	Brabham	BT10	Ford Cosworth	4		3
03/08	British Eagle Airways Trophy (Brit F2)	Brands Hatch	46	Brabham	BT10	Ford Cosworth	4		6
23/08	AUSTRIAN GP	Zeltweg	12	Brabham	BT11	BRM	V8	first F1 WC Grand Prix/steering	DNF
13/09	Grand Prix d'Albi (Trophées/Fra)	Albi	10	Brabham	BT10	Ford Cosworth	4	battery	DNF
19/09	International Gold Cup (Brit F2)	Oulton Park	11	Brabham	BT10	Ford Cosworth	4	clutch	DNF
27/09	Grand Prix de L'Île de France (Trophées/Fra)	Montlhéry	6	Brabham	BT10	Ford Cosworth	4	front row/suspension	DNF

Date	Country/ event	Circuit	No	Car	Model	Engine	Configuration	Notes	Result

1965

Date	Country/ event	Circuit	No	Car	Model	Engine	Configuration	Notes	Result
01/01	SOUTH AFRICAN GP	East London	10	Cooper	T73	Coventry Climax	V8	electrics	DNF
13/03	Daily Mail Race of Champions (non-ch F1)	Brands Hatch	10	Cooper	T77	Coventry Climax	V8	13th (heat 1), 7th (heat 2)	7
03/04	Daily Express Spring Trophy (F2)	Oulton Park	25	Brabham	BT16	Ford Cosworth	4	f lap/gearbox	DNF
10/04	Autocar 'Daily Mirror' Trophy (F2)	Snetterton	6	Brabham	BT16	Ford Cosworth	4	pole/18th (heat 1), engine (heat 2)	NC
11/04	Preis von Wien	Aspern	67	Abarth Simca	2000 GT	Simca	4		1
19/04	Sunday Mirror International Trophy (non-ch F1)	Goodwood	10	Cooper	T77	Coventry Climax	V8	missed chicane	DQ
25/04	Grand Prix de Pau (Trophées/Fra)	Pau	38	Brabham	BT16	Ford Cosworth	4		3
15/05	BRDC 'Daily Express' Int Trophy (non-ch F1)	Silverstone	10	Cooper	T77	Coventry Climax	V8	con rod	DNF
16/05	Gran Premio di Roma (It F2)	Vallelunga	10	Brabham	BT16	Ford Cosworth	4	3rd (heat 1), 3rd (heat 2)	3
23/05	ADAC 1000 km-Rennen (World Sports)	Nürburgring	20	Porsche	Carrera 8	Porsche	F8	with Jo Bonnier	3
30/05	MONACO GP	Monte-Carlo	8	Cooper	T77	Coventry Climax	V8		DNQ
07/06	London Trophy (F2)	Crystal Palace	5	Brabham	BT16	Ford Cosworth	4	4th (heat 1), 4th (heat 2)	4
13/06	BELGIAN GP	Spa-Francorchamps	5	Cooper	T77	Coventry Climax	V8		11
19-20/06	24 Heures du Mans (World Sports)	Le Mans	21	Ferrari	250LM	Ferrari	V12	with Masten Gregory	1
27/06	FRENCH GP	Clermont-Ferrand	20	Cooper	T77	Coventry Climax	V8	accident	DNF
04/07	Grand Prix de Reims (Trophées/Fra)	Reims	34	Brabham	BT16	Ford Cosworth	4	pole/f lap	1
10/07	BRITISH GP	Silverstone	10	Cooper	T77	Coventry Climax	V8	engine	14DNF
18/07	DUTCH GP	Zandvoort	20	Cooper	T77	Coventry Climax	V8	oil pressure	DNF
01/08	GERMAN GP	Nürburgring	12	Cooper	T77	Coventry Climax	V8		4
08/08	Gran Premio di Pergusa (It F2)	Enna-Pergusa	16	Brabham	BT16	Ford Cosworth	4	1st (heat 1), pole (final)	2
15/08	Gran Premio del Mediterraneo (non-ch F1)	Enna-Pergusa	14	Brabham	BT16	Ford Cosworth	4	driveshaft	DNF
22/08	200 mile Zeltweg (Austrian GP, non-ch Sports)	Zeltweg	10	Ferrari	250LM	Ferrari	V12		1
12/09	ITALIAN GP	Monza	18	Cooper	T73	Coventry Climax	V8	drove T77 in practice	8
18/09	International Gold Cup (non-ch F2)	Oulton Park	18	Brabham	BT16	Ford Cosworth	4	driveshaft	DNF
26/09	Grand Prix d'Albi (Trophées/Fra)	Albi	15	Brabham	BT16	Ford Cosworth	4		4
03/10	USA GP	Watkins Glen	10	Cooper	T77	Coventry Climax	V8		6
10/10	Preis von Tirol Saloon car race	Innsbruck	17	Alfa Romeo	GTA	Alfa Romeo	4		1
10/10	Preis von Tirol GT race	Innsbruck	6	Abarth Simca	2000 GT	Simca	4		1
10/10	Preis von Tirol Sports car race	Innsbruck	7	FIAT-Abarth	2000 OT S	FIAT	4	front row	1
17/10	Donau-Pokal Saloon car race	Aspern	30	Alfa Romeo	GTA	Alfa Romeo	4		DNF
17/10	Donau-Pokal GT race	Aspern	70	Abarth Simca	2000 GT	Simca	4		3
17/10	Donau-Pokal Sports car race	Aspern	90	FIAT-Abarth	2000 OT S	FIAT	4		1
24/10	MEXICAN GP	Mexico City	10	Cooper	T77	Coventry Climax	V8	ignition	DNF

1966

Date	Country/ event	Circuit	No	Car	Model	Engine	Configuration	Notes	Result
05-06/02	Daytona Continental 24 hours (World Sports)	Daytona	22	Ferrari	250LM	Ferrari	V12	with Bob Bondurant	9
19-20/03	4 ore del Jolly Club (Saloon)	Monza	64	Alfa Romeo	GTA	Alfa Romeo	4	with Roberto Bussinello	DNF
25/03	4-hr Trans-Am (Saloon)	Sebring	36	Alfa Romeo	GTA	Alfa Romeo	4		1
11/04	Sunday Mirror International Trophy (non-ch F2)	Goodwood	16	Brabham	BT18	Ford Cosworth	4		3
17/04	Grand Prix de Pau (Trophées/Fra)	Pau	26	Brabham	BT18	Ford Cosworth	4	engine/accident	DNF
24/04	Internationales ADAC-Eifelrennen (non-ch F2)	Nürburgring	9	Brabham	BT18	Ford Cosworth	4	pole/f lap	1
08/05	Grote Prijs van Limborg (non-ch F2)	Zolder	21	Brabham	BT18	Ford Cosworth	4	3rd (heat 1), 3rd (heat 2)	3
14/05	Daliy Express International Trophy (non-ch F1)	Silverstone	6	Cooper	T81	Maserati	V12		5
22/05	MONACO GP	Monte-Carlo	10	Cooper	T81	Maserati	V12	engine	DNF
30/05	London Trophy (Brit F2)	Crystal Palace	9	Brabham	BT18	Ford Cosworth	4	4th (heat 1), 4th (heat 2)	4
05/06	ADAC 1000 km-Rennen (World Sports)	Nürburgring	5	Porsche	Carrera P8	Porsche	F8	with Nino Vaccarella/ clutch/accident	DNF
12/06	BELGIAN GP	Spa-Francorchamps	19	Cooper	T81	Maserati	V12	front row	2
18-19/06	24 Heures du Mans (World Sports)	Le Mans	12	Ford	GT40	Ford	V8	with Innes Ireland/engine	DNF
02/07	Grand Prix de Reims (Trophées/Fra)	Reims	30	Brabham	BT18	Ford Cosworth	4	front row/boiling fuel	DNF
03/07	FRENCH GP	Reims	6	Cooper	T81	Maserati	V12		4
10/07	Grand Prix de Rouen (Trophées/Fra)	Rouen-les-Essarts	22	Brabham	BT18	Ford Cosworth	4	gearbox	DNF
16/07	BRITISH GP	Brands Hatch	11	Cooper	T81	Maserati	V12		5
24/07	DUTCH GP	Zandvoort	26	Cooper	T81	Maserati	V12	accident	DNF
30/07	Snetterton 500 km (Euro saloon)	Snetterton	38	Alfa Romeo	GTA	Alfa Romeo	4	spin	DNF
07/08	GERMAN GP	Nürburgring	8	Cooper	T81	Maserati	V12		3
21/08	Kanonloppet (non-ch F2)	Karlskoga	6	Brabham	BT18	Ford Cosworth	4	accident	DNF
24/08	Suomen GP (non-ch F2)	Keimola	10	Brabham	BT18	Ford Cosworth	4	4th (heat 1), 4th (heat 2)	4
04/09	ITALIAN GP	Monza	16	Cooper	T81	Maserati	V12		4
11/09	500 km Zeltweg (Austrian GP, World Sports)	Zeltweg	1	Ford	GT40	Ford	V8		9
18/09	Trophées Craven 'A' (Trophées/Fra)	Bugatti au Mans	24	Brabham	BT18	Ford Cosworth	4	throttle linkage	DNF
25/09	Grand Prix d'Albi (Trophées/Fra)	Albi	36	Brabham	BT18	Ford Cosworth	4	engine	DNF
02/10	USA GP	Watkins Glen	8	Cooper	T81	Maserati	V12		2
09/10	Preis von Tirol Sports car race	Innsbruck	94	Porsche	Carrera 6	Porsche	F6	f lap	2
09/10	Preis von Tirol Saloon car race	Innsbruck	32	Alfa Romeo	GTA	Alfa Romeo	4		1
16/10	Donau-Pokal Sports car race	Aspern	76	Porsche	Carrera 6	Porsche	F6	pole	2
16/10	Donau-Pokal Saloon car race	Aspern	31	Alfa Romeo	GTA	Alfa Romeo	4	gear lever	DNF
23/10	MEXICAN GP	Mexico City	8	Cooper	T81	Maserati	V12	front suspension	DNF
30/10	Motor Show 200 (non-champ F2)	Brands Hatch	6	Brabham	BT18	Ford Cosworth	4	pole/1st (heat 1), pole (final)	1
04/12	Nassau Speed Week	Nassau	2	VW	1500 Sport	Volkswagen	V8	1st in class	5

1967

Date	Country/ event	Circuit	No	Car	Model	Engine	Configuration	Notes	Result
02/01	SOUTH AFRICAN GP	Kyalami	3	Cooper	T81	Maserati	V12	engine	DNF
04-05/02	Daytona Continental 24 hours (World Sports)	Daytona	51	Porsche	Carrera 6	Porsche	F6	with Gerhard Mitter/suspension/accident	DNF
10/03	Carolina 500	Rockingham	66	Ford	Fairlane	Ford	V8	Rindt qualified/Jim Clark raced	DNS
12/03	Daily Mail Race of Champions (non-ch F1)	Brands Hatch	3	Cooper	T81	Maserati	V12	retired (heat 1/2), steering/ gearbox (final)	DNF
24/03	International Guards 100 (Euro/Brit F2)	Snetterton	3	Brabham	BT23	Ford Cosworth	4	pole/1st (h1), pole/elecs (h2), pole/f lap (fin)	1
27/03	BARC 200 'Wills Trophy (Euro/Brit F2)	Silverstone	4	Brabham	BT23	Ford Cosworth	4	pole/f lap / 1st (both heats)	1
02/04	Grand Prix de Pau (Trophées/Fra)	Pau	26	Brabham	BT23	Ford Cosworth	4		1
09/04	Gran Premio de Barcelona (non-ch F2)	Montjuïc	8	Brabham	BT23	Ford Cosworth	4		2
23/04	Internationales ADAC-Eifelrennen (Euro F2)	Nürburgring	2	Brabham	BT23	Ford Cosworth	4	f lap	1
25/04	1000km di Monza (World Sports)	Monza	15	Porsche	910	Porsche	F8	with Gerhard Mitter	3
07/05	MONACO GP	Monte-Carlo	10	Cooper	T81B	Maserati	V12	gearbox	DNF
30-31/05	Indianapolis 500 (IndyCar)	Indianapolis	48	Eagle		Gurney Weslake	V8	valve	24DNF
04/06	DUTCH GP	Zandvoort	12	Cooper	T81B	Maserati	V12	front suspension/handling	DNF
10-11/06	24 Heures du Mans (World Sports)	Le Mans	40	Porsche	907LH	Porsche	F8	with Gerhard Mitter/camshaft	DNF
18/06	BELGIAN GP	Spa-Francorchamps	29	Cooper	T81B	Maserati	V12		4
25/06	Grand Prix de Reims (Trophées/Fra)	Reims	20	Brabham	BT23	Ford Cosworth	4		1
02/07	FRENCH GP	Bugatti au Mans	12	Cooper	T81B	Maserati	V12	piston	DNF
09/07	Grand Prix de Rouen (Trophées/Fra)	Rouen-les-Essarts	12	Brabham	BT23	Ford Cosworth	4	pole/f lap	1
15/07	BRITISH GP	Silverstone	11	Cooper	T86	Maserati	V12	engine (drove T81B in practice)	DNF
16/07	Internationales Flugplatzrennen (Euro F2)	Tulln-Langenlebarn	8	Brabham	BT23	Ford Cosworth	4	front row	1
23/07	Gran Premio de Madrid (Euro F2)	Jarama	6	Brabham	BT23	Ford Cosworth	4	puncture	DNF
30/07	International BOAC 500 (World Sports)	Brands Hatch	25	Porsche	910	Porsche	F8	with Udo Schütz	11
30/07	International BOAC 500 (World Sports)	Brands Hatch	10	Porsche	910	Porsche	F8	with Graham Hill/ valve	DNF
06/08	GERMAN GP	Nürburgring	5	Cooper	T86	Maserati	V12	engine (drove T81B in practice)	DNF
13/08	Sveriges Grand Prix (Kanonloppet) (non-ch F2)	Karlskoga	6	Brabham	BT23	Ford Cosworth	4	pole/f lap	2
20/08	500 km Zeltweg (Austrian GP, World Sports)	Zeltweg	10	Porsche	Carrera 6	Porsche	F6	with Rolf Stommelen	10
27/08	CANADIAN GP	Mosport Park	71	Cooper	T81	Maserati	V12	ignition wet (drove car 7, T86 in practice)	DNF
28/08	Guards Int Trophy (Euro/Brit F2)	Brands Hatch	4	Brabham	BT23	Ford Cosworth	4	pole/f lap/ 1st (heat 1), pole/f lap (final)	1
03/09	Suomen GP (non-ch F2/F3)	Keimola	5	Brabham	BT23	Ford Cosworth	4	pole/ 2nd (heat)	2
05/09	Hämeenlinnan Ajot (non-ch F2)	Ahvenisto	5	Brabham	BT23	Ford Cosworth	4		1
10/09	ITALIAN GP	Monza	30	Cooper	T86	Maserati	V12	drove T81 in practice	4
16/09	International Gold Cup (non-ch F1/F2)	Oulton Park	21	Brabham	BT23	Ford Cosworth	4	front row, 5th in F2 class	6
24/09	Grand Prix d'Albi (Trophées/Fra)	Albi	14	Brabham	BT23	Ford Cosworth	4		2
01/10	USA GP	Watkins Glen	4	Cooper	T81B	Maserati	V12	engine (drove Ickx's T86 car 21 in practice)	DNF

1968

Date	Country/ event	Circuit	No	Car	Model	Engine	Configuration	Notes	Result
01/01	SOUTH AFRICAN GP	Kyalami	3	Brabham	BT24	Repco	V8		3
31/03	Gran Premio de Barcelona (non-ch F2)	Montjuïc	4	Brabham	BT23C	Ford Cosworth	4	f lap/fuel line	DNF
15/04	BARC 200 Thruxton Trophy (Euro F2)	Thruxton	8	Brabham	BT23C	Ford Cosworth	4	pole/f lap/ 1st (heat 2), pole/f lap (final)	1
21/04	Grand Prix de Pau (non-ch F2)	Pau	4	Brabham	BT23C	Ford Cosworth	4	pole/radiator hose	DNF
28/04	Gran Premio de Madrid (Euro F2)	Jarama	3	Brabham	BT23C	Ford Cosworth	4	pole	2
05/05	Grote Prijs van Limborg (non-ch F2)	Zolder	16	Brabham	BT23C	Ford Cosworth	4	pole/f lap/ 1st and 3rd (heats)	1
12/05	SPANISH GP	Jarama	4	Brabham	BT24	Repco	V8	oil pressure	DNF
26/05	MONACO GP	Monte-Carlo	3	Brabham	BT24	Repco	V8	accident	DNF
30/05	Indianapolis 500 (IndyCar)	Indianapolis	35	Brabham	BT25	Repco	V8	piston	32DNF
03/06	London 'Holts' Trophy (Euro F2)	Crystal Palace	1	Brabham	BT23C	Ford Cosworth	4	f lap/1st (heat 1), pole/f lap (final)	1
09/06	BELGIAN GP	Spa-Francorchamps	19	Brabham	BT26	Repco	V8	valve insert	DNF
16/06	Rhein-Pokal-Rennen (non-ch F2)	Hockenheim	1	Brabham	BT23C	Ford Cosworth	4	f lap	1
23/06	DUTCH GP	Zandvoort	6	Brabham	BT26	Repco	V8	front row/ignition damp	DNF
07/07	FRENCH GP	Rouen-les-Essarts	2	Brabham	BT26	Repco	V8	first F1 WC pole/fuel tank	DNF
14/07	OAMTC Flugplatzrennen (Euro F2)	Tulln-Langenlebarn	1	Brabham	BT23C	Ford Cosworth	4	pole/ f lap/ 1st (both heats)	1
20/07	BRITISH GP	Brands Hatch	4	Brabham	BT26	Repco	V8	fuel electrics/fire (drove BT24 in practice)	DNF
04/08	GERMAN GP	Nürburgring	5	Brabham	BT26	Repco	V8		3
17/08	Guards International Gold Cup (non-ch F1)	Oulton Park	7	Brabham	BT26	Repco	V8	oil seal/engine	DNF
25/08	Gran Premio del Mediterraneo (Euro F2)	Enna-Pergusa	7	Brabham	BT23C	Ford Cosworth	4	f lap	1
08/09	ITALIAN GP	Monza	11	Brabham	BT26	Repco	V8	dropped valve	DNF
15/09	Grand Prix de Reims (non-ch F2)	Reims	2	Brabham	BT23C	Ford Cosworth	4	pole/fuel pipe	DNF
22/09	CANADIAN GP	Mont-Tremblant	6	Brabham	BT26	Repco	V8	pole/engine overheating	DNF
06/10	USA GP	Watkins Glen	4	Brabham	BT26	Repco	V8	engine	DNF
13/10	ADAC-Preis von Württemberg (Euro F2)	Hockenheim	1	Brabham	BT23C	Ford Cosworth	4	pole/accident	DNF
20/10	Grand Prix d'Albi (non-ch F2)	Albi	2	Brabham	BT23C	Ford Cosworth	4	pole/f lap/ignition	11DNF
03/11	MEXICAN GP	Mexico City	4	Brabham	BT26	Repco	V8	ignition	DNF
01/12	Gran Premio YPF (Temporada)	Buenos Aires	30	Brabham	BT23C	Ford Cosworth	4	pole/wing	DNF
08/12	Gran Premio Ciudad de Cordoba (Temporada)	Cordoba	30	Brabham	BT23C	Ford Cosworth	4		2
15/12	Gran Premio Ciudad de San Juan (Temporada)	San Juan	30	Brabham	BT23C	Ford Cosworth	4	f lap	3
22/12	Gran Premio Argentina Airlines (Temporada)	Buenos Aires	30	Brabham	BT23C	Ford Cosworth	4		2

Date	Country/ event	Circuit	No	Car	Model	Engine	Configuration	Notes	Result

1969

Date	Country/ event	Circuit	No	Car	Model	Engine	Configuration	Notes	Result
04/01	New Zealand International Grand Prix (Tasman)	Pukekohe	4	Lotus	49T	Ford Cosworth	V8	f lap	2
11/01	Levin International (Tasman)	Levin	4	Lotus	49T	Ford Cosworth	V8	pole/f lap/ 4th (heat 1), f lap/accident (final)	DNF
18/01	International Lady Wigram Trophy (Tasman)	Christchurch	4	Lotus	49T	Ford Cosworth	V8	pole/f lap/ 2nd (heat 2), pole/f lap (final)	1
25/01	International Teretonga (Tasman)	Invercargill	4	Lotus	49T	Ford Cosworth	V8	pole/f lap/ 1st (heat), pole/driveshaft (final)	DNF
02/02	Australian GP (Tasman)	Lakeside	2	Lotus	49T	Ford Cosworth	V8	engine	DNF
09/02	Warwick Farm International (Tasman)	Warwick Farm	2	Lotus	49T	Ford Cosworth	V8	pole	1
16/02	Sandown International (Tasman)	Sandown Park	2	Lotus	49T	Ford Cosworth	V8	pole	2
01/03	SOUTH AFRICAN GP	Kyalami	2	Lotus	49B	Ford Cosworth	V8	front row/fuel pump	DNF
16/03	Race of Champions (non-ch F1)	Brands Hatch	2	Lotus	49B	Ford Cosworth	V8	f lap/oil pressure	DNF
30/03	BRDC 'Daily Express' Int Trophy (non-ch F1)	Silverstone	2	Lotus	49B	Ford Cosworth	V8	f lap	2
07/04	BARC 200 'Wills Trophy' (Euro F2)	Thruxton	2	Lotus	59B	Ford Cosworth	4	pole/f lap/puncture (heat 2), f lap (final)	1
20/04	Grand Prix de Pau (non-ch F2)	Pau	4	Lotus	59B	Ford Cosworth	4	pole/f lap	1
27/04	Internationales ADAC-Eifelrennen (Euro F2)	Nürburgring	2	Lotus	59B	Ford Cosworth	4	suspension	DNF
04/05	SPANISH GP	Montjuïc	2	Lotus	49B	Ford Cosworth	V8	pole/f lap/aerofoil/accident	DNF
30/05	Indianapolis 500 (IndyCar)	Indianapolis	80	Hawk	III	Ford Cosworth	V8	withdrew	EW
08/06	Grote Prijs van Limborg (non-ch F2)	Zolder	2	Lotus	59B	Ford Cosworth	4	1st (heat 1), pole/1st (heat 2)	1
21/06	DUTCH GP	Zandvoort	2	Lotus	49B	Ford Cosworth	V8	pole/cv joint	DNF
29/06	Grand Prix de Reims (Trophées/Fra)	Reims	2	Lotus	59B	Ford Cosworth	4	accident	DNF
06/07	FRENCH GP	Clermont-Ferrand	15	Lotus	49B	Ford Cosworth	V8	driver had double vision	DNF
13/07	OAMTC Flugplatzrennen (Euro F2)	Tulln-Langenlebarn	2	Lotus	59B	Ford Cosworth	4	pole/f lap/1st (both heats)	1
19/07	BRITISH GP	Silverstone	2	Lotus	49B	Ford Cosworth	V8	pole	4
03/08	GERMAN GP	Nürburgring	2	Lotus	49B	Ford Cosworth	V8	ignition	DNF
16/08	Guards International Gold Cup (non-ch F1)	Oulton Park	2	Lotus	63	Ford Cosworth	V8		2
24/08	Nordic Challenge Cup round 1	Keimola	12	Porsche	908	Porsche	F8	pole/f lap	1
07/09	ITALIAN GP	Monza	4	Lotus	49B	Ford Cosworth	V8	pole	2
14/09	Grand Prix d'Albi (Trophées/Fra)	Albi	2	Lotus	59B	Ford Cosworth	4	pole/f lap	3
20/09	CANADIAN GP	Mosport Park	2	Lotus	49B	Ford Cosworth	V8	drove Lotus 63 in practice	3
05/10	USA GP	Watkins Glen	2	Lotus	49B	Ford Cosworth	V8	pole/f lap/first F1 WC victory	1
12/10	Gran Premio di Roma (Euro F2)	Vallelunga	32	Lotus	59B	Ford Cosworth	4	brakes/accident (heat 1)	NC
19/10	MEXICAN GP	Mexico City	2	Lotus	49B	Ford Cosworth	V8	front suspension	DNF
26/10	6 hours of Jarama (non-ch Sports)	Jarama	1	Porsche	908	Porsche	F8	with Alex Soler-Roig/pole/f lap	1

1970

Date	Country/ event	Circuit	No	Car	Model	Engine	Configuration	Notes	Result
11/01	Buenos Aires 1000 km (non-ch Sports)	Buenos Aires	12	Porsche	908	Porsche	F8	with Alex Soler-Roig	2
07/03	SOUTH AFRICAN GP	Kyalami	9	Lotus	49C	Ford Cosworth	V8	engine	13DNF
22/03	Daily Mail Race of Champions (non-ch F1)	Brands Hatch	8	Lotus	49C	Ford Cosworth	V8		2
30/03	BARC 200 'Wills Trophy' (Euro F2)	Thruxton	24	Lotus	69	Ford Cosworth	4	pole/f lap (heat 2/final)	1
05/04	Grand Prix de Pau (non-ch F2)	Pau	2	Lotus	69	Ford Cosworth	4	pole/f lap	1
12/04	Deutschland Trophäe (Euro F2)	Hockenheim	1	Lotus	69	Ford Cosworth	4	pole/accident damage	DNF
19/04	SPANISH GP	Jarama	3	Lotus	72	Ford Cosworth	V8	ignition	DNF
26/04	BRDC 'Daily Express' Int Trophy (non-ch F1)	Silverstone	8	Lotus	72	Ford Cosworth	V8	5th (heat 1), ignition (heat 2)	NC
03/05	Internationales ADAC-Eifelrennen (non-ch F2)	Nürburgring	1	Lotus	69	Ford Cosworth	4	pole/f lap	1
10/05	MONACO GP	Monte-Carlo	3	Lotus	49C	Ford Cosworth	V8	f lap	1
24/05	Grote Prijs van Limborg (non-ch F2)	Zolder	1	Lotus	69	Ford Cosworth	4	pole/f lap/ 1st (both heats)	1
25/05	London 'Alcoa' Trophy (Euro F2)	Crystal Palace	2	Lotus	69	Ford Cosworth	4	pole/f lap (heat 2), pole/battery (final)	DNF
07/06	BELGIAN GP	Spa-Francorchamps	20	Lotus	49C	Ford Cosworth	V8	front row/piston (drove Lotus 72C in pract)	DNF
14/06	Rhein-Pokal-Rennen (Euro F2)	Hockenheim	1	Lotus	69	Ford Cosworth	4	universal joint	DNF
21/06	DUTCH GP	Zandvoort	10	Lotus	72C	Ford Cosworth	V8	pole	1
28/06	Grand Prix de Rouen (Euro F2)	Rouen-les-Essarts	1	Lotus	69	Ford Cosworth	4	2nd (heat 2)	9
05/07	FRENCH GP	Clermont-Ferrand	6	Lotus	72C	Ford Cosworth	V8		1
18/07	BRITISH GP	Brands Hatch	5	Lotus	72C	Ford Cosworth	V8	pole	1
26/07	Trophées de France (non-ch F2)	Paul Ricard	2	Lotus	69	Ford Cosworth	4	fuel leak	DNF
02/08	GERMAN GP	Hockenheim	2	Lotus	72C	Ford Cosworth	V8	front row	1
16/08	AUSTRIAN GP	Österreichring	6	Lotus	72C	Ford Cosworth	V8	pole/engine	DNF
22/08	International Gold Cup (non-ch F1)	Oulton Park	2	Lotus	72C	Ford Cosworth	V8	3rd (heat 1), 1st (heat 2)	2
23/08	Stainzer Bergrennen (hill climb)	Stainz		Lotus	69	Ford Cosworth	4		2
30/08	Festspielpreis der Salzburg (non-ch F2)	Salzburgring	1	Lotus	69	Ford Cosworth	4	pole/engine (heat1), f lap/1st (heat 2)	NC
06/09	ITALIAN GP	Monza	22	Lotus	72C	Ford Cosworth	V8	fatal accident in practice (05/09)	DNS

Key :	
DNF	Did not finish
DNQ	Did not qualify
DNS	Did not start
DQ	Disqualified
EW	Entry withdrawn
f lap	Fastest lap
NC	Non-classified

INDEX